EASY PIANO

SONGS OF THE 60'S

THE DECADE SERIES

ISBN 0-7935-2670-1

7777 W. BLUEMOUND RD. P.O. BOX 13819 MILWAUKEE, WI 53213

EASY PIANO

SONGS OF THE 60's

THE DECADE SERIES

The Sixties

by Stanley Green

The New York Times.

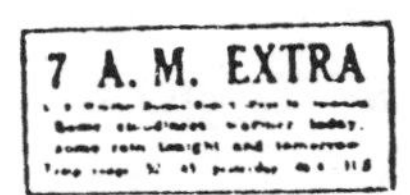

NEW YORK, WEDNESDAY, NOVEMBER 9, 1960 FIVE CENTS

KENNEDY IS APPARENT VICTOR; LEAD CUT IN TWO KEY STATES; DEMOCRATS RETAIN CONGRESS

"Let the word go forth from this time and place, to friend and foe alike, that the torch has been passed to a new generation of Americans — born in this century, tempered by war, disciplined by a hard and bitter peace, proud of our ancient heritage — and unwilling to witness or permit the slow undoing of those human rights to which this nation has always been committed, and to which we are committed today at home and around the world."

John F. Kennedy

Those bold, eloquent words of the nation's 35th President, John F. Kennedy, rang out from the Capitol steps on a raw January 20, 1961. But far from inaugurating an era of unity, idealism and action, they would, ironically, usher in the most divisive decade of the 20th Century. For the Sixties were years of turbulence and conflict as the American people suffered through three traumatic assassinations, the ongoing struggle for civil rights, and the deepening involvement in the war in Vietnam.

EXTRA The Washington Post EXTRA

Times Herald

President Kennedy Shot Dead By Assassin in Dallas Parade

Lyndon Johnson Sworn; Texas Gov. Connally Is Woun[ded]

The motorcade in Dallas after President Kennedy had been shot

The vision of Kennedy's inaugural address was followed in short order by the reality of the disastrous Bay of Pigs operation which resulted in some 1,400 anti-Castro Cubans, trained in Guatemala and equipped by the C.I.A., being routed in the attempted invasion of their homeland. We were, however, soon heartened by the suborbital mission of Astronaut Alan Shepard and of the Earth-orbiting flight of Col. John Glenn, a feat he accomplished three times in a period of four hours 55 minutes.

Kennedy's firm resolve helped end the Soviet missile crisis in Cuba, but this was to be his last major achievement. On November 22, 1963, while riding in a motorcade in Dallas, he was assassinated by Lee Harvey Oswald who, two days later, was gunned down by a local nightclub owner.

A march on the 1st Anniversary of Rev. Martin Luther King's death

The death of Kennedy and his succession by Vice President Lyndon Johnson came amidst the growing, often violent confrontations resulting from the efforts of Rev. Martin Luther King and his followers to protest the policy of racial segregation then being enforced in the South. Among the events of the Sixties that marked the struggle: the admission of James Meredith as the first black student at the University of Mississippi; the murder of civil-rights leader Medgar Evans; the killing of three white activists — Goodman, Schwerner and Cheney — in Philadelphia, Mississippi; the mammoth rally in Washington where 250,000 heard King's stirring "I have a dream" speech; the bombing that cost the lives of four black girls in a Birmingham church; the adoption of the Civil Rights Act barring discrimination in public accommodations; the arrest of Dr. King and 2,600 demonstrators in Selma, Alabama; the riots in the nation's ghettos during the long hot summers from 1964 through 1967; and the assassination of Dr. King the following year that fanned the flames of more violence and looting. Then, as the country seemed to be reeling from one tragic event to another, Sen. Robert Kennedy was shot to death in a Los Angeles hotel.

Demonstrators both for and against the Vietnam War.

Overseas, the United States was finding itself mired deeper and deeper in the rice paddies of Vietnam. At the beginning of the decade, there were 1,000 military advisers, a figure that rose to 543,400 combat troops before a phased withdrawal was begun in 1969. During the war — the longest in U.S. history — the country was rent by continued anti-war demonstrations, including student protests on college campuses and the disruption of the 1968 Democratic National Convention in Chicago. Beset by Communist troops of North Vietnam and guerrilla units of the Vietcong in the South, the American forces were ill-equipped to wage jungle warfare and the many bombings of the North were unable to force the Communist leader, Ho Chi Minh, to the conference table. Following the Tet offensive and the My Lai massacre, however, the United States ordered a unilateral cease-fire of the bombings and Hanoi finally agreed to peace talks. By the end of the Sixties — with the war still on — American combat deaths had risen to almost 34,000.

Other areas of the world were also exploding with strife. In the former Belgian Congo, the newly established Republic of the Congo underwent severe birth pains when Premier Patrice Lumumba was murdered and Katanga Province leader Moise Tshombe tried to establish an independent nation. In the Dominican Republic, Dictator Rafael Trujillo was shot to death. In Ghana, Premier Kwami Nkruma was ousted in a coup and the military junta that took over was soon crushed by another coup. In Indonesia, tens of thousands were massacred in a government crackdown to foil a Communist takeover. In South Africa, Prime Minister Verwoerd was stabbed to death. In the Middle East, the Six-Day War between Israel and it's neighbors, Egypt, Jordan, Syria, and Iraq, ended with the Jewish state occupying territory four times its own size. In Czechoslovakia, the liberal policies of Premier Alexander Dubcek were brutally halted by the invasion of Soviet Union and Warsaw Pact troops. And in Libya, a fanatic army captain, Muammar al-Qadaffi, put an end to the reign of King Idris.

Lyndon B. Johnson

The Sixties also saw such vivid events as the shooting down of Gary Francis Power's U-2 spy plane over Russia, the erection of the Berlin Wall, the power blackout of the northeastern states in November 1965 (and the resultant increase in the birth rate nine months later), the year-long internment of the U.S. Navy ship Pueblo by the North Korean government, and the Chappaquiddick tragedy involving Sen. Edward Kennedy. In addition, the decade gave us such diverse heroes as heavyweight champ Muhammed Ali (formerly Cassius Clay), heart-transplant pioneer Christiaan Barnard, sailboat skipper Francis Chichester, whose solo voyage around the world on the Gypsy Moth IV took 226 days, and Astronaut Neil Armstrong, the first man to set foot on the moon. Lest we forget, the era also provided a number of visual innovations and pleasures, including pop art, mini skirts, and the phenomenon known as Twiggy.

"All the News That's Fit to Print"

The New York Times.

LATE CITY EDITION

Sunny today; clear tonight. Fair and milder tomorrow.

VOL. CXIV. No. 39,001. NEW YORK, WEDNESDAY, NOVEMBER 4, 1964. TEN CENTS

JOHNSON SWAMPS GOLDWATER AND KENNEDY BEATS KEATING; DEMOCRATS WIN LEGISLATURE

KENNEDY EDGE 6-5

Keating's Defeat Is Termed a 'Tragedy' by Rockefeller

UPSET AT ALBANY

Carlino and M[illegible]

[TUR]NOUT IS HEAVY

[illegible] Margin Expected [P]resident, Victor [in G]O.P. Bastions

[By] TOM WICKER

IN PHILADELPHIA NEARLY EVERYBODY READS THE BULLETIN

The Evening Bulletin WITH SUNDAY MORNING EDITION

4 ★★★★ SPORTS

TEN CENTS

PHILADELPHIA, PA. 19101, MONDAY, JULY 21, 1969

Eagle Boosts Self From Moon's Surface, Heads for Linkup With Command Ship

Kennedy Faces Car Complaint In Fatal Crash

Police Accuse Him Of Leaving Scene Where Woman Died

By LAWRENCE M. O'ROURKE
Of The Bulletin Staff

Edgartown, Martha's Vineyard, Mass. — Police today asked formally for a complaint charging Sen. Edward M. Kennedy (D-Mass) with leaving the scene of an accident that took the life of 28-year-old secretary Mary Jo Kopechne.

STEPPING TO THE MOON for the first time is Astronaut Neil A. Armstrong, who swings his left foot from lunar lander.

Armstrong and Aldrin Make Risky Landing On Rock-Strewn Plain

By EARL ABRAHAM and GARY BROOTEN
Of The Bulletin Staff

Spacecraft Center, Houston—Astronauts Neil A. Armstrong and Edwin E. (Buzz) Aldrin Jr., safely launched from the lunar surface this afternoon after putting the imprint of mankind on the moon.

The upper half of Tranquility Base, as the lunar lander was called from the moment it landed in the Sea of Tranquility yesterday, became Eagle once more at 1.54 P. M.

As the two astronauts rose through the lunar heights to rejoin Michael Collins in the command ship Columbia, orbiting 70 miles up, they knew the homeward journey to earth on Thursday had begun.

They had landed on the moon, cavorted and worked on it and were carrying home pieces of it after 21 hours and 38 minutes.

They had raised the Stars and Stripes over it. Afterward, President Nixon told Armstrong, 38, and Aldrin, 39, that their achievement "inspires us to redouble our efforts to bring peace and tranquility to earth."

On Rocky Plain

The two first explorers of the moon set their Eagle down on a bleak, rock-strewn plain in the Sea of Tranquility at 4.18 P. M. yesterday.

In the final seconds, Armstrong had to maneuver the gawky craft clear of a large crater ringed with boulders. He made it to firm, gently sloping ground, where the round foot pads of Eagle barely indented the surface.

"Hou[st]on, Tranquility Base here. The Eagle has landed," Armstrong radioed to earth.

The astronauts reached their immediate goal—and if they return safely, the one set for America in 1961 by President Kennedy — 102 hours and 46 minutes after they had left the blue-white earth that hung 241,500 miles over their heads.

Their firm, excited voices assured earth they were keen to press on with the daring venture. And the healthy condition they displayed via telemetry to doctors here brought them an early "go" to step to the

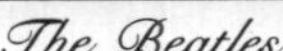
The Beatles

The tunes — as well as the times — were a-changin' in the Sixties. Rock and roll was declared dead only to be reborn with the arrival of the mop-headed foursome known as The Beatles (from Liverpool, no less). The folk music craze twanged in and out. Songs preaching social justice and expressing anti-war sentiments brought adherents to Bob Dylan and Joan Baez. Big bands showed no signs of a comeback, except for those with the near-symphonic sounds of Mantovani and Henry Mancini. And glitzy discothèques became the rage, introducing such dancefloor gyrations as the twist, the frug, the mashed potato, the Watusi, and the monkey.

Anthony Newley in "Stop The World — I Want To Get Off"

Perhaps the most noticeable influence was the British invasion led by The Beatles ("I Want to Hold Your Hand," "She Loves You"). In their wake came Marian Faithfull ("As Tears Go By"), Petula Clark ("Downtown"), Gerry and the Pacemakers ("Ferry Cross the Mersey"), Tom Jones ("It's Not Unusual"), and The Seekers ("Georgy Girl"). Even that traditional American form, the musical theatre, made way for the arrival of such British writers as Lionel Bart with *Oliver!* (featuring "As Long as He Needs Me") , and Anthony Newley and Leslie Bricusse with two shows, *Stop the World — I Want to Get Off* ("What Kind of Fool Am I?") and *The Roar of the Greasepaint — The Smell of the Crowd* ("Who Can I Turn To?").

England wasn't the only foreign country to supply songs for the U.S. pop market during the decade. A German folk song, "Muss I Denn Zum Stadtele Haus," was turned into "Wooden Heart," one of Elvis Presley's successes, and a Russian folk song provided the source for Mary Hopkin's hit, "Those Were the Days." The Danish singer Bent Fabric (né Bent Fabricus Bjerre) brought over his "Alley Cat" (né "Omkring et Flygel"), the Belgian Singing Nun Soeur Sourire achieved fame with her own "Dominique," Roy Clark scored impressively with "Yesterday When I Was Young," the English version of the French "Hier encore," and French composer-conductor André Popp's "L'Amour est bleu" became — not too surprisingly — "Love Is Blue," a hit single for Claudine Longet. The bossa nova beat proliferated for a while thanks to the appeal of Astrud Gilberto's recording of the Brazilian "Girl from Ipanema," written by Antonio Carlos Jobim, and Frank Sinatra returned auspiciously to the top of the charts with "Strangers in the Night" ("Zoobee zoobee zoo"), indited by German orchestra leader Bert Kaempfert. Also winning favor were songs emanating from foreign films, notably "More," the theme of the Italian documentary *Mondo Cane,* and Michel Legrand's "Watch What Happens," adapted from the love duet in the French *Umbrellas of Cherbourg.*

Barbra Streisand in "Funny Girl"

Very much a part of the spirit of the Sixties were the vocal and instrumental groups that appealed primarily — but not exclusively — to teenagers. These went by such fanciful rubrics as Ruby and the Romantics ("Our Day Will Come"), The Dixie Cups ("Chapel of Love"), Little Anthony and the Imperials ("Goin' Out of My Head"), The Mamas and the Papas ("California Dreamin'," "Monday, Monday"), Booker T. and the MG's ("Groovin'"), The McCoys ("Hang on Sloopy"), The Turtles ("Happy Together"), Steam ("Na Na Hey Hey, Kiss Him Goodbye"), and The Fifth Dimension ("Up, Up and Away").

There were, of course, the more traditional, melodic songs, mostly from Broadway musicals, that continued to catch the public fancy. Among them: "Try to Remember," a haunting ballad still being sung in *The Fantasticks,* which — at this writing — has been running Off Broadway for over 26 years!); "Sunrise, Sunset," a wistful rumination about the passing of time that was introduced in *Fiddler on the Roof*; the philosophical "People," sung by Barbra Streisand in *Funny Girl;* "Cabaret," an insinuating invitation first proffered in the show of the same name; and "My Cup Runneth Over," an expression of love that served as a duet for Mary Martin and Robert Preston in *I Do! I Do!* Also in the canorous vein were two romantic standards, "Fly Me to the Moon" and "I Left My Heart in San Francisco," both benefiting from Tony Bennett's distinctive interpretations.

A number of songwriters of the Sixties gave voice to their feelings about contemporary issues. In the forefront was Pete Seeger, whose output included such pieces as "If I Had a Hammer," a rollicking proclamation of brotherhood "all over this land"; "Turn! Turn! Turn!," a call for peace based on the Bible's "Book of Ecclesiastes"; and "Where Have All the Flowers Gone?," a somber reflection on the lives lost in battle. In addition, there was "One Tin Soldier," an ironic, allegorical message about the futility of war, and "San Francisco (Be Sure to Wear Some Flowers in Your Hair)," a paean to the lifestyle of hippies and flower children.

"The Fantasticks"

Robert Preston and Mary Martin in "I Do! I Do!"

Woodstock

AP Photo

Probably never before this decade had music played such an important part in the lives of young people. Deeply affected by the tumult and turmoil all around them, their anti-establishment attitude was marked by long hair and slovenly dress, strong opposition to war, and their advocacy of civil rights, sexual freedom, and drugs. As something of a symbol of the age, some 300,000 converged on the town of Bethel, New York, for a three-day marathon rock concert known as Woodstock. They may not have been exactly what President Kennedy had in mind in his inaugural address, but they were unquestionably a new generation of Americans.

ALLEY CAT SONG

Words by JACK HARLEN
Music by FRANK BJORN

Moderately, in 2

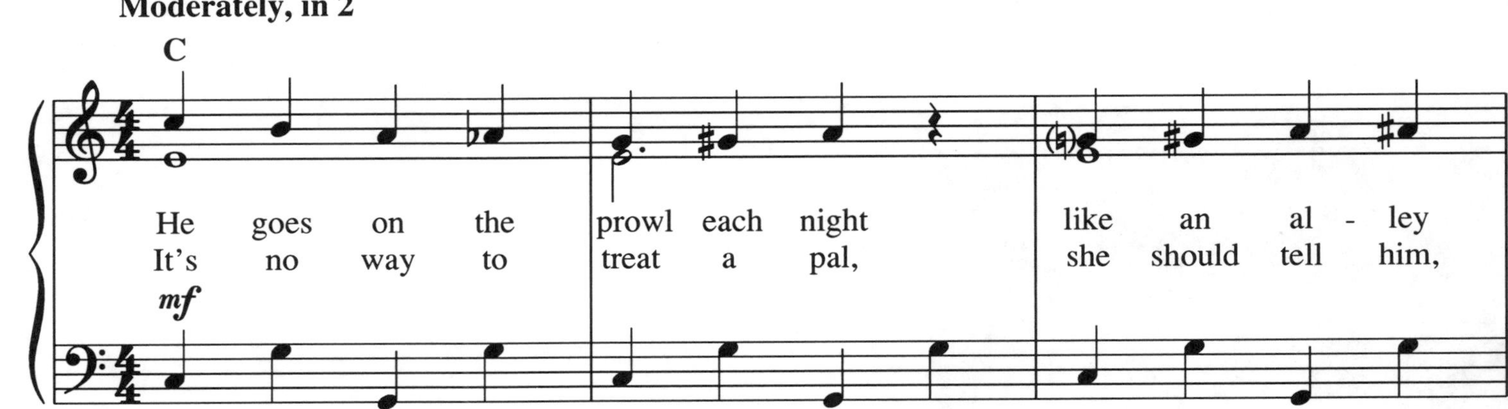

To Coda
C
F
like an al - ley
like an al - ley
cat. He
meets 'em
and
C
D7
loves 'em
and
leaves 'em,
G7
D.C. al Coda
that's what Cat - sa - nov - a does.
CODA
C
cat. And that's the
F
F#dim
C/G
A
D7
G7
C
sad, sad, tale of a
lone - some frail,
and her al - ley
cat.

AS LONG AS HE NEEDS ME

(From the Columbia Pictures-Romulus film "OLIVER!")

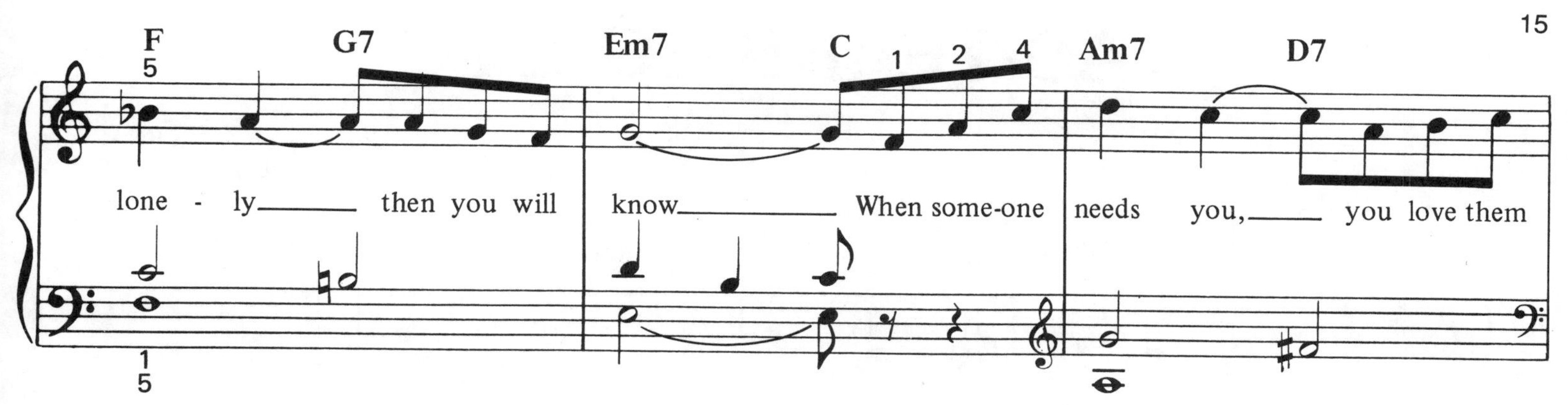
F
G7
Em7
C
Am7
D7
lone - ly then you will
know When some-one
needs you, you love them

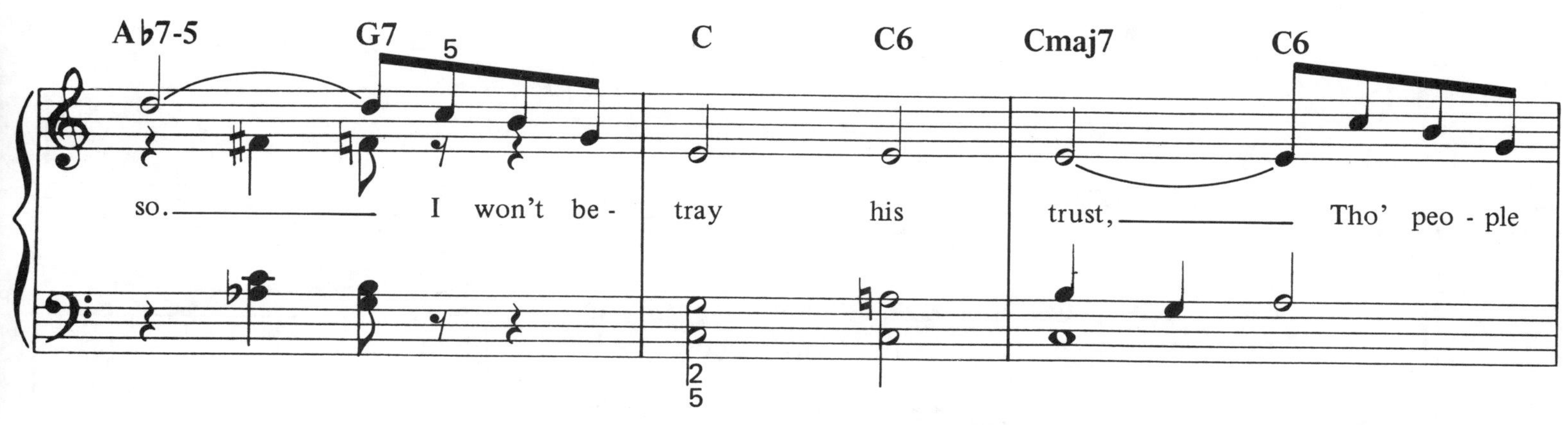
A♭7-5
G7
C
C6
Cmaj7
C6
so. I won't be -
tray his
trust, Tho' peo - ple

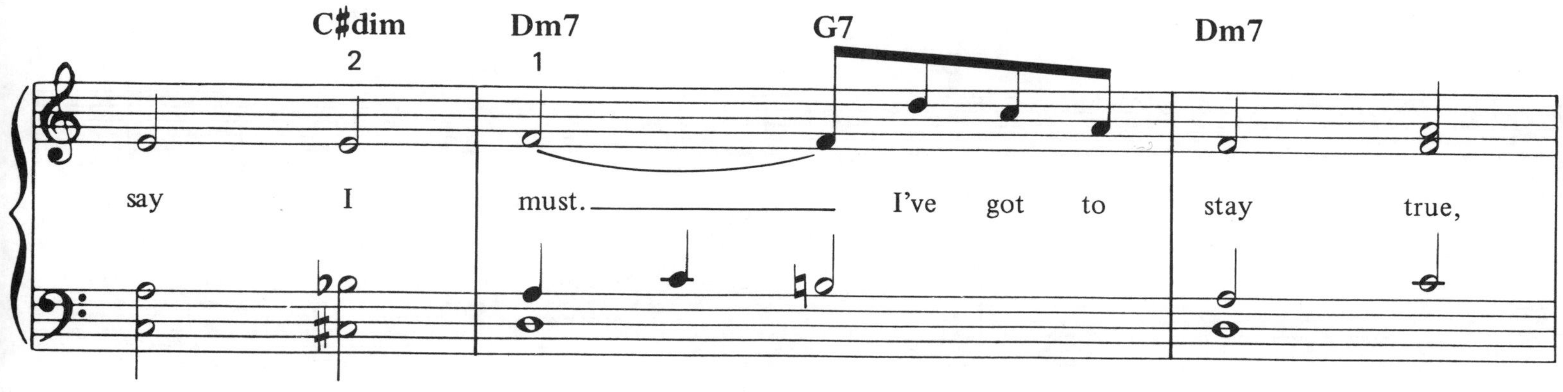
C♯dim
Dm7
G7
Dm7
say I
must. I've got to
stay true,

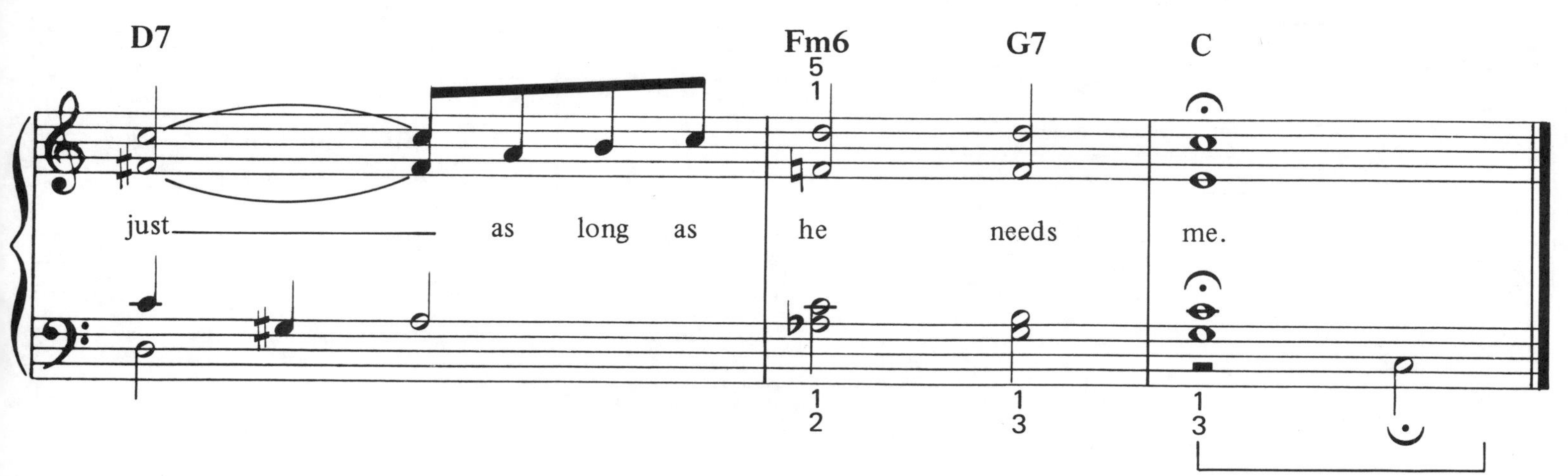
D7
Fm6
G7
C
just as long as
he needs
me.

AS TEARS GO BY

Words and Music by MICK JAGGER,
KEITH RICHARD and ANDREW LOOG OLDHAM

Moderately

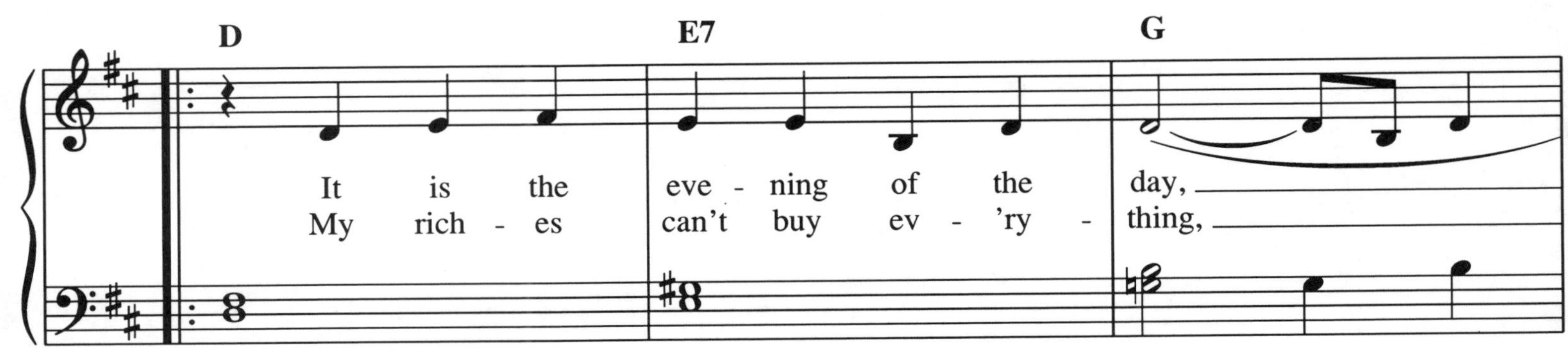

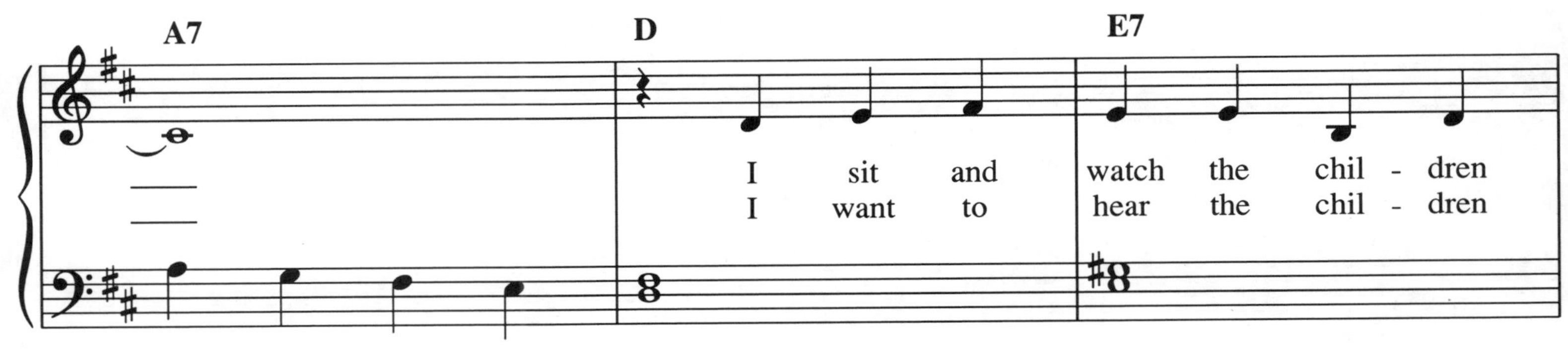

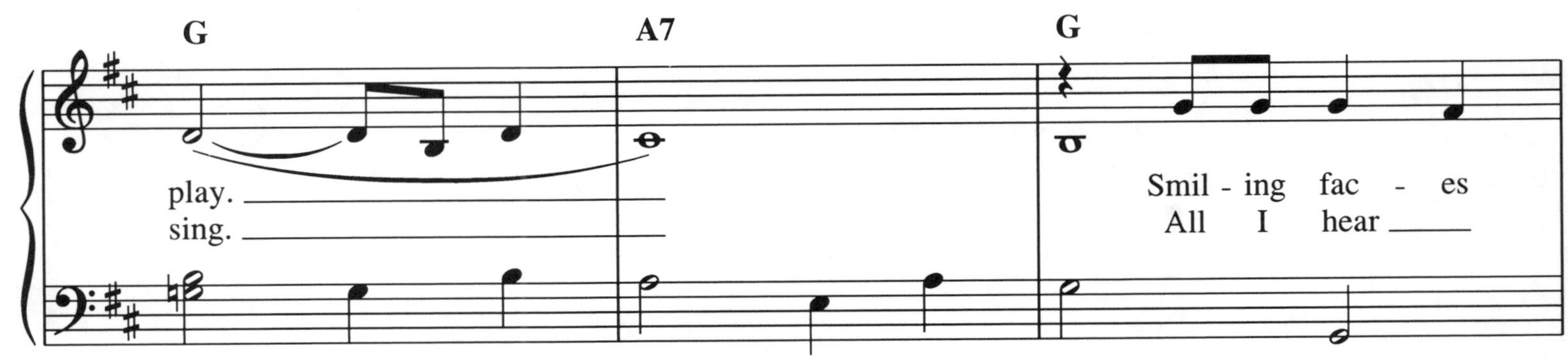

A7
1.
D
Bm
I can see,
is the sound
but not for
me,
G
F♯m
Em7
A7
I sit and
watch as tears go
by.
2.
D
Bm
of rain fal - ling
on the ground,
G
F♯m
Em7
A7
I sit and
watch as tears go
by.

D
E7
It is the eve - ning of the

G
A7
D
day,
I sit and

E7
G
A7
watch the chil - ren play,

G
A7
D
Do - in' things I used to do
they think are

Bm
G
F♯m
Em7
new,
I sit and watch as tears go
A7
D
by.
Mm
E7
G
A7
D
Mm
E7
G
A7
D
Mm

BY THE TIME I GET TO PHOENIX

Gm7
E♭
C7
left that girl so many times before.
By the

Gm7
E♭
C7
wall, that's all.
By the

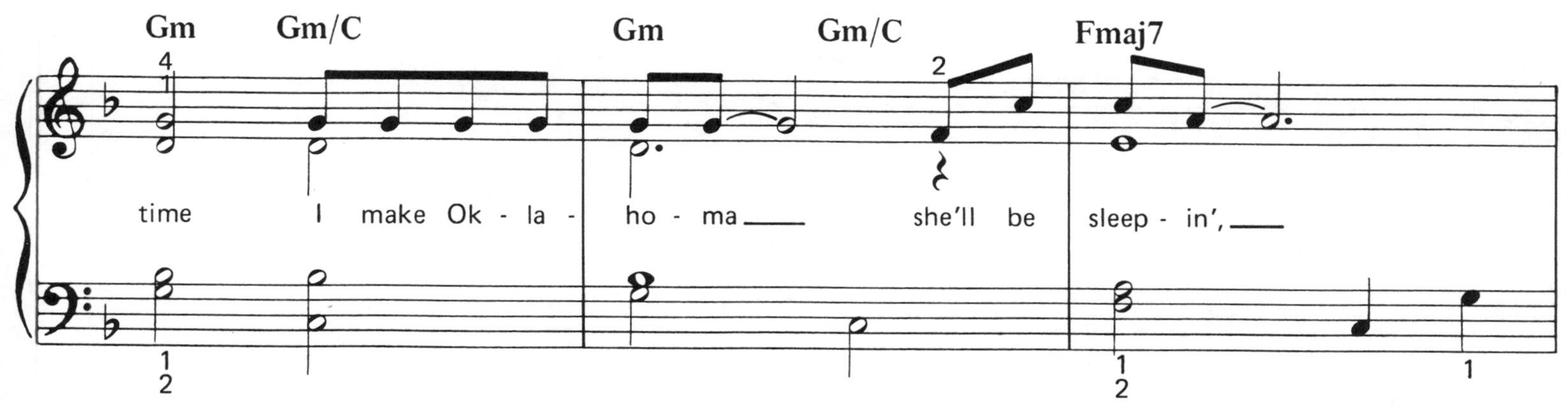
Gm
Gm/C
Gm
Gm/C
Fmaj7
time I make Ok - la - ho - ma she'll be sleep - in',

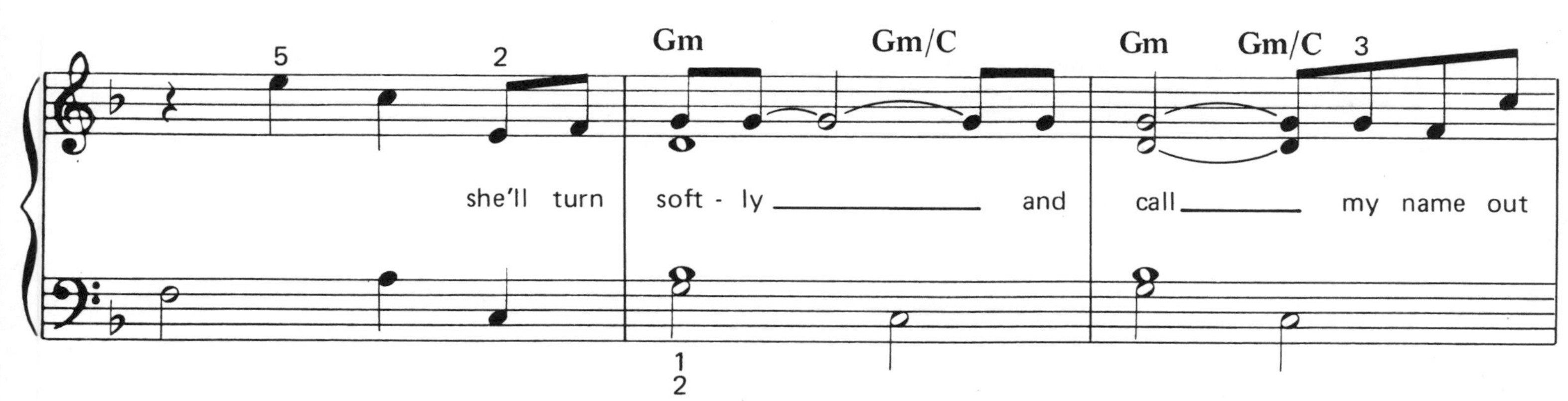
Gm
Gm/C
Gm
Gm/C
she'll turn soft - ly and call my name out

Fmaj7
B♭maj7
low. And she'll cry just to

C9
Am7
Dm7
think I'd real - ly leave her, tho'

Gm7
C7
Fmaj7
time and time I've tried to tell her so,

B♭maj7
Gm
A7
D
she just did - n't know I would real - ly go.
ritard.

CHAPEL OF LOVE

Words and Music by PHIL SPECTOR,
ELLIE GREENWICH and JEFF BARRY

love you and we're gon - na get mar - ried,

Gm
C7
F
To Coda
go - in' to the chap - el of love.

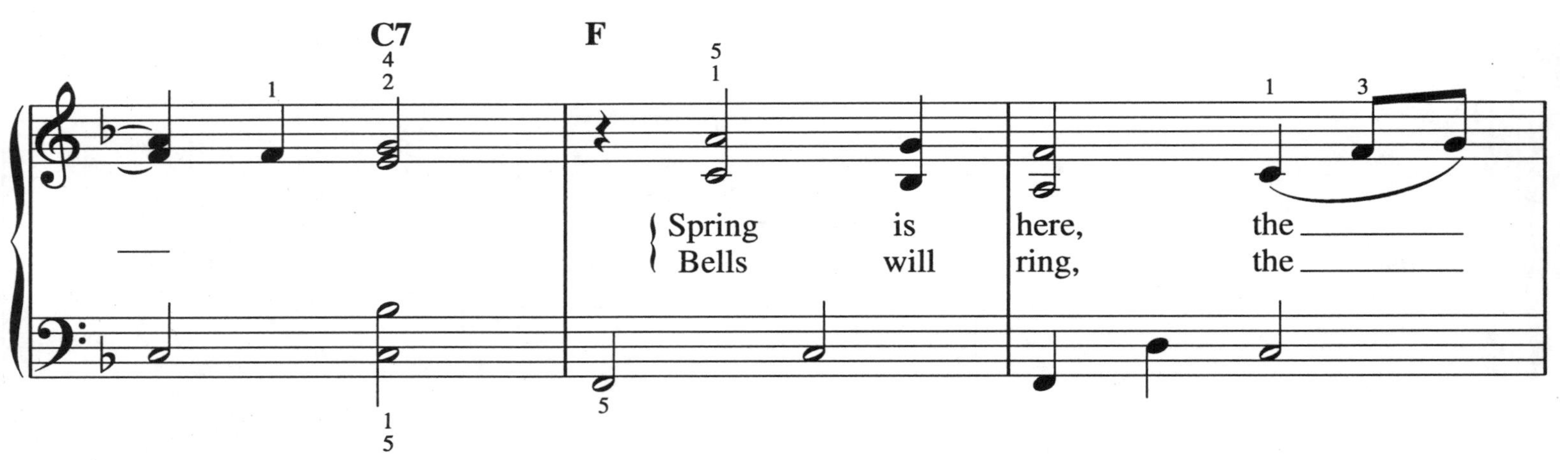
C7
F
Spring is here, the
Bells will ring, the

Gm
sky is blue. Woe, birds will
sun will shine. Woe, I'll be

C7
Gm
C7
F
5
1
5
1
sing as if they knew. To - day's the
his and he'll be mine. We'll love un -

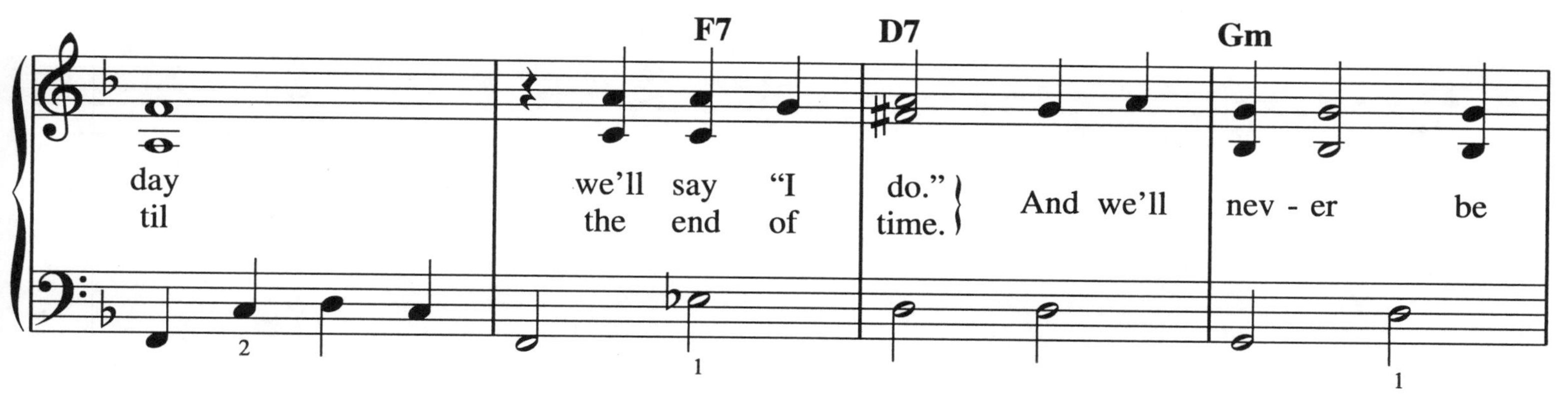
F7
D7
Gm
day we'll say "I do."
til the end of time.
And we'll nev - er be

C7
1.
F
2.
F
lone - ly an - y - more. Be - cause we're more.

D.S. al Coda
Be - cause we're

CODA
F
B♭
F
love.

CABARET
(From the Musical "CABARET")

Music by JOHN KANDER
Words by FRED EBB

Moderately, in 2 (𝅗𝅥 = 1 beat)

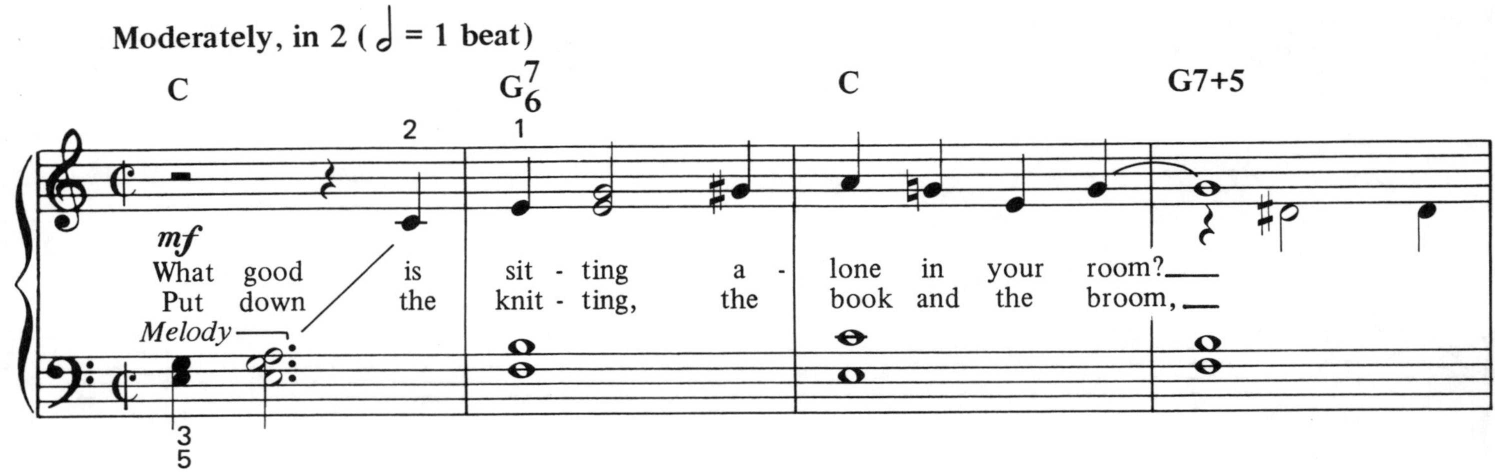

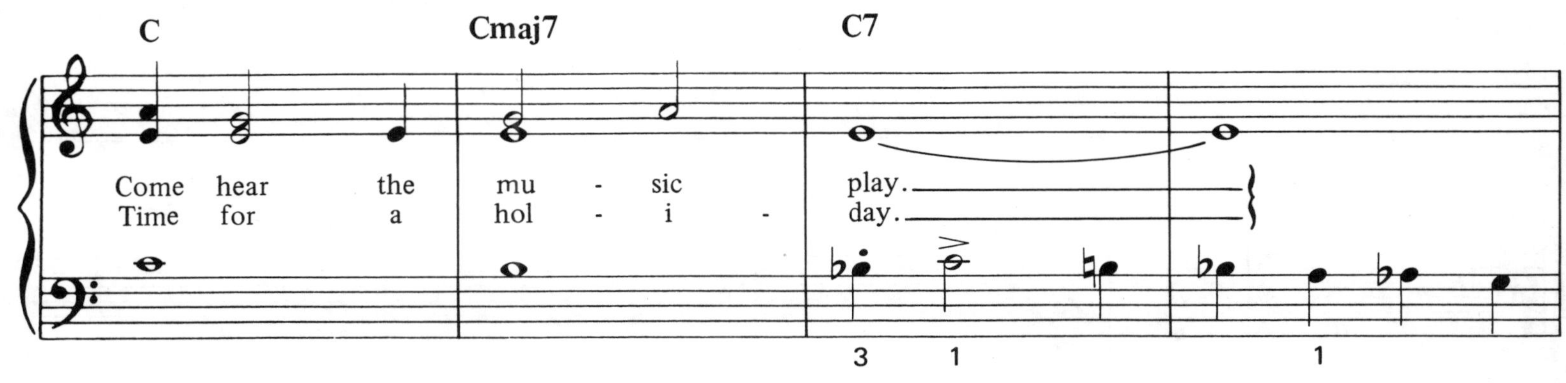

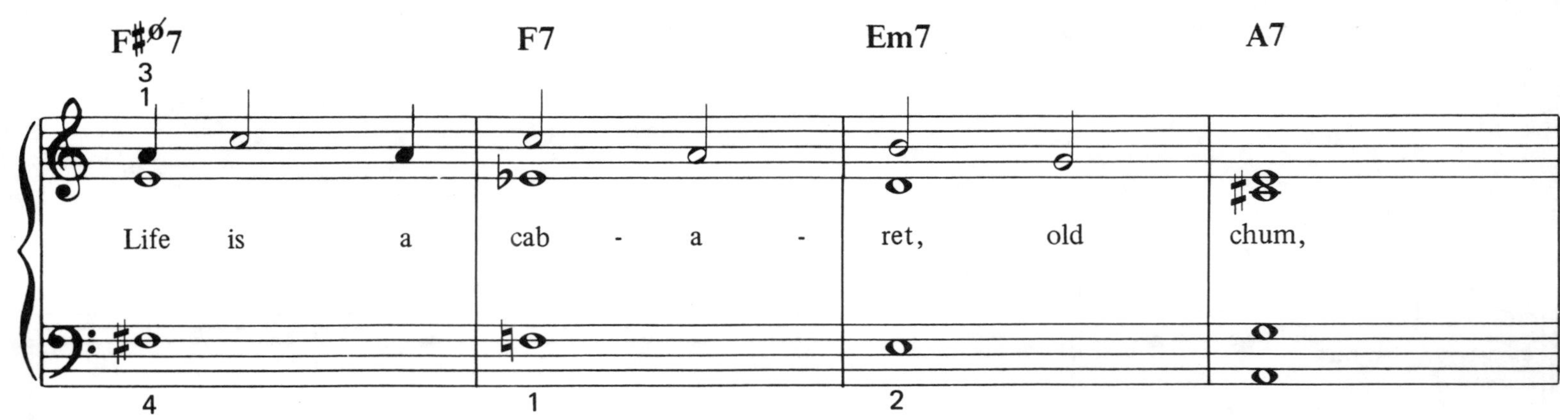

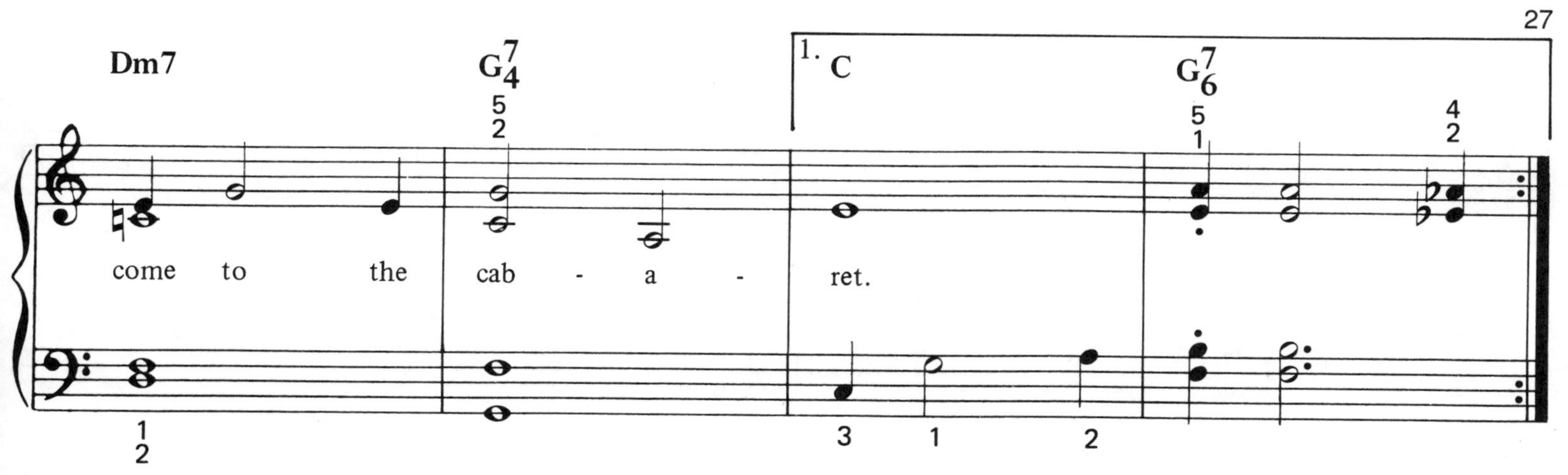
Dm7
G7/4
1.
C
G7/6
come to the cab - a - ret.

2.
C
Fm6
ret.
Come taste the
wine,

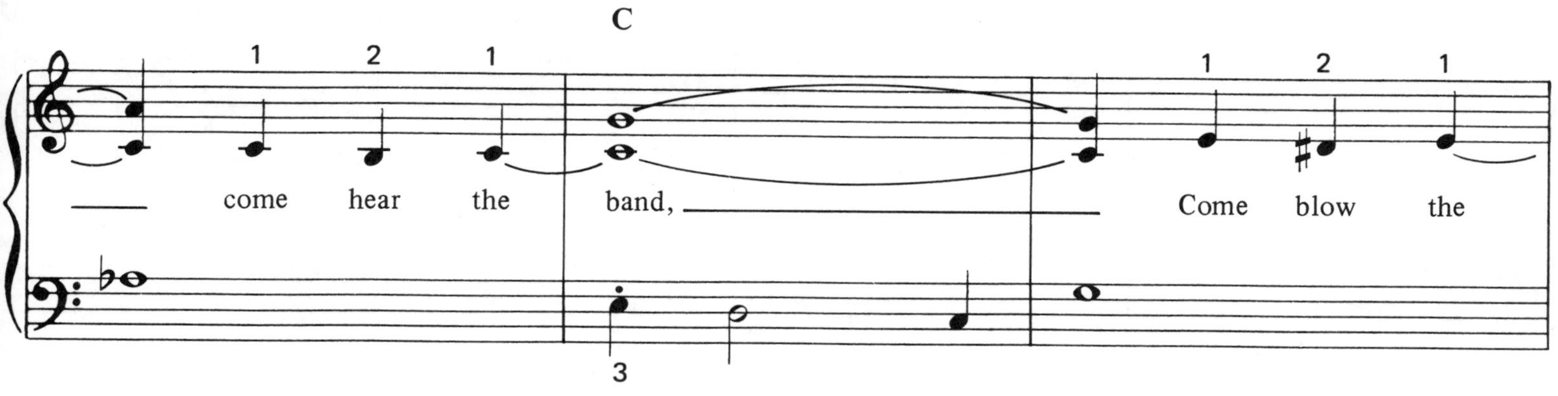
C
come hear the
band,
Come blow the

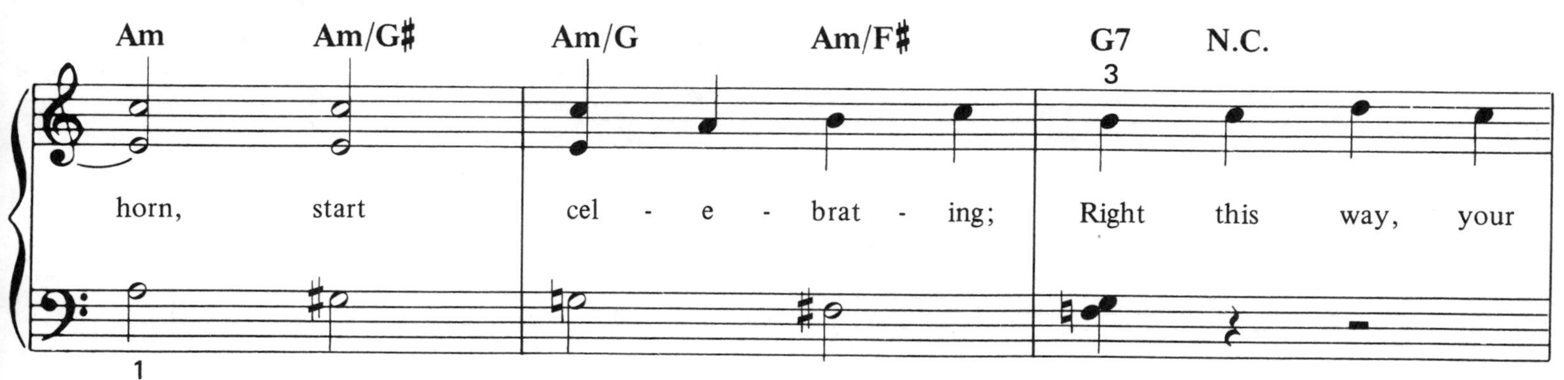
Am
Am/G♯
Am/G
Am/F♯
G7
N.C.
horn, start
cel - e - brat - ing;
Right this way, your

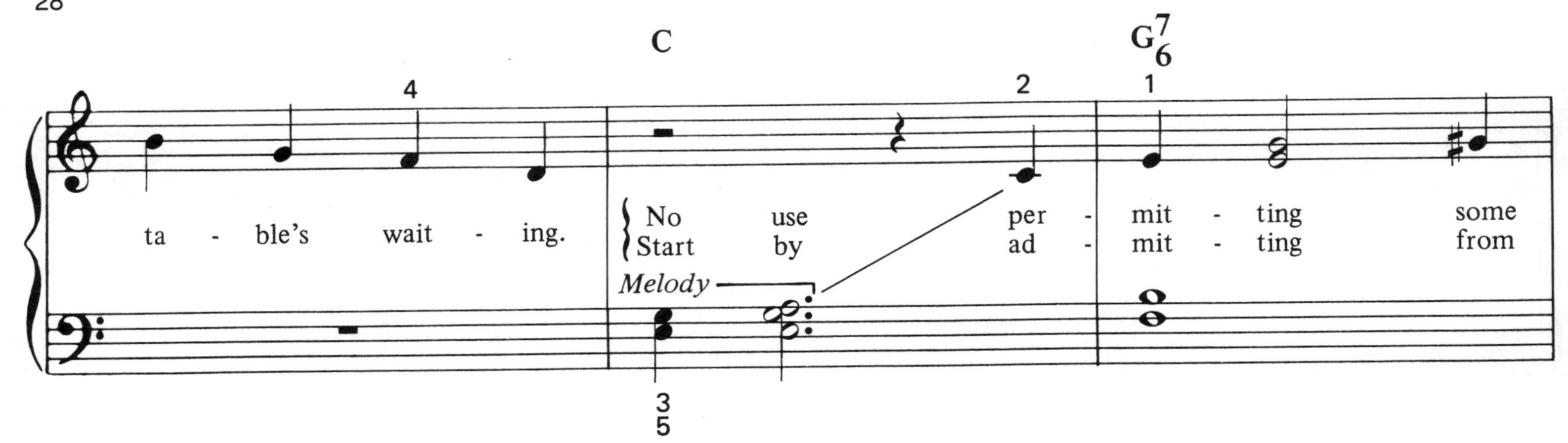
C
G7/6
ta - ble's wait - ing.
No use per - mit - ting some
Start by ad - mit - ting from
Melody

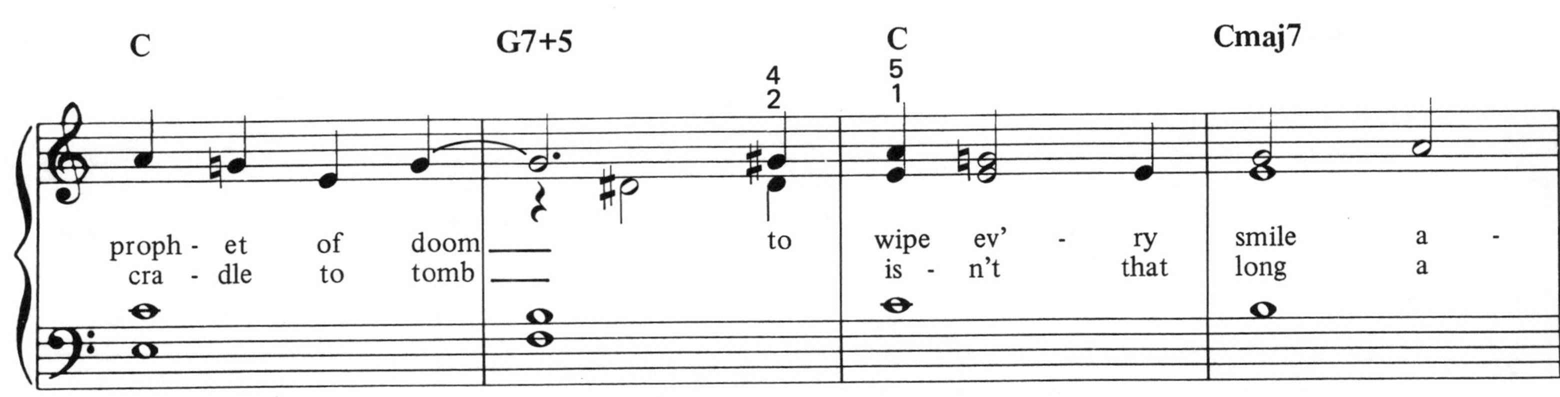
C
G7+5
C
Cmaj7
proph - et of doom to wipe ev' - ry smile a -
cra - dle to tomb is - n't that long a

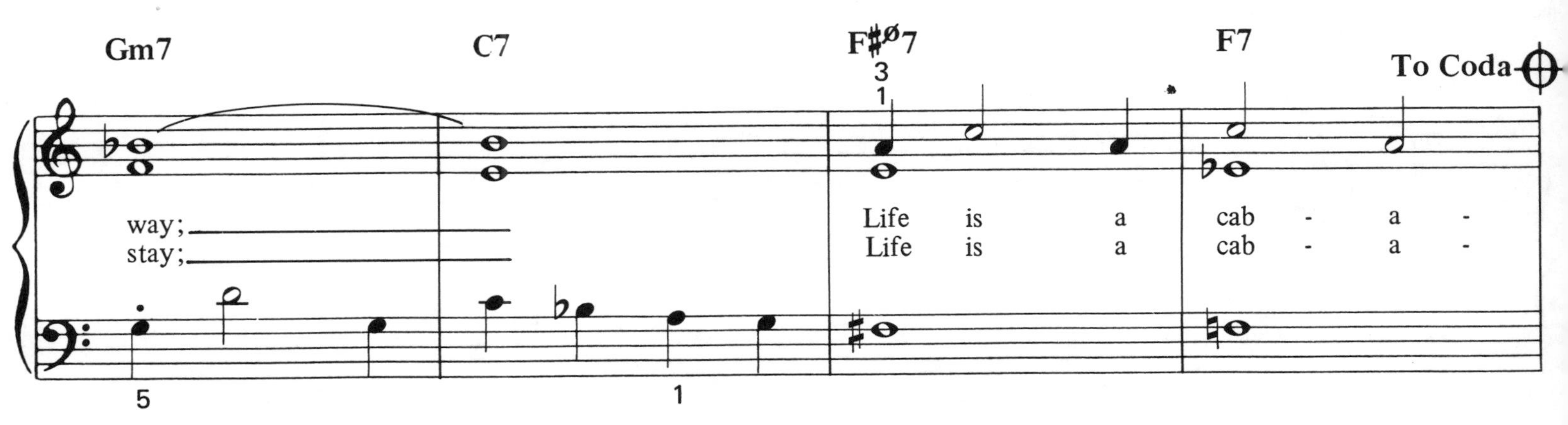
Gm7
C7
F#ø7
F7
To Coda
way;
stay;
Life is a cab - a -
Life is a cab - a -

Em7
A7
Dm7
F/G
ret, old chum, come to the cab - a -

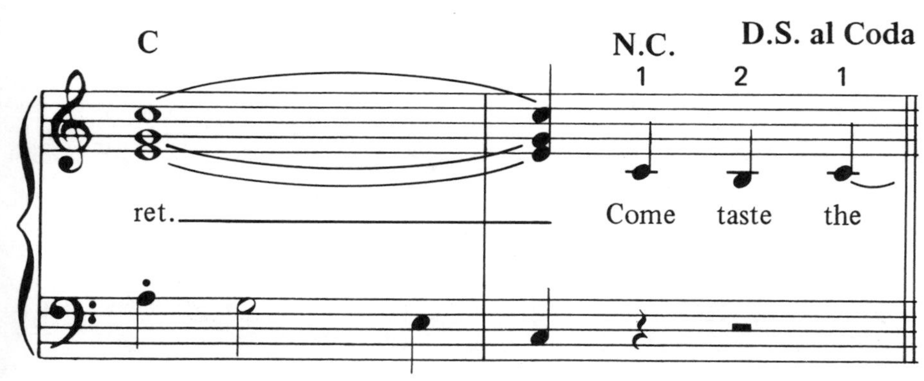
C
N.C.
D.S. al Coda
1 2 1
ret.
Come taste the

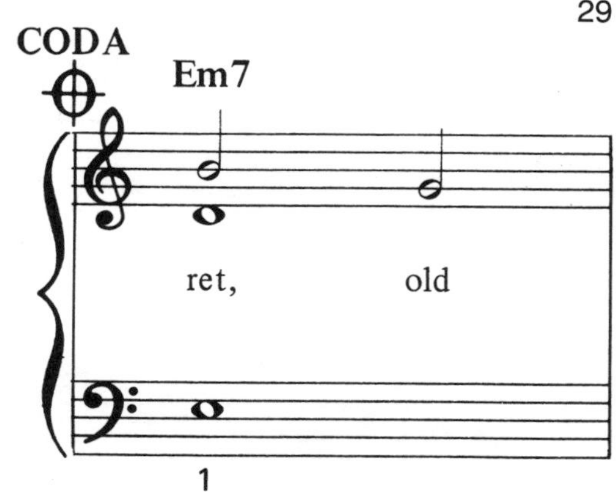
CODA
Em7
ret, old
1

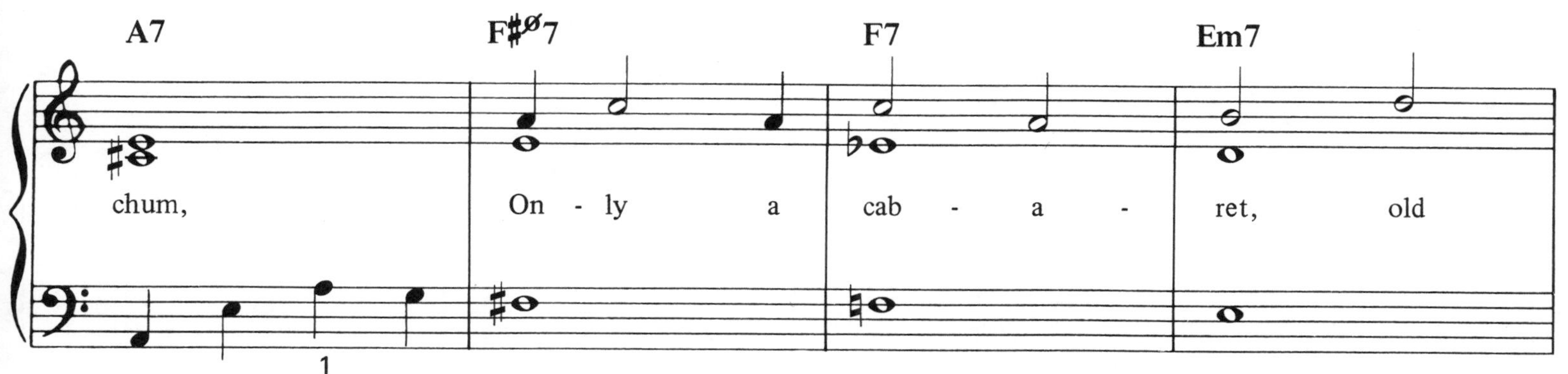
A7
F♯ø7
F7
Em7
chum,
On - ly a
cab - a -
ret, old
1

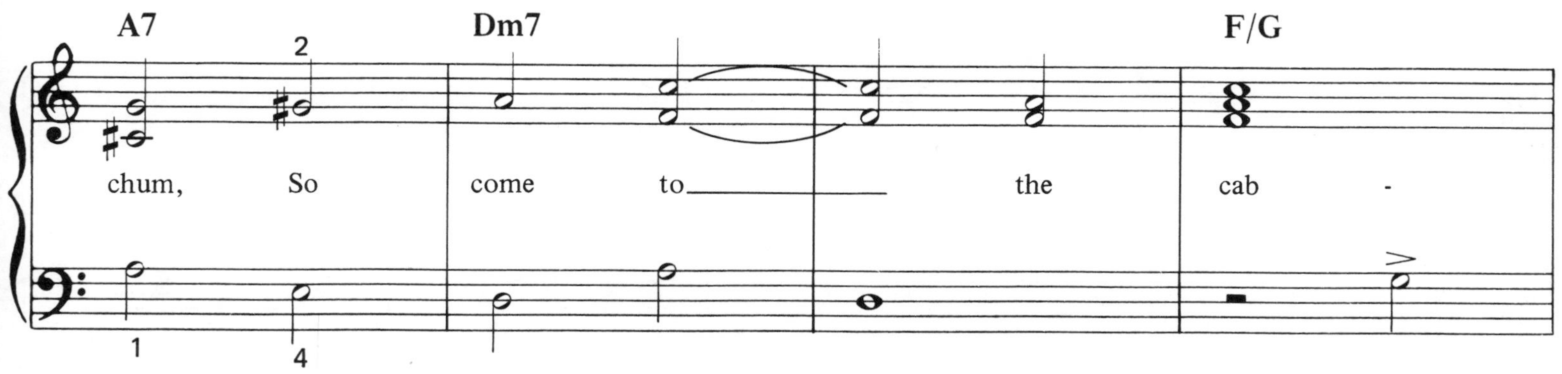
A7
2
Dm7
F/G
chum, So
come to
the
cab -
1
4

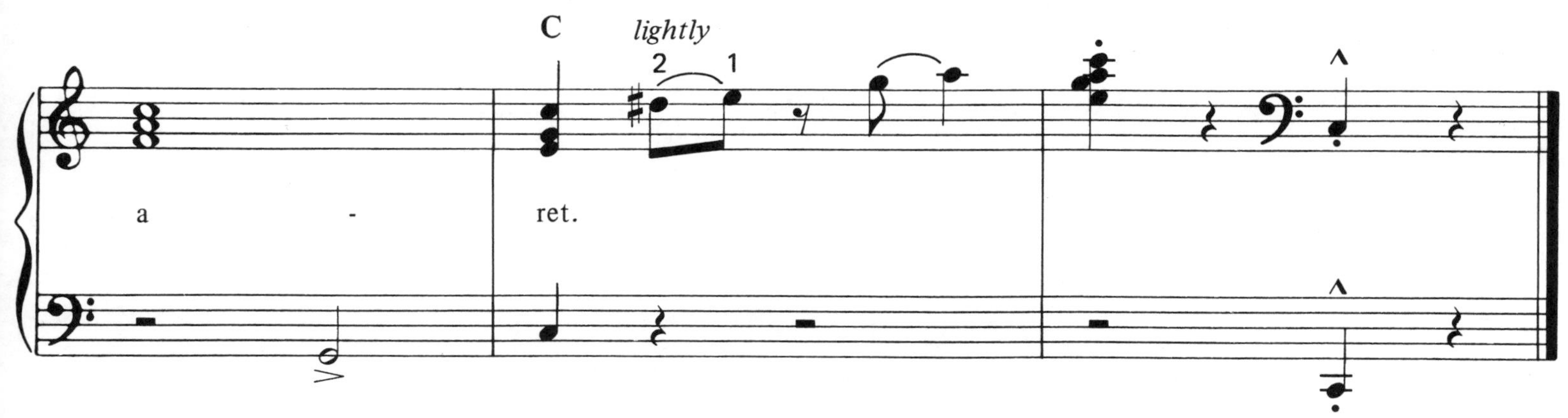
C
lightly
2 1
a -
ret.

CALIFORNIA DREAMIN'

Words and Music by JOHN PHILLIPS
and MICHELLE PHILLIPS

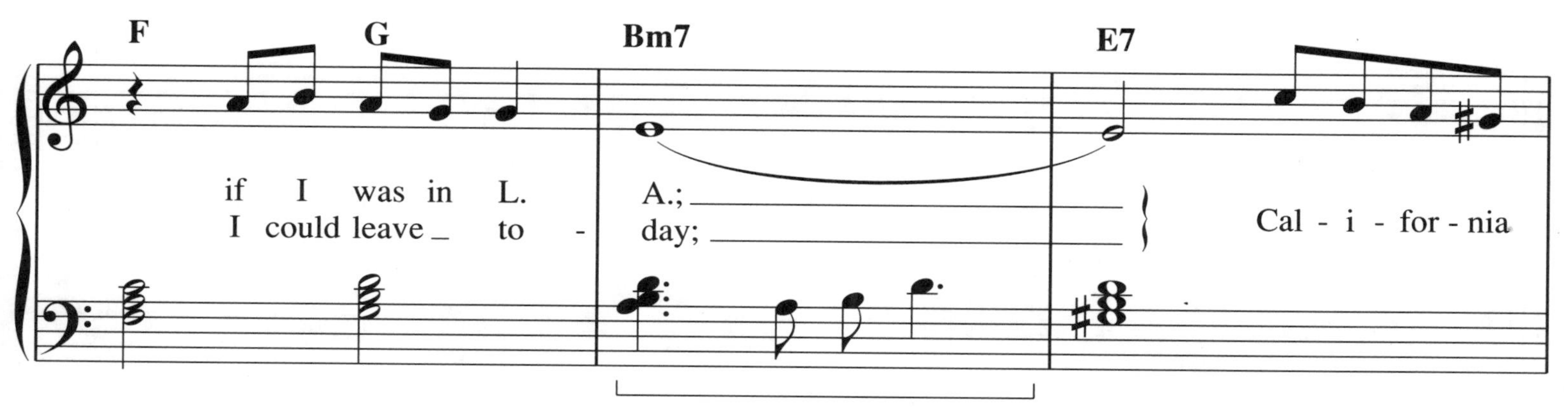
F
G
Bm7
E7
if I was in L. A.;
I could leave to - day;
Cal - i - for - nia

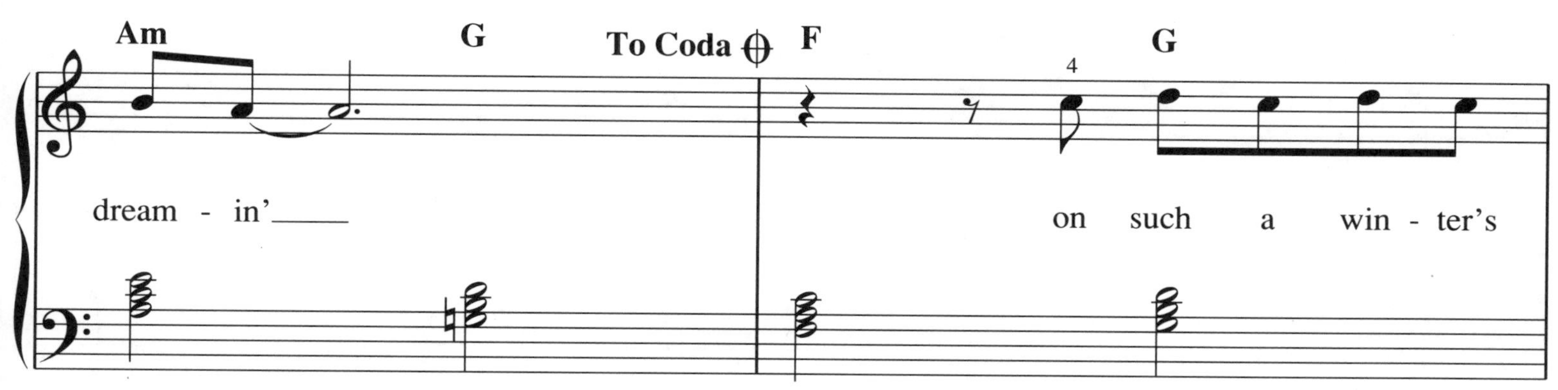
Am
G
To Coda
F
G
dream - in'
on such a win - ter's

E7sus4
E7
Am
G
day.
Stopped in - to a
church

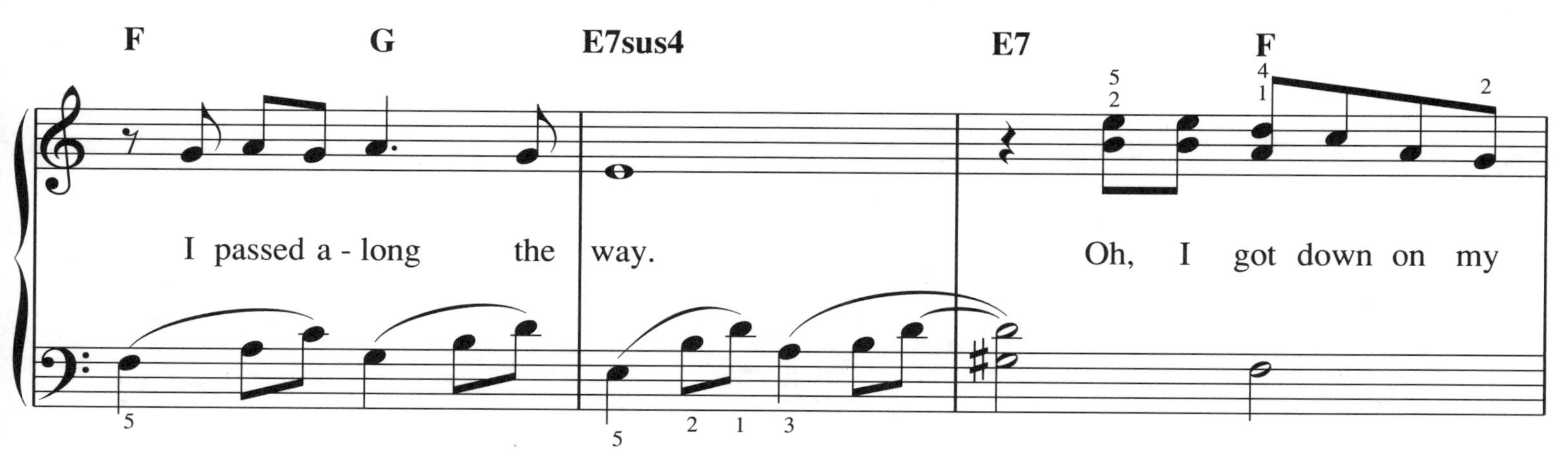
F
G
E7sus4
E7
F
I passed a - long the
way.
Oh, I got down on my

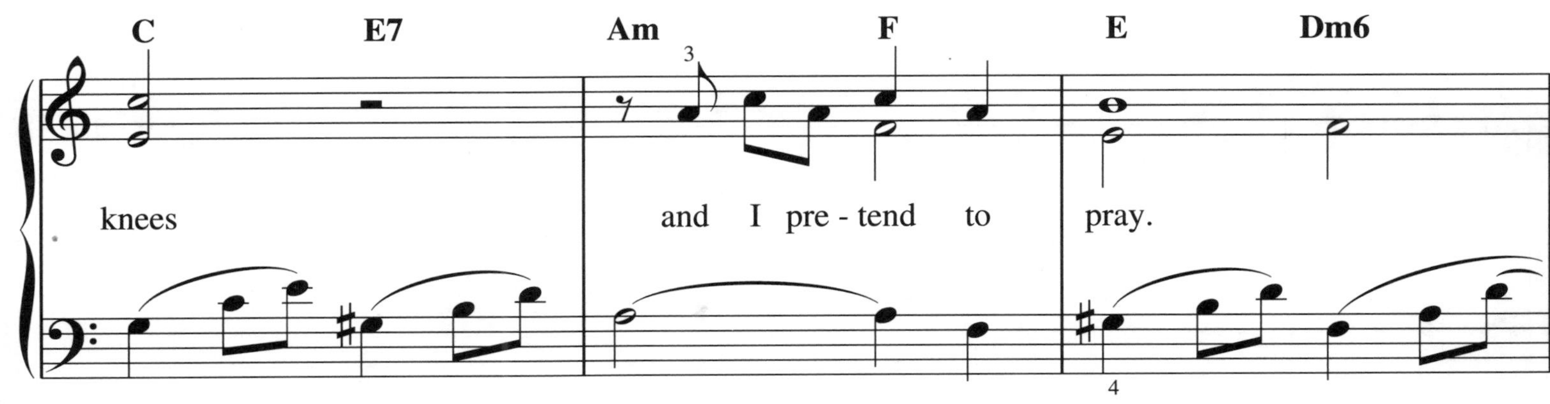
C
E7
Am
F
E
Dm6
knees
and I pre - tend to
pray.

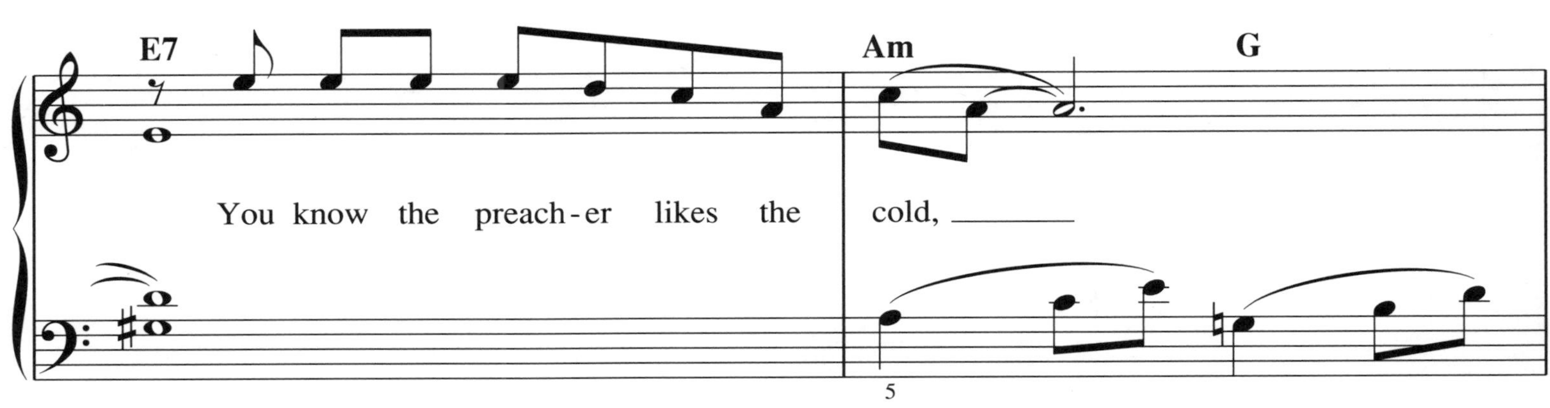
E7
Am
G
You know the preach - er likes the
cold,

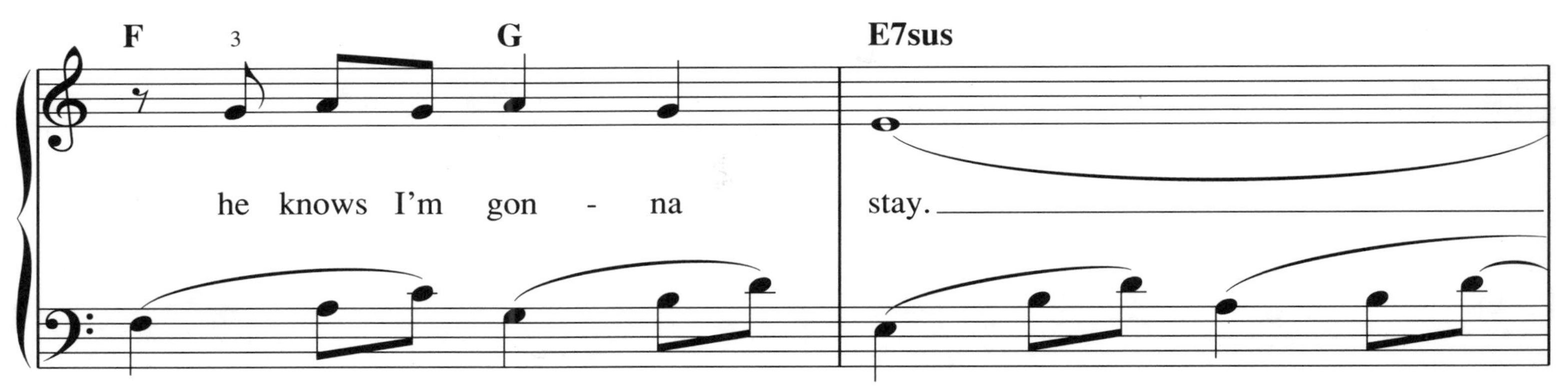
F
G
E7sus
he knows I'm gon - na
stay.

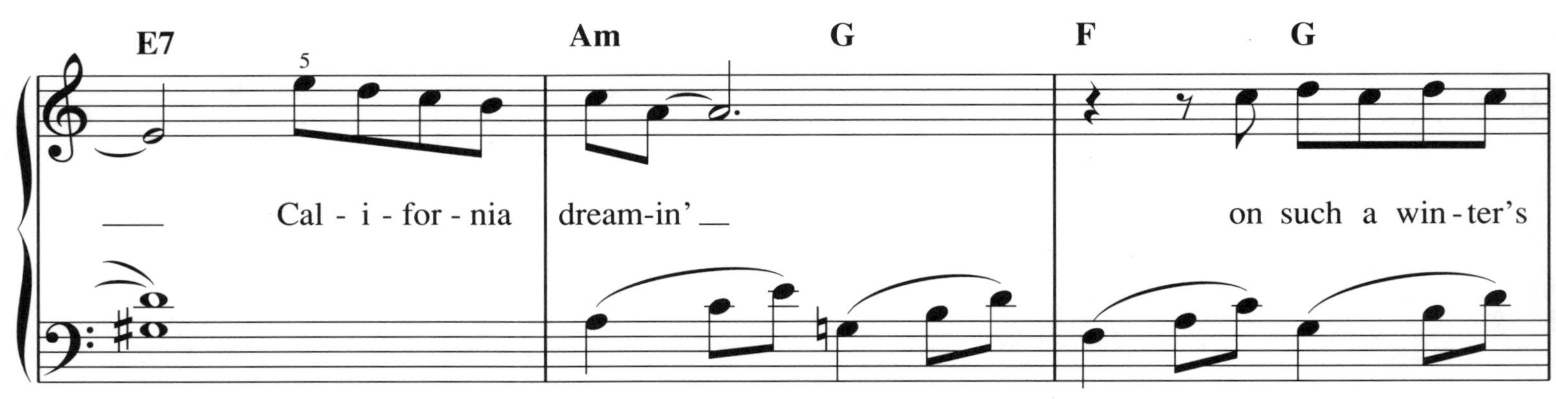
E7
Am
G
F
G
Cal - i - for - nia
dream-in'
on such a win - ter's

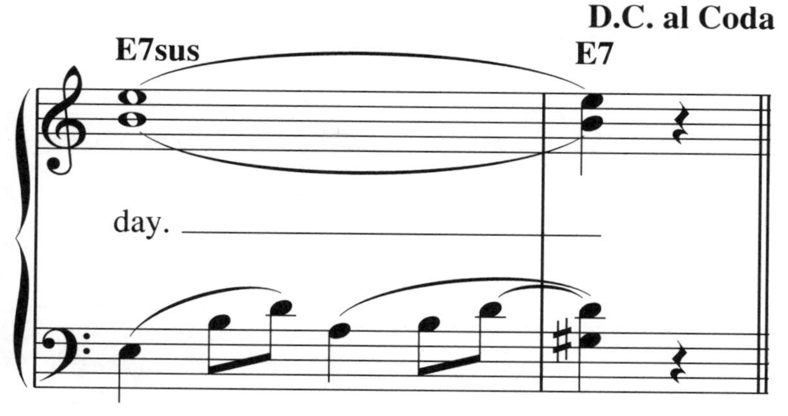
D.C. al Coda
E7sus
E7
day.

CODA
F
G
4
on such a win-ter's

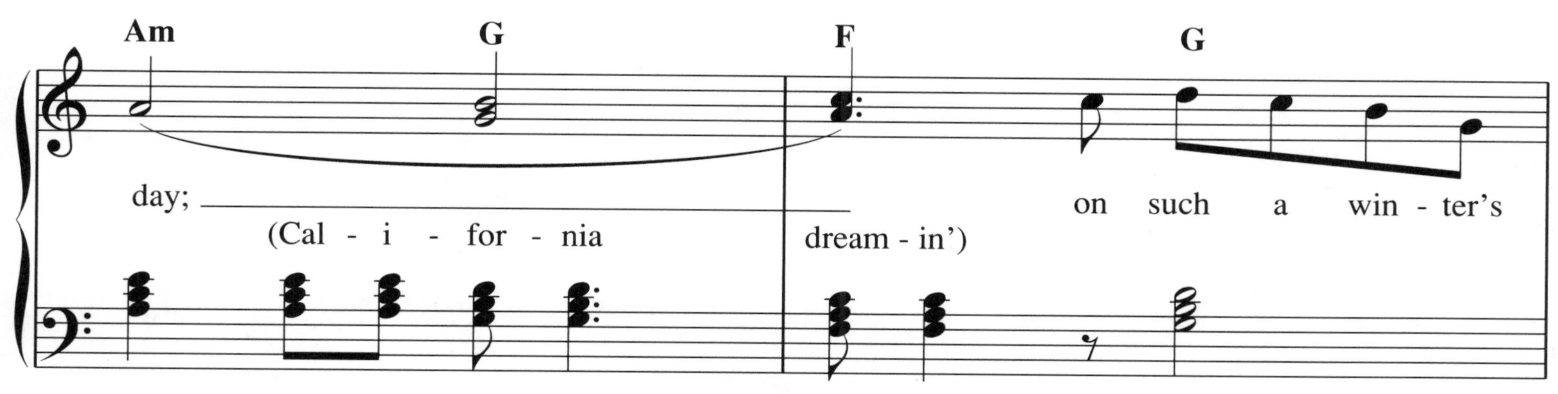
Am
G
F
G
day;
(Cal - i - for - nia
dream - in')
on such a win - ter's

Am
G
F
G
Fmaj7
5
3
1
day,
(Cal - i - for - nia
dream-in')
on such a win-ter's
day.

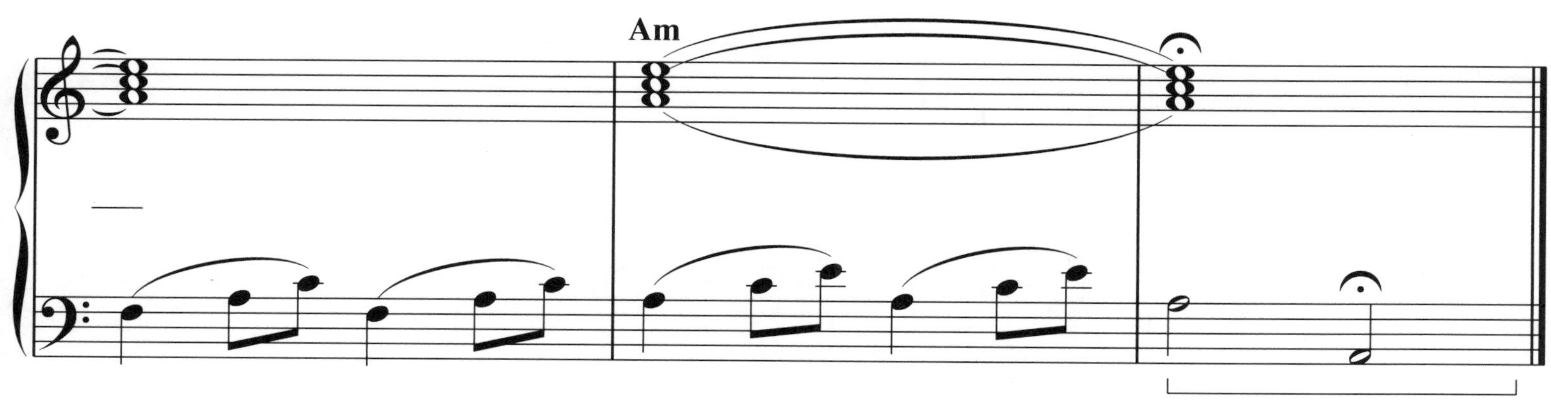
Am

CAN'T HELP FALLING IN LOVE

Words and Music by GEORGE DAVID WEISS,
HUGO PERETTI and LUIGI CREATORE

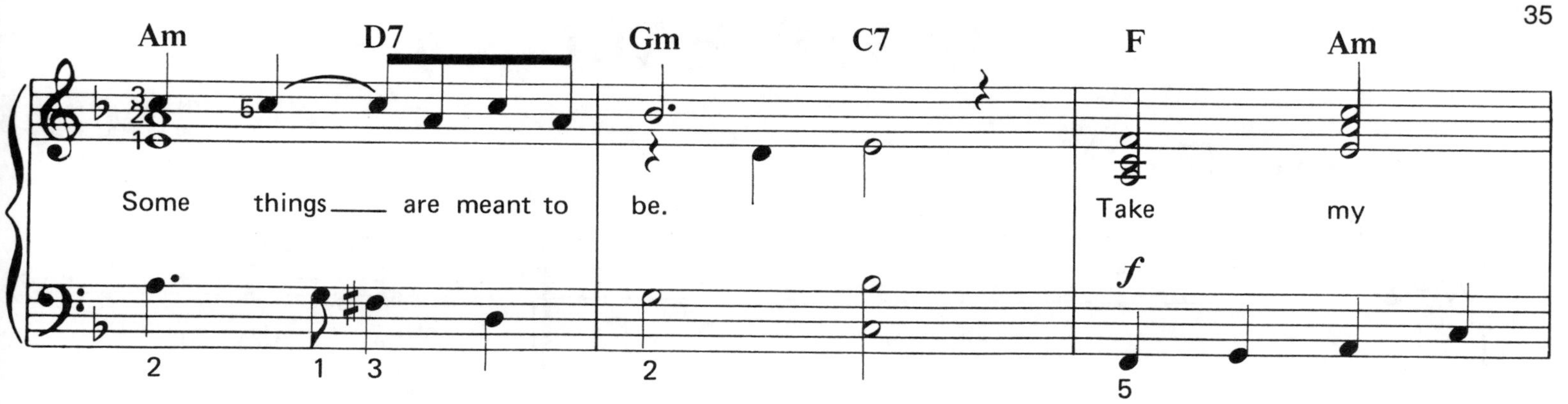
Am D7 Gm C7 F Am
Some things ___ are meant to be. Take my
f
3 2 1 5
2 1 3 2 5

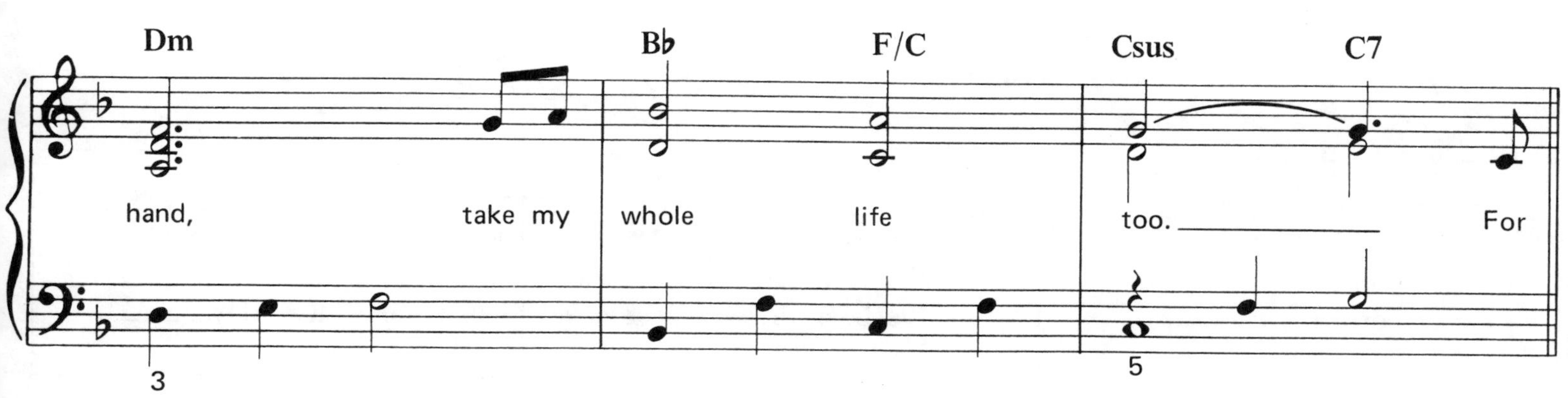
Dm B♭ F/C Csus C7
hand, take my whole life too. ___ For
3 5

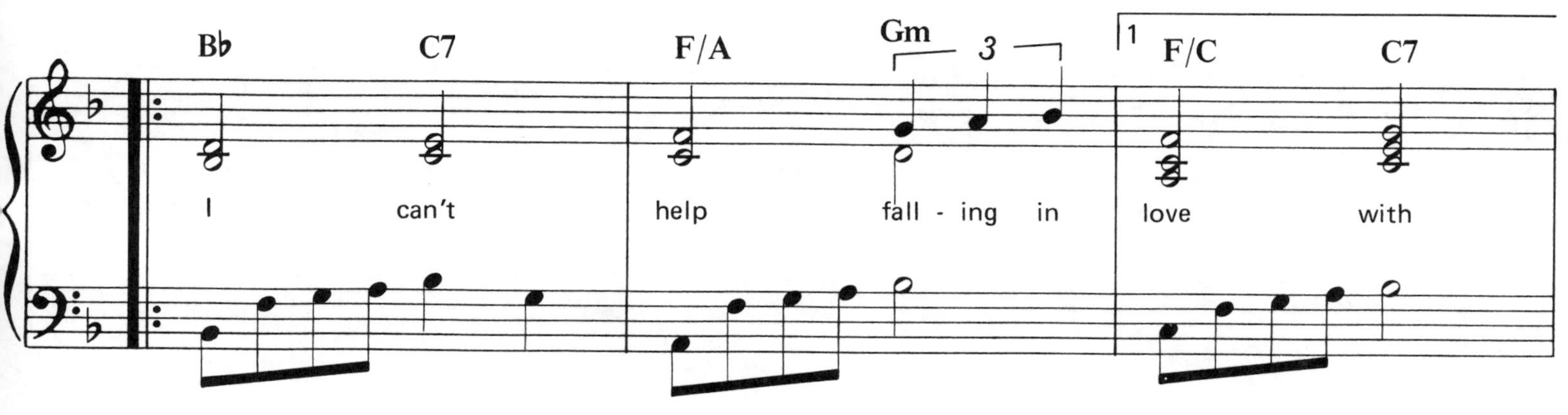
B♭ C7 F/A Gm F/C C7
3
1
I can't help fall - ing in love with

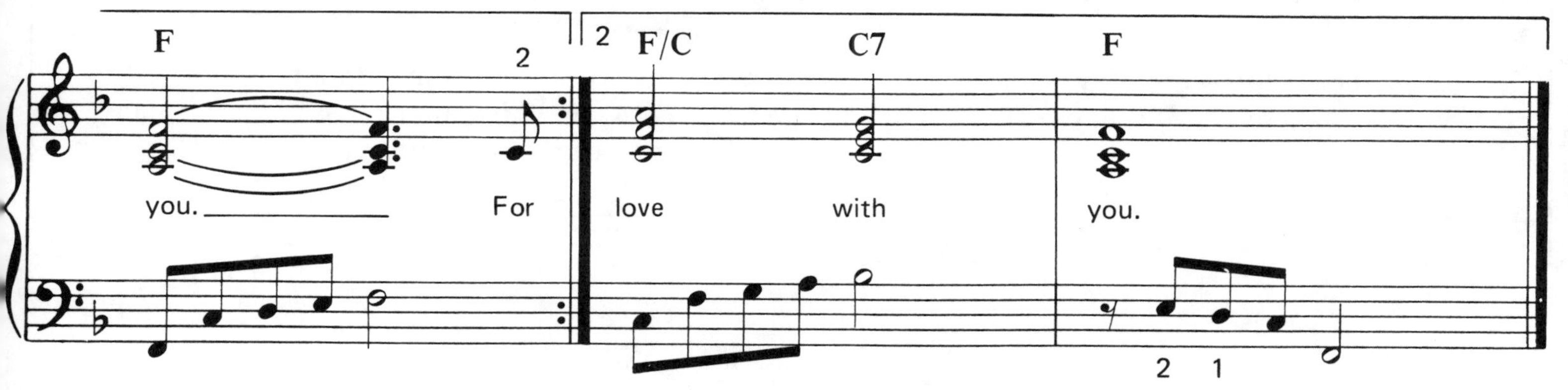
F F/C C7 F
2
2
you. ___ For love with you.
2 1

DAYDREAM

Words and Music by
JOHN SEBASTIAN

C/G A7 F D7/F♯
on my side, It's one of those days for tak - ing a
by a - lot, I could - n't care less a - bout the
feel - ing right, A day - dream will last a - long
C/G A7 F D7/F♯
walk out - side, I'm blow - ing the day to take a
dues you say I got. To - mor - row I'll pay the dues for
into the night. To - mor - row at break - fast you may
To Coda
C/G A7 Dm7
walk in the sun, and fall on my face on some - bod - y's
drop - ping my load, a pie in the face for be - ing a
prick up your ears,
1. G7sus G7
new - mowed lawn.
2. G7sus G7 D.S. al Coda
sleep - y bull - toad.

CODA
Dm7
G7
3
3
or you may be day-dream-in' for a
thou - sand years.

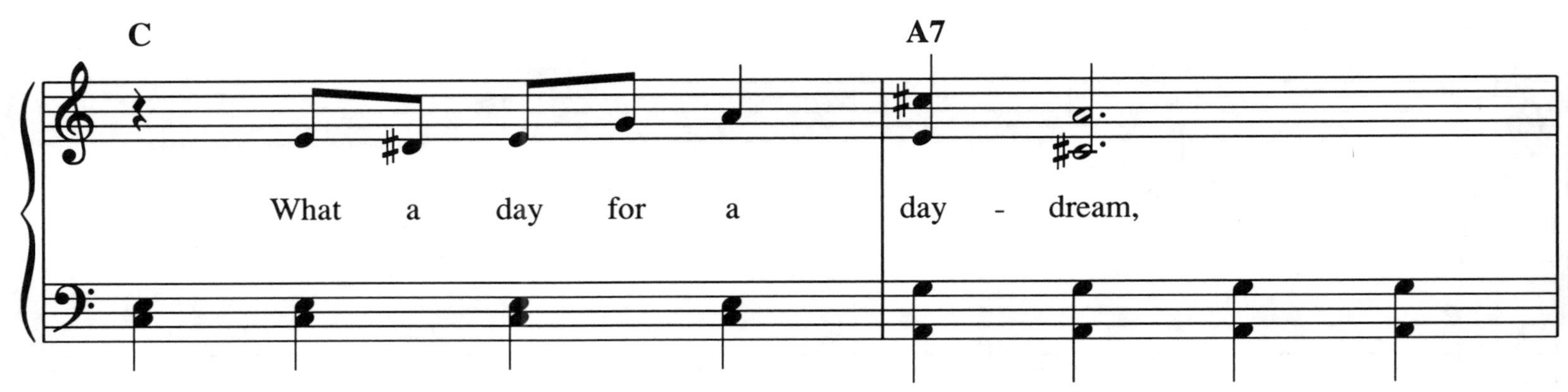
C
A7
What a day for a
day - dream,

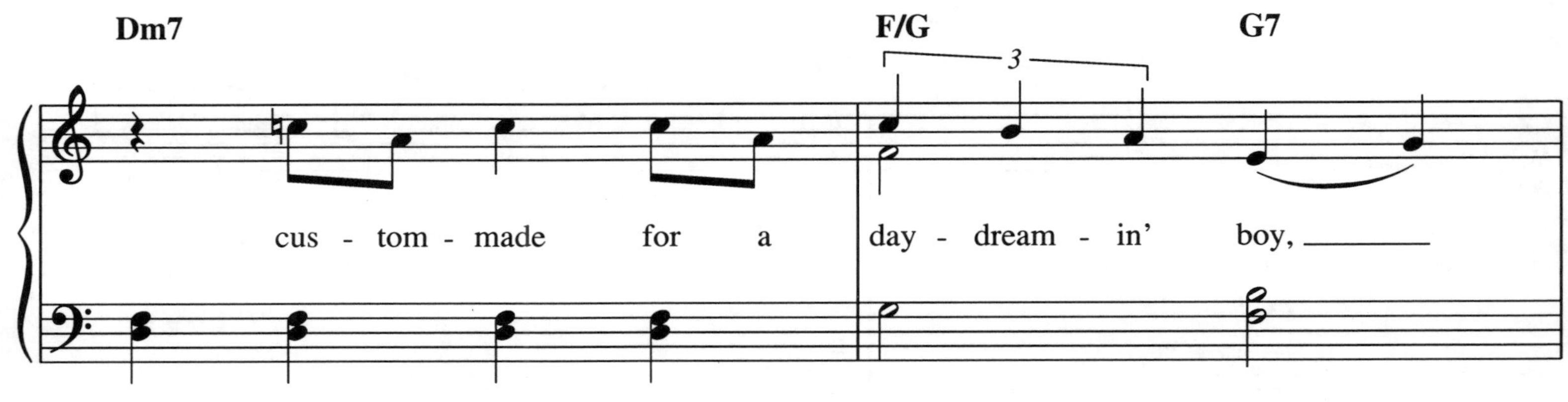
Dm7
F/G
G7
3
cus - tom - made for a
day - dream - in' boy,

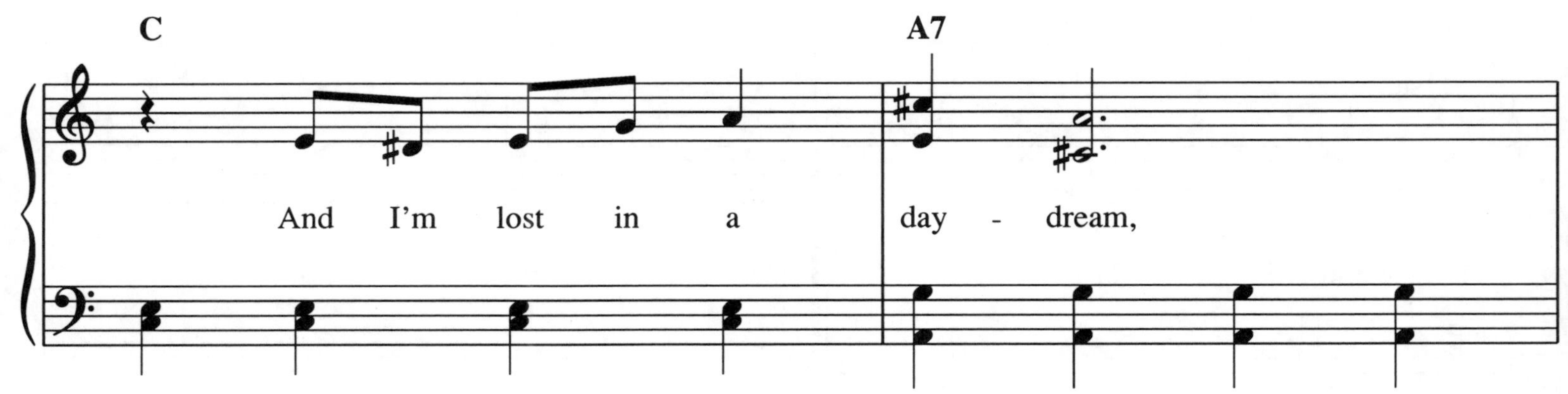
C
A7
And I'm lost in a
day - dream,

Dm7
F/G
G7
dream - in' 'bout my
bun - dle of joy.

F
D7/F♯
C/G
A7
(Whistle)

Repeat ad lib.
F
D7/F♯
C/G
A7

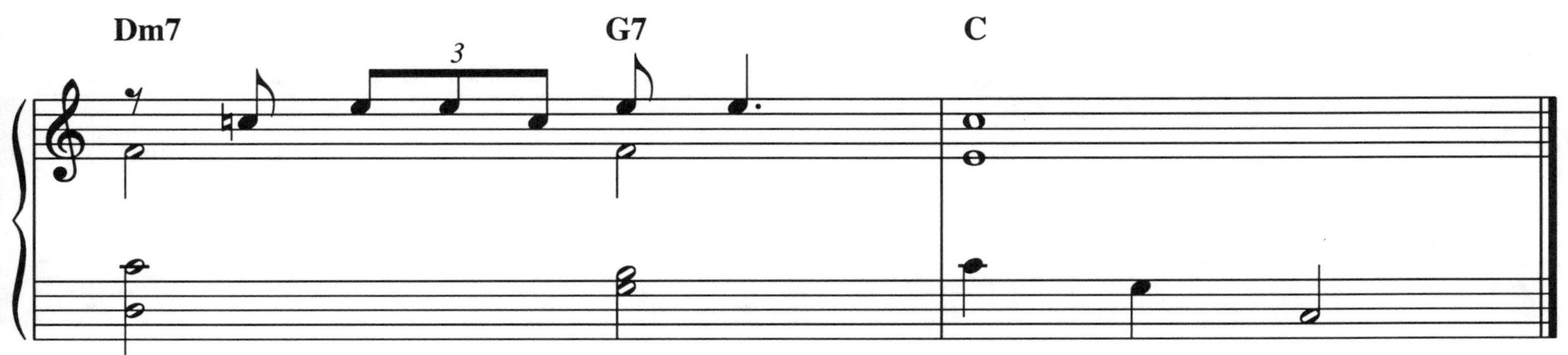
Dm7
G7
C

DOMINIQUE

English Lyrics by NOEL REGNEY
By SOEUR SOURIRE, O.P.

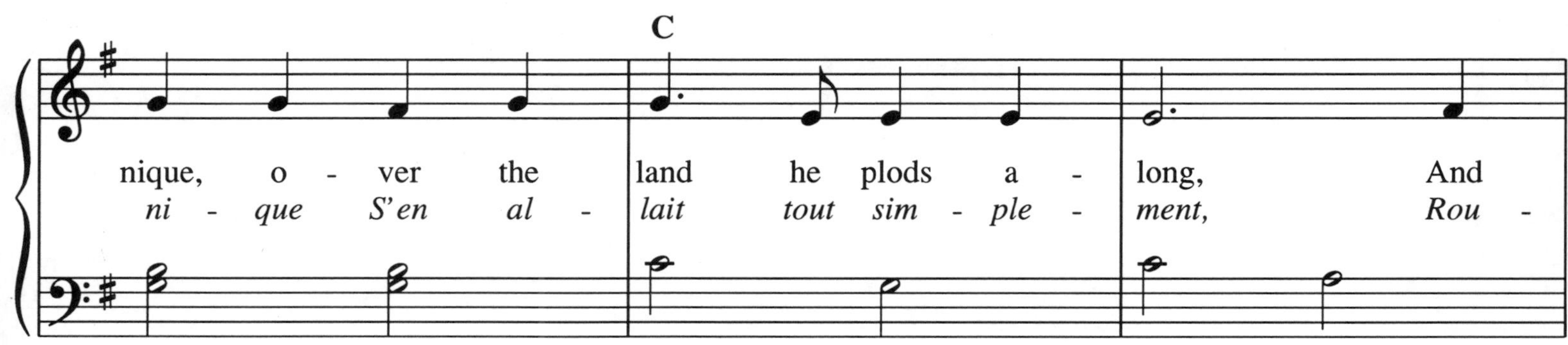

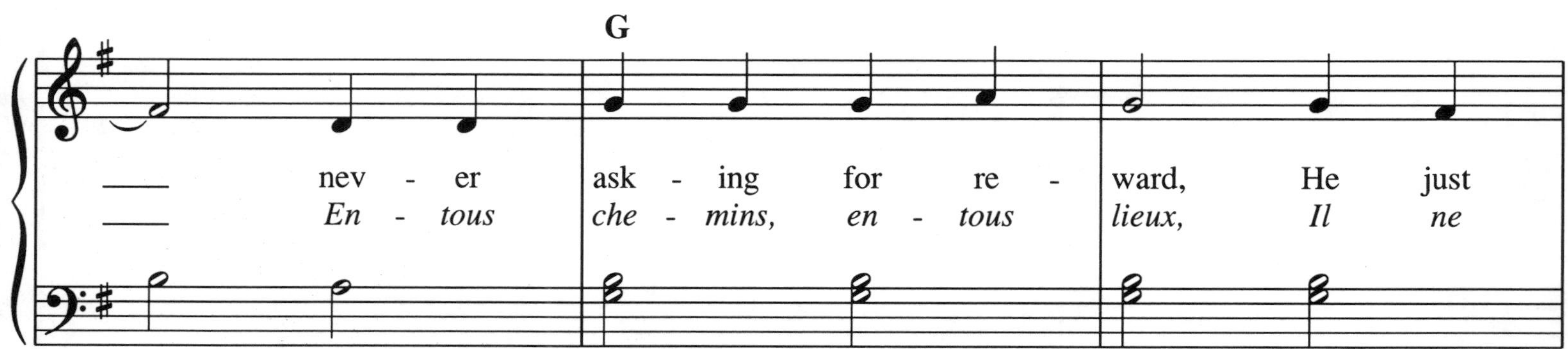

C
G
talks a - bout the Lord, He just talks a -
parle que du bon Dieu, Il ne parle que

To Coda
D7
G
bout the Lord.
du bon Dieu.

VERSE
C
G
mf 1. At a time when John - ny Lack - land o - ver
1. A l'e - poque ou Jean - sans - Ter - re D'An - gle
2.-7. (See additional lyrics)

D7
G
A
Eng - land was the King, Do - mi - nique was in the
ter - re é - tait roi, Do - mi - in - que, no - tre

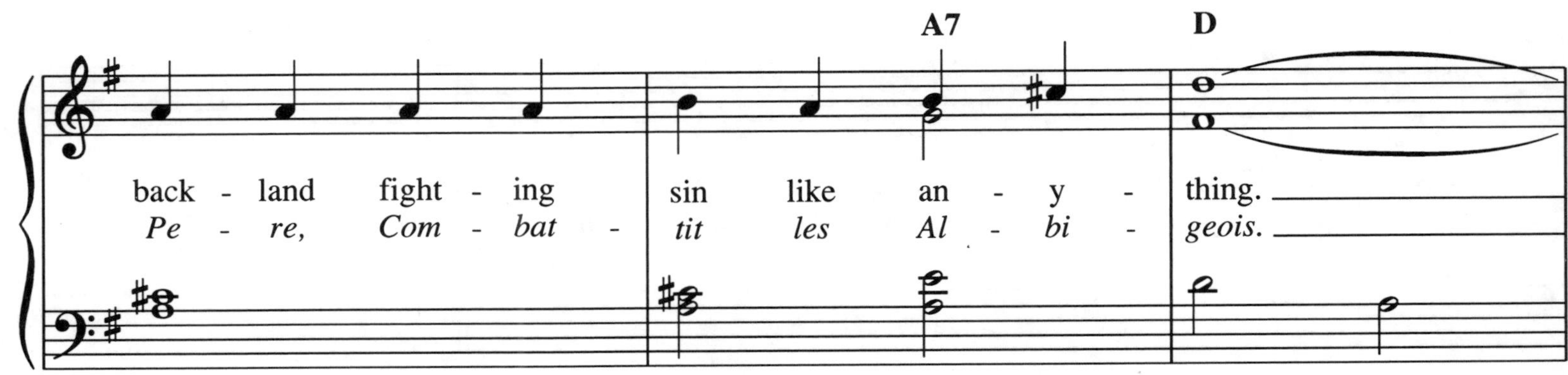

ENGLISH

2. Now a heretic, one day,
   Among the thorns forced him to crawl.
   Dominique with just one prayer,
   Made him hear the good Lord call. (Chorus)

3. Without horse or fancy wagon,
   He crossed Europe up and down.
   Poverty was his companion,
   As he walked from town to town. (Chorus)

4. To bring back the straying liars
   And the lost sheep to the fold,
   He brought forth the Preaching Friars,
   Heaven's soldiers, brave and bold. (Chorus)

5. One day, in the budding Order,
   There was nothing left to eat.
   Suddenly two angels walked in
   With a load of bread and meat. (Chorus)

6. Dominique once, in his slumber,
   Saw the Virgin's coat unfurled
   Over Friars without number
   Preaching all around the world. (Chorus)

7. Grant us now, oh Dominique,
   The grace of love and simple mirth,
   That we all may help to quicken
   Godly life and truth on earth. (Chorus)

FRENCH

2. *Certain jour un hérétique*
   Par de ronces le conduit
   Mais notre Père Dominique
   Par sa joie le convertit. (Au refrain)

3. *Ni chameau, ni diligence*
   Il parcourt l'Europe à pied.
   Scandinavie ou Provence
   Dans la sainte pauvretè. (Au refrain)

4. *Enflamma de toute école*
   Filles et garçons pleins d'ardeur,
   Et pour semer la Parole
   Inventa les Frères-Prêcheurs. (Au refrain)

5. *Chez Dominique et ses frères*
   Le pain s'en vint à manquer
   Et deux anges se présentèrent
   Portant de grands pains dorés. (Au refrain)

6. *Dominique vit en rêve*
   Les prêcheurs du monde entier
   Sous le manteau de la Vierge
   En grand nombre rassemblés. (Au refrain)

7. *Dominique, mon bon Père,*
   Garde-nous simples et gais
   Pour annoncer à nos frères
   La Vie et la Vérité. (Au refrain)

DOWNTOWN

Words and Music by
TONY HATCH

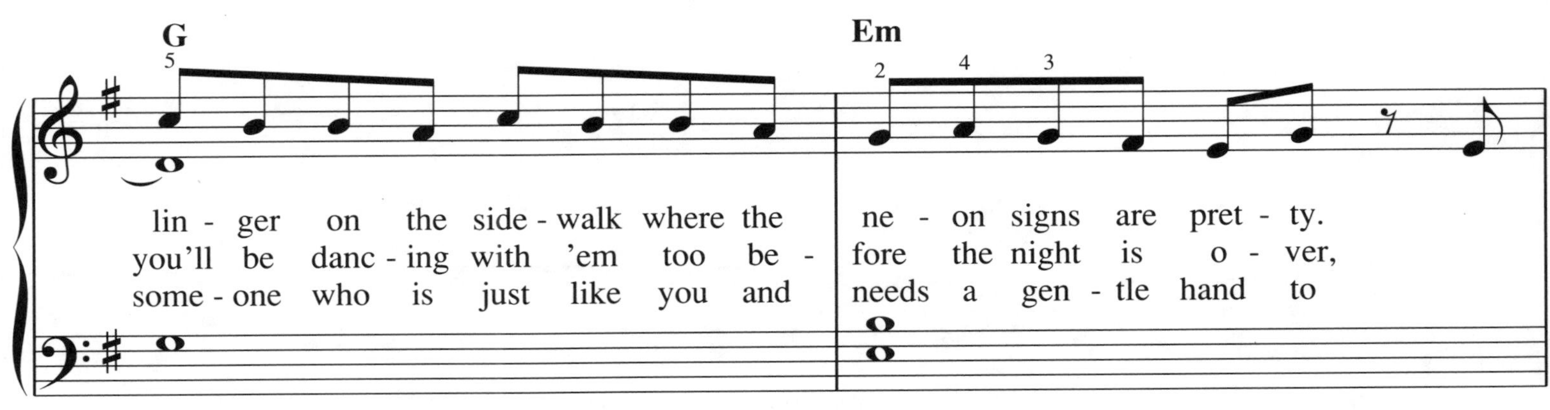

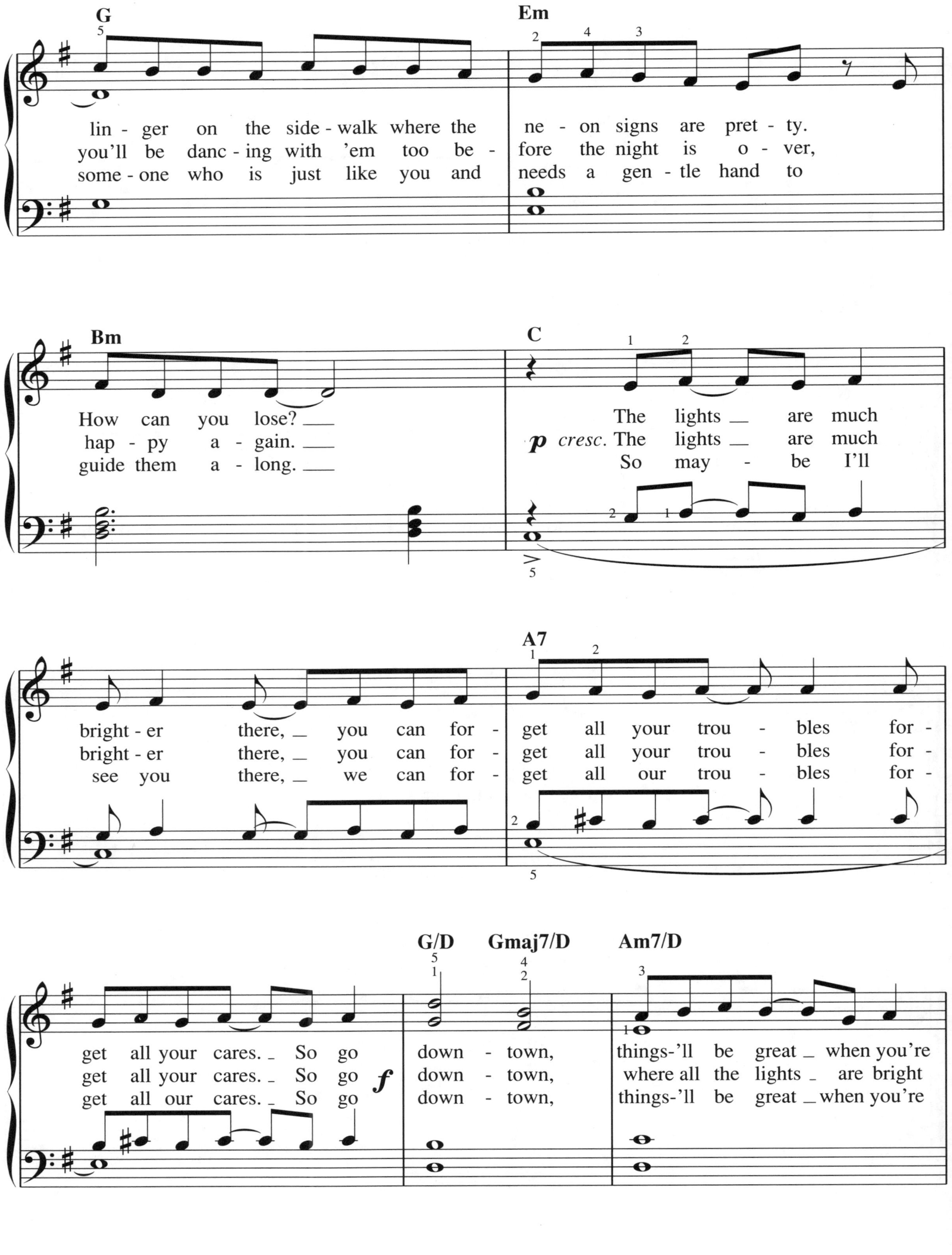

Bm
C
How can you lose?
hap - py a - gain.
guide them a - long.
The lights are much
p *cresc.* The lights are much
So may - be I'll

A7
bright - er there, you can for -
bright - er there, you can for -
see you there, we can for -
get all your trou - bles for -
get all your trou - bles for -
get all our trou - bles for -

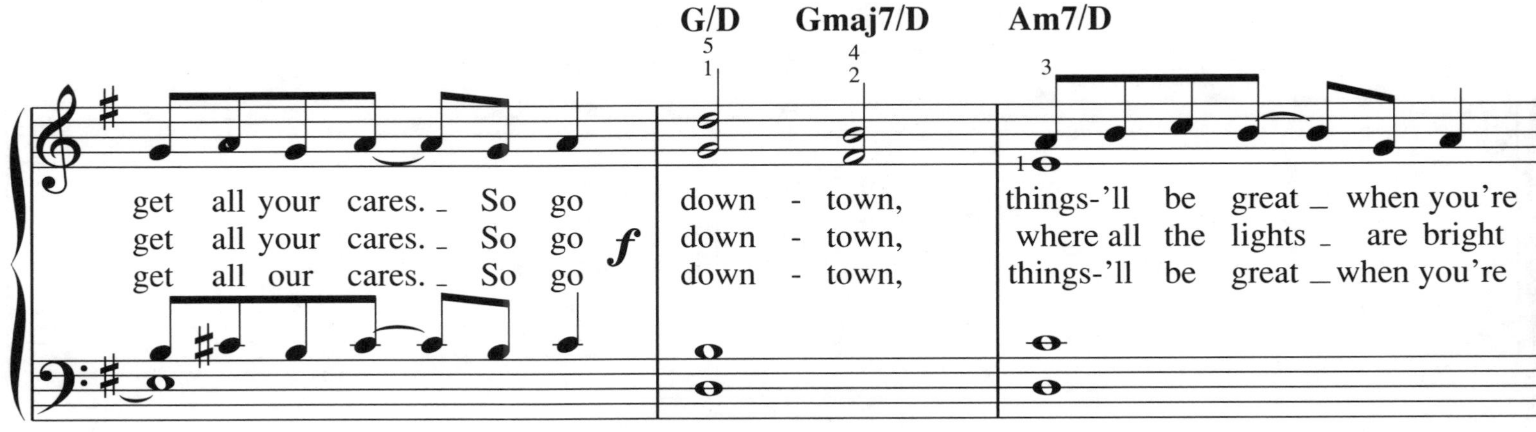

G/D
Gmaj7/D
Am7/D
G/D
Gmaj7/D
down - town,
no fin - er place for sure,
down - town,
down - town,
wait - ing for you to - night,
down - town,
down - town,
don't wait a min - ute more,
down - town,

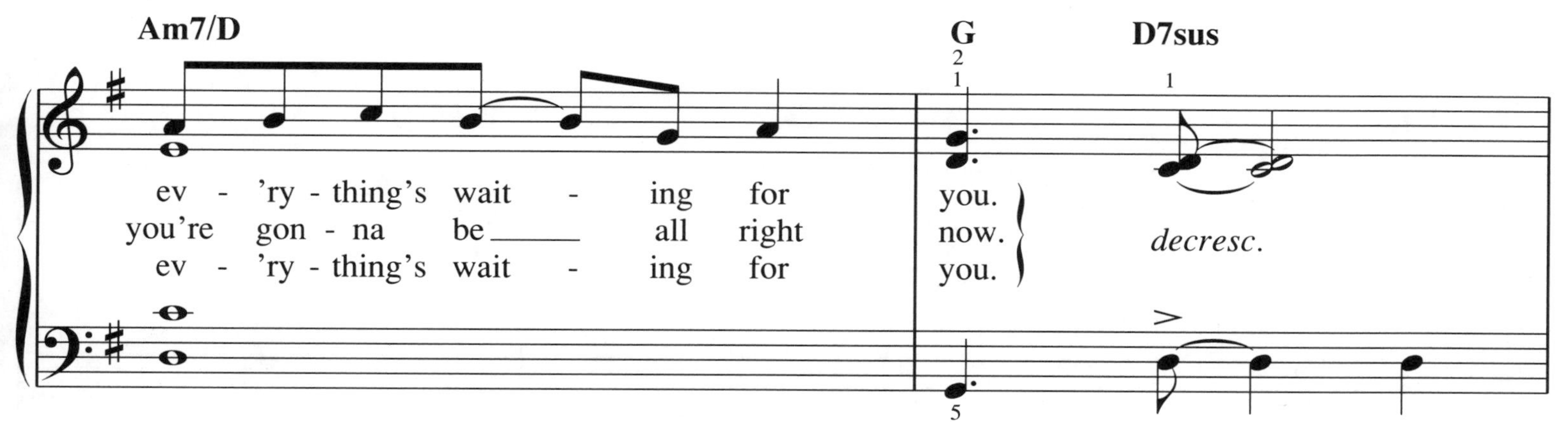
Am7/D
G
D7sus
ev - 'ry - thing's wait - ing for you.
you're gon - na be all right now.
ev - 'ry - thing's wait - ing for you.
decresc.

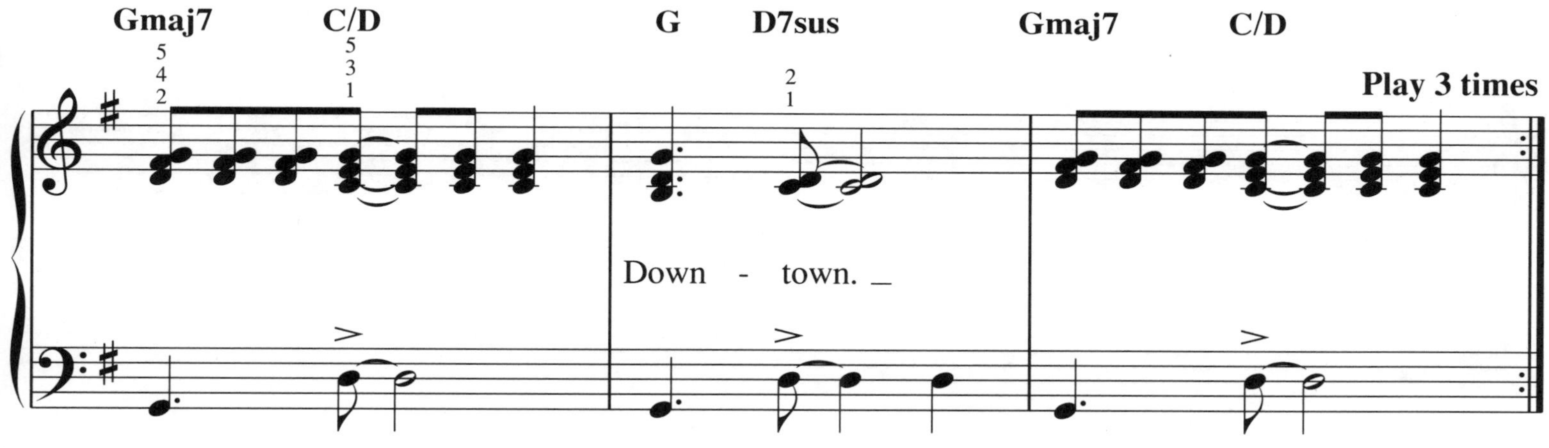
Gmaj7
C/D
G
D7sus
Gmaj7
C/D
Play 3 times
Down - town.

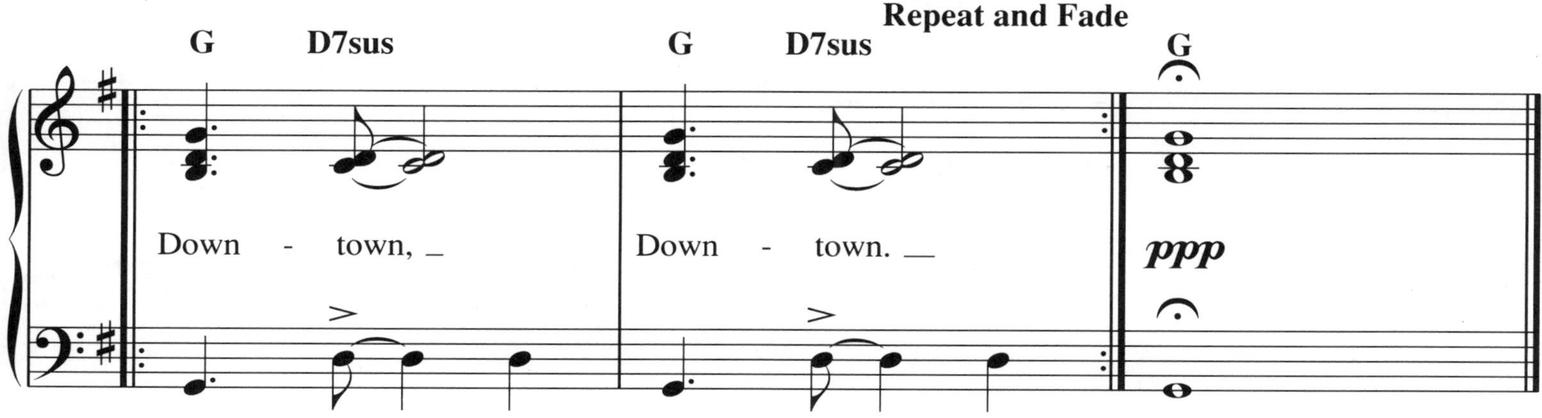
Repeat and Fade
G
D7sus
G
D7sus
G
Down - town,
Down - town.
ppp

THE EXODUS SONG

Words by PAT BOONE
Music by ERNEST GOLD

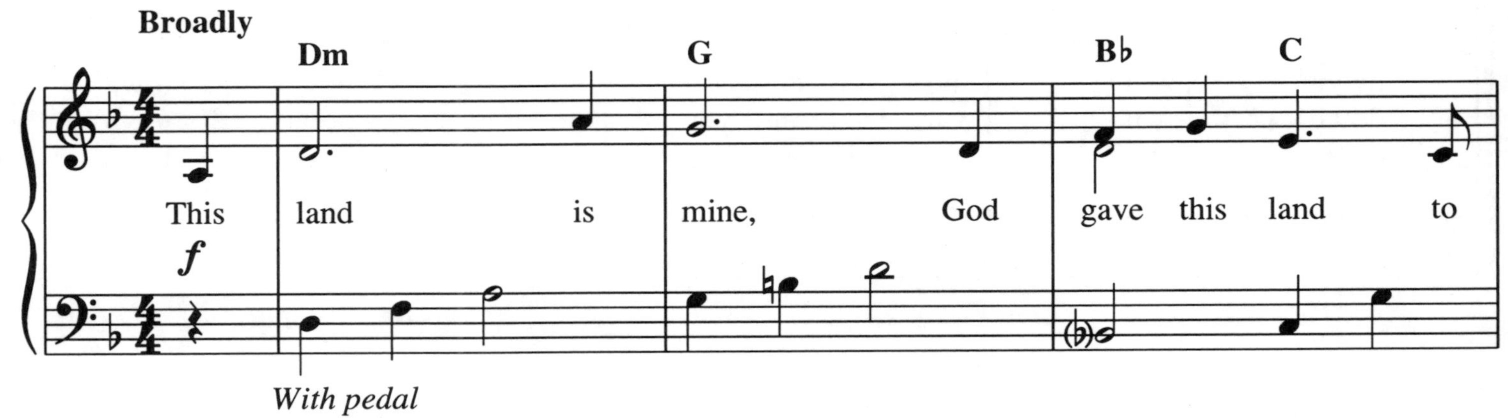

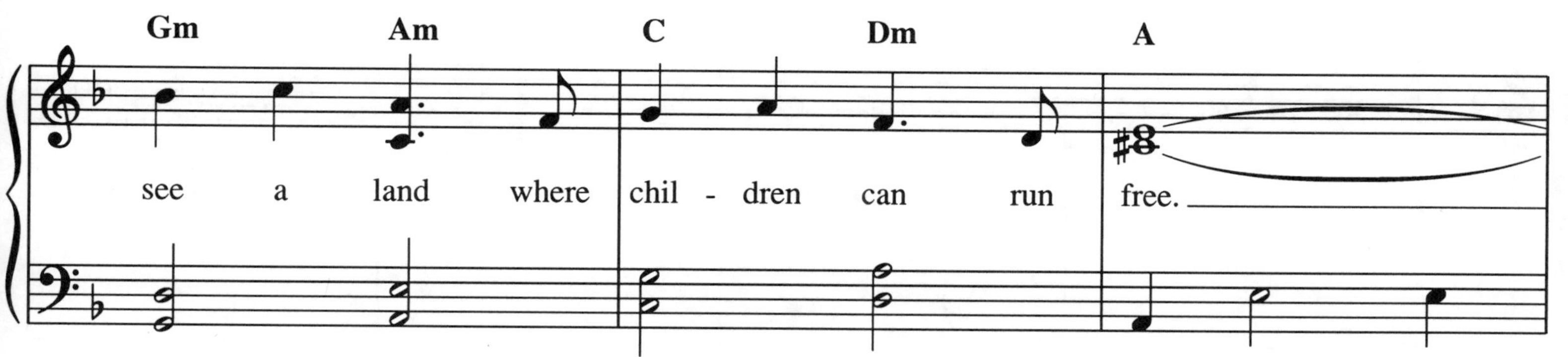
Gm Am C Dm A
see a land where chil - dren can run free.

Dm G B♭ C
So take my hand and walk this land with

Dm Am F G A
me, And walk this love - ly land with me.

Am D Dm
Tho I am just a man, when you are

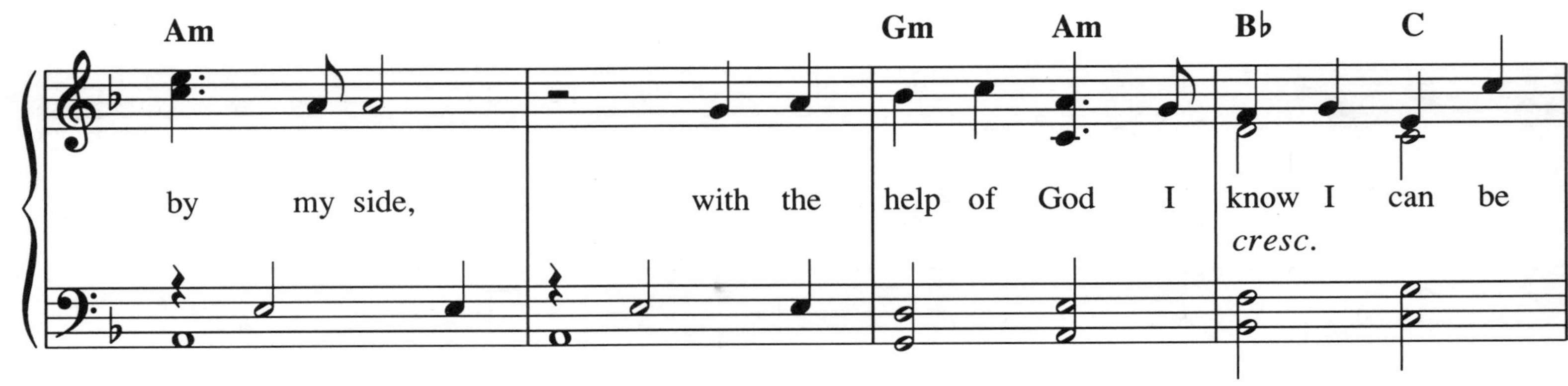
Am
Gm
Am
B♭
C
by my side, with the help of God I know I can be
cresc.

Dm
Am
Am7
strong. To make this land our home, If
f

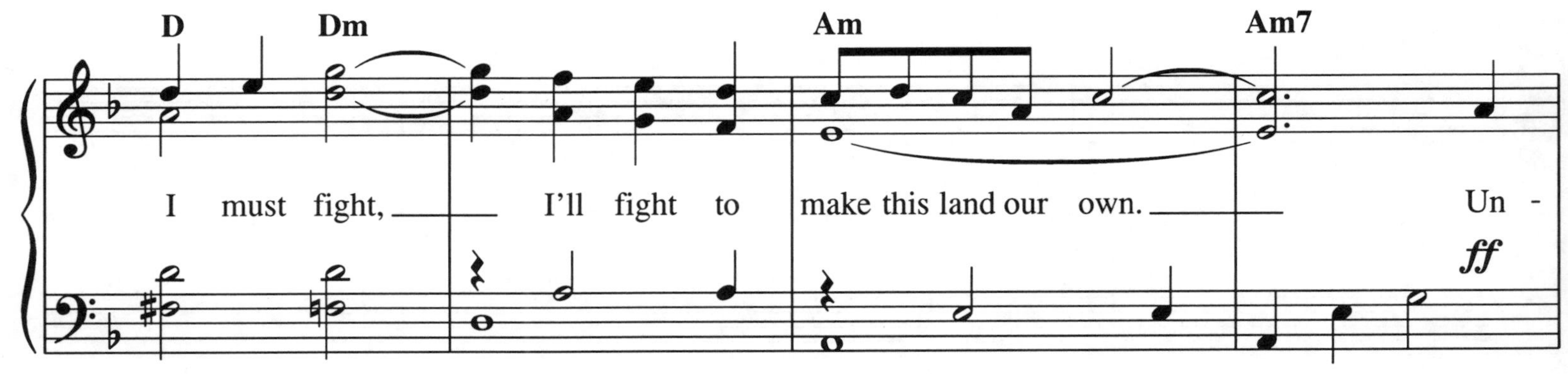
D
Dm
Am
Am7
I must fight, I'll fight to make this land our own. Un -
ff

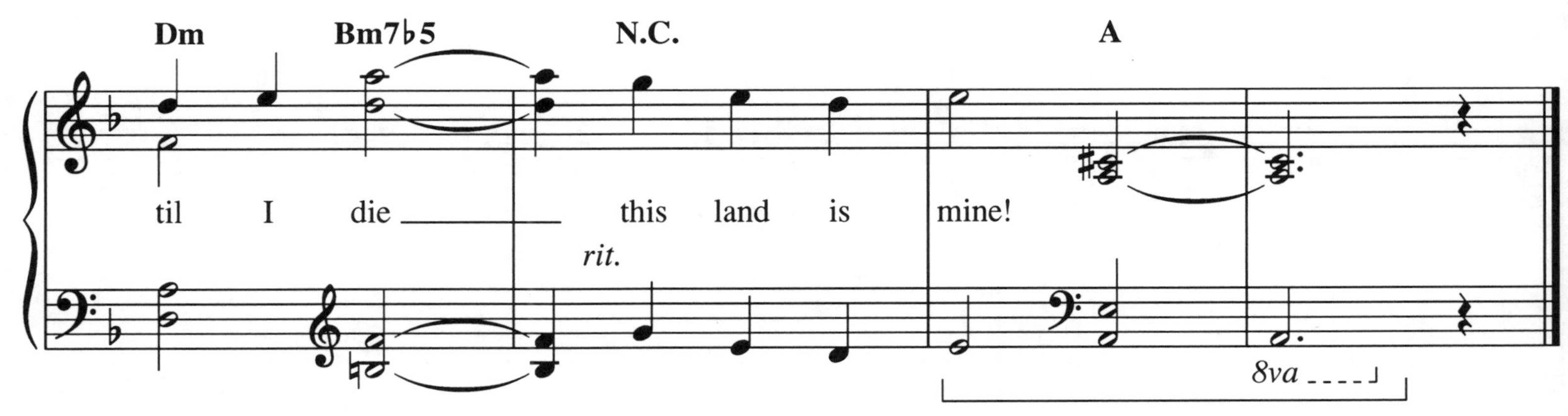
Dm
Bm7♭5
N.C.
A
til I die this land is mine!
rit.
8va

FERRY CROSS THE MERSEY

Words and Music by
GERRARD MARSDEN

With a beat

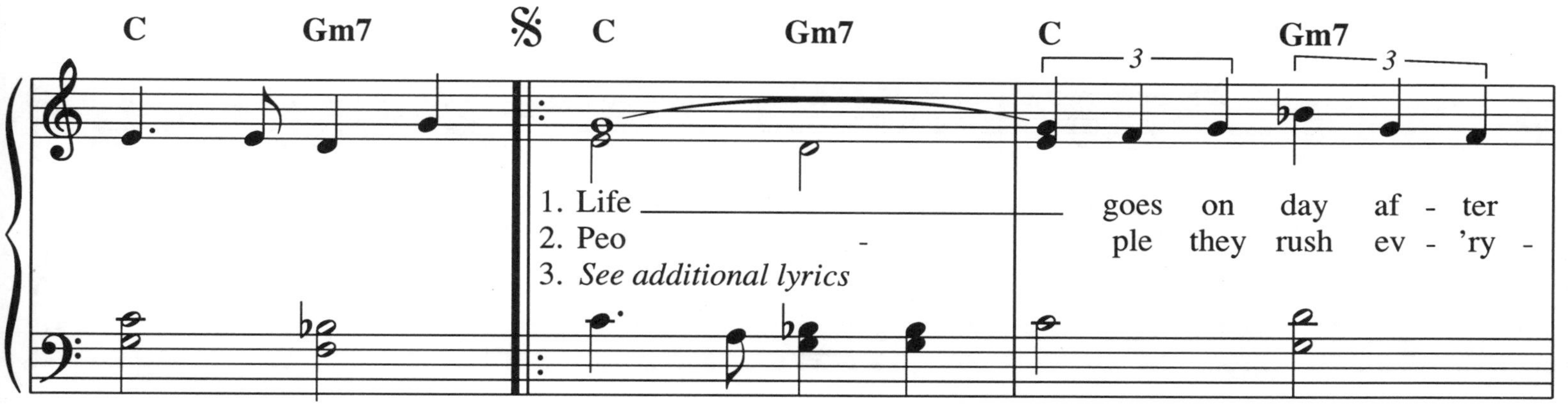

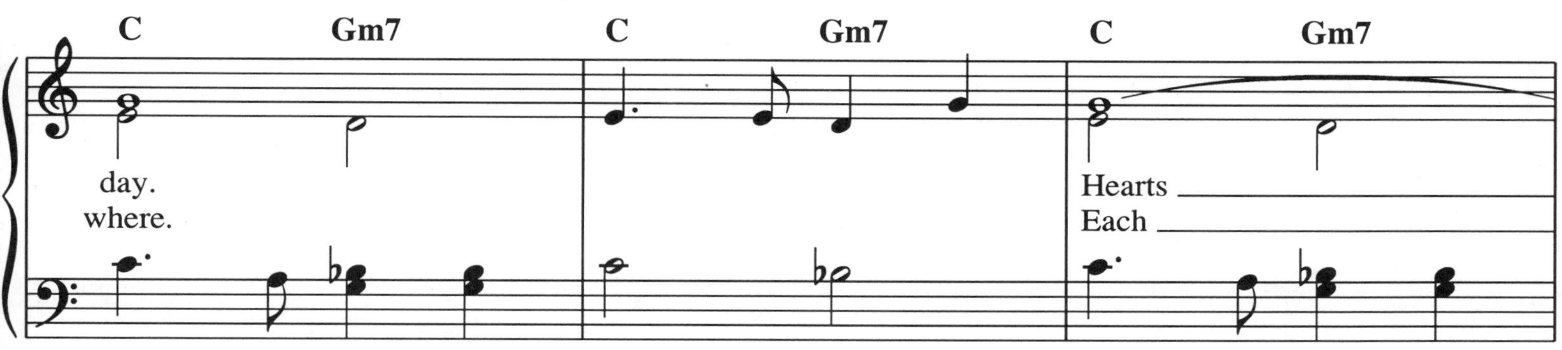

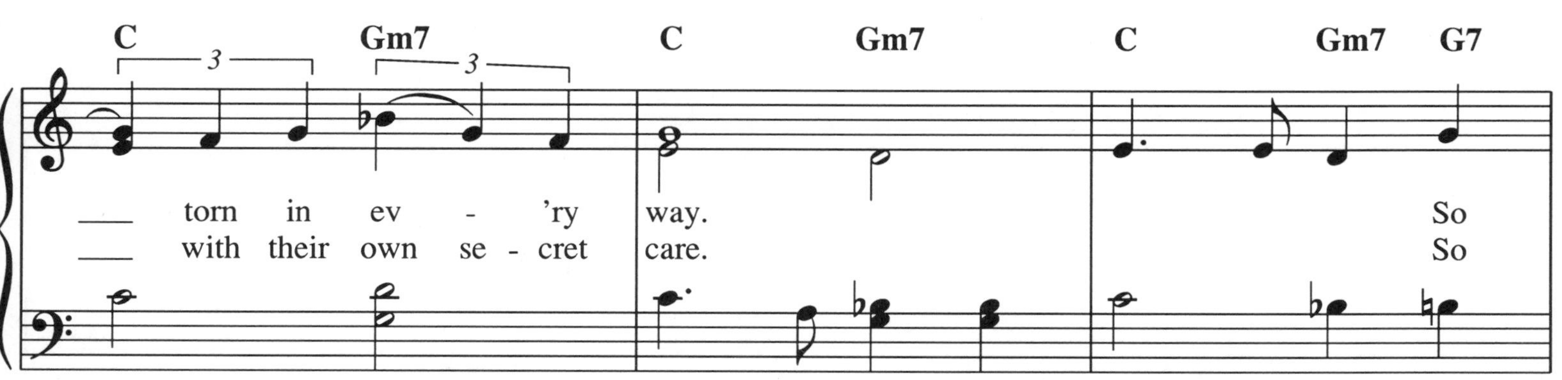

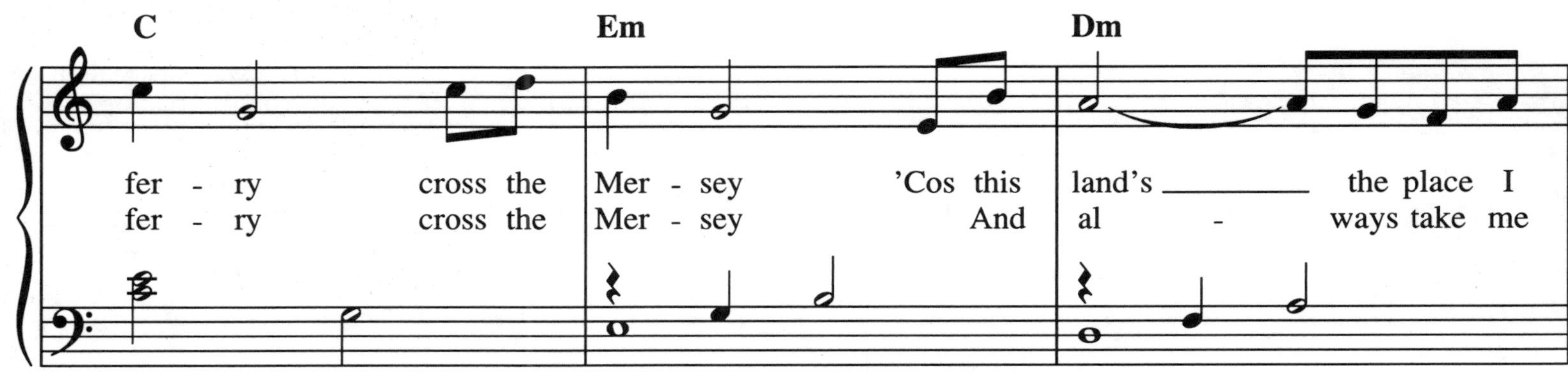
C
Em
Dm
fer - ry cross the Mer - sey 'Cos this land's the place I
fer - ry cross the Mer - sey And al - ways take me

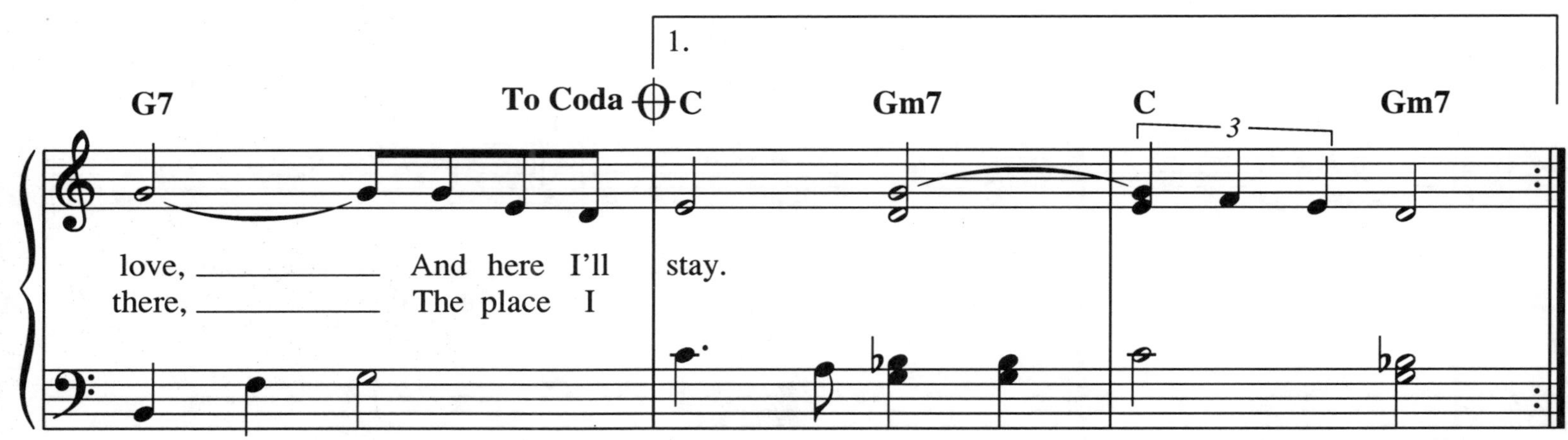
G7
To Coda
C
Gm7
C
Gm7
1.
3
love, And here I'll stay.
there, The place I

2.
C
Dm
G7
love.
Peo - ple a - round ev - 'ry

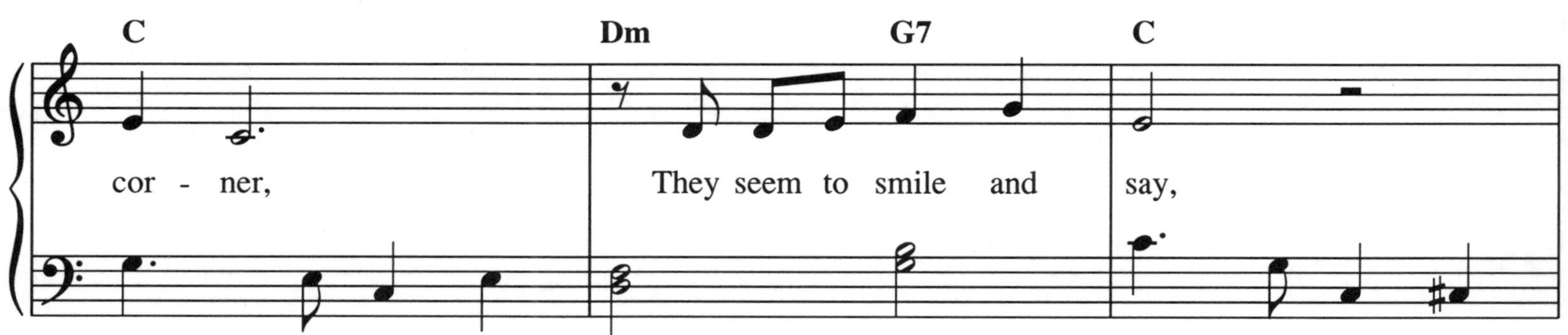
C
Dm
G7
C
cor - ner, They seem to smile and say,

Additional Lyrics

3. So I'll continue to say,
   Hope I always will stay.
   So ferry cross the Mersey
   'Cos this land's the place I love
   And here I'll stay.

FLY ME TO THE MOON
(In Other Words)

Words and Music by
BART HOWARD

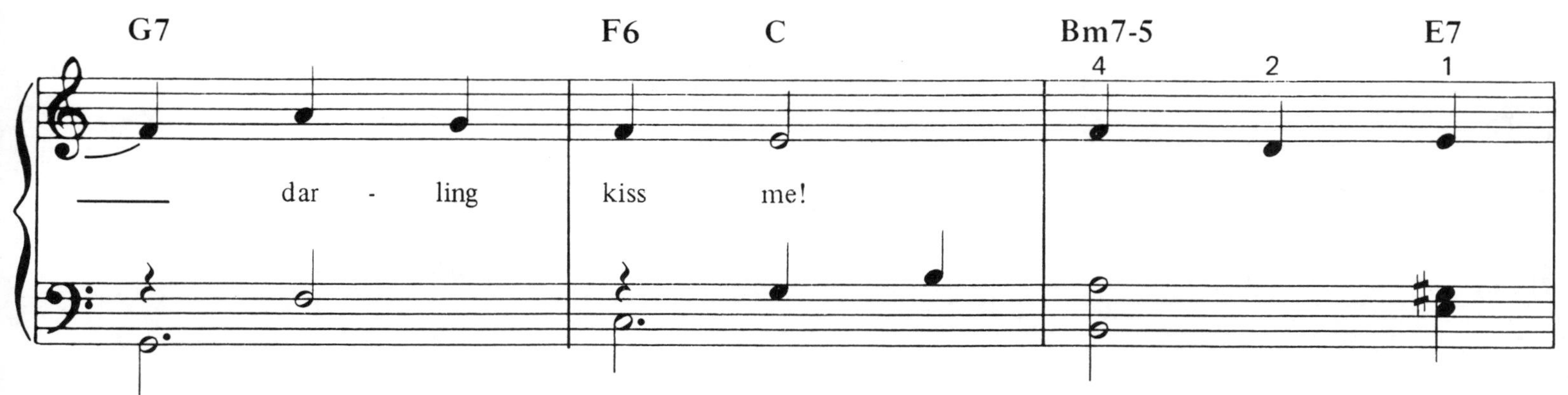
G7
F6
C
Bm7-5
E7
4
2
1
dar - ling
kiss me!

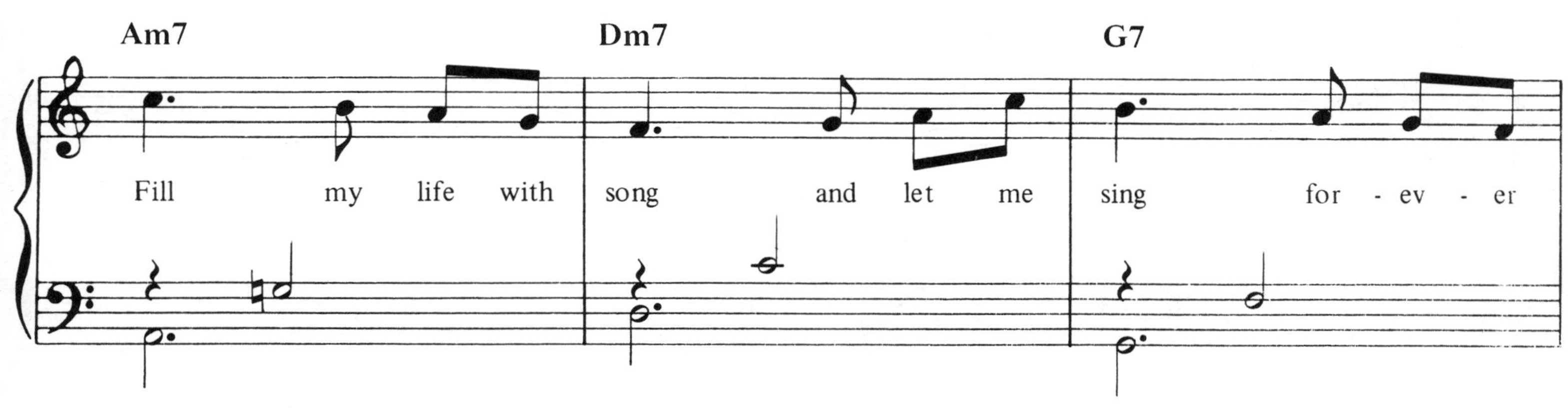
Am7
Dm7
G7
Fill my life with
song and let me
sing for - ev - er

C
C7
F
Bm7-5
more;
You are all I
long for, all I

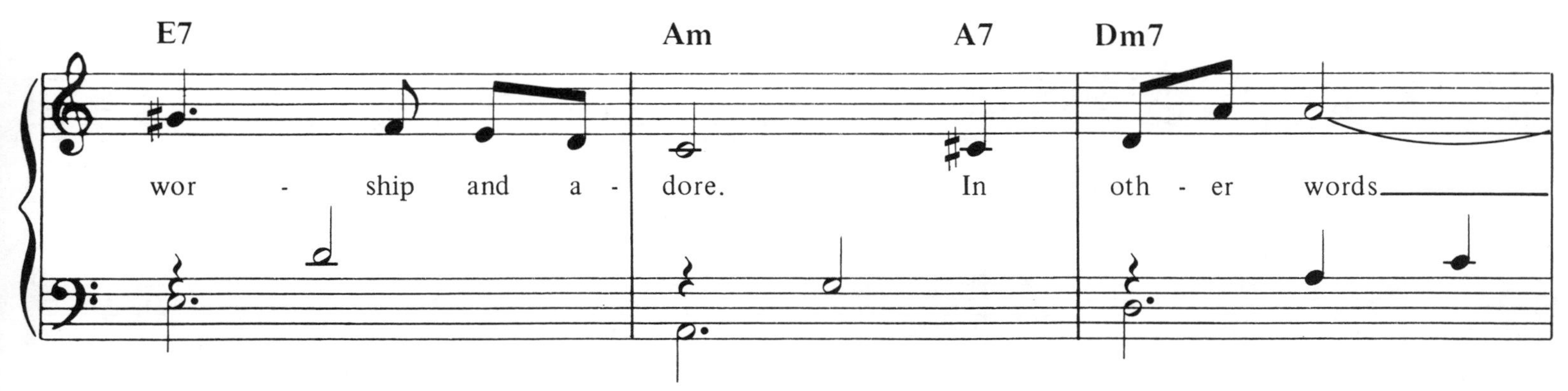
E7
Am
A7
Dm7
wor - ship and a -
dore. In
oth - er words

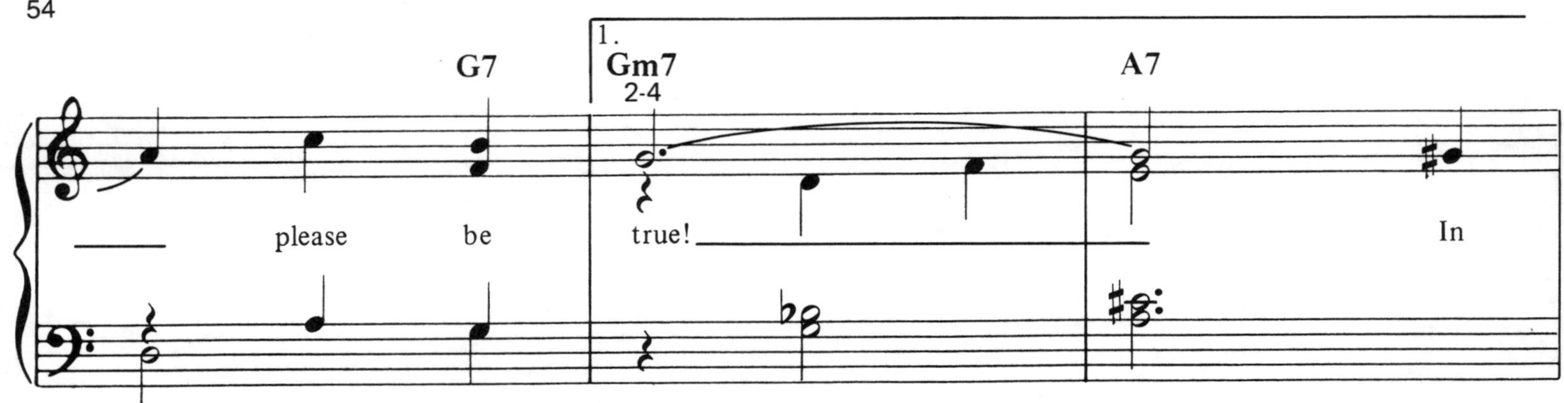
G7
1.
Gm7
2-4
A7
please be
true!
In

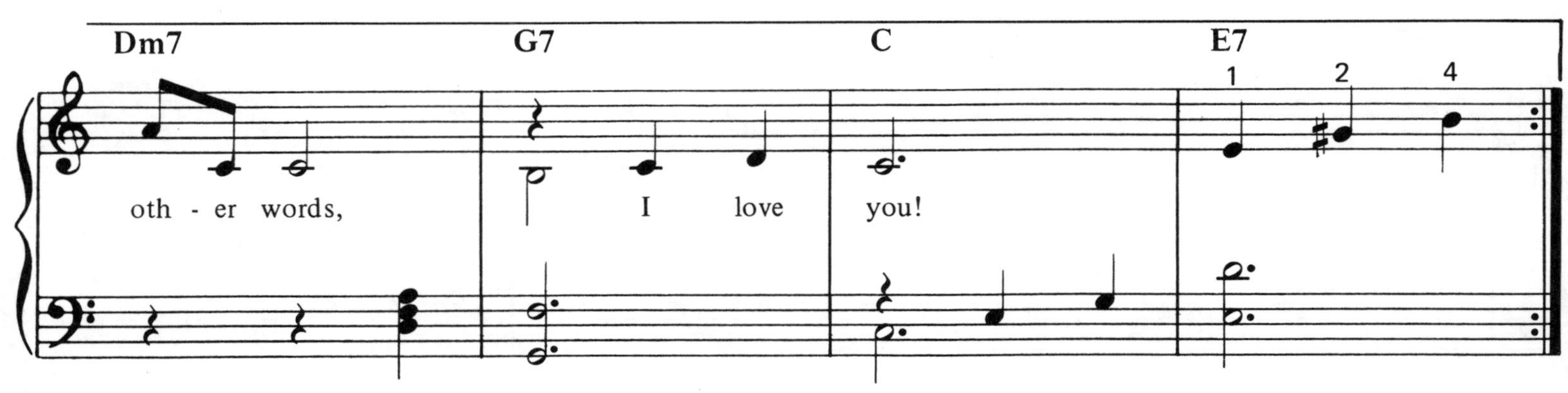
Dm7
G7
C
E7
1 2 4
oth - er words,
I love
you!

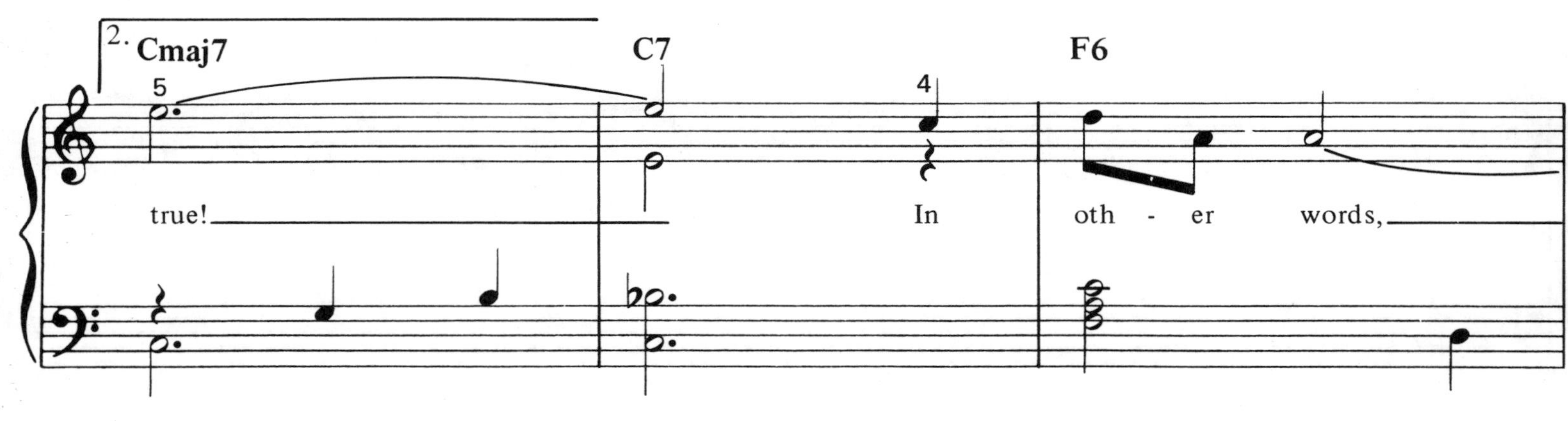
2.
Cmaj7
5
C7
4
F6
true!
In
oth - er words,

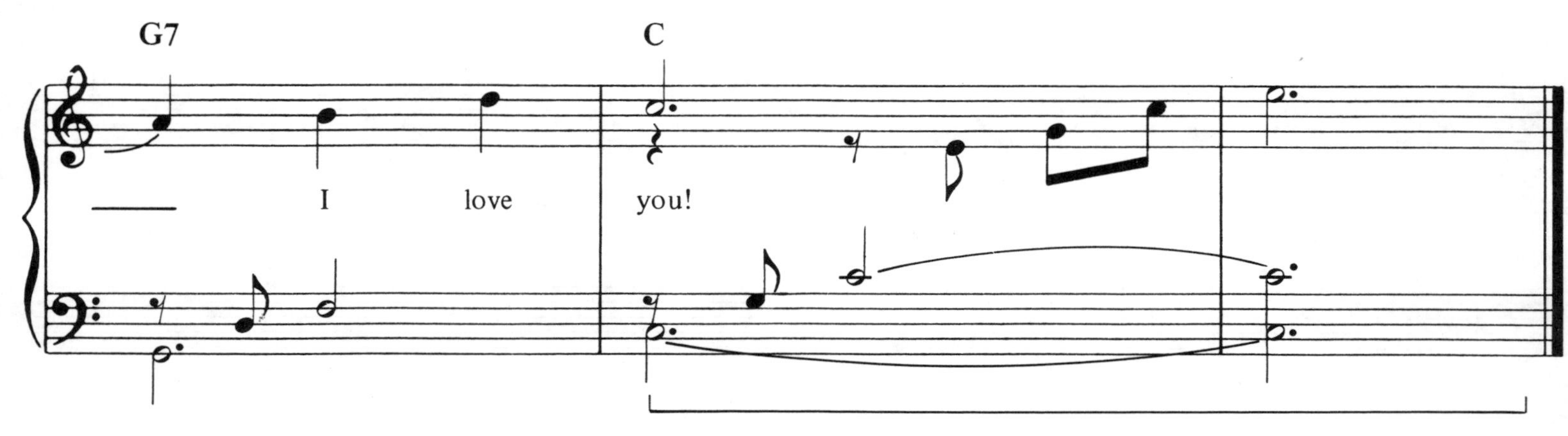
G7
C
I love
you!

THE GIRL FROM IPANEMA

(Garôta De Ipanema)

Original Words by VINICIUS DE MORAES
English Words by NORMAN GIMBEL
Music by ANTONIO CARLOS JOBIM

B9
F♯m7
sad - ly.
How

D9
can I tell her I love her?

Gm7
E♭9
Yes, I would give my heart glad - ly,

Am7
D7-5
-9
but each day when she walks to the sea, she

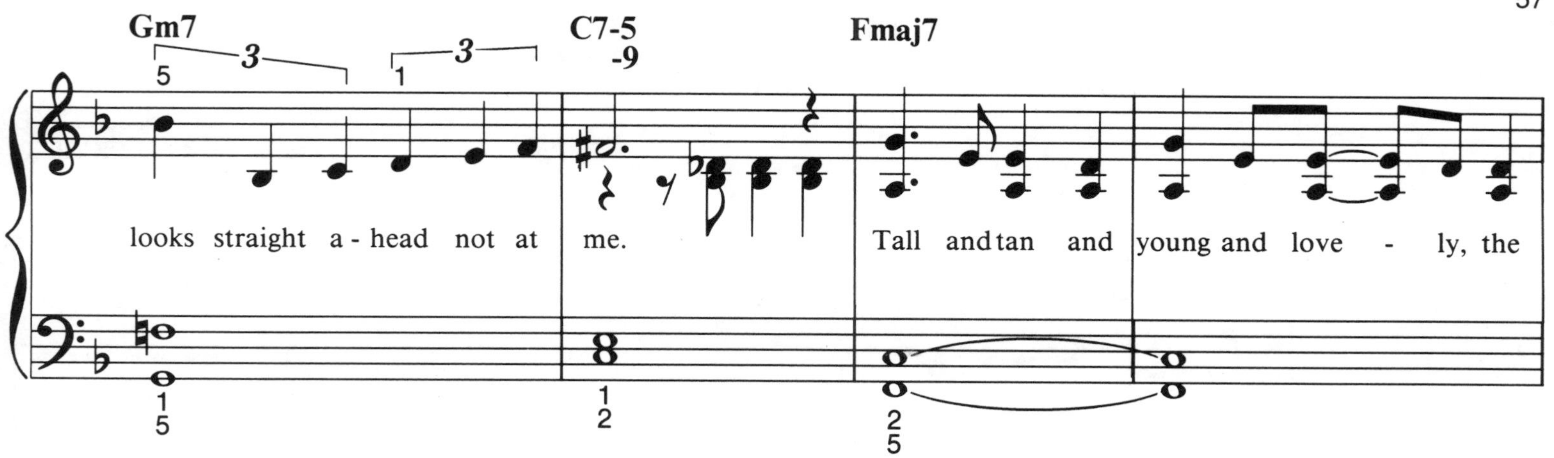
Gm7
C7-5
-9
Fmaj7
looks straight a - head not at me. Tall and tan and young and love - ly, the

G7
Gm7
girl from I - pa - ne - ma goes walk - ing, and when she pass - es I

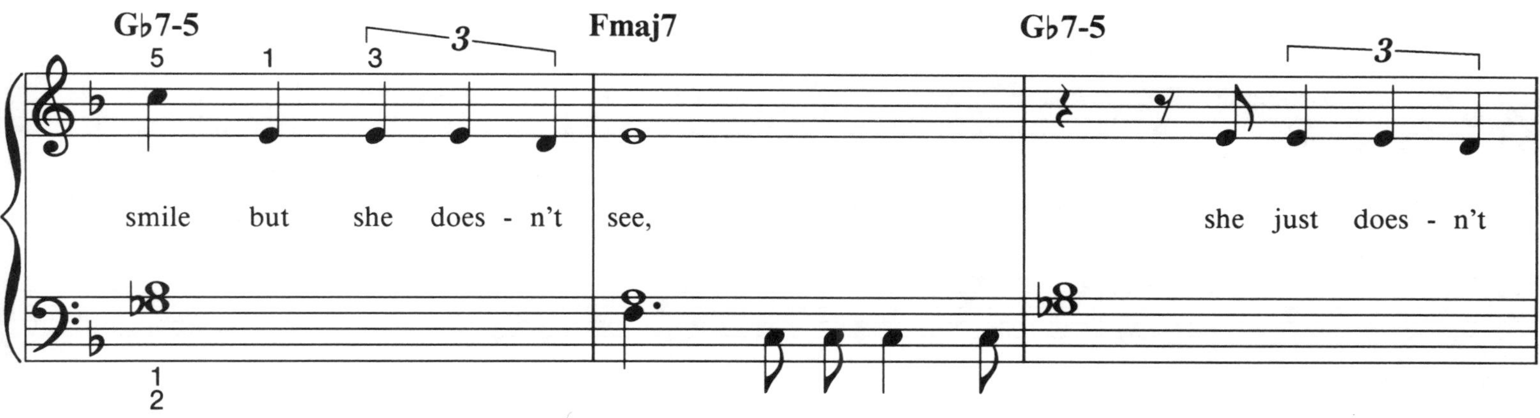
G♭7-5
Fmaj7
G♭7-5
smile but she does - n't see, she just does - n't

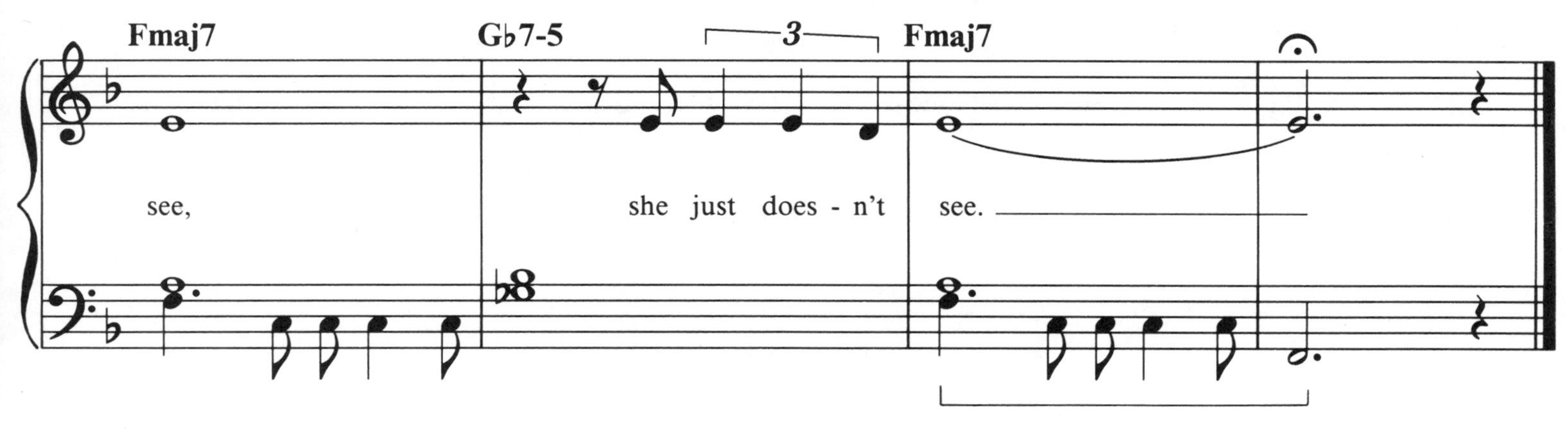
Fmaj7
G♭7-5
Fmaj7
see, she just does - n't see.

GEORGY GIRL

Words by JIM DALE
Music by TOM SPRINGFIELD

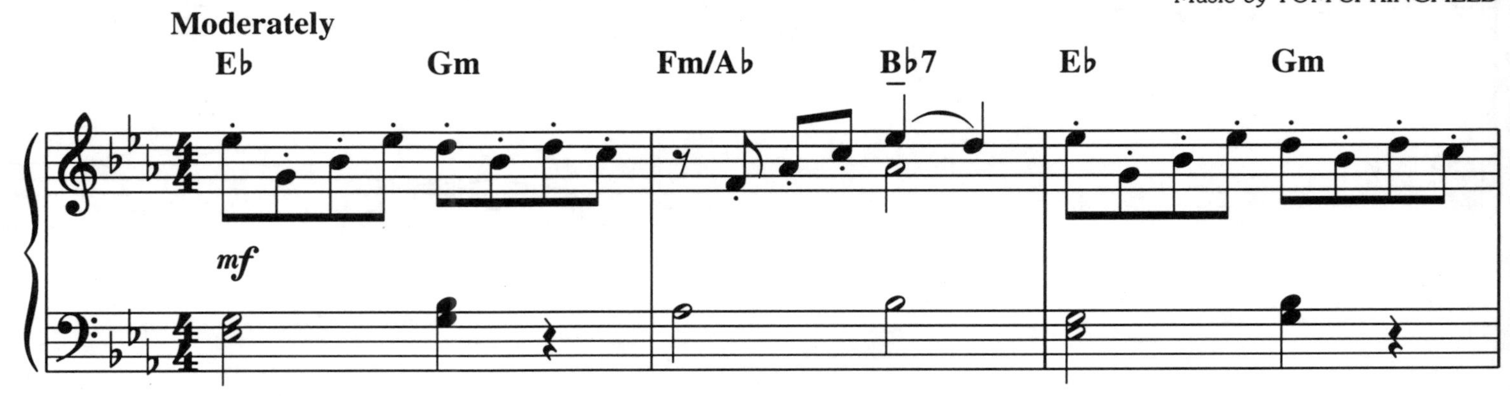

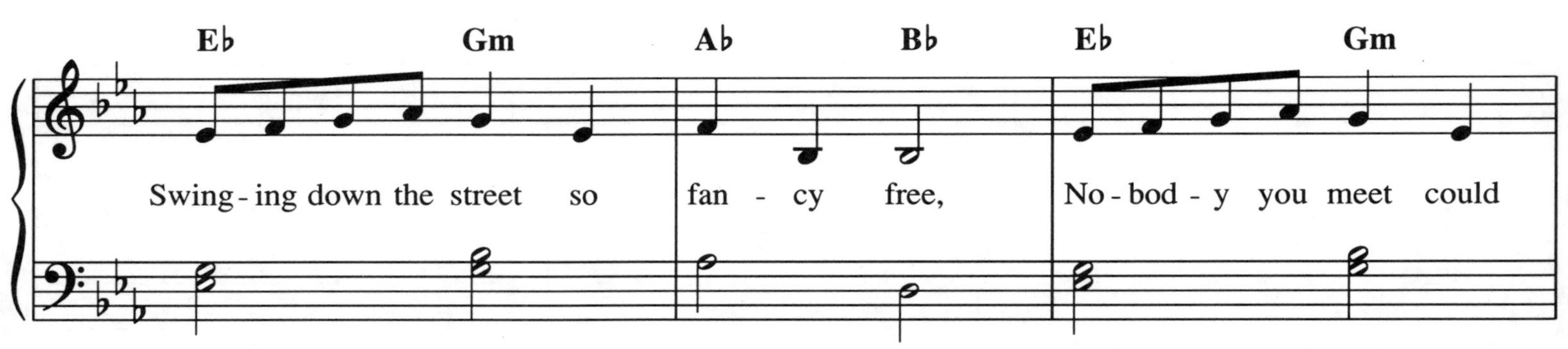

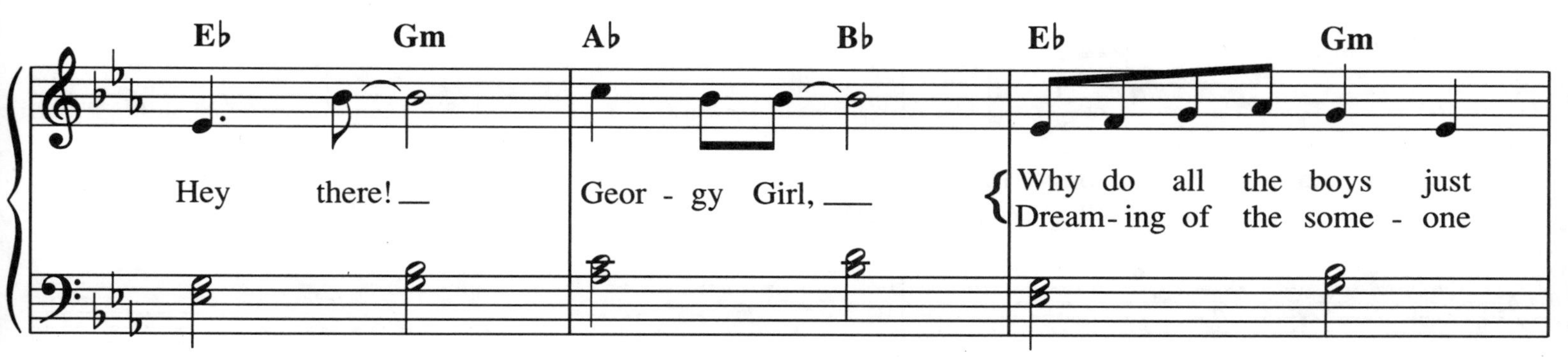
E♭
Gm
A♭
B♭
E♭
Gm
Hey there! __
Geor - gy Girl, __
Why do all the boys just
Dream - ing of the some - one

A♭
B♭
E♭
Gm
pass you by?
you could be.
Could it be you just don't
Life is a re - al - i -

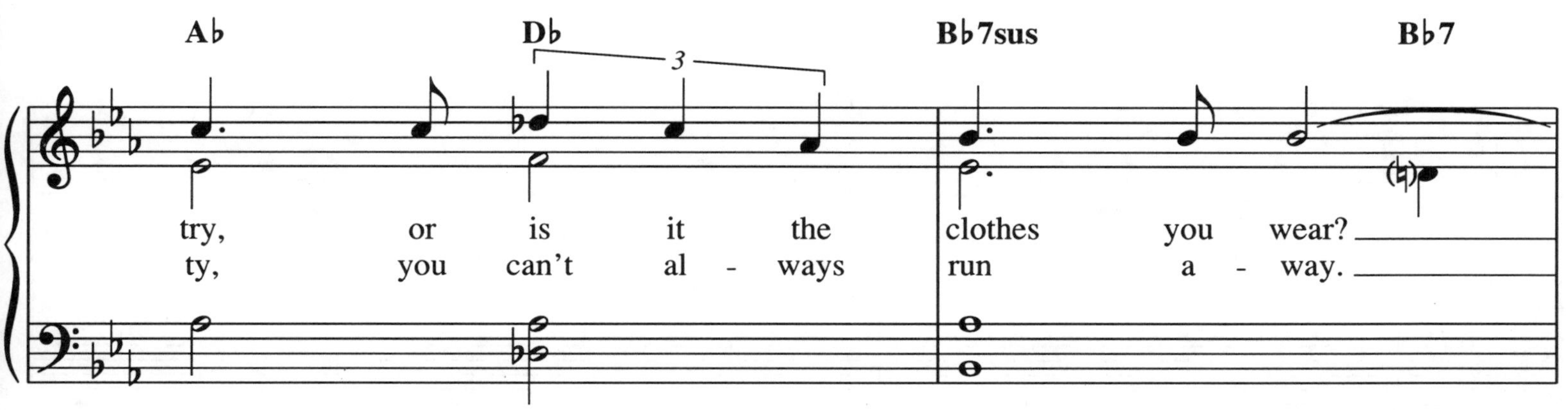
A♭
D♭
B♭7sus
B♭7
3
try, or is it the
ty, you can't al - ways
clothes you wear? __
run a - way. __

Cm
Gm
You're al - ways
Don't be so
win - dow shop - ping but
scared of chang - ing and

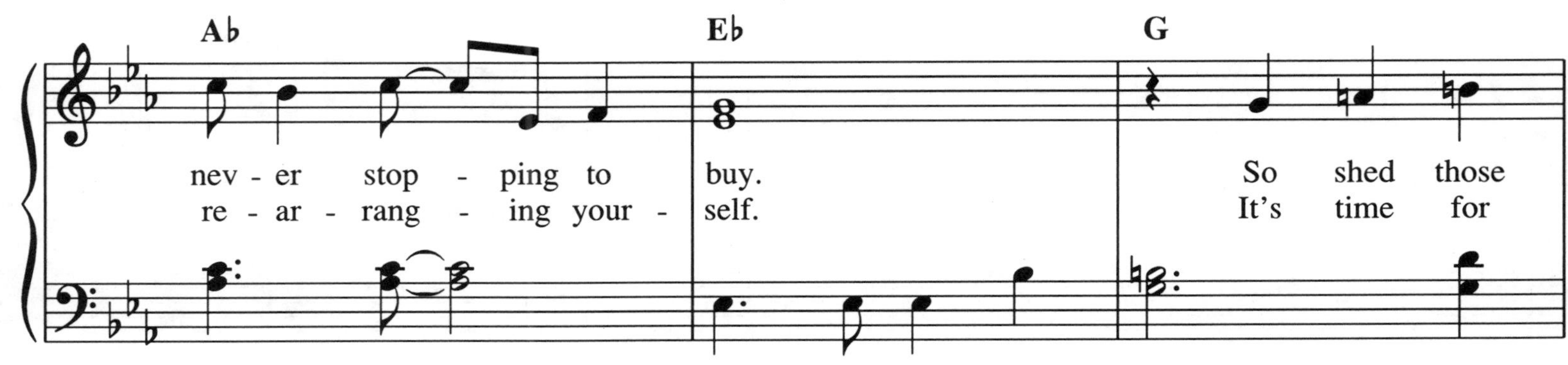
A♭
E♭
G
nev - er stop - ping to buy.
re - ar - rang - ing your - self.
So shed those
It's time for

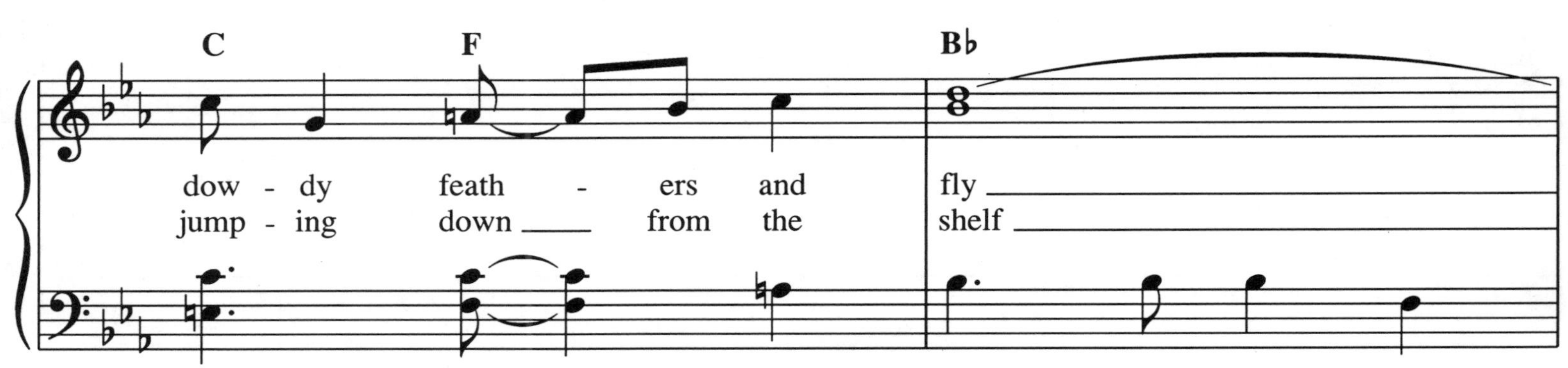
C
F
B♭
dow - dy feath - ers and fly
jump - ing down from the shelf

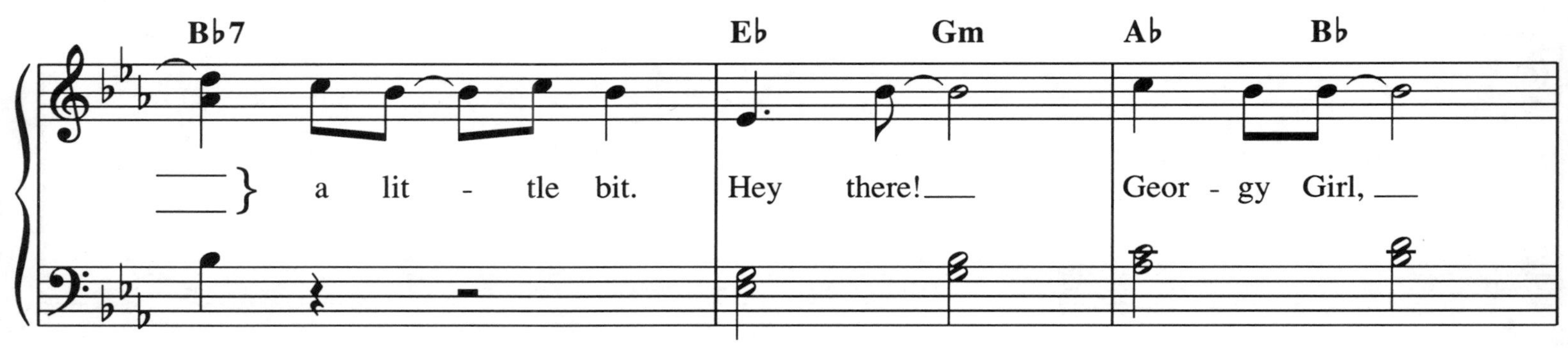
B♭7
E♭
Gm
A♭
B♭
} a lit - tle bit.
Hey there!
Geor - gy Girl,

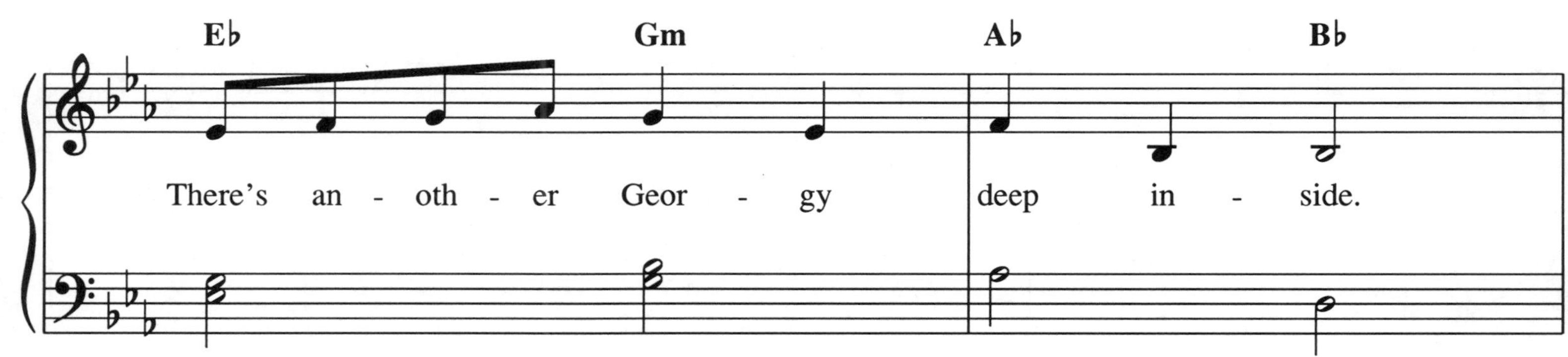
E♭
Gm
A♭
B♭
There's an - oth - er Geor - gy deep in - side.

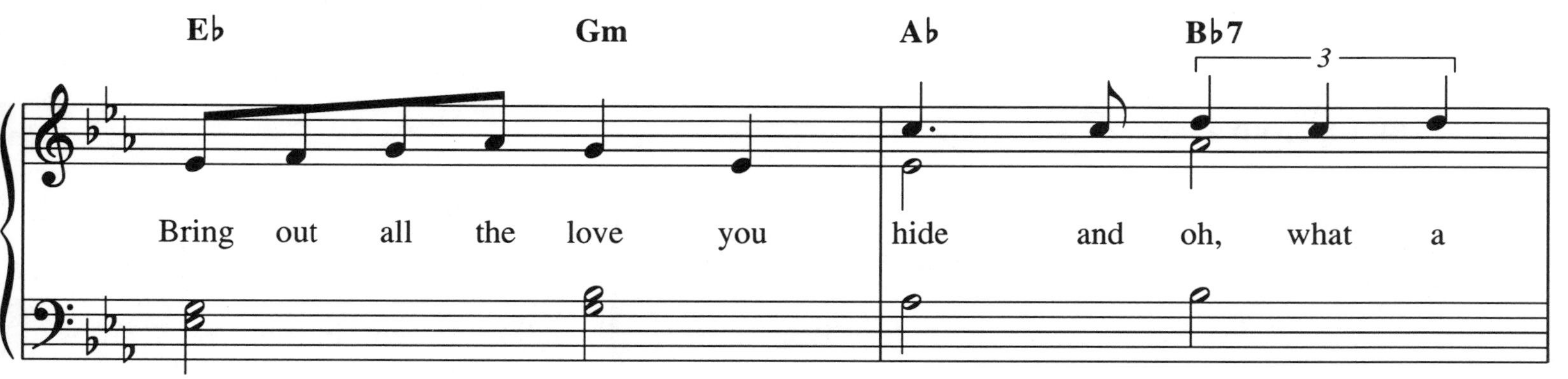
E♭ Gm A♭ B♭7
3
Bring out all the love you hide and oh, what a

Cm Cm/B♭ A♭
change there'd be, The world would see

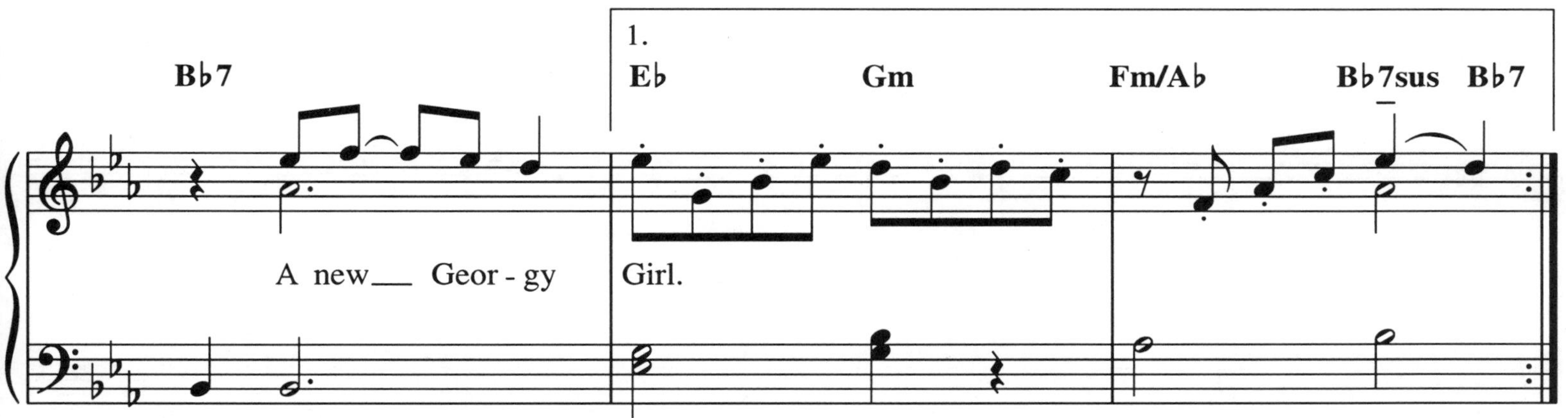
B♭7
1.
E♭ Gm Fm/A♭ B♭7sus B♭7
A new Geor - gy Girl.

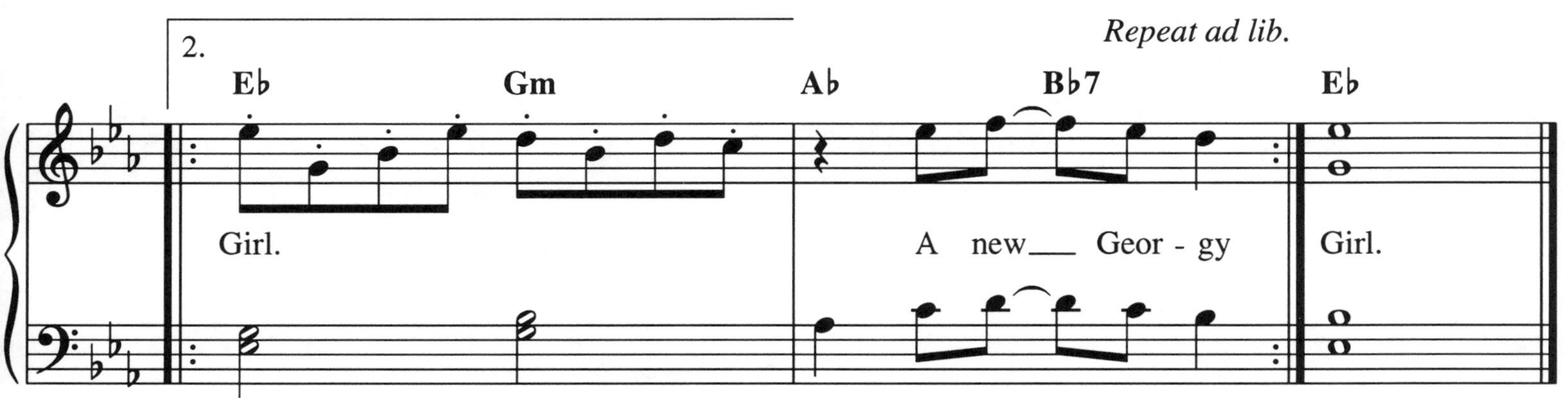
2.
Repeat ad lib.
E♭ Gm A♭ B♭7 E♭
Girl. A new Geor - gy Girl.

GOIN' OUT OF MY HEAD

Words and Music by TEDDY RANDAZZO
and BOBBY WEINSTEIN

Gm
Eb
Gm
want me, I
need you so bad - ly, I
morn - ing; But
you just walk past me, you
Ab
Bb
1.
Cmaj7
can't think of an - y - thing but
you.
don't e - ven know that I ex -
And I
2.
Cmaj7
ist.
F/G
G7
Go - in' out of my
mf
Cmaj7
Dm7
F/G
G7
head o - ver
you,
Out of my

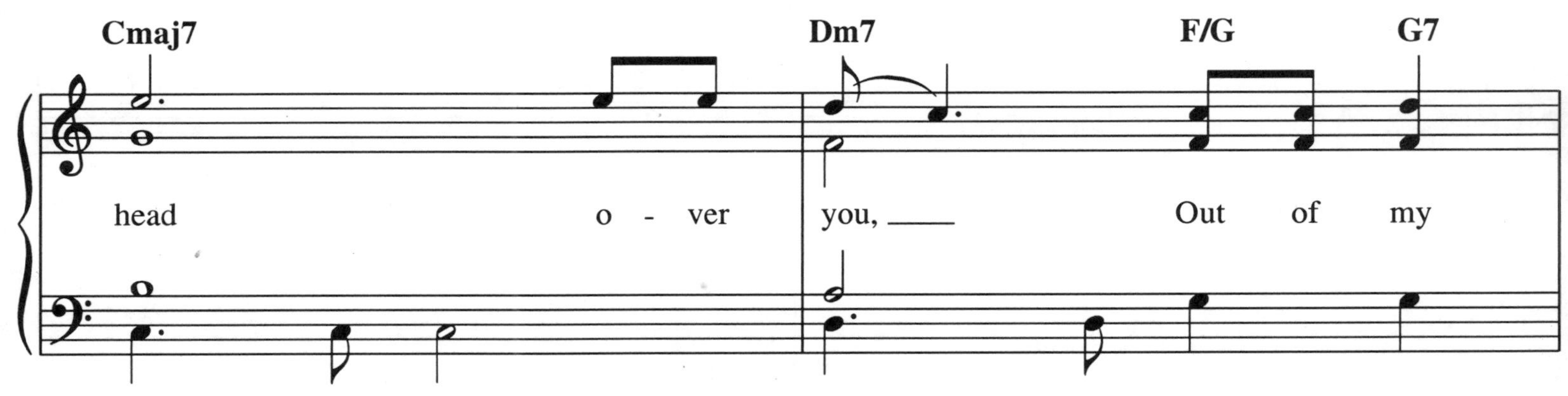
Cmaj7
Dm7
F/G
G7
head o - ver you, Out of my

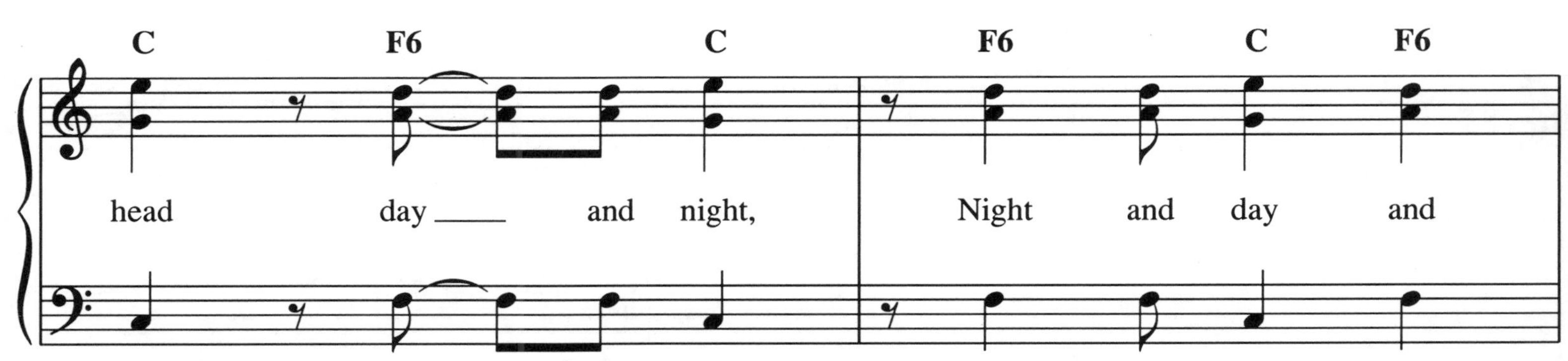
C
F6
C
F6
C
F6
head day and night, Night and day and

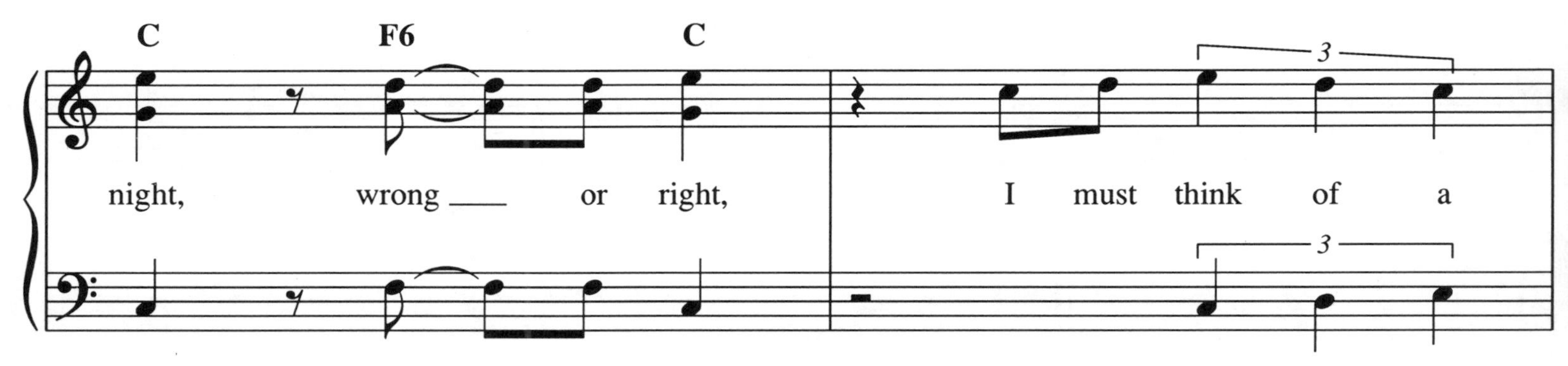
C
F6
C
3
night, wrong or right, I must think of a

D
Dm7(♭5)
3
C
way in - to your heart,

Cdim
G
There's no rea - son why my be - ing

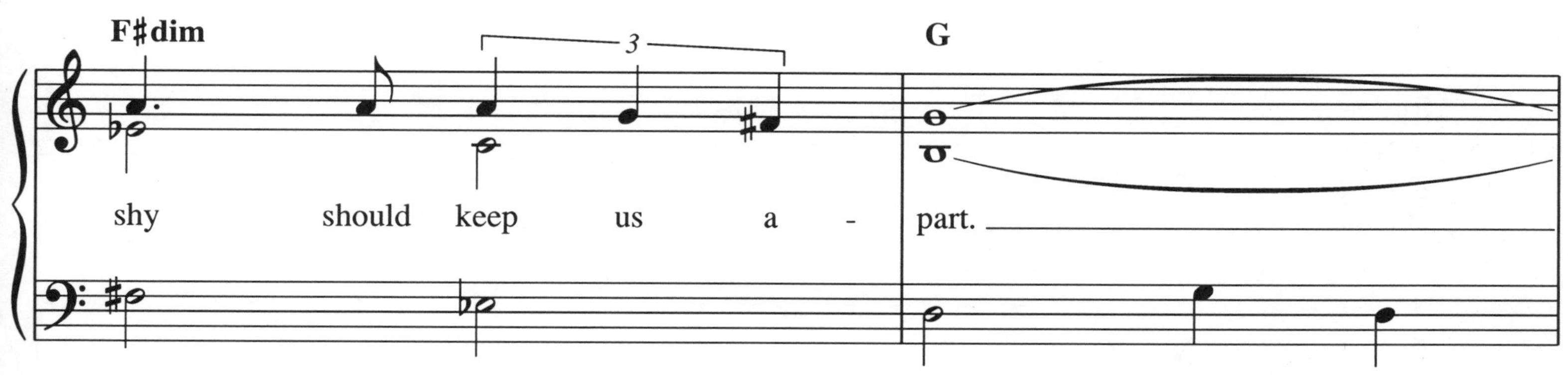
F♯dim
G
shy should keep us a - part.

Cm7
Cmaj7
Repeat ad lib.
And I think I'm go - ing out of my head. Yes, I

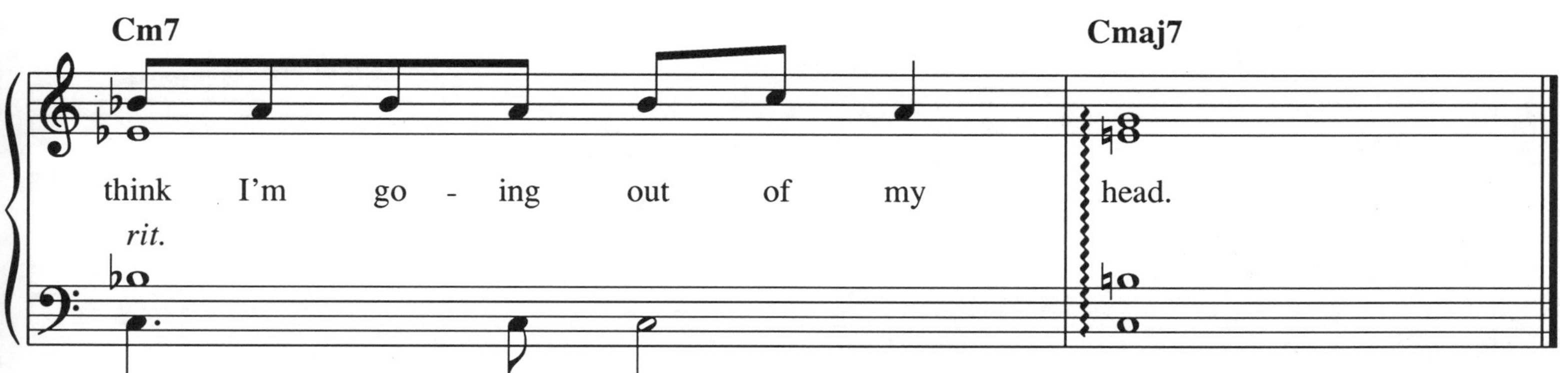
Cm7
Cmaj7
think I'm go - ing out of my head.
rit.

GROOVIN'

Words and Music by FELIX CAVALIERE
and EDWARD BRIGATI, JR.

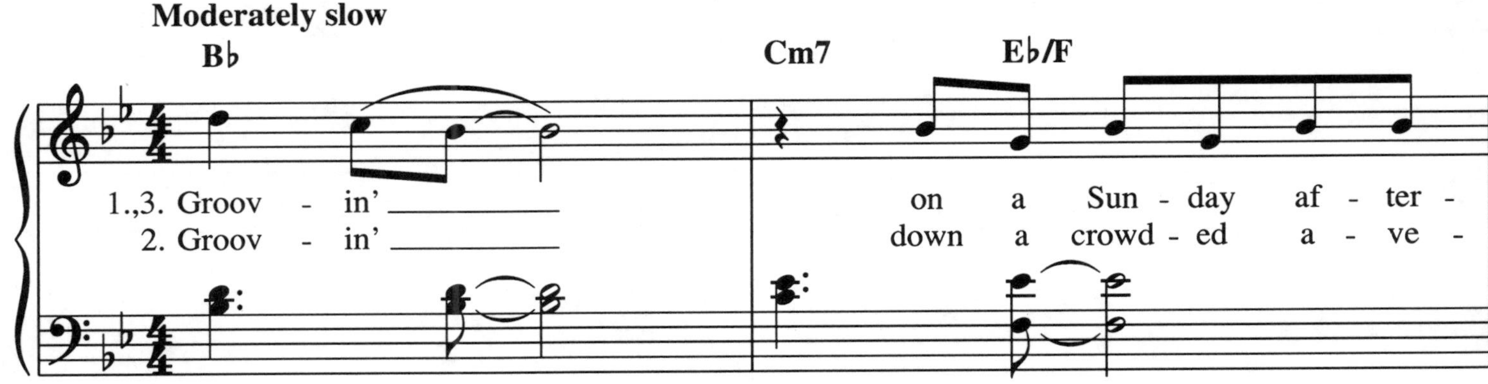

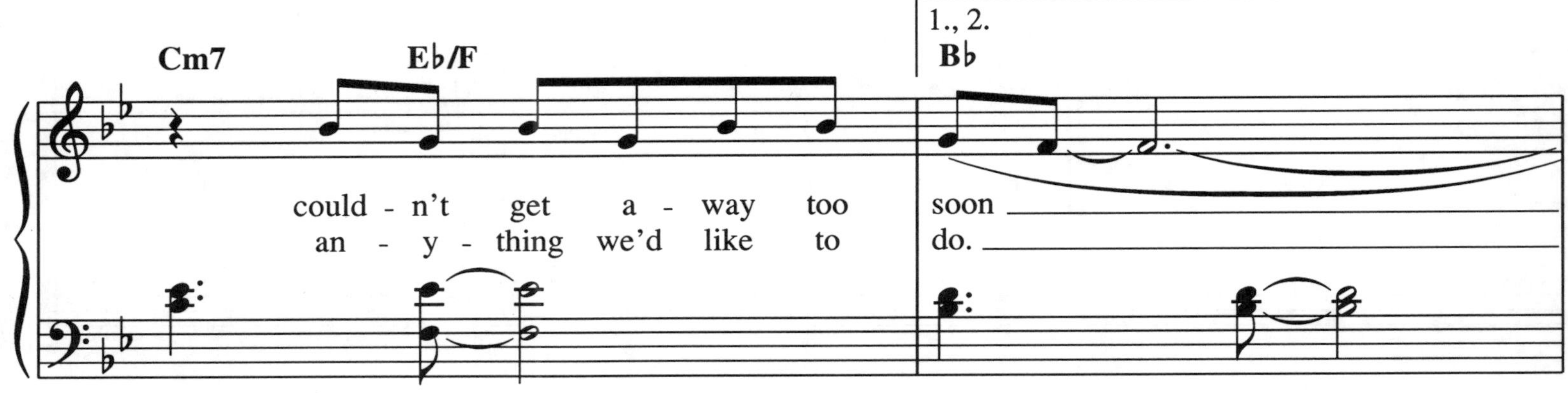

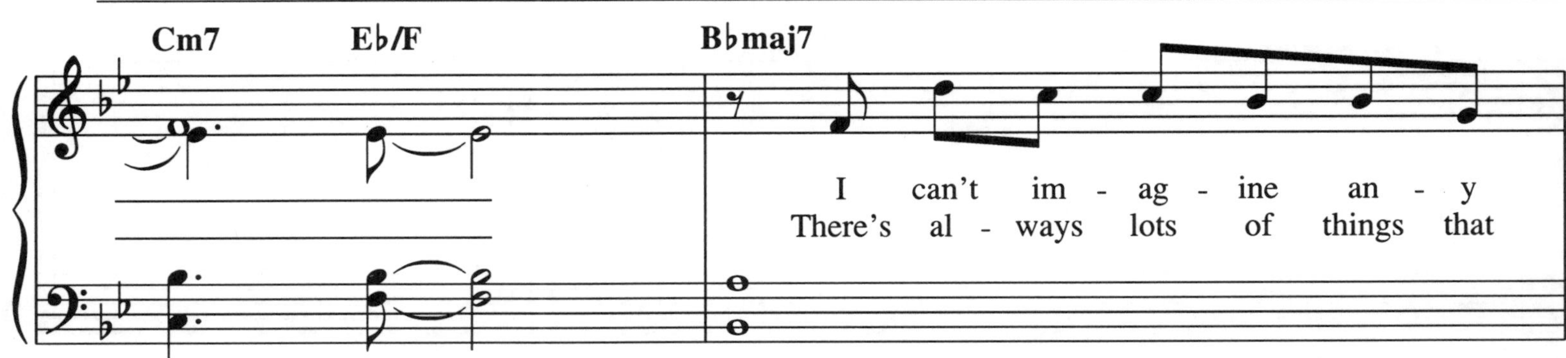

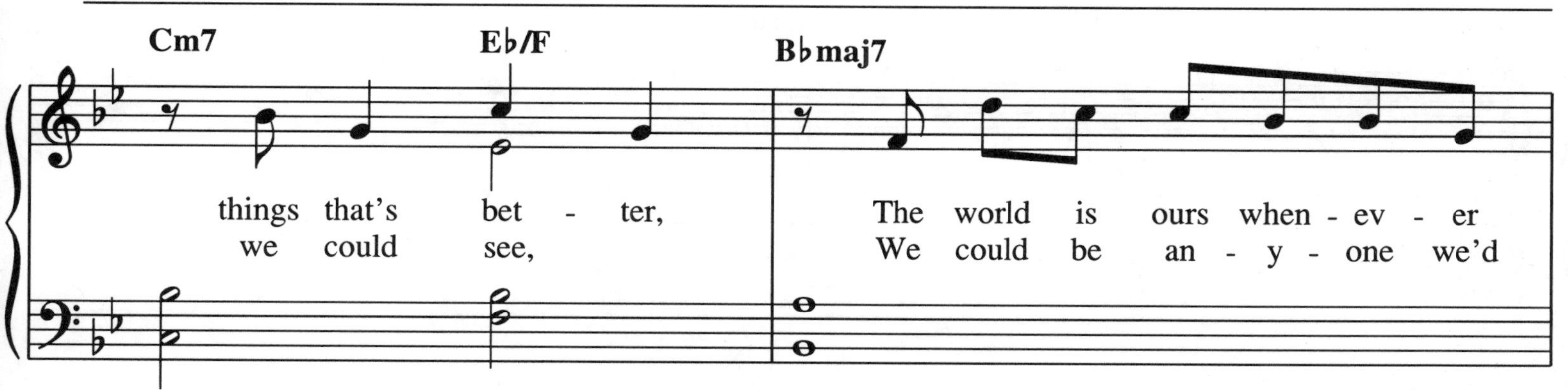
Cm7
Eb/F
Bbmaj7
things that's bet - ter,
we could see,
The world is ours when - ev - er
We could be an - y - one we'd

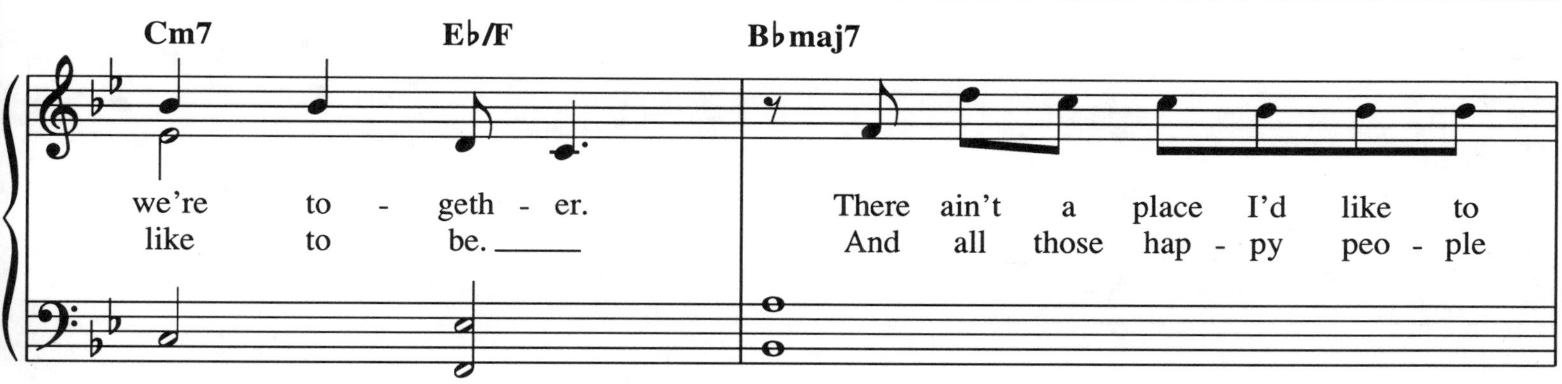
Cm7
Eb/F
Bbmaj7
we're to - geth - er.
like to be.
There ain't a place I'd like to
And all those hap - py peo - ple

Cm7
Ebmaj7
F9
3.
Bb
3
be in - stead of
we could meet just
soon, no no, no,

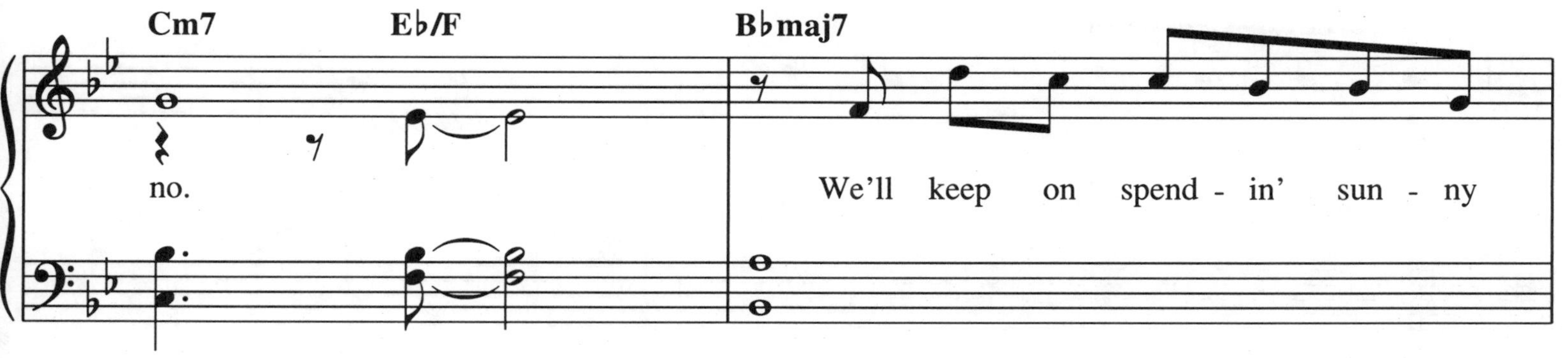
Cm7
Eb/F
Bbmaj7
no.
We'll keep on spend - in' sun - ny

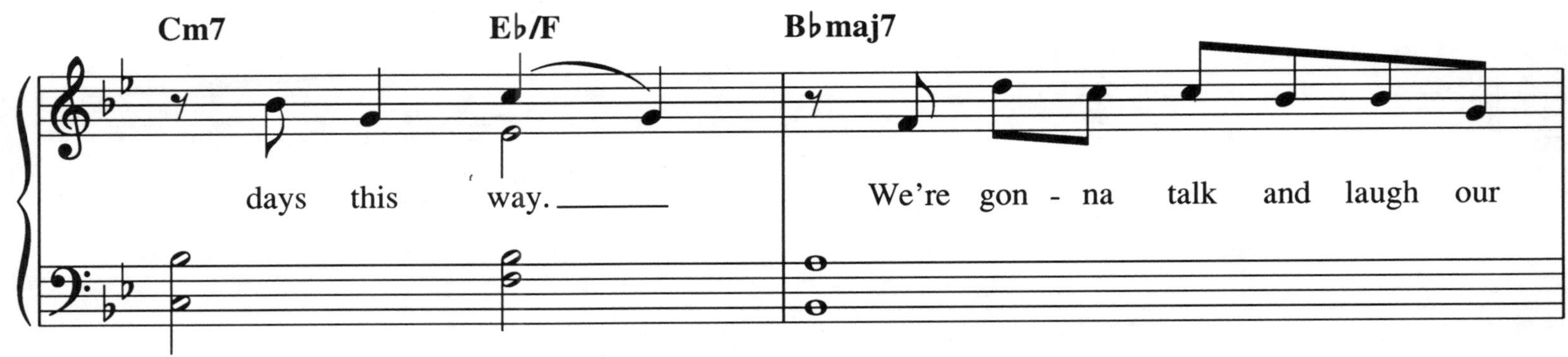
Cm7
Eb/F
Bbmaj7
days this way.
We're gon - na talk and laugh our

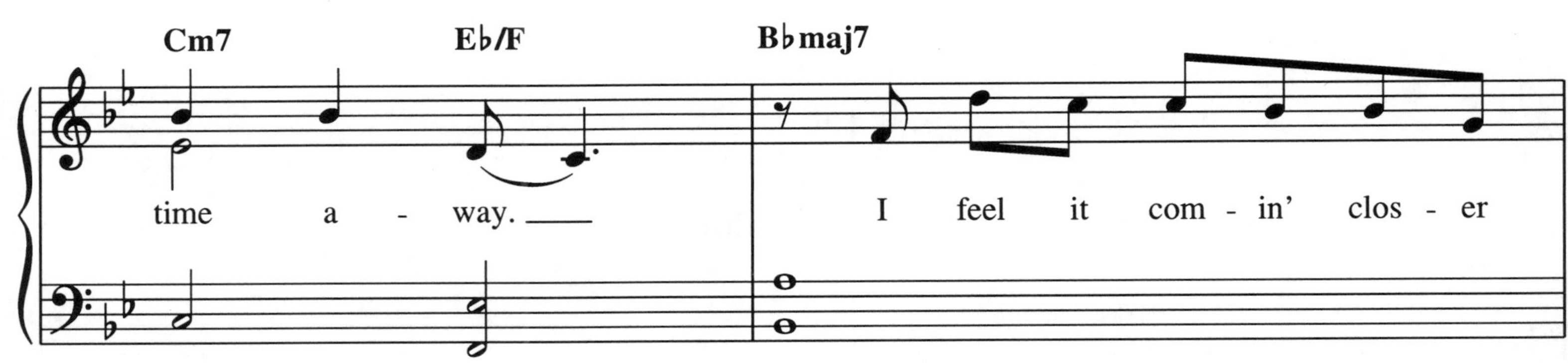
Cm7
Eb/F
Bbmaj7
time a - way.
I feel it com - in' clos - er

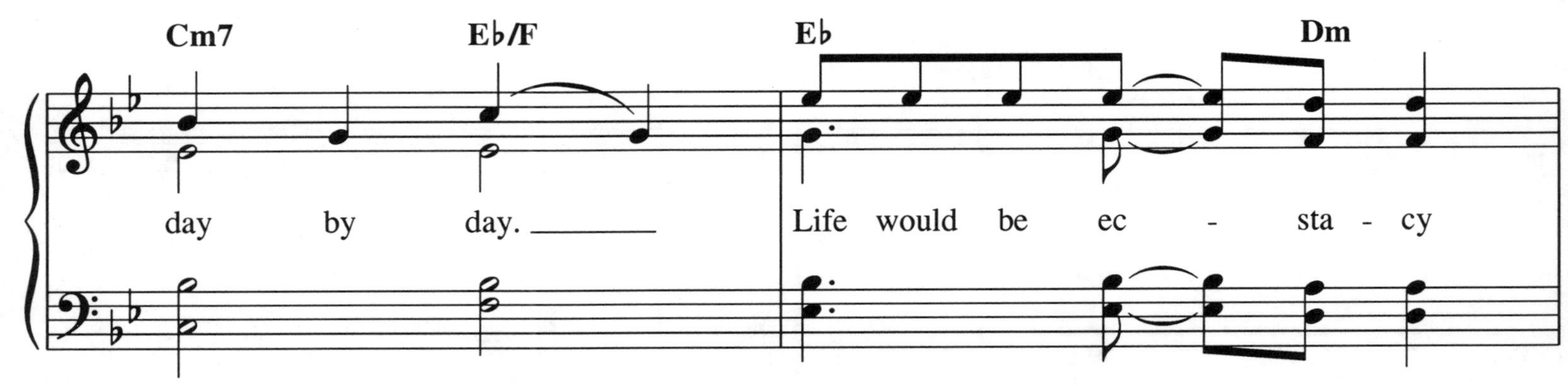
Cm7
Eb/F
Eb
Dm
day by day.
Life would be ec - sta - cy

Cm7
Eb/F
Bb
you and me end - less - ly
Groov - in',

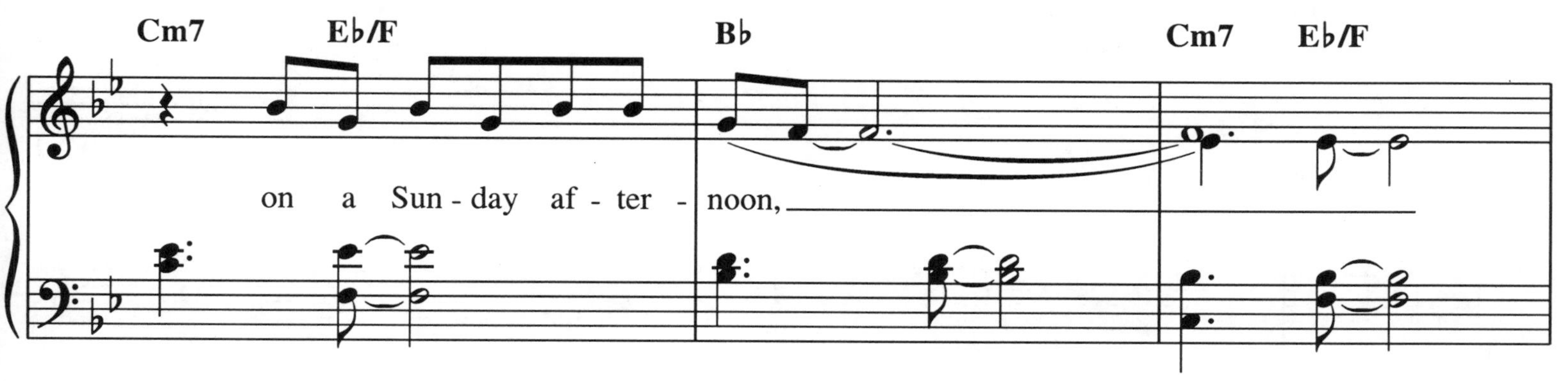
Cm7
Eb/F
Bb
Cm7
Eb/F
on a Sun - day af - ter - noon,

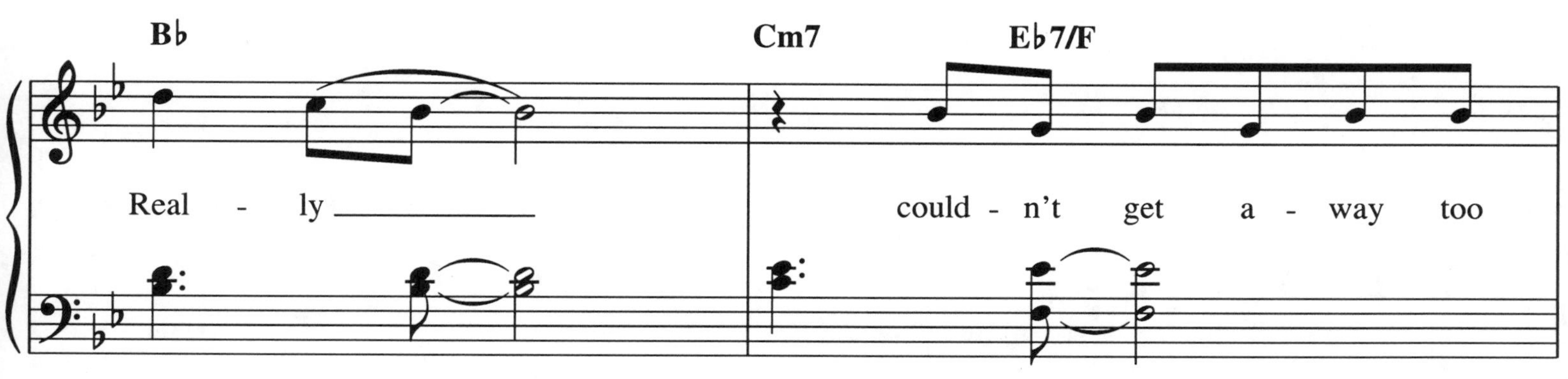
Bb
Cm7
Eb7/F
Real - ly
could - n't get a - way too

Bb
3
Cm7
Eb/F
soon, no, no, no, no.

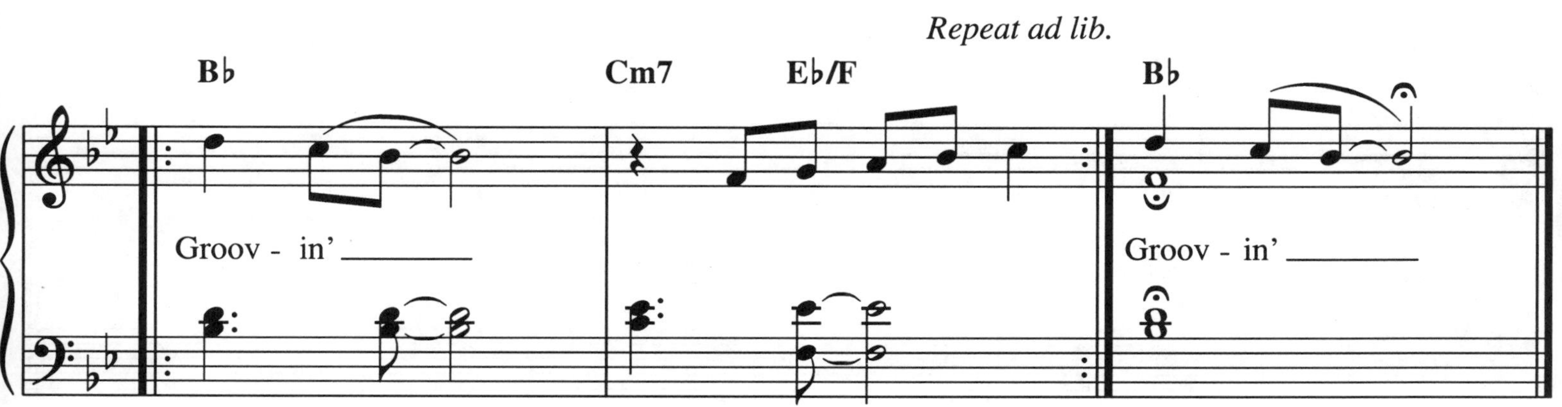
Repeat ad lib.
Bb
Cm7
Eb/F
Bb
Groov - in'
Groov - in'

GREEN GREEN GRASS OF HOME

Words and Music by
CURLY PUTMAN

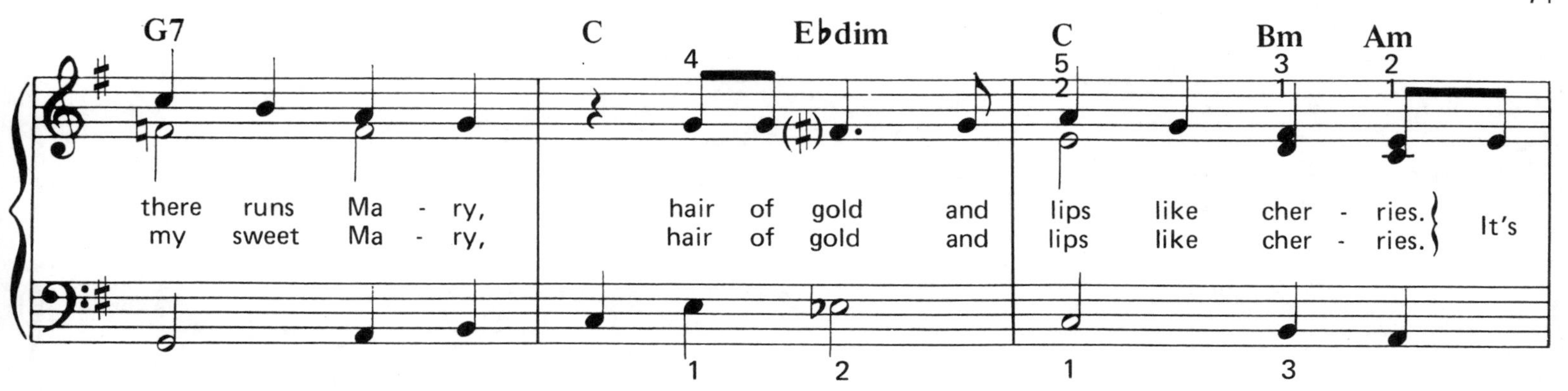
G7
C
E♭dim
C
Bm
Am
there runs Ma - ry,
my sweet Ma - ry,
hair of gold and
hair of gold and
lips like cher - ries.
lips like cher - ries.
It's

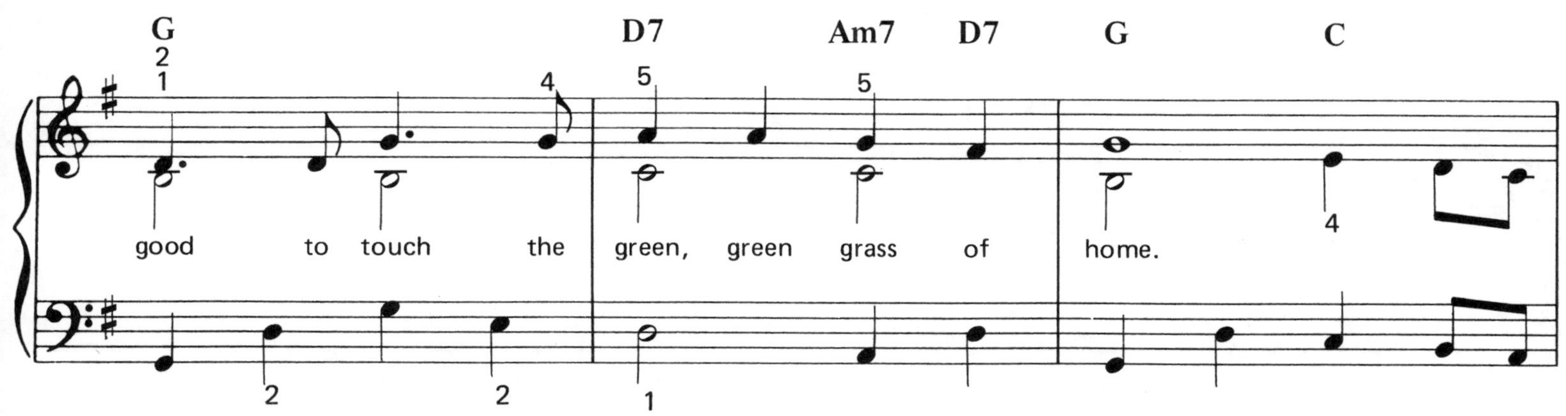
G
D7
Am7
D7
G
C
good to touch the green, green grass of home.

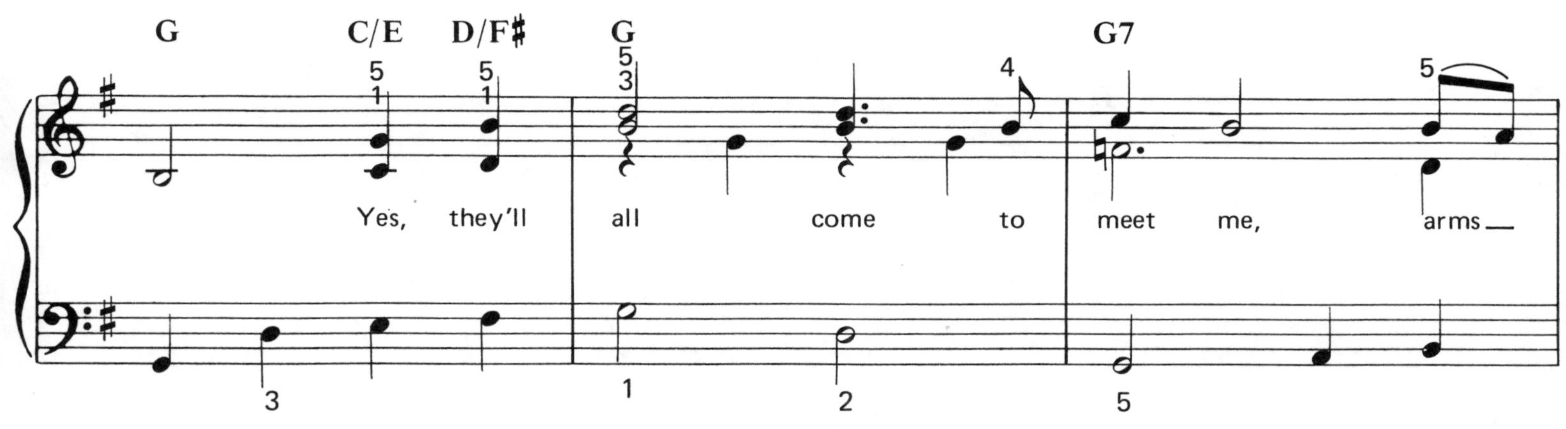
G
C/E
D/F♯
G
G7
Yes, they'll all come to meet me, arms

1,2
C
Am
G
reach - ing, smil - ing sweet - ly. It's good to touch the

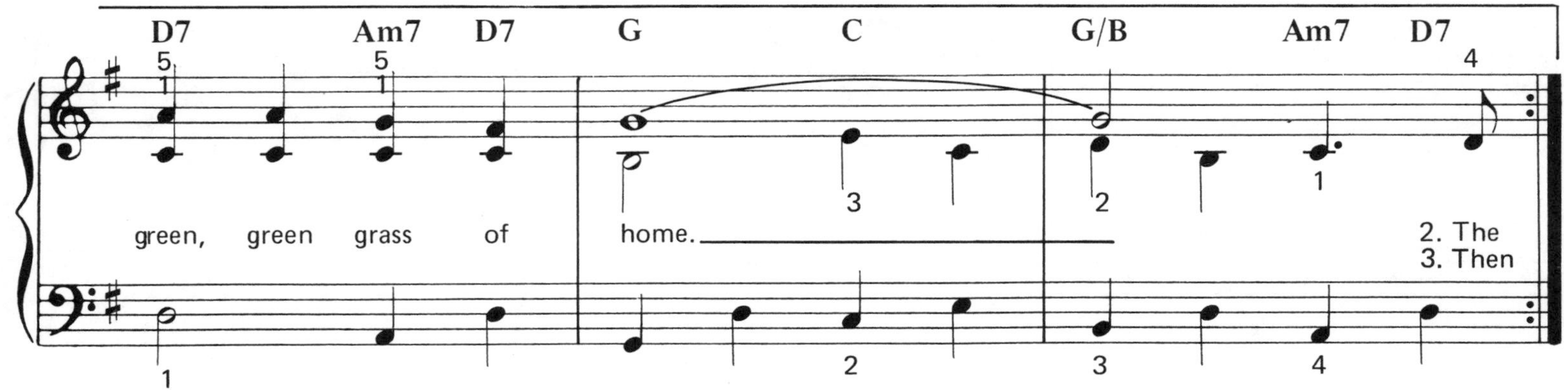

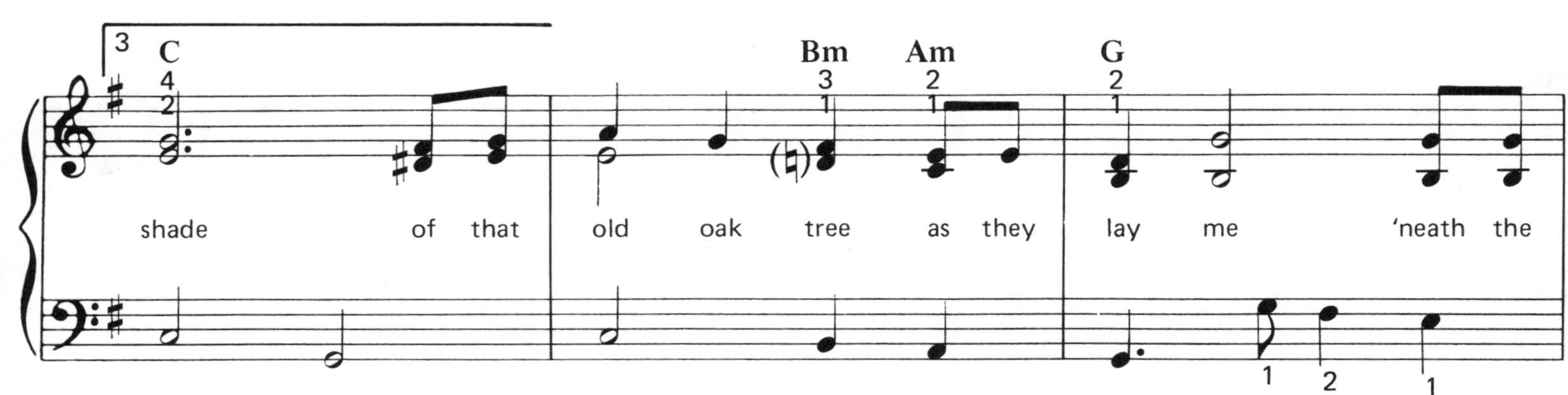

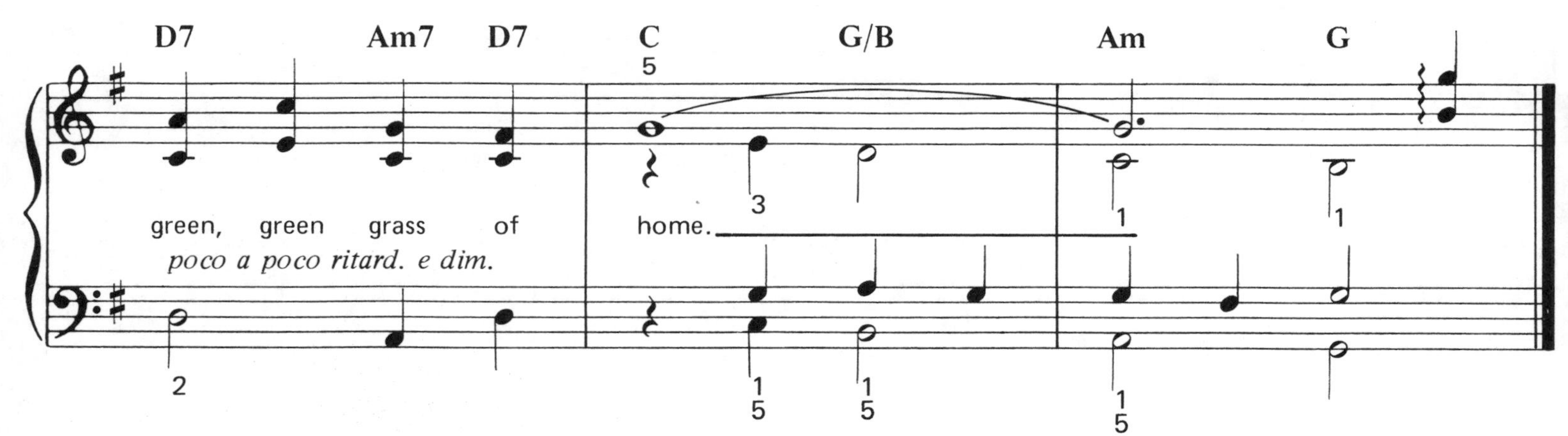

Verse 3.
Then I awake and look around me
At four gray walls that surround me,
And I realize that I was only dreaming.
For there's a guard and there's a sad old padre,
Arm in arm we'll walk at daybreak,
Again I'll touch the green, green grass of home.

Yes, they'll all come to see me
In the shade of that old oak tree
As they lay me 'neath the green, green grass of home.

HANG ON SLOOPY

Words and Music by BURT RUSSELL
and WES FARRELL

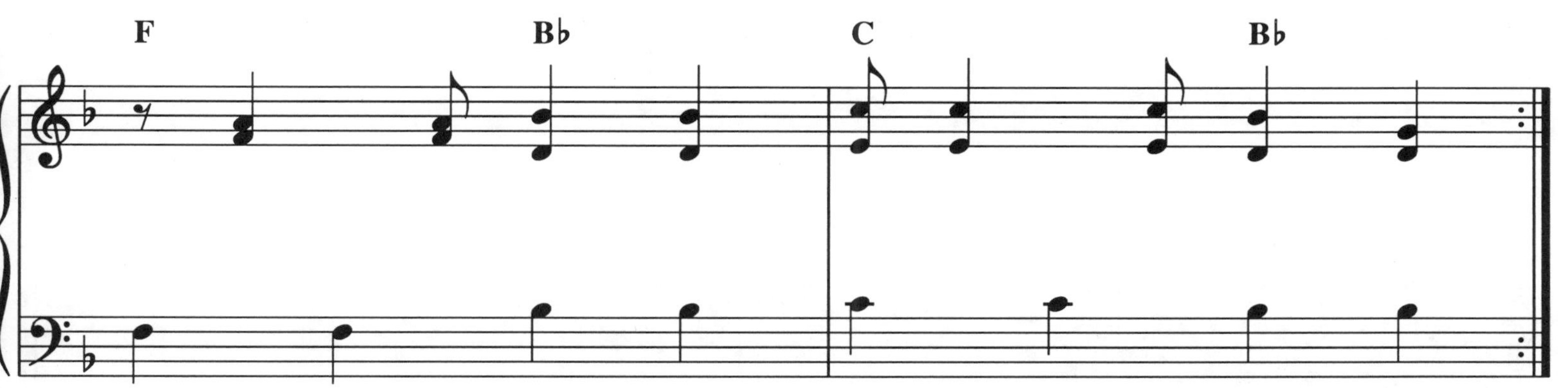

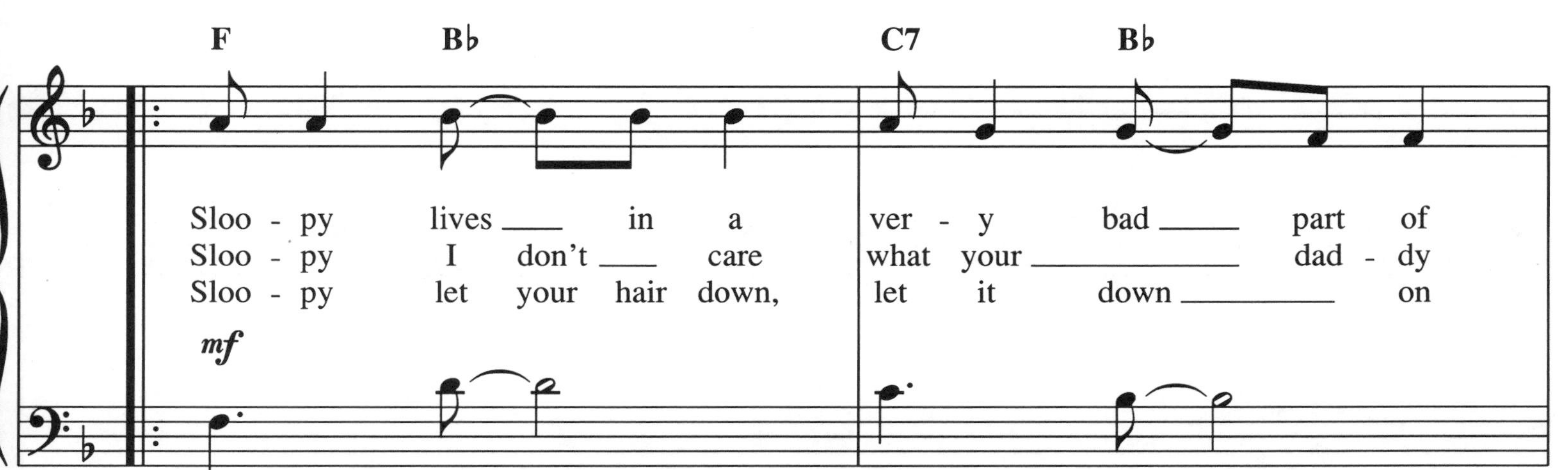

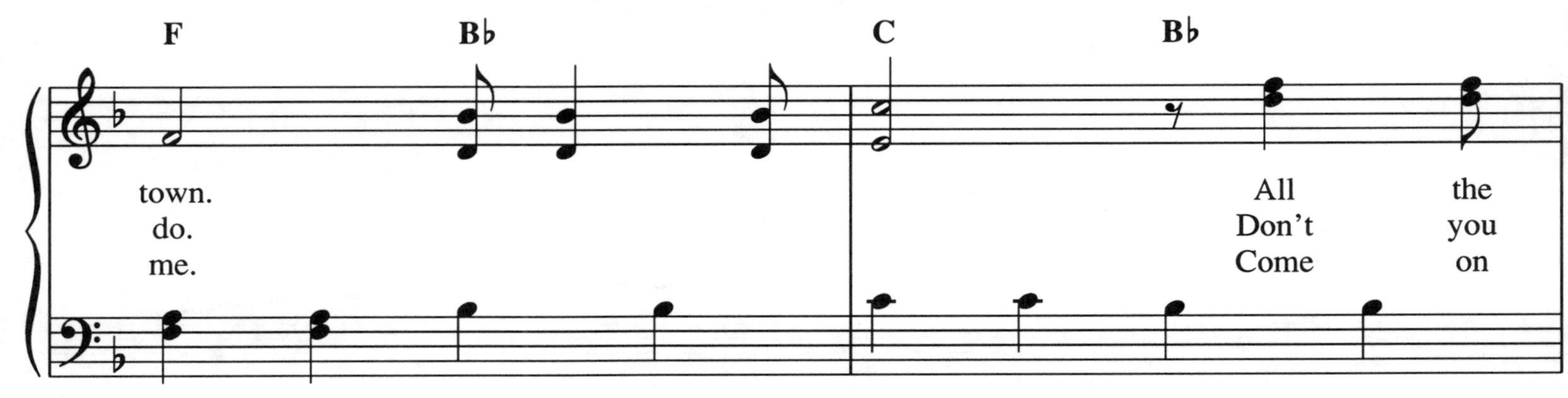
F
B♭
C
B♭
town.
do.
me.
All the
Don't you
Come on

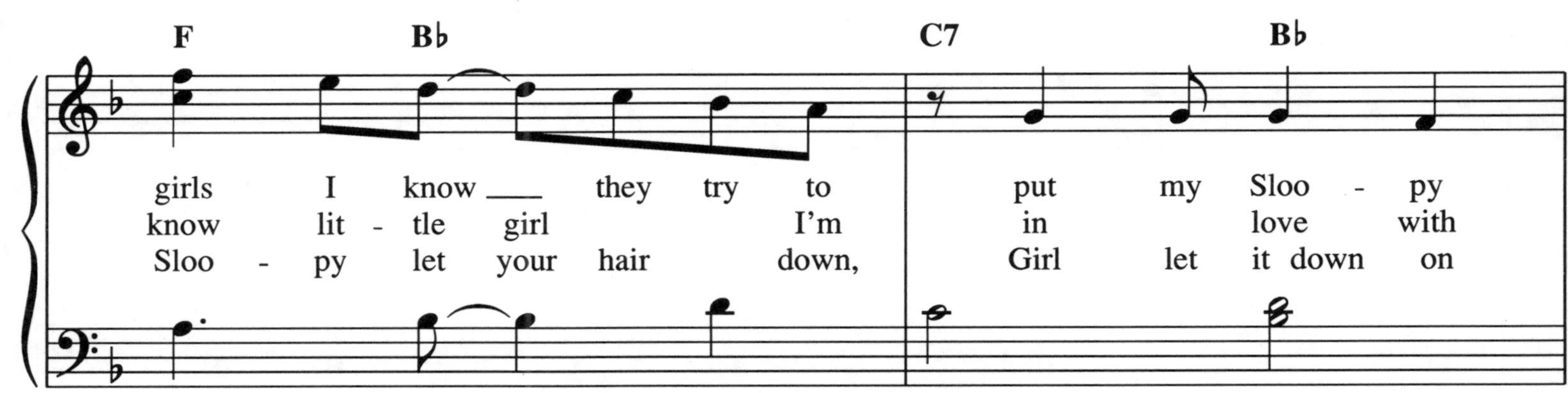
F
B♭
C7
B♭
girls I know ___ they try to put my Sloo - py
know lit - tle girl I'm in love with
Sloo - py let your hair down, Girl let it down on

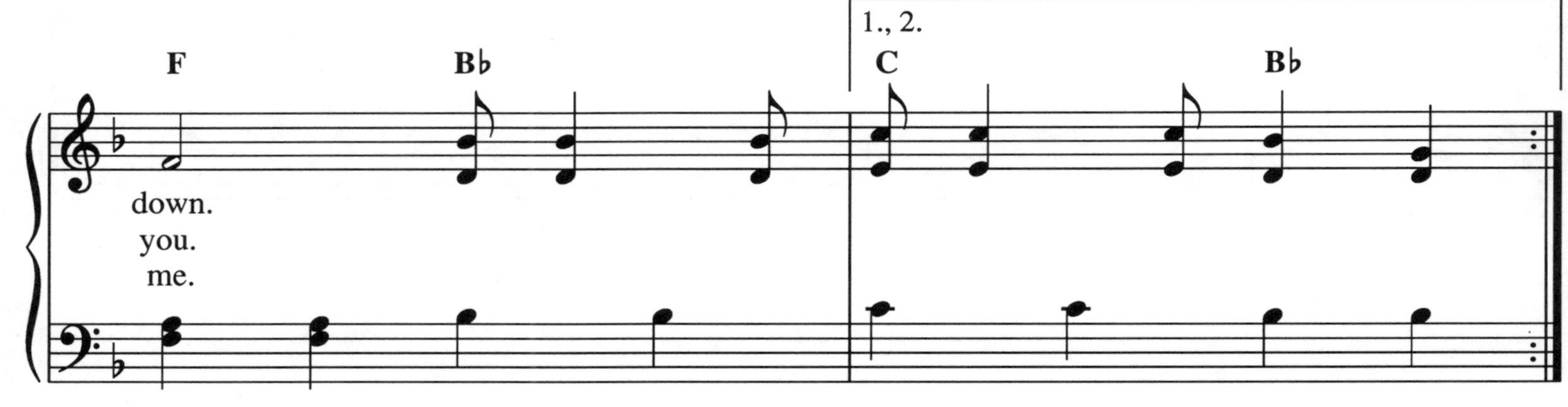
F
B♭
1., 2.
C
B♭
down.
you.
me.

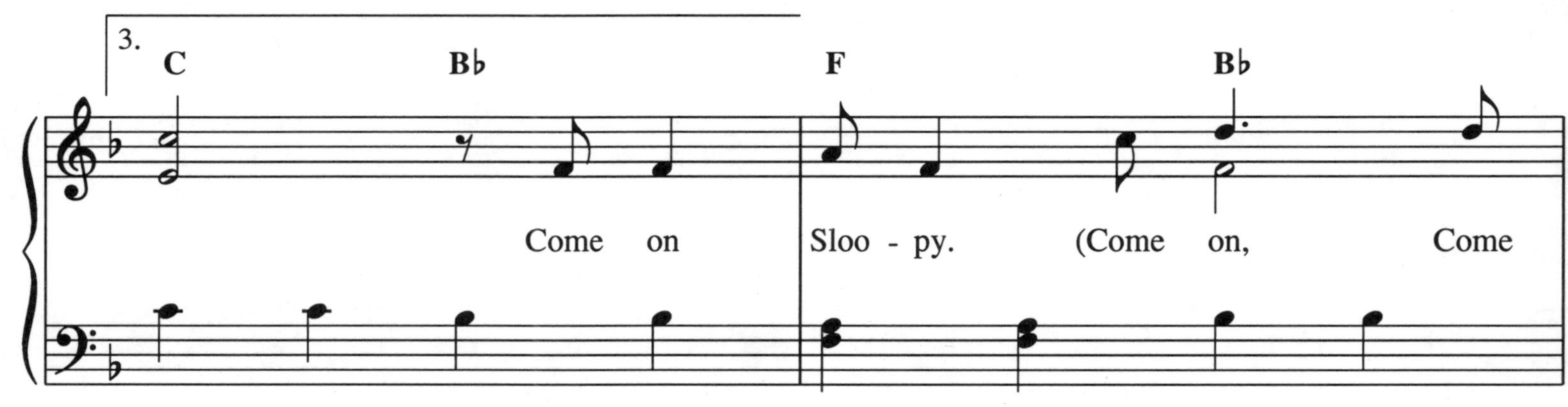
3.
C
B♭
F
B♭
Come on Sloo - py. (Come on, Come

C7
B♭
F
B♭
on.) Come on
girl. (Come on, Come

C7
B♭
F7
on.) Say
Yeah, Yeah, Yeah.

(Yeah, Yeah, Yeah.) Good,
Good, Good, Good. (Good,

Good, Good, Good.) Good,
Good, Good, Good. (Good, Good,

F
cresc.
Good.) Now I wan - na say
Ah

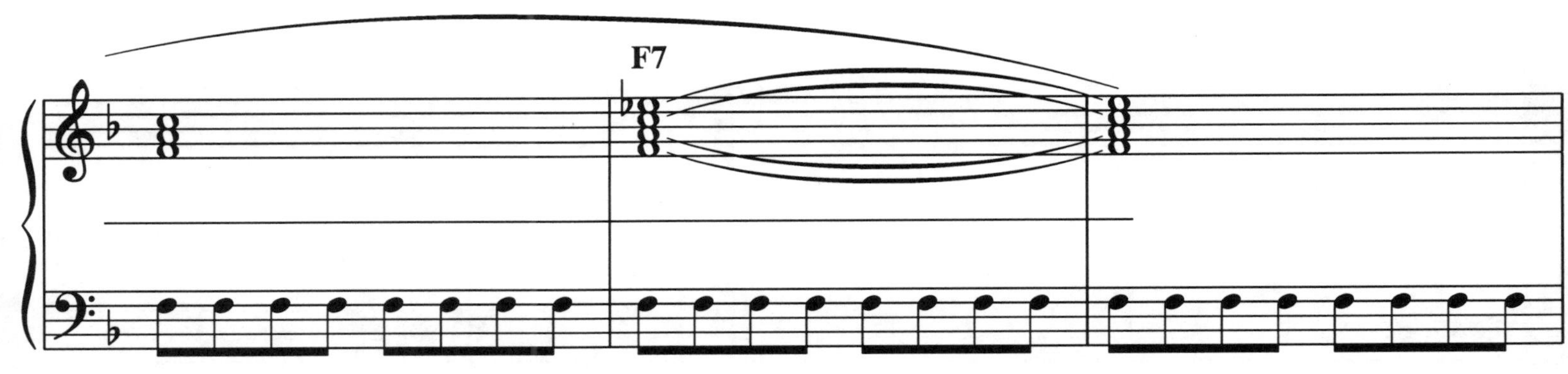
F7

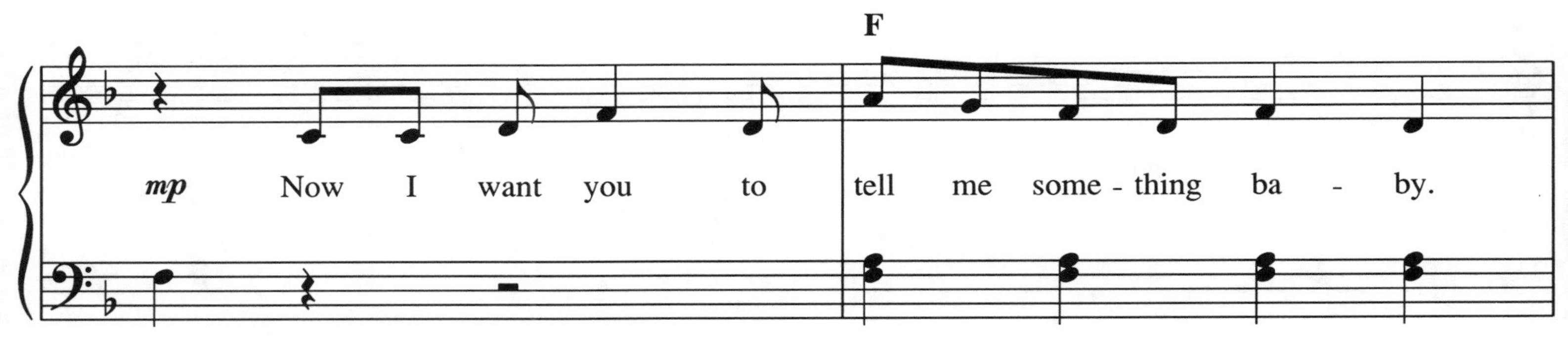
F
mp
Now I want you to
tell me some - thing ba - by.

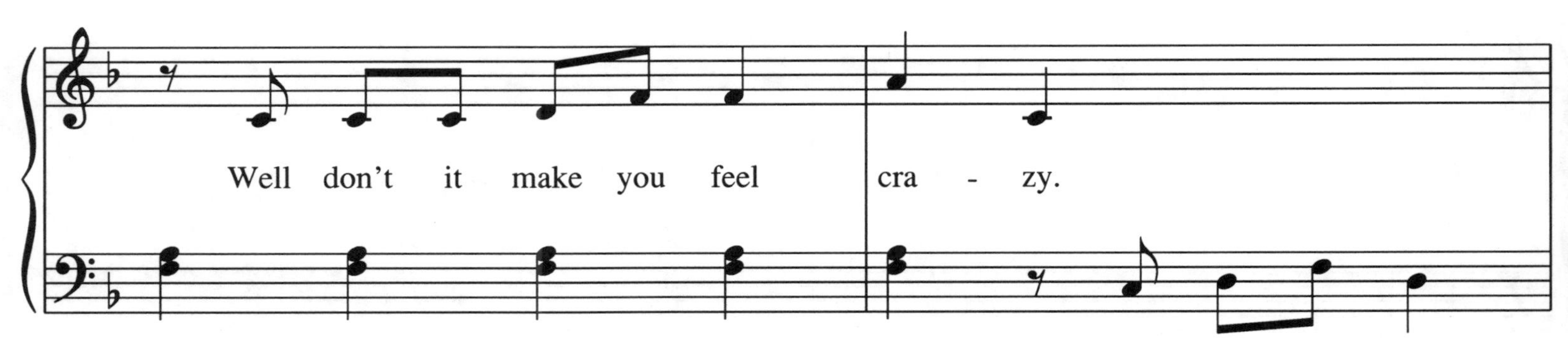
Well don't it make you feel
cra - zy.

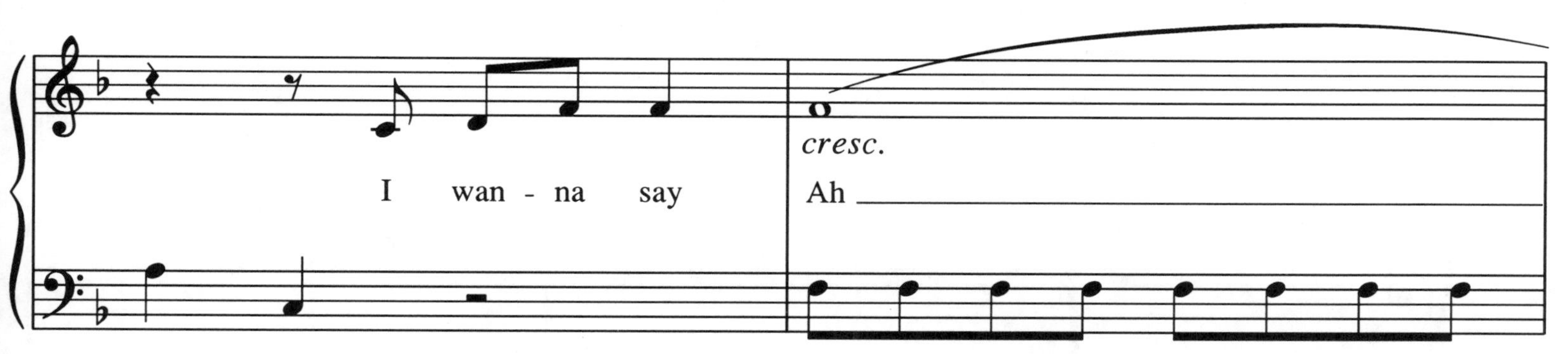
cresc.
I wan - na say
Ah

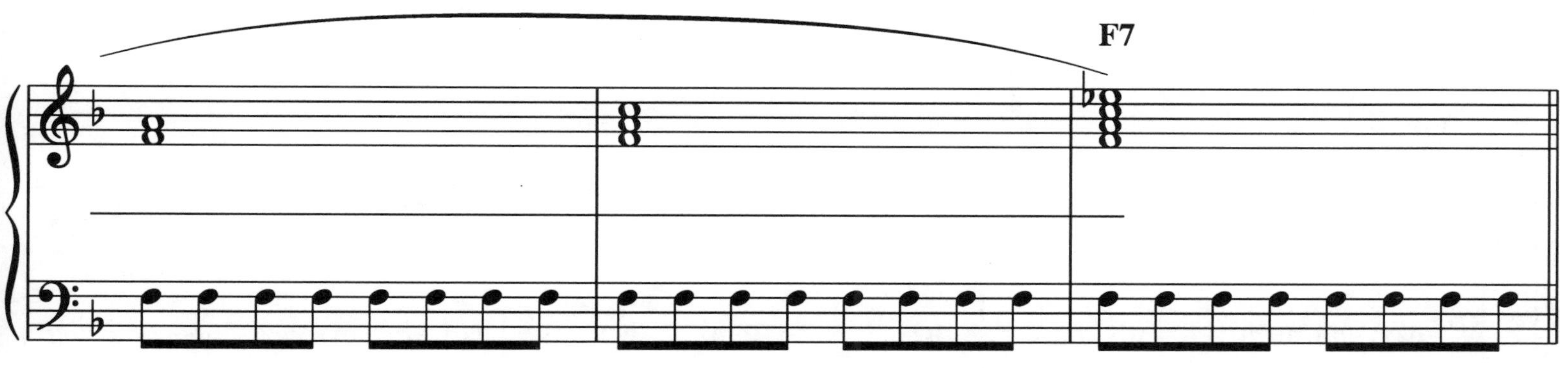
F7

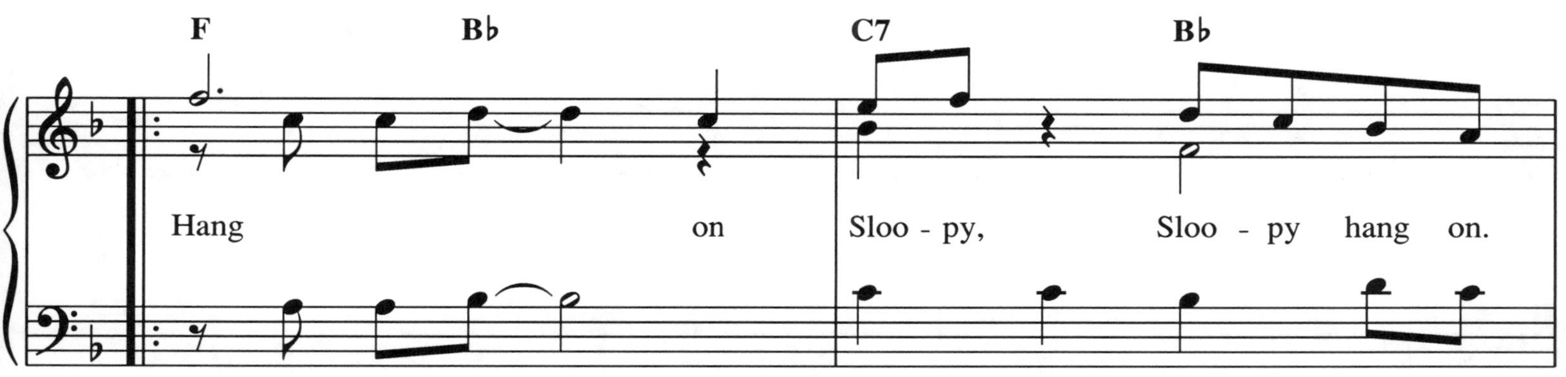
F
B♭
C7
B♭
Hang on
Sloo - py,
Sloo - py hang on.

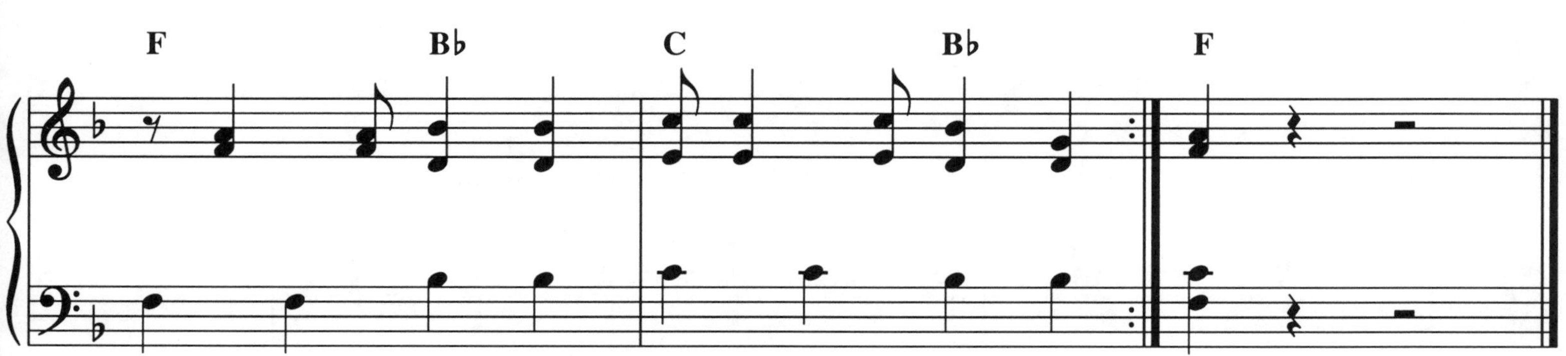
F
B♭
C
B♭
F

HAPPY TOGETHER

Words and Music by GARRY BONNER
and ALAN GORDON

C
mind, im- ag - ine how the world would be so ver - y fine, so hap - py to -
B
E
alt. fing.
geth - er.
I can see me
Bm7
E
G
lov - in' no - bod - y but you for all my life.
E
Bm7
E
When you're with me, ba - by, the skies will be blue for all my

G
Em
life.
Me and you and you and me, no mat - ter how they

D
C
toss the dice, it has to be. The on - ly one for me is you, and you for

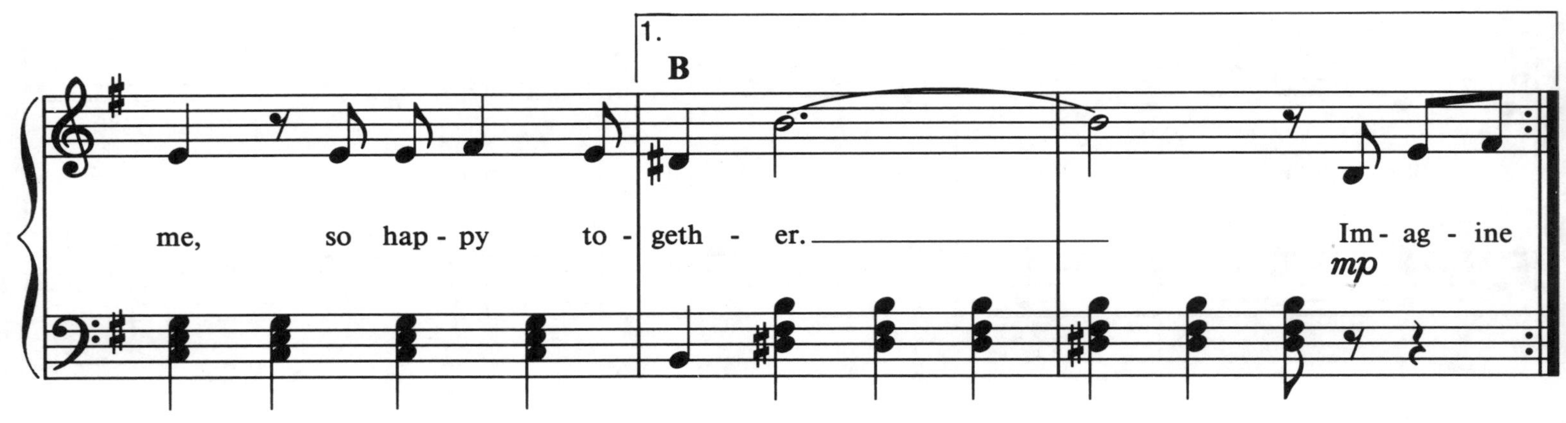
1.
B
me, so hap - py to - geth - er. Im - ag - ine
mp

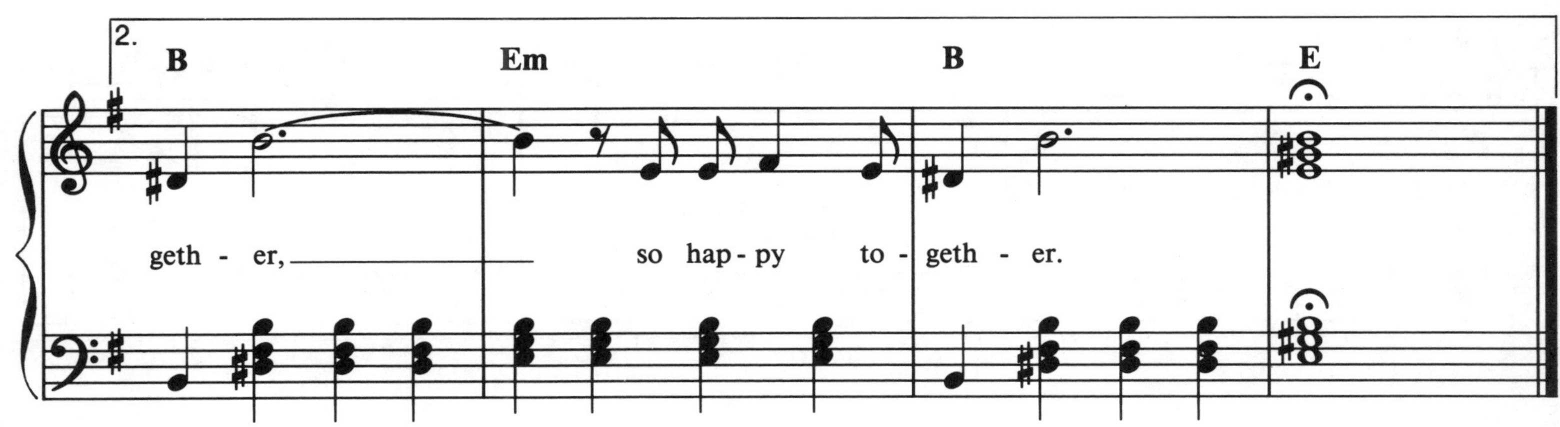
2.
B
Em
B
E
geth - er, so hap - py to - geth - er.

HELLO MARY LOU

Words and Music by GENE PITNEY
and C. MANGIARACINA

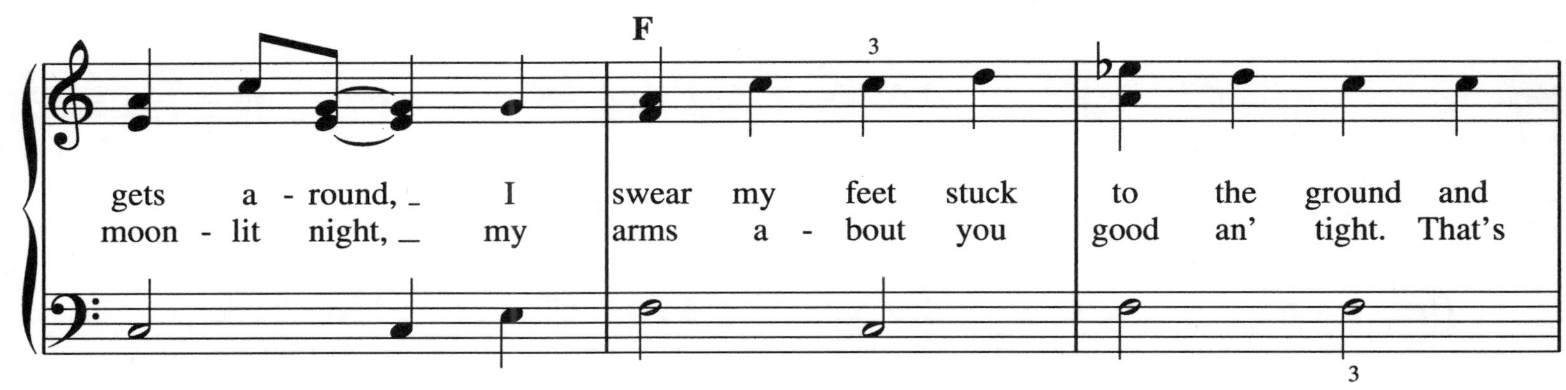
F
3
gets a - round, _ I swear my feet stuck to the ground and
moon - lit night, _ my arms a - bout you good an' tight. That's
3

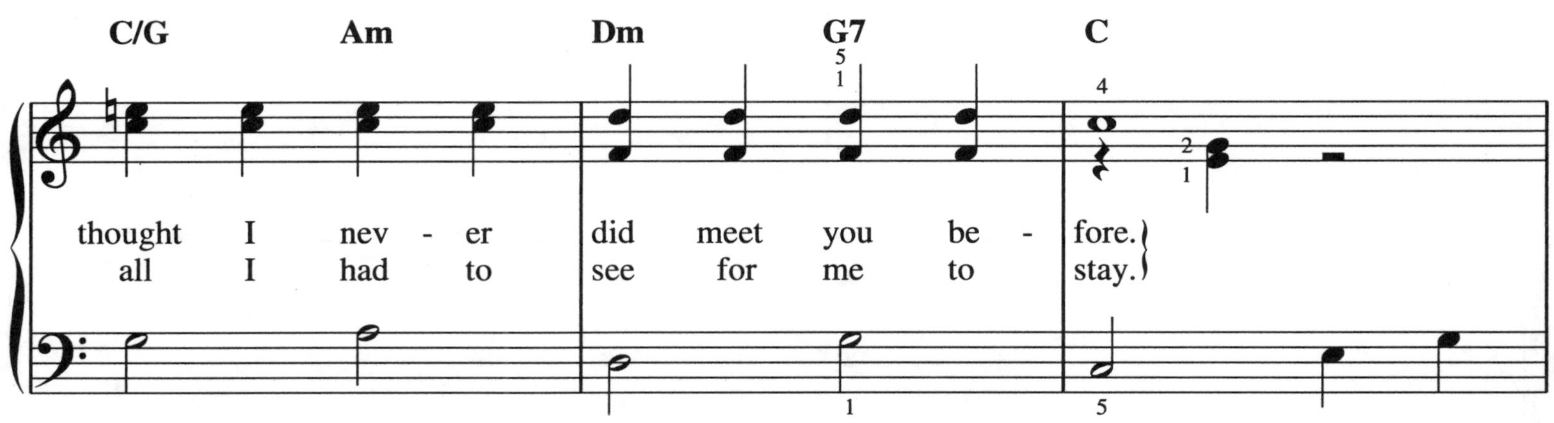
C/G Am Dm G7 C
thought I nev - er did meet you be - fore.
all I had to see for me to stay.

I said, "Hel - lo, Mar - y Lou,

F C
good - bye, heart. Sweet Mar - y Lou, I'm

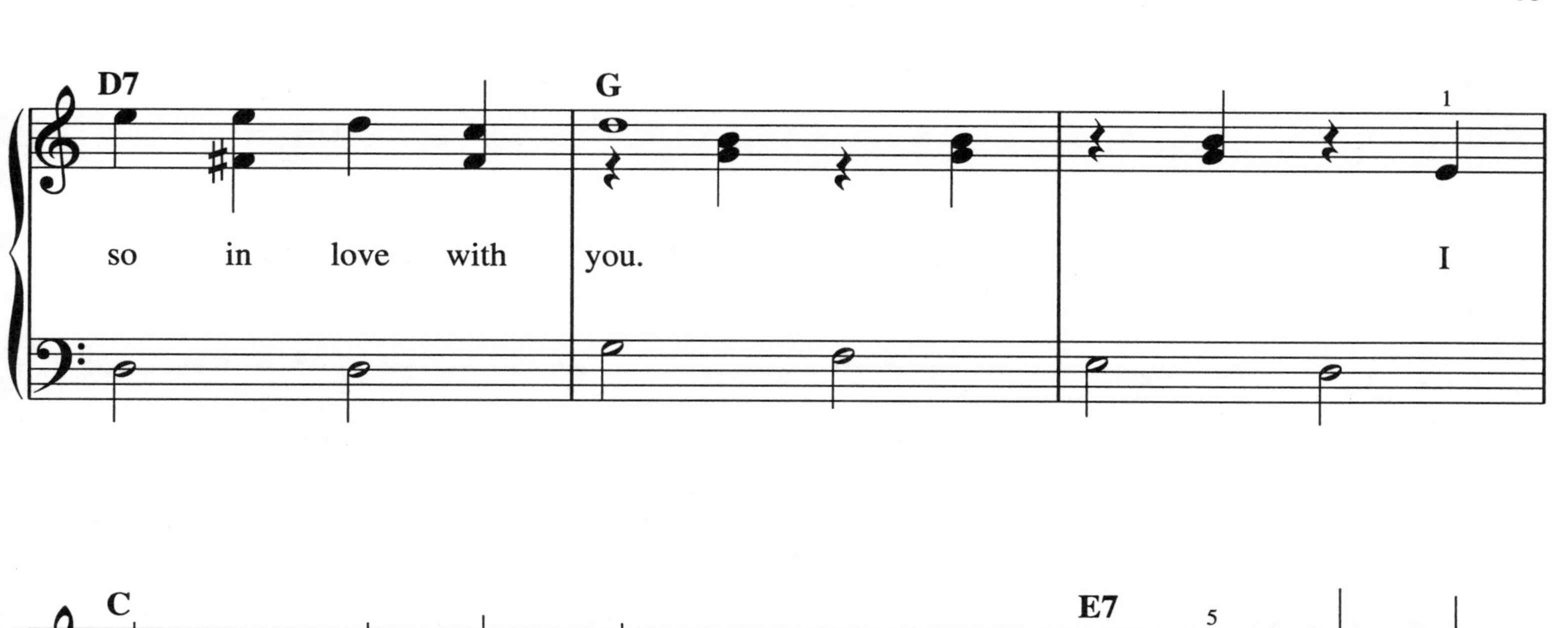
D7
G
1
so in love with you. I

C
E7
5
knew, Mar - y Lou, we'd nev - er
4

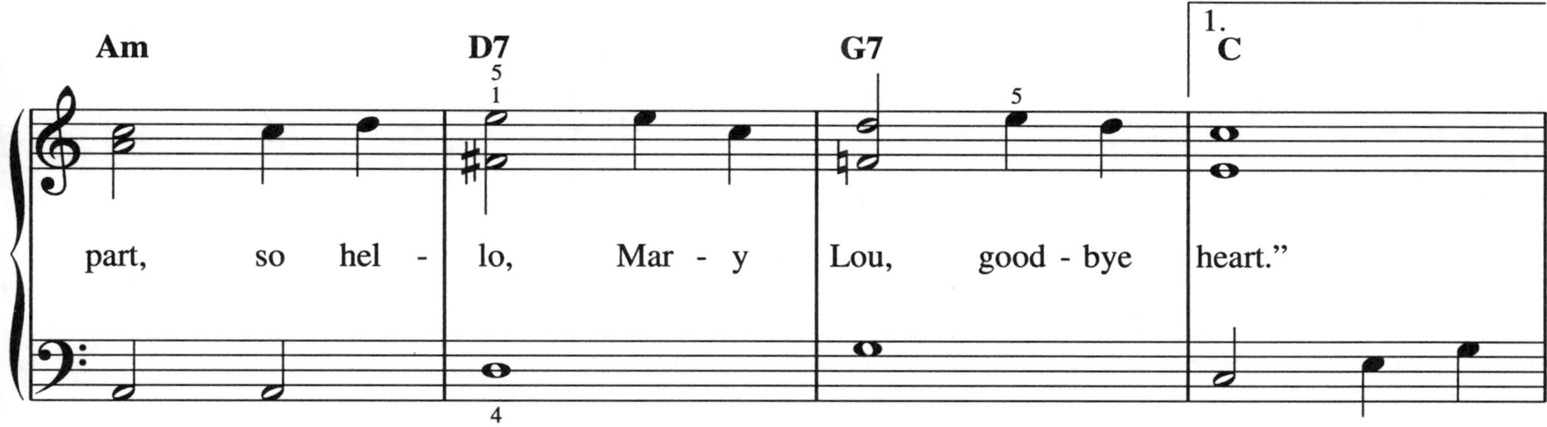
Am
D7
G7
1.
C
5
1
5
part, so hel - lo, Mar - y Lou, good - bye heart."
4

2
2.
C
3 - 5
I heart."

HONEY

Words and Music by BOBBY RUSSELL

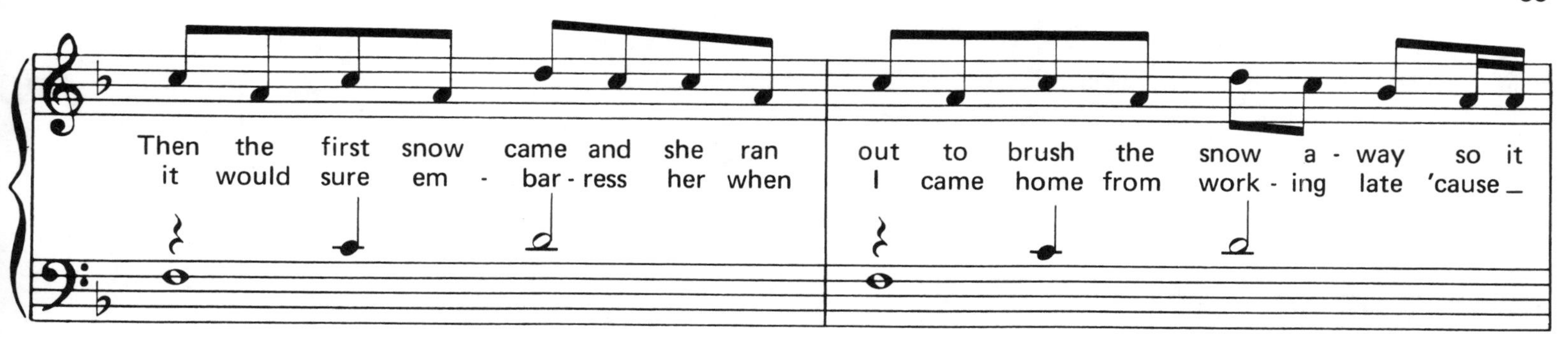
Then the first snow came and she ran out to brush the snow a - way so it
it would sure em - bar - ress her when I came home from work - ing late 'cause

Gm/F
C7/E
would - n't die, Came run - nin' in all ex - cit - ed,
I would know That she's been sit-tin' there and cry - in'

1 F6
slipped and al - most hurt her - self, I laughed 'til I cried.
o - ver some sad and sil - ly

2 F6
Chorus
Gm7
late, late show. And Hon - ey, I miss you.

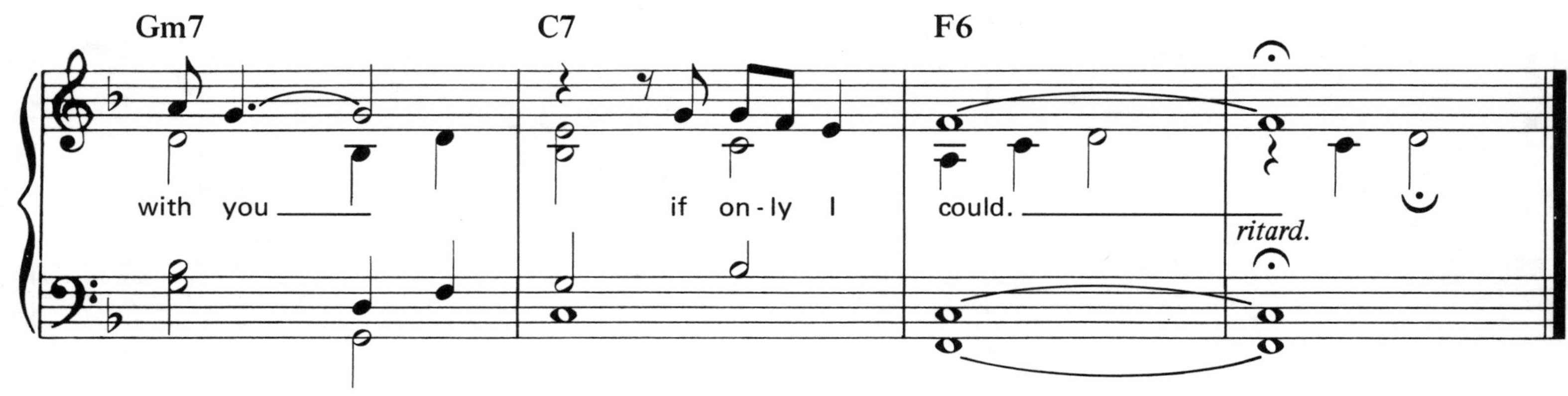

3rd Verse: She wrecked the car and she was sad
And so afraid that I'd be mad,
But what the heck.
Though I pretended hard to be,
Guess she could say she saw through me
And hugged my neck.

I came home unexpectedly
And found her crying needlessly
In the middle of the day,
And it was in the early spring,
When flowers bloom and robins sing
She went away.

To Chorus

4th Verse: Yes, one day, while I wasn't home,
While she was there and all alone
The angels came.
Now all I have is memories of Honey,
And I wake up nights and call her name.

Now my life's an empty stage,
Where Honey lived and Honey played,
And love grew up.
A small cloud passes over head
And cries down in the flower bed
That Honey loved.

To Chorus

I LEFT MY HEART IN SAN FRANCISCO

Words by DOUGLAS CROSS
Music by GEORGE CORY

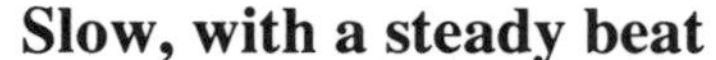

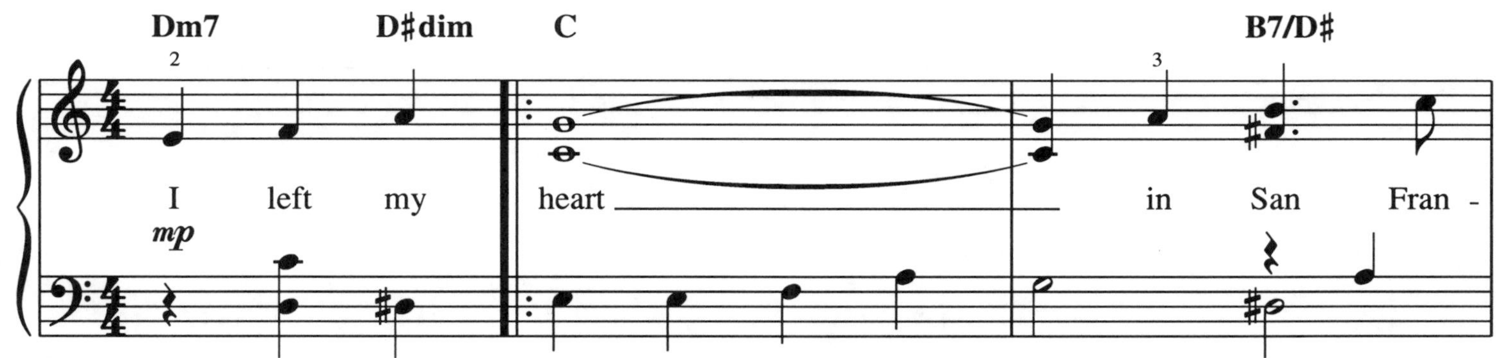

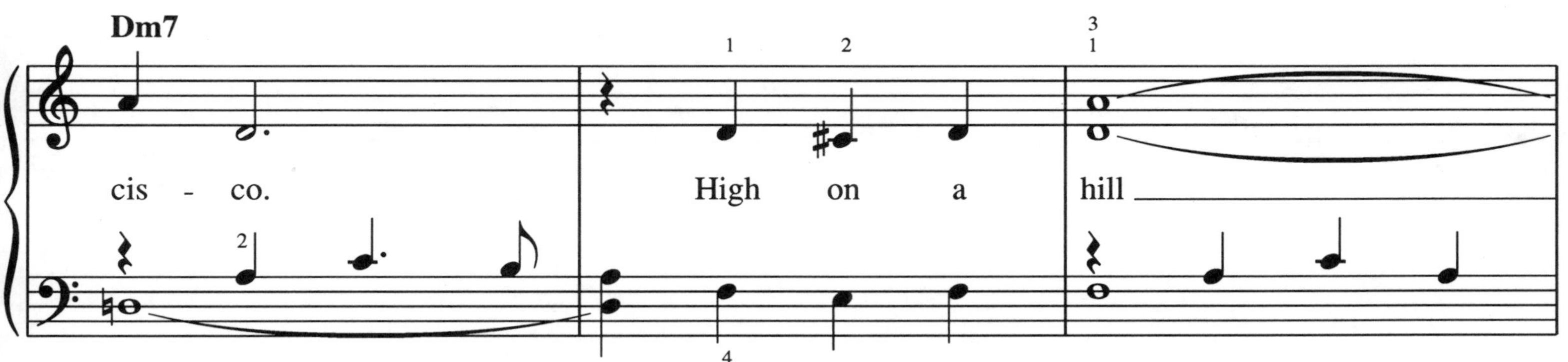

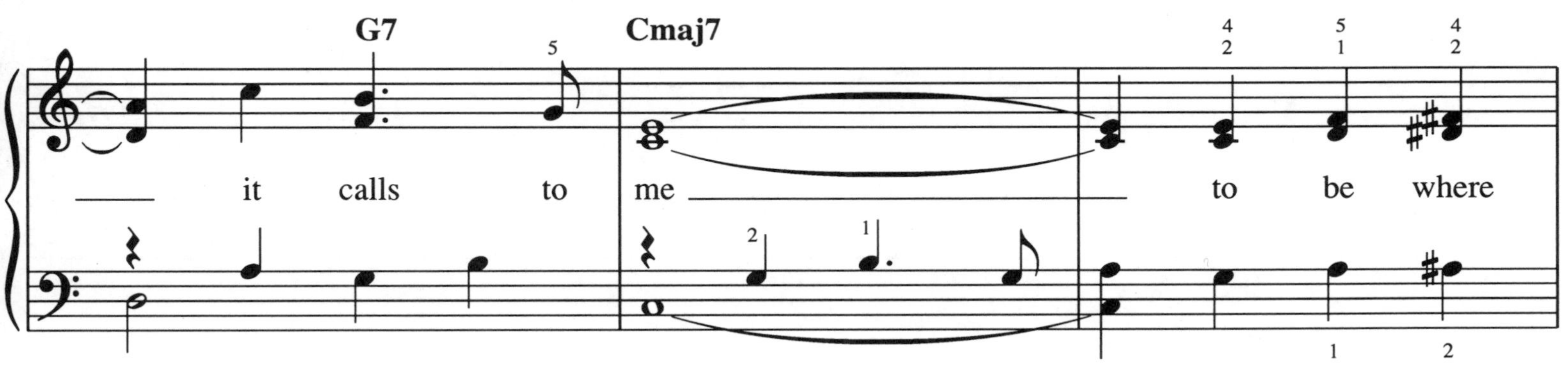

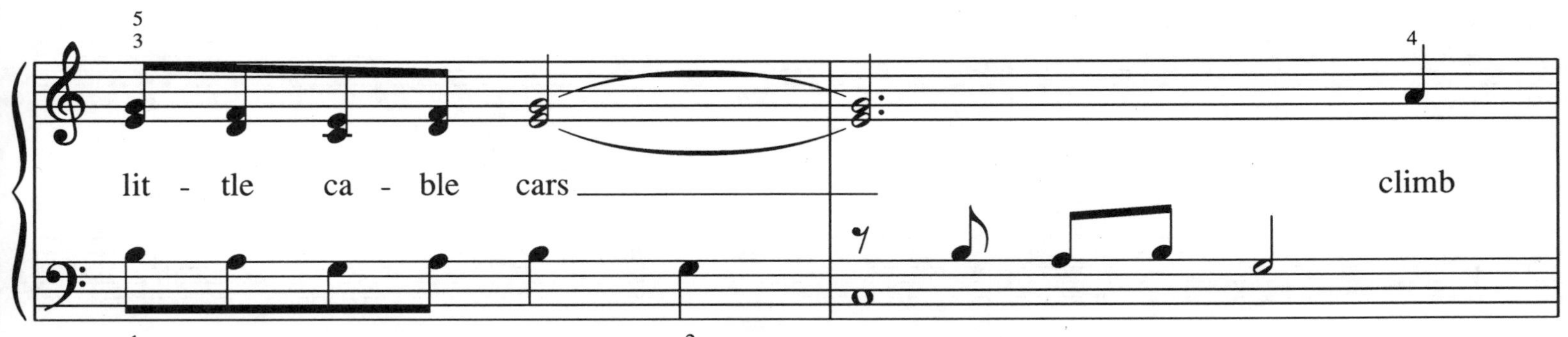

Bm/E
E7♭9
half - way to the stars!
The morn - ing

Am
D7
G7sus
G7
fog may chill the air, I don't

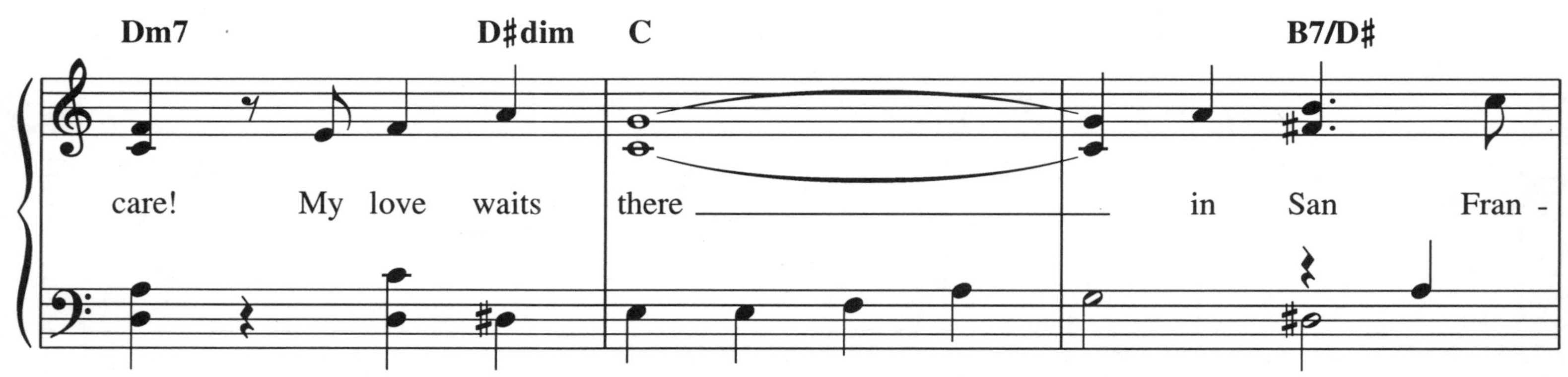
Dm7
D♯dim
C
B7/D♯
care! My love waits there in San Fran -

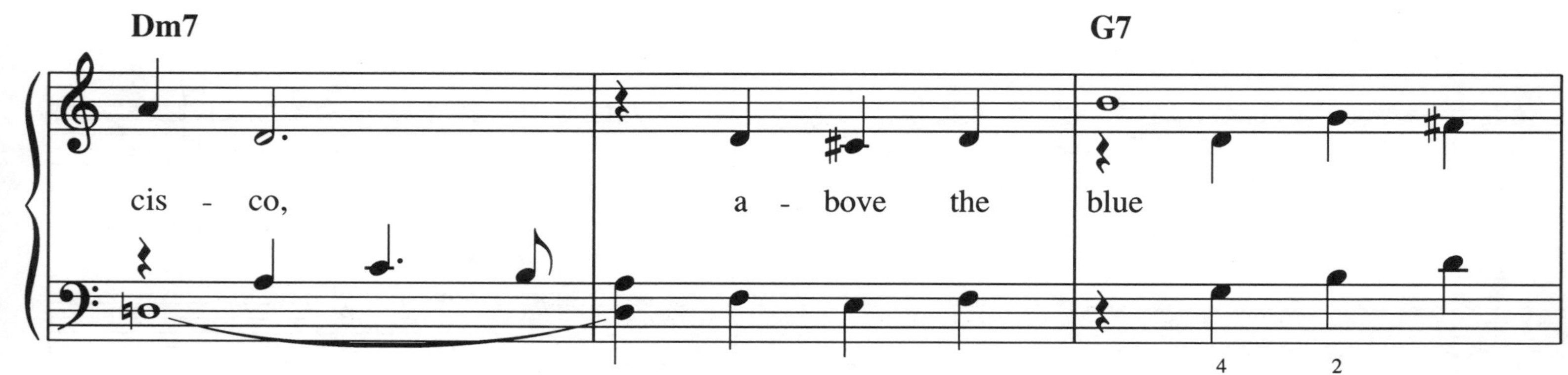
Dm7
G7
cis - co, a - bove the blue

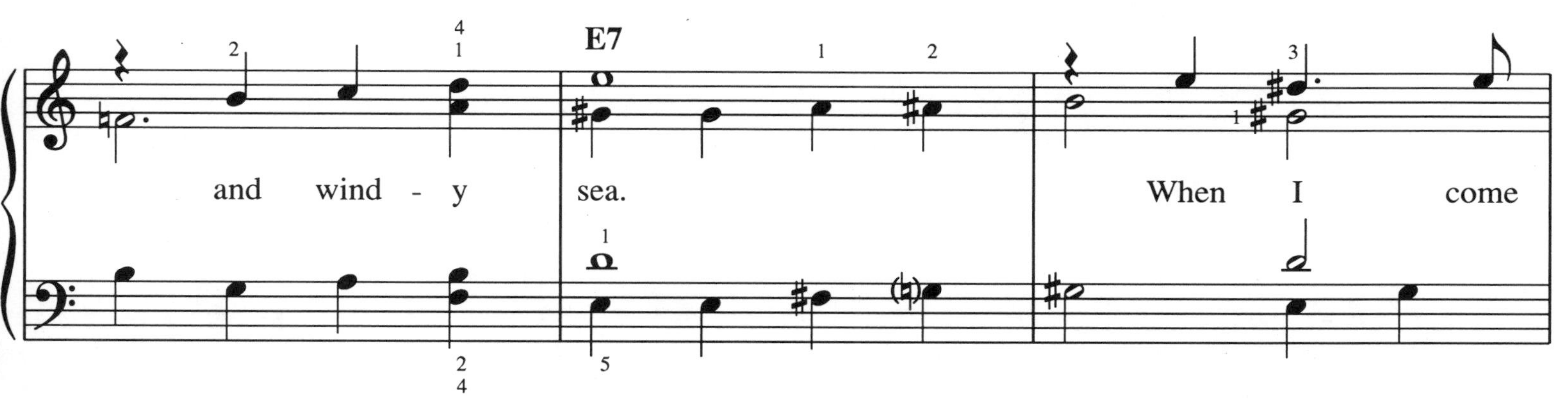
E7
and wind - y
sea.
When I come

A7
D7sus
home to
you, San Fran -
cis - co,

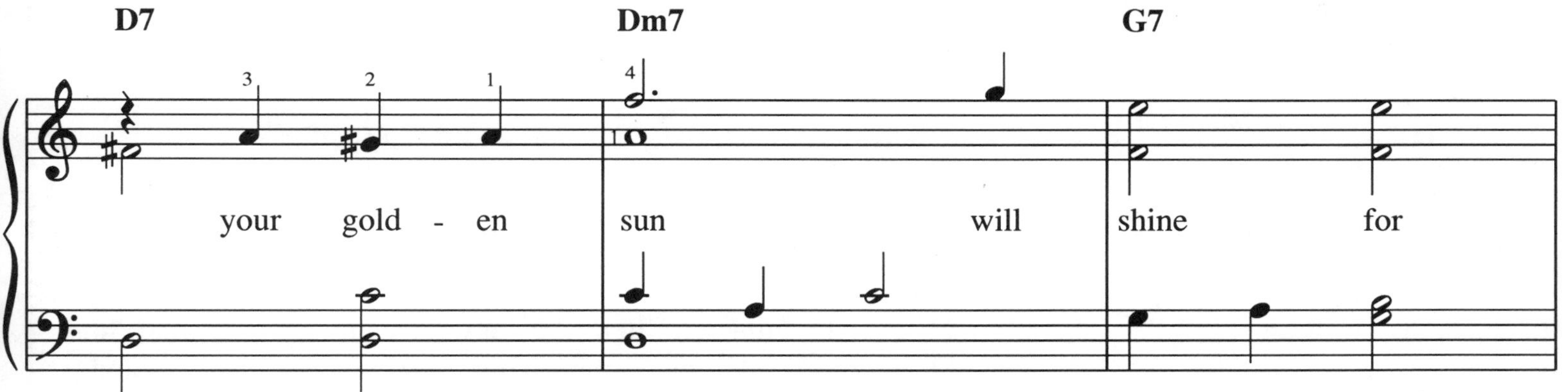
D7
Dm7
G7
your gold - en
sun will
shine for

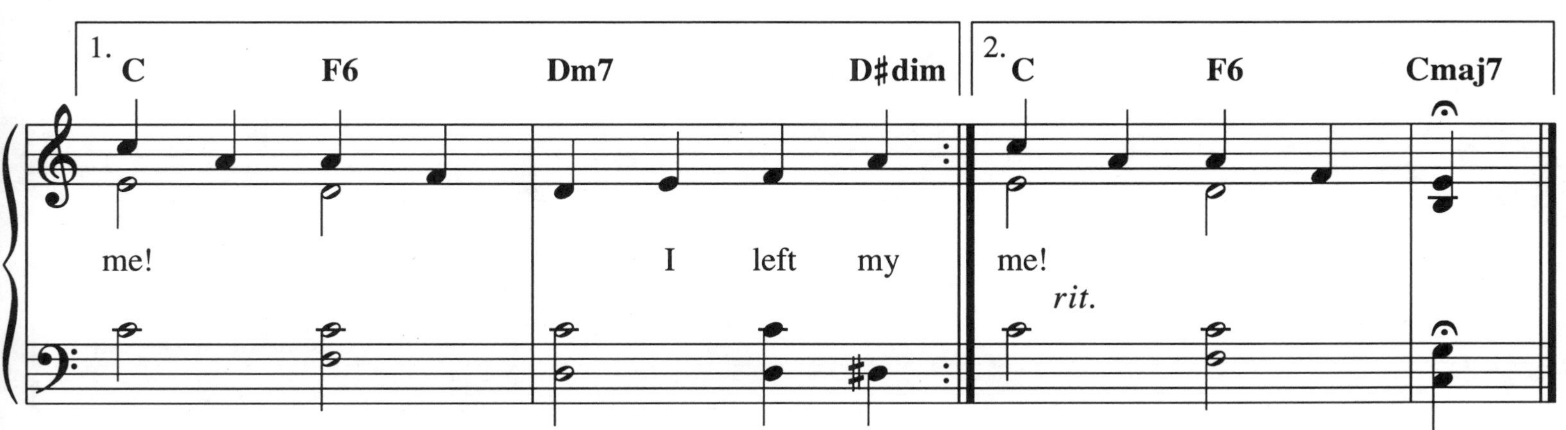
1. C
F6
Dm7
D♯dim
2. C
F6
Cmaj7
me!
I left my
me!
rit.

I WANT TO HOLD YOUR HAND

Em Bm C D
I want to hold your hand, I want to hold your
you'll let me hold your hand. Now let me hold your
G Em C D
hand, I want to hold your
hand, I want to hold your
1. G 2. G Dm7
hand. Oh, hand. And when I
G C Am
touch you I feel hap - py in - side.

Dm7
G
C
It's such a
feel - ing that my
love I can't hide,

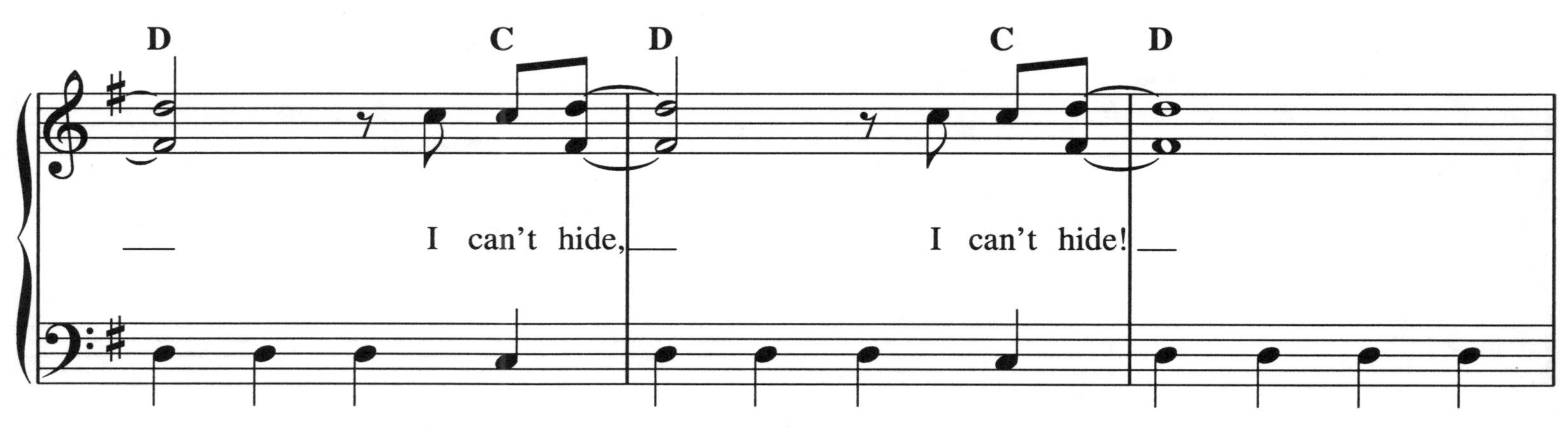
D
C
D
C
D
I can't hide,
I can't hide!

G
D
Yeah, you got that some - thing
Yeah, you got that some - thing

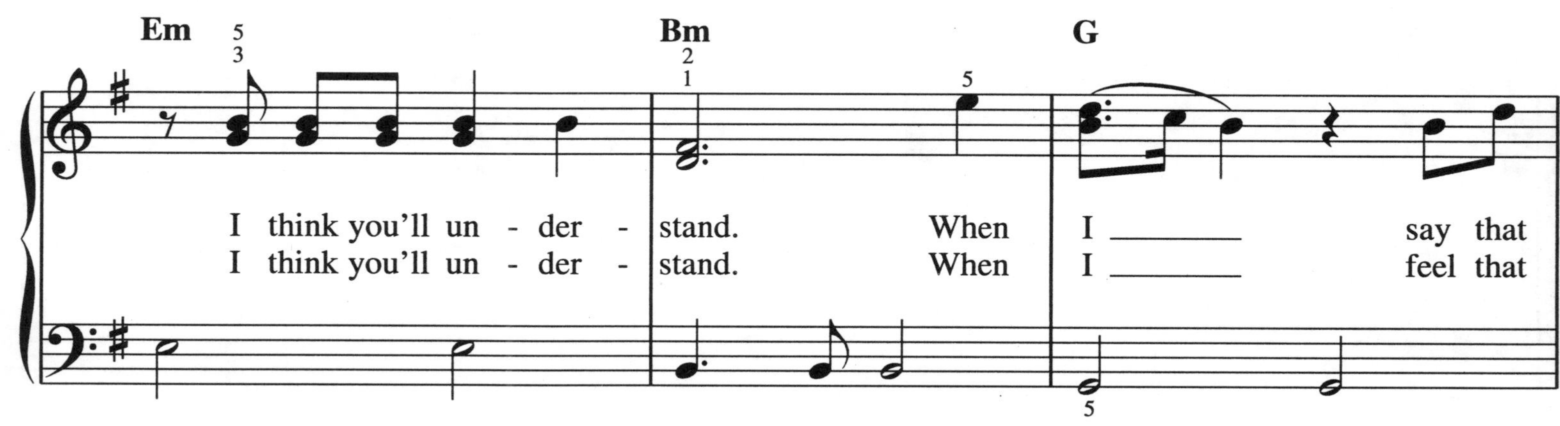
Em
Bm
G
I think you'll un - der - stand. When I say that
I think you'll un - der - stand. When I feel that

D
Em
Bm
some - thing,
some - thing,
I want to hold your hand,
C
D
G
Em
I want to hold your
hand,
1.
C
D
G
I want to hold your
hand.
2.
C
D
I want to hold your
B
C
D
C
G
hand,
I want to hold your
hand.

IF I HAD A HAMMER

(The Hammer Song)

Words and Music by LEE HAYS
and PETE SEEGER

Moderately

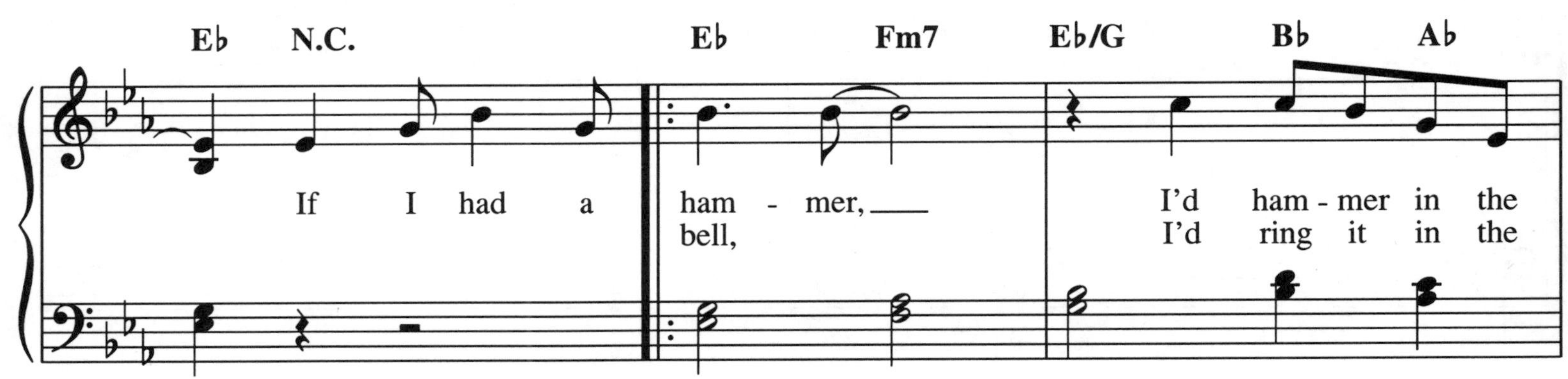

B♭7
Fm7
B♭7
B♭7/D
land;
I'd ham - mer out
land;
I'd ring out
E♭
Fm7
E♭/G
E♭7
dan - ger,
I'd ham - mer out a
dan - ger,
I'd ring out a
Cm7
A♭maj7
warn - ing,
I'd ham - mer out
warn - ing,
I'd ring out
E♭
Fm7
E♭/G
B♭7
love be - tween my bro - thers and my sis - ters,
love be - tween my bro - thers and my sis - ters,

1.
2.
Eb
Ab
Eb/Bb
Bb7
Ab/Bb
N.C.
Fm7
Eb/G
Bb
All _____ o - ver this land. _____
All _____ o - ver this
_____ If I had a
land. _____ If I had a
song, I'd sing it in the
ham-mer, And I've _____ got a
morn - ing, _____ I'd sing it in the
bell, _____ And I've got _____ a

E♭ Fm7 E♭7/G E♭7
ev - 'ning all o - ver this
song all o - ver this
B♭7 Fm7 B♭7 B♭7/D
land; I'd sing out
land; It's the ham - mer of
E♭ Fm7 E♭/G E♭7
dan - ger, I'd sing out a
jus - tice, It's the bell of
Cm7 A♭maj7
warn - ing, I'd sing out
free - dom, It's the song a - bout

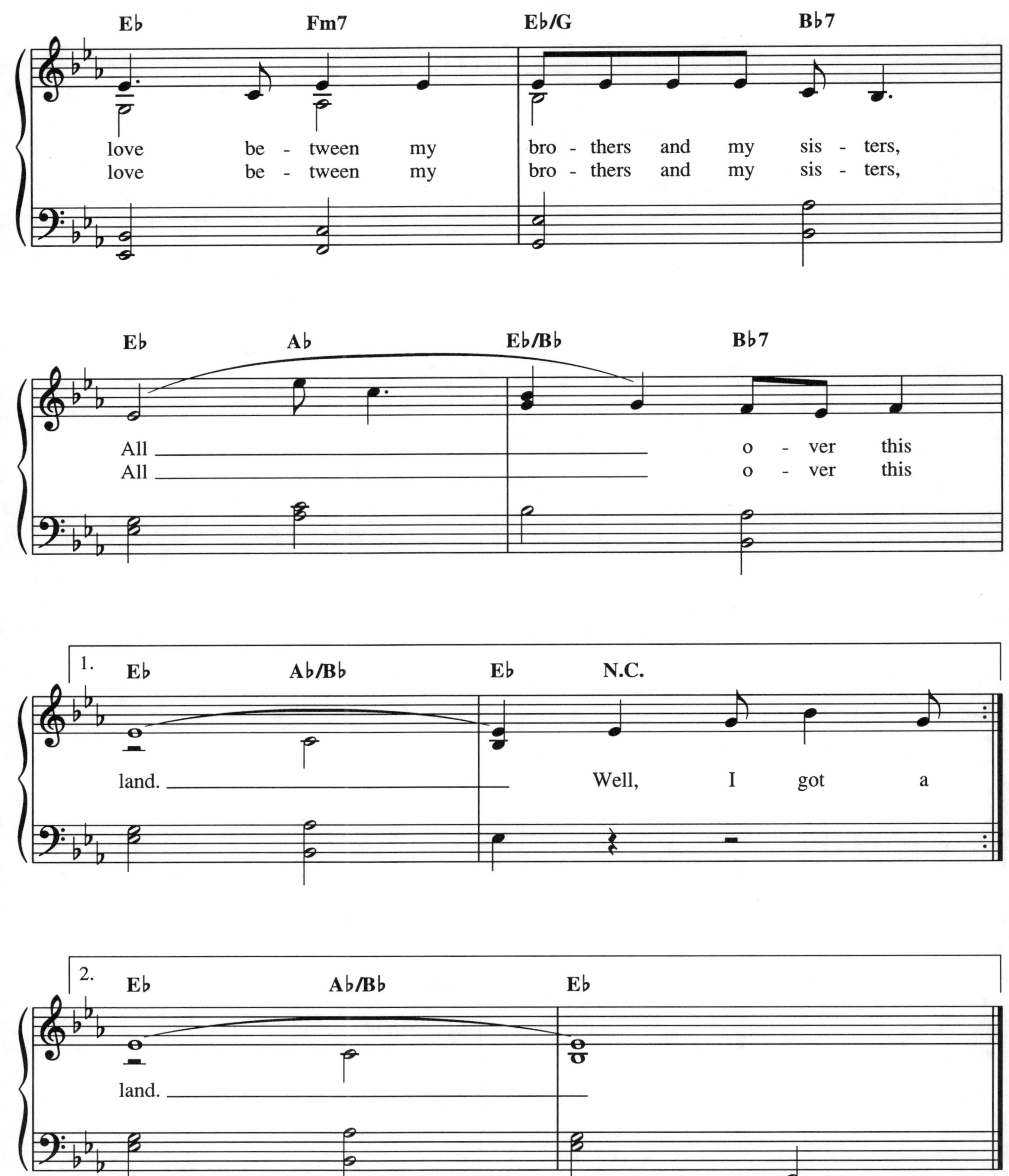
Eb
Fm7
Eb/G
Bb7
love be - tween my bro - thers and my sis - ters,
love be - tween my bro - thers and my sis - ters,
Eb
Ab
Eb/Bb
Bb7
All o - ver this
All o - ver this
1.
Eb
Ab/Bb
Eb
N.C.
land. Well, I got a
2.
Eb
Ab/Bb
Eb
land.

IF I WERE A CARPENTER

Words and Music by
TIM HARDIN

Eb
ba - by?
bove me."
If a tin - ker
If I were a
Db
Ab
Ab/Eb
Eb
were my trade,
mil - ler,
would you still love me,
at a mill wheel grind - ing,
car - ry - ing the
would you miss your
Db
pots I made
col - lored box
Ab
Eb
Eb
fol - low - ing be - hind me?
your soft shoes shin - ing?

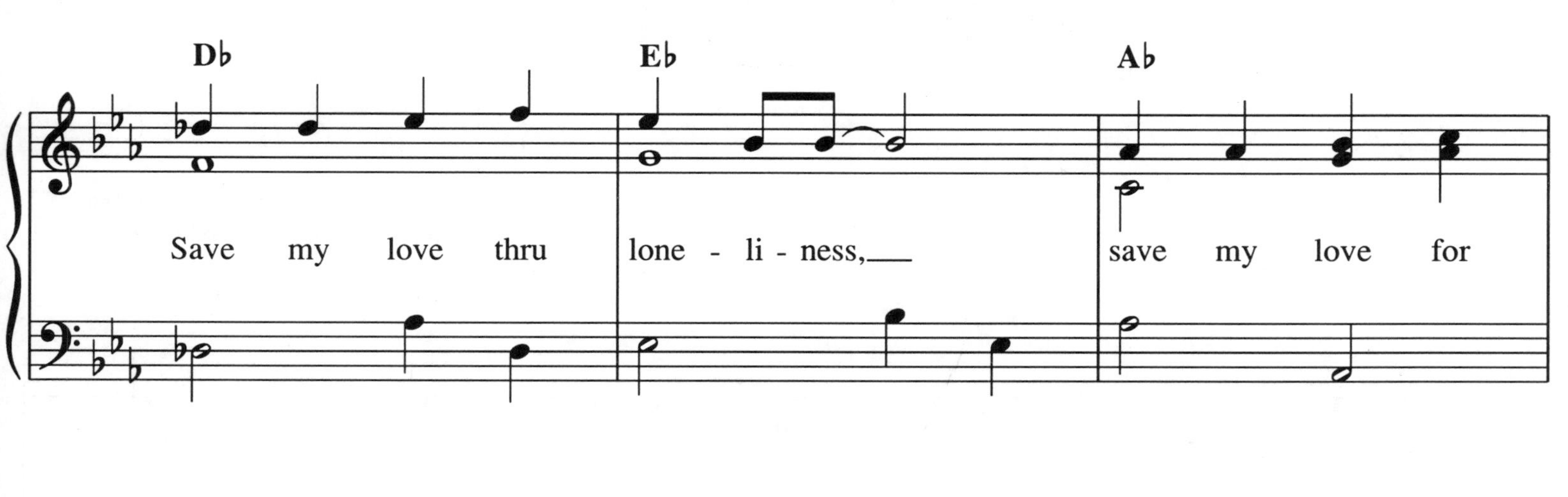
D♭
E♭
A♭
Save my love thru lone - li - ness,
save my love for

E♭
sor - row,
I've gi - ven you my

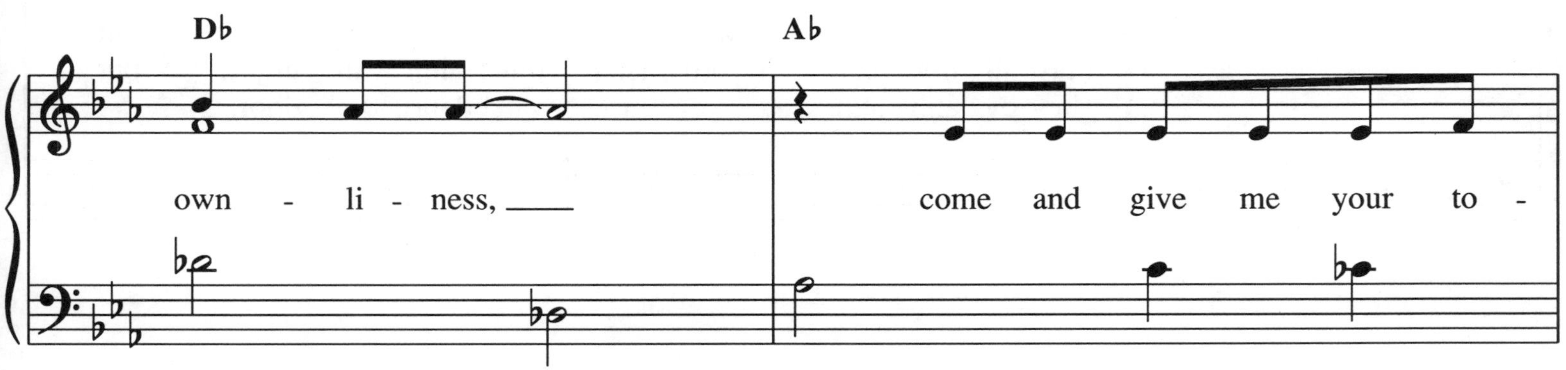
D♭
A♭
own - li - ness,
come and give me your to -

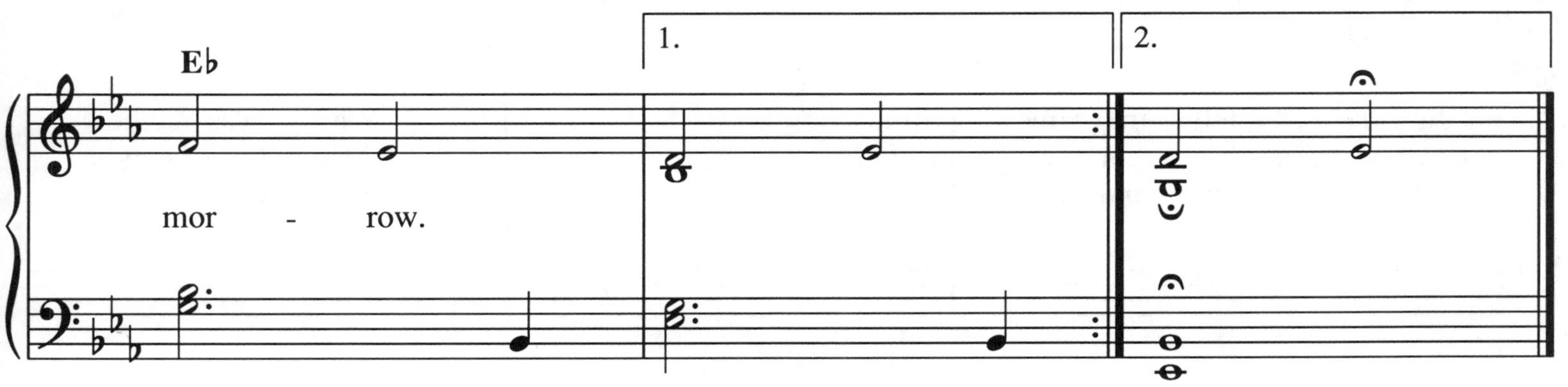
E♭
1.
2.
mor - row.

IT'S MY PARTY

Words and Music by HERB WIENER,
WALLY GOLD and JOHN GLUCK, Jr.

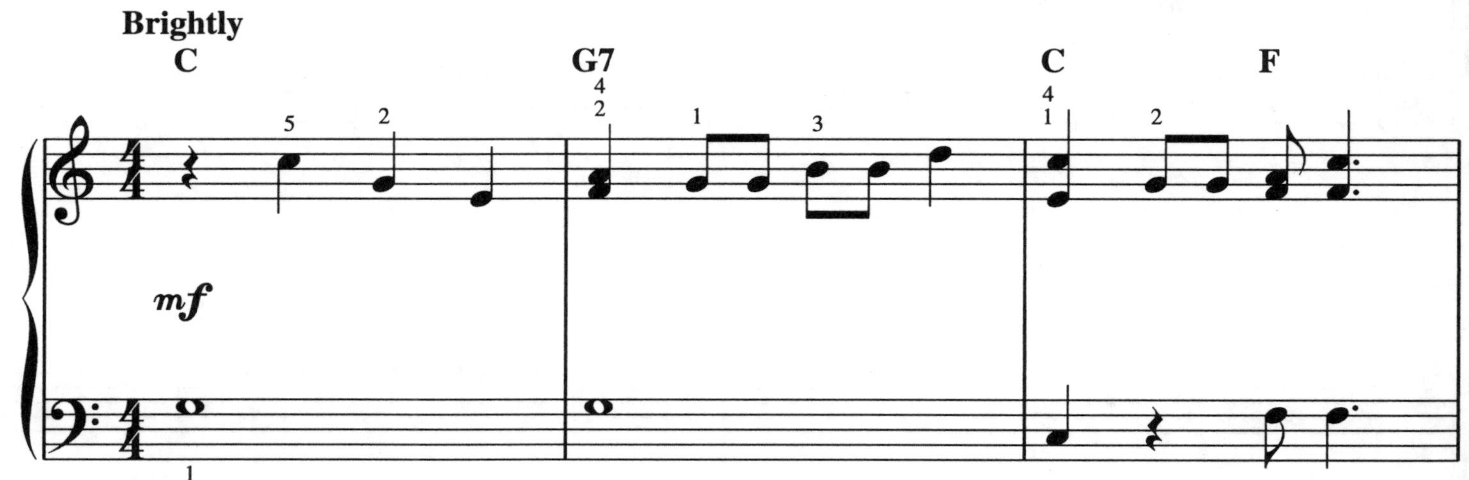

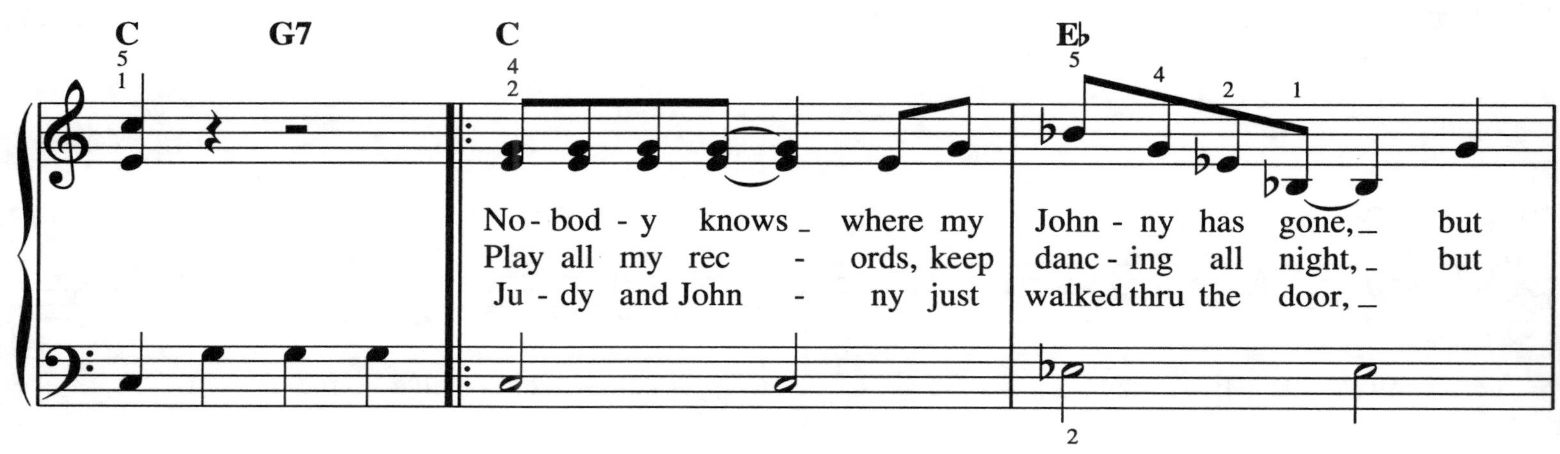

C
D7
G7
hold-ing her hand _ when he's sup-posed _ to be mine?
danc-ing with me, _ I've got no rea - son to smile.
birth-day sur - prise, _ Ju - dy's wear - ing his ring.
C
Caug
F
It's my par - ty and I'll cry if I want _ to, cry if I want _ to,
Fm
C
Dm
G7
cry if I want _ to. You would cry too, if it hap-pened to
C
F
1.,2.
C
G7
3.
C
you.
8va

IT'S NOT UNUSUAL

Words and Music by GORDON MILLS
and LES REED

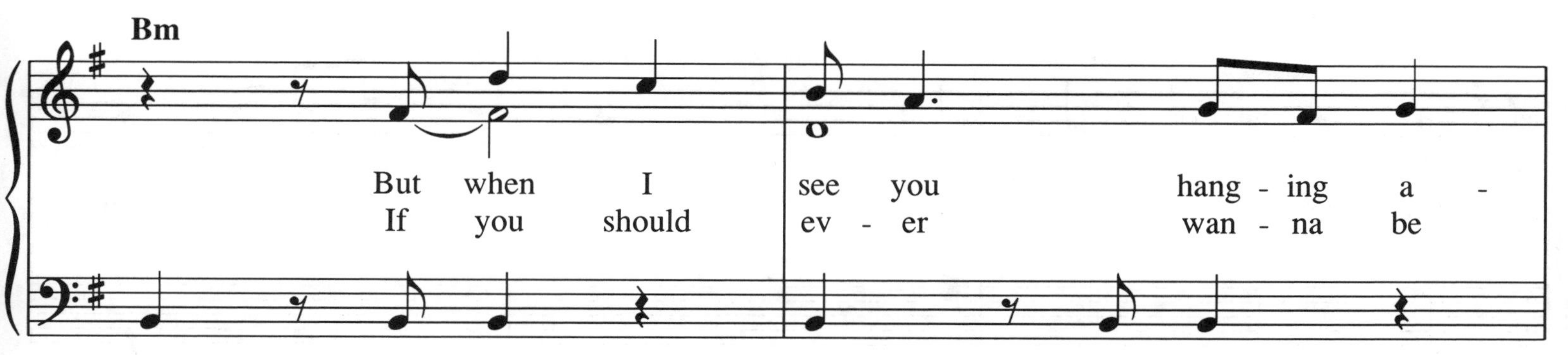
Bm
But when I see you hang - ing a -
If you should ev - er wan - na be

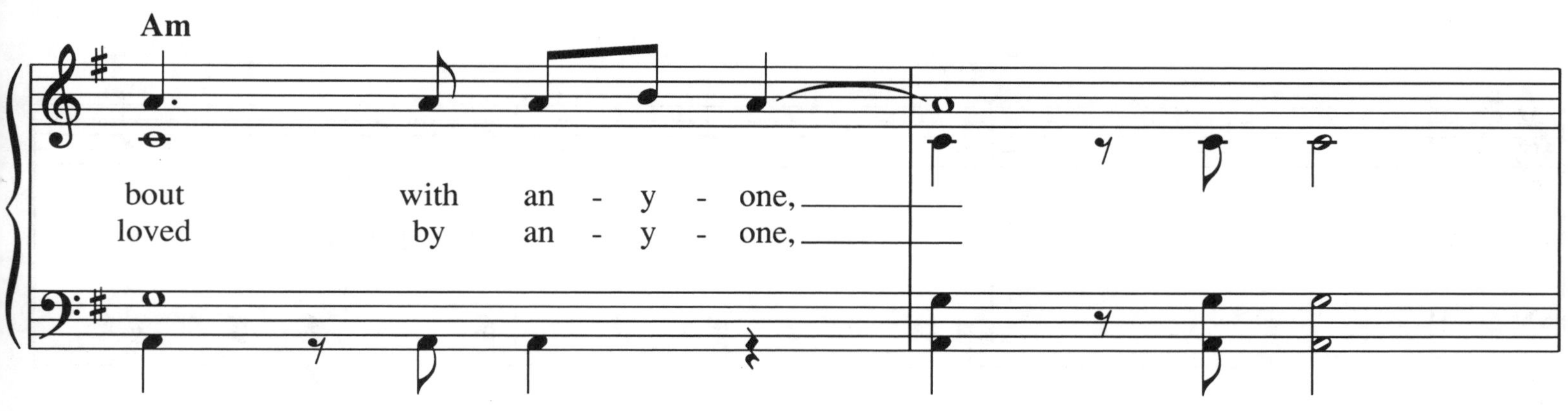
Am
bout with an - y - one,
loved by an - y - one,

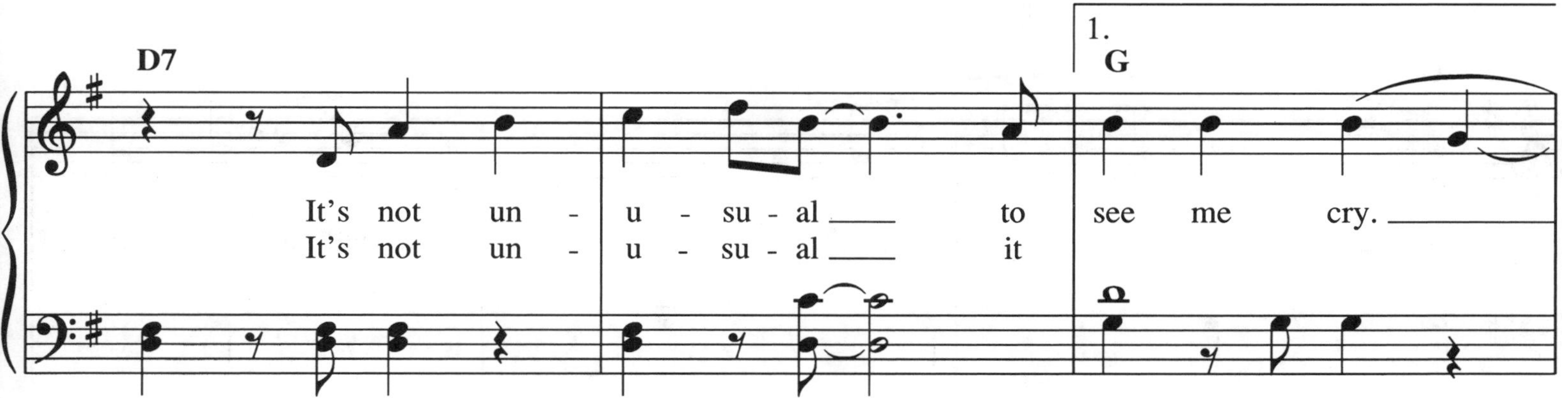
D7
1.
G
It's not un - u - su - al to see me cry.
It's not un - u - su - al it

Am7
D7
I wan - na die.

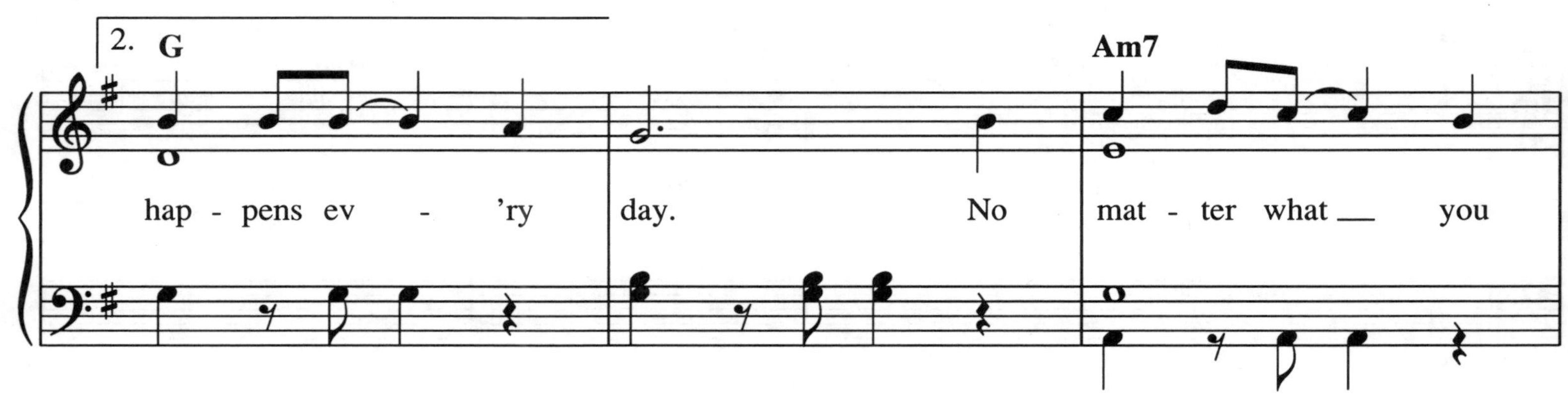
2.
G
Am7
hap - pens ev - 'ry day. No mat - ter what __ you

D7
say, you'll find it hap - pens all the

G
time. __
Love will nev - er

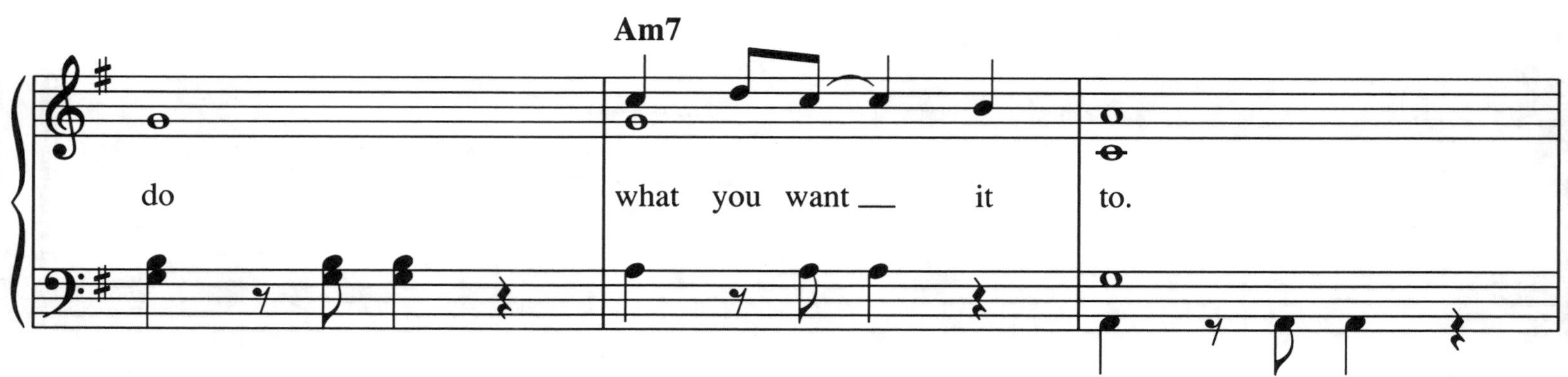
Am7
do what you want __ it to.

D7
Why can't this cra - zy love be
Bm7
mine?
B♭7
Am7
D7
G
It's not un - u - su - al to be
Am7
mad with an - y - one.
D7
G
It's not un - u - su - al to be

Am7
Bm
sad with an - y - one.
But if I

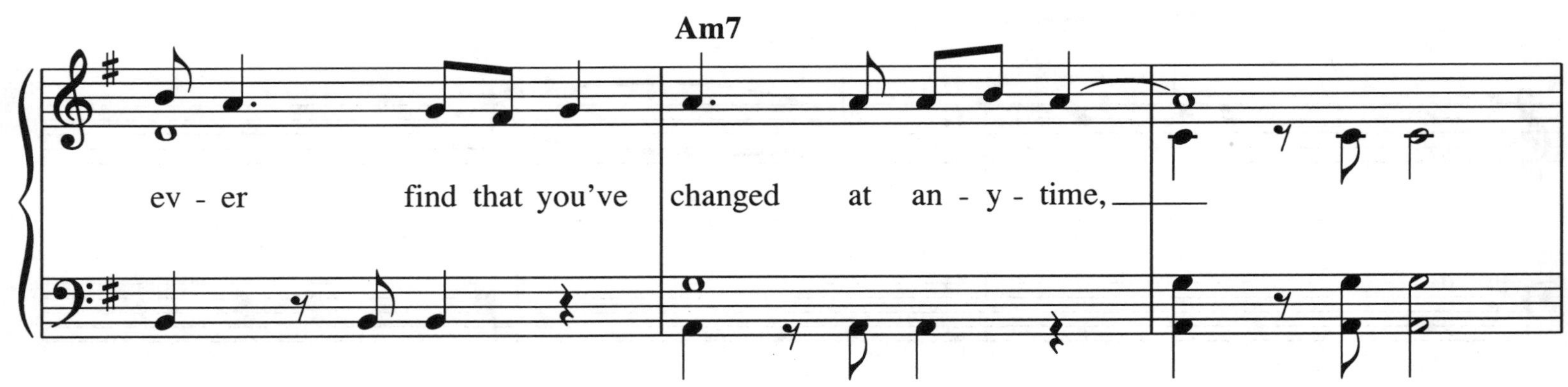
Am7
ev - er find that you've changed at an - y - time,

D7
G
It's not un - u - su - al to find that I'm in

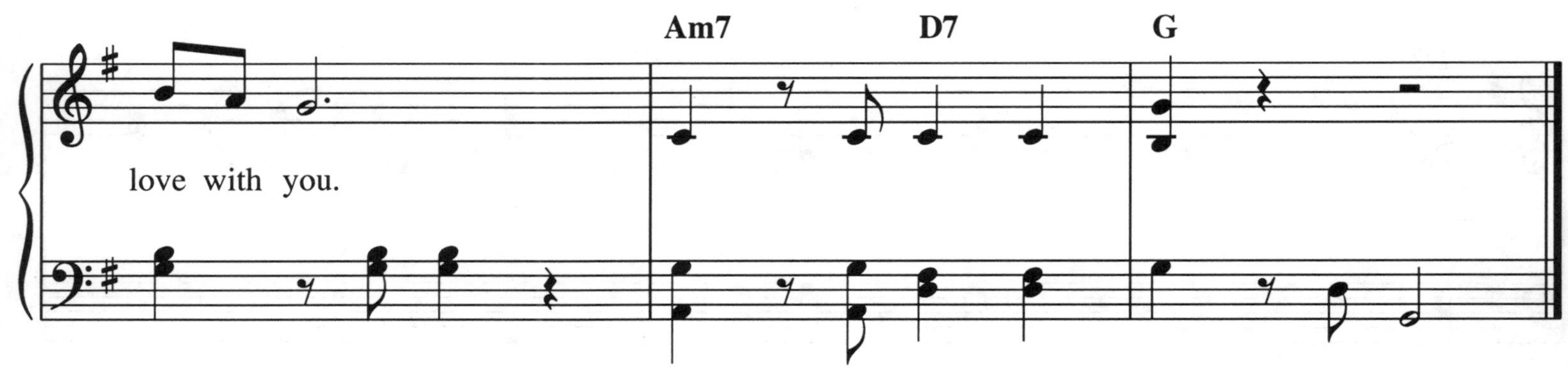
Am7
D7
G
love with you.

MONDAY, MONDAY

Words and Music by
JOHN PHILLIPS

F
B♭
be. ___
way. ___
Oh, Mon - day
Oh, Mon - day
morn - in', Mon - day
morn - in', you gave me no

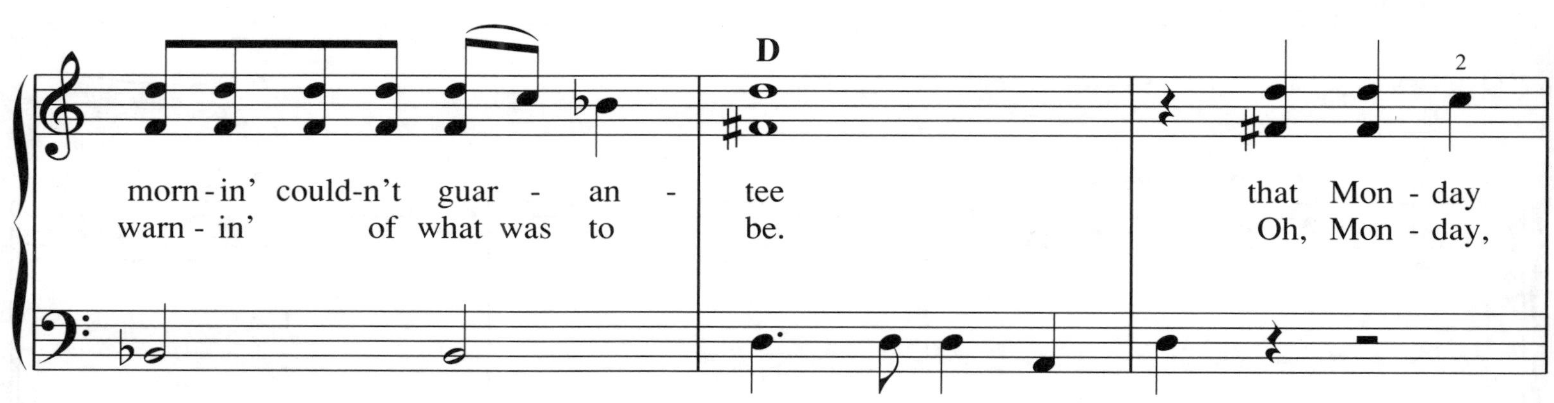
D
morn - in' could-n't guar - an -
warn - in' of what was to
tee
be.
that Mon - day
Oh, Mon - day,

1.
G
C
eve - nin' you would
Mon-day, how could you
still be here__ with
leave and not __ take
me.

2.
G
C
G
2. Mon - day,
me.

A♭
3
2
Ev - 'ry oth - er day, ev - 'ry oth - er day, ev-'ry oth-er day of the week is
3

F
2
A♭
fine, yeah!
But when-ev-er Mon-day comes,

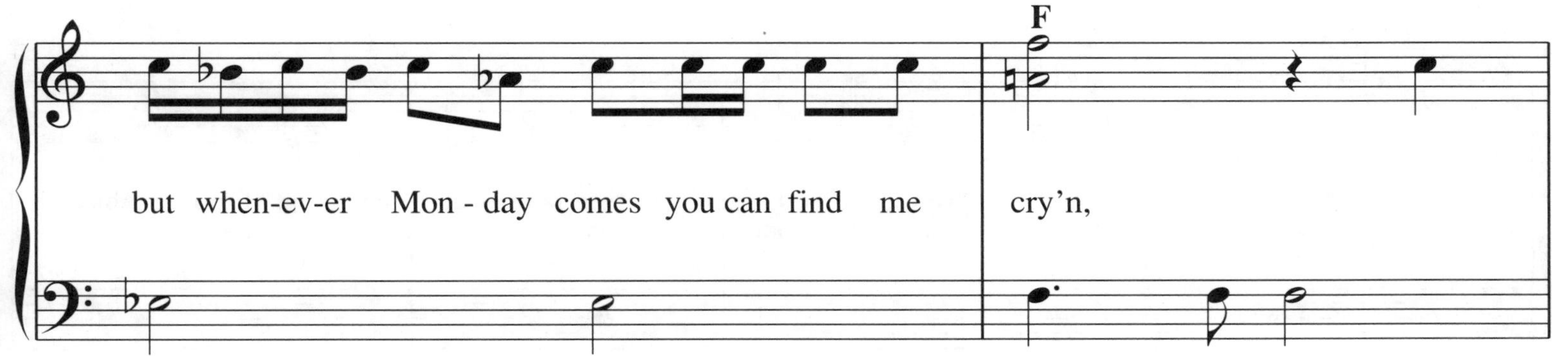
F
but when-ev-er Mon - day comes you can find me cry'n,

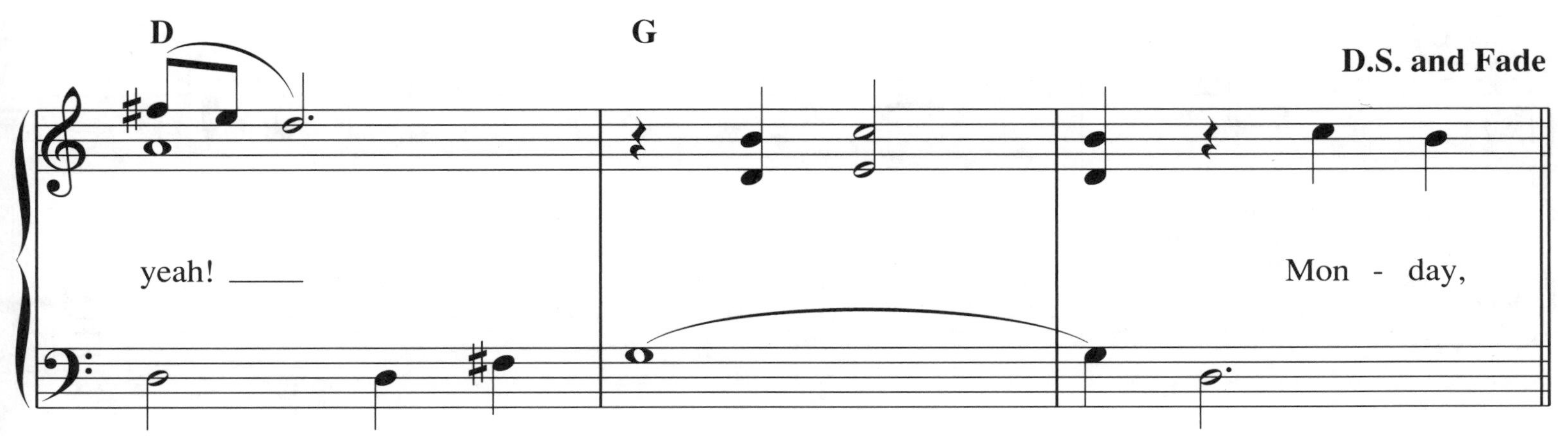
D
G
D.S. and Fade
yeah!
Mon - day,

KING OF THE ROAD

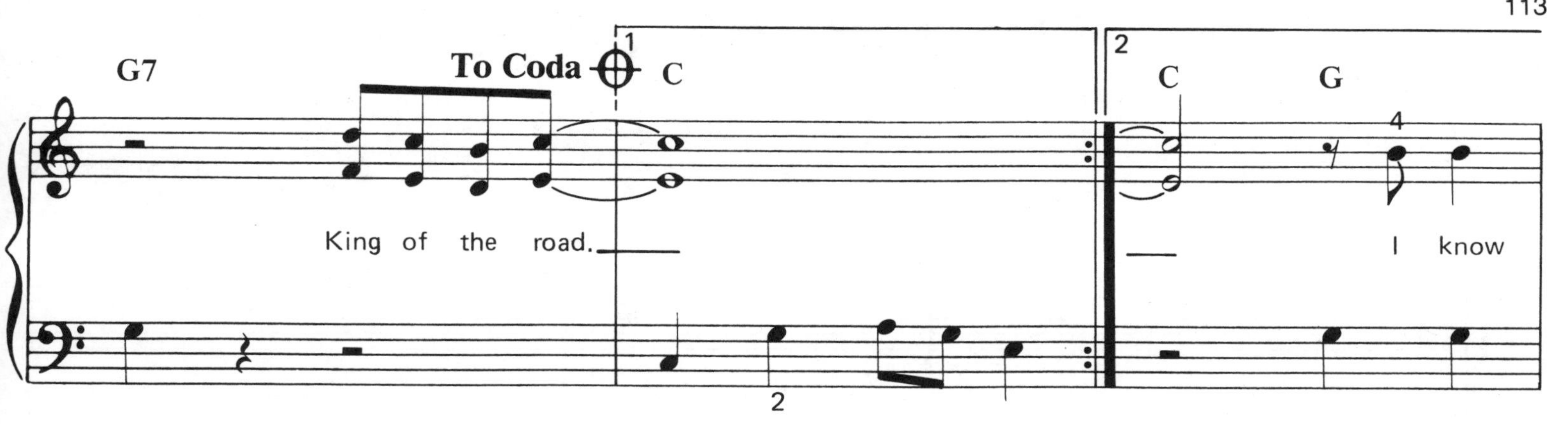
G7
To Coda
C
1
2
C
G
4
King of the road.
I know
2

C
F
G7
ev - er - y en - gi - neer on
ev - er - y train,
all of the chil - dren and

C
1
F
4
all of their names,
and
ev - er - y hand - out in
ev - er - y town.
And

G7
2
3
D.S. al Coda
(verse 1)
CODA
C
ev'-ry lock that ain't locked when
no one's a - round. I sing
2

LITTLE GREEN APPLES

Words and Music by
BOBBY RUSSELL

Moderately

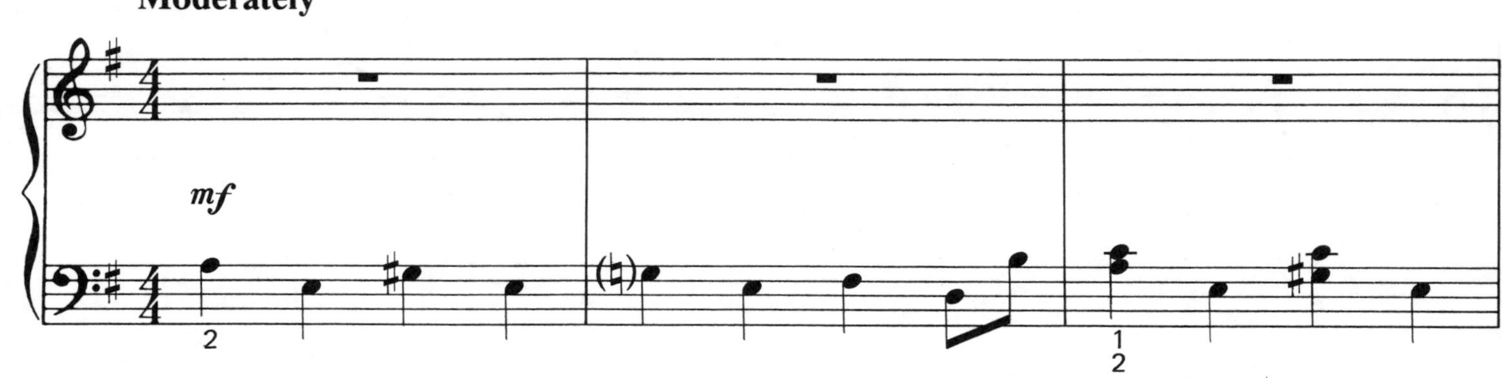

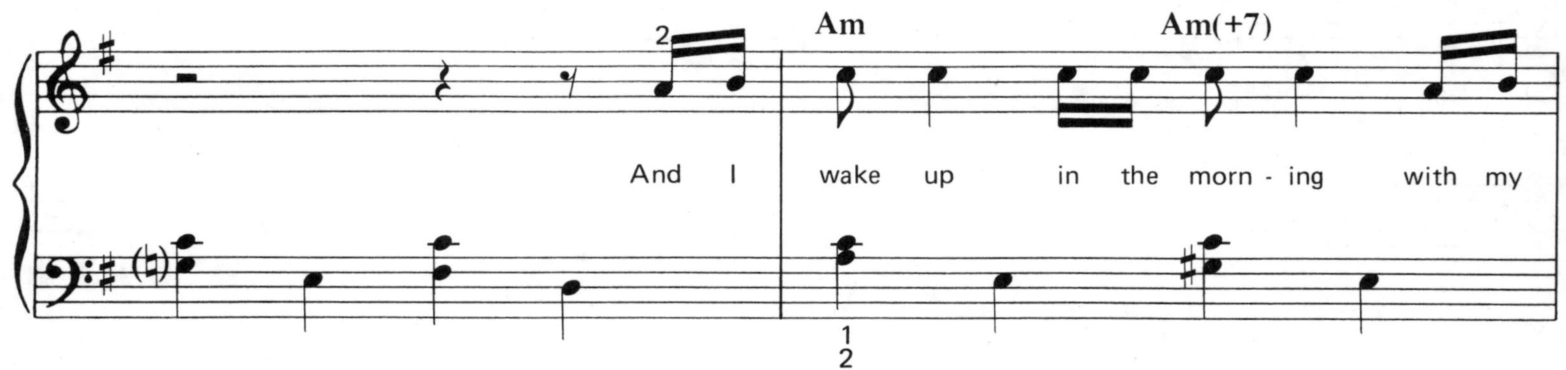

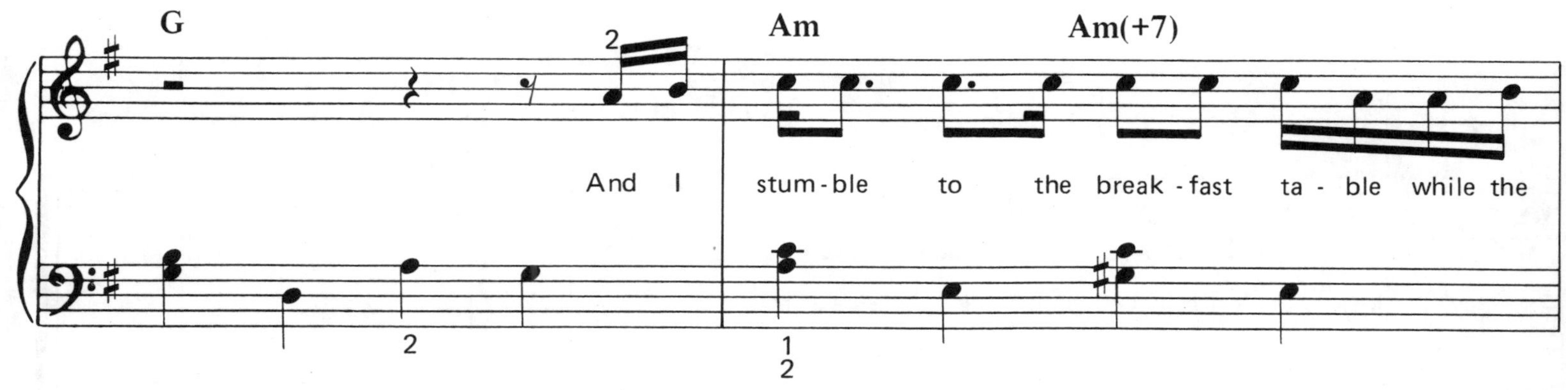

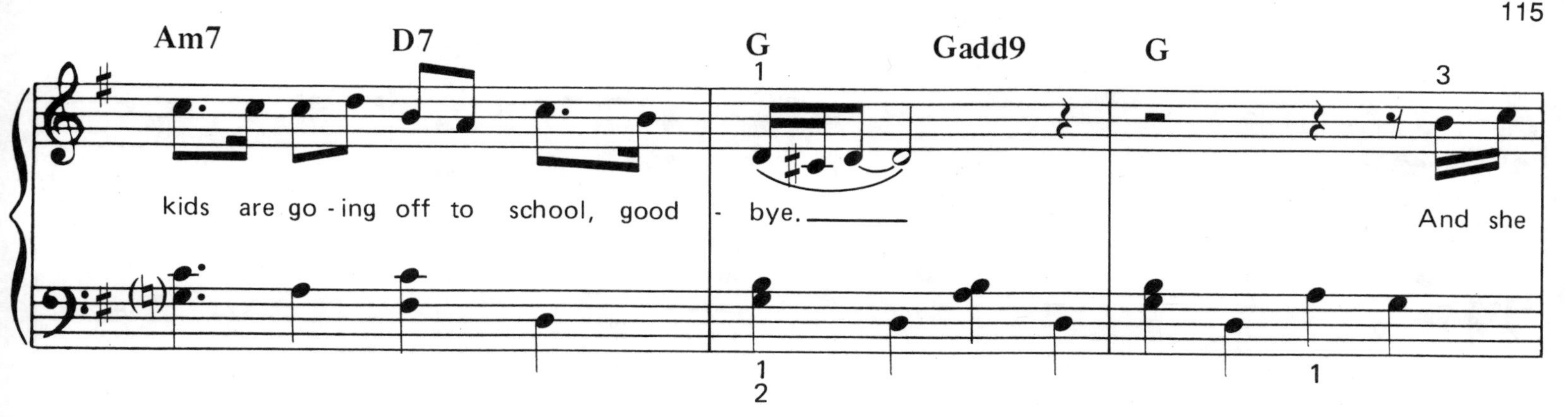
Am7 D7 G Gadd9 G
kids are go - ing off to school, good - bye.
And she

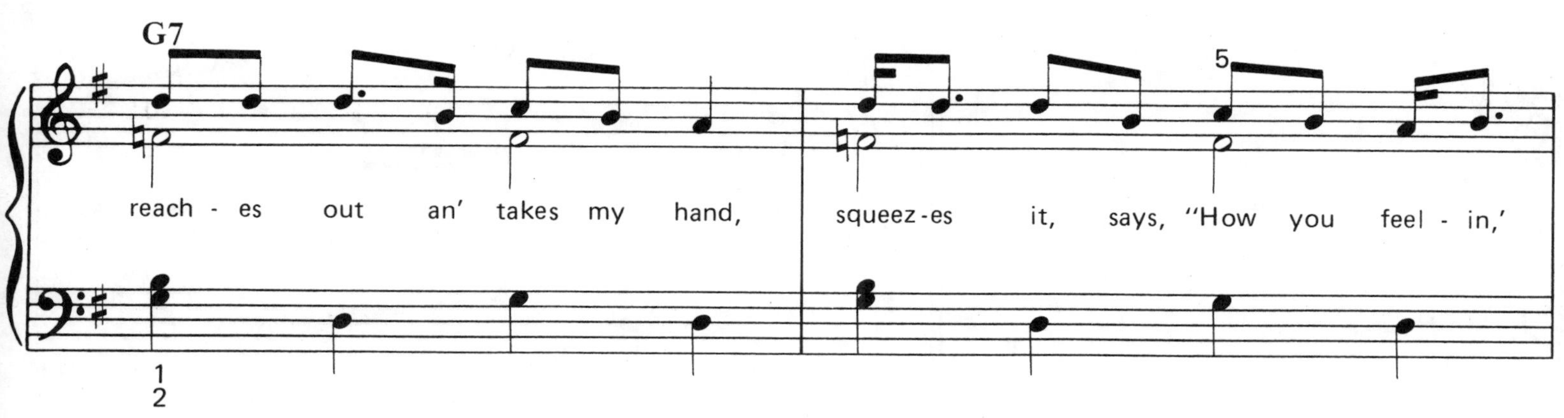
G7
reach - es out an' takes my hand,
squeez - es it, says, "How you feel - in,'

C6 Cm Am D7
hon?"
And I
look a - cross at smil - ing lips that

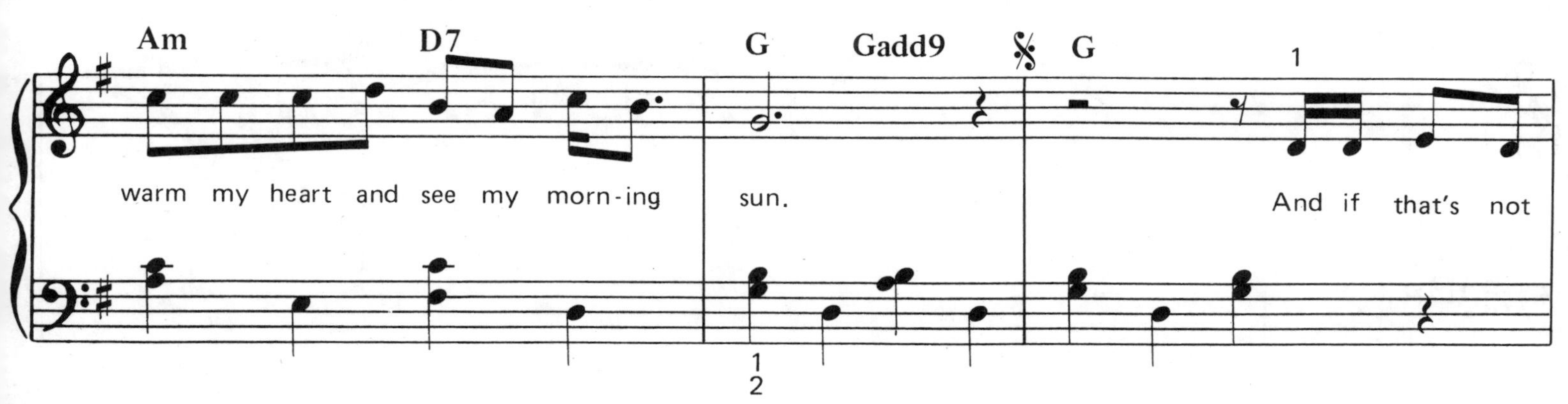
Am D7 G Gadd9 G
warm my heart and see my morn - ing sun.
And if that's not

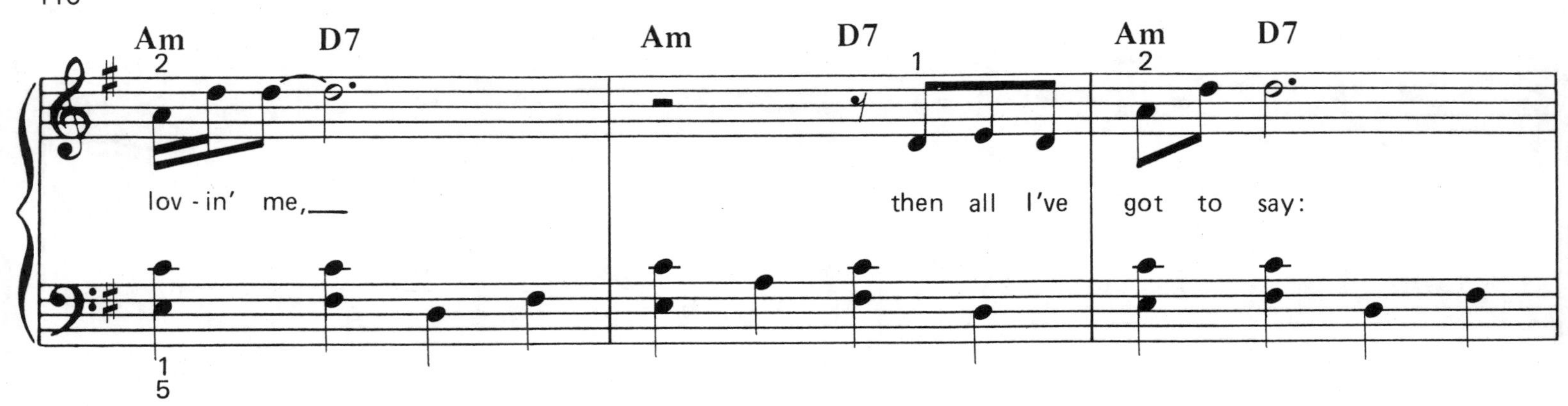
Am D7 Am D7 Am D7
lov - in' me,
then all I've got to say:

Am D7 Gadd9 G
God did - n't make lit - tle green ap - ples and
God did - n't make lit - tle green ap - ples and

Gadd9 G Am Am(+7)
it don't rain in In - di'an - ap - 'lis in the sum - mer time,
it don't snow in Min - ne - ap - 'lis when the win - ter comes,

Am7 D7 Am Am(+7)
There's no such thing as Doc - tor Seuss,
There's no such thing as make be - lieve,

Am7
D7
G
Dis - ney - land and Moth - er Goose is no nurs - 'ry rhyme.
pup - py dogs and au - tumn leaves and B. B. guns.

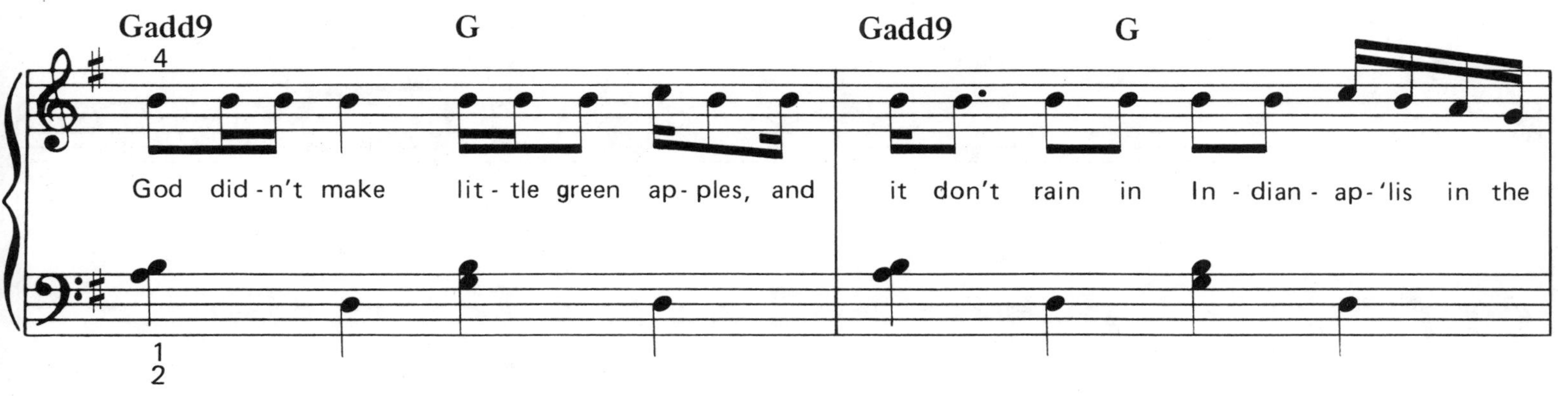
Gadd9
G
Gadd9
G
God did - n't make lit - tle green ap - ples, and it don't rain in In - dian - ap - 'lis in the

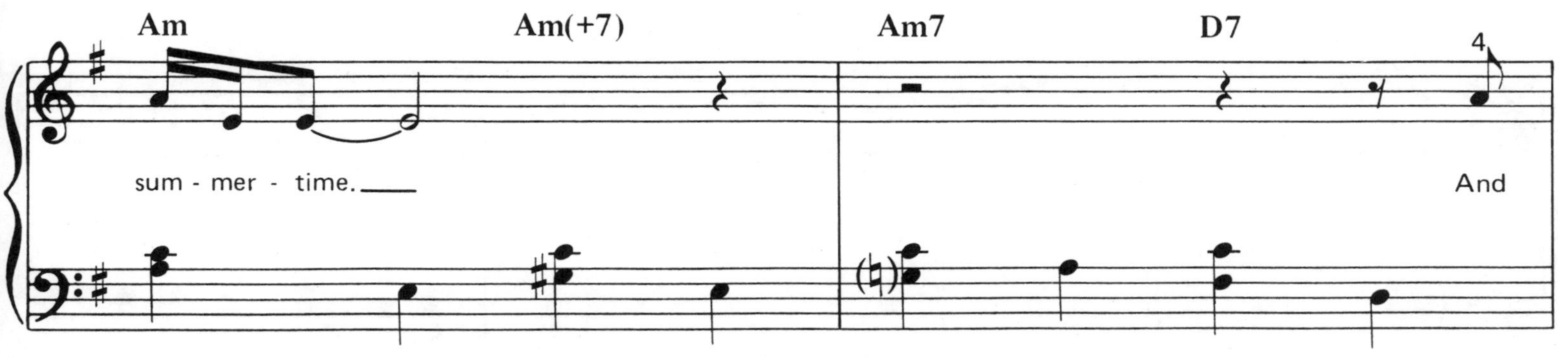
Am
Am(+7)
Am7
D7
sum - mer - time.
And

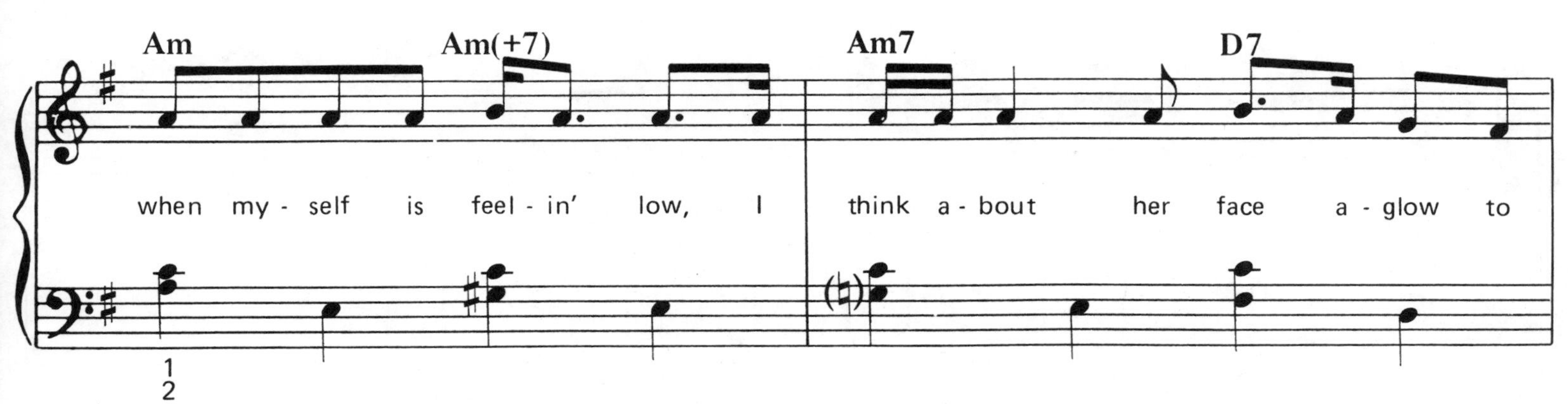
Am
Am(+7)
Am7
D7
when my - self is feel - in' low, I think a - bout her face a - glow to

G
Gadd9
1 G
To next strain
2 G
Am
G
Fine
ease my mind.

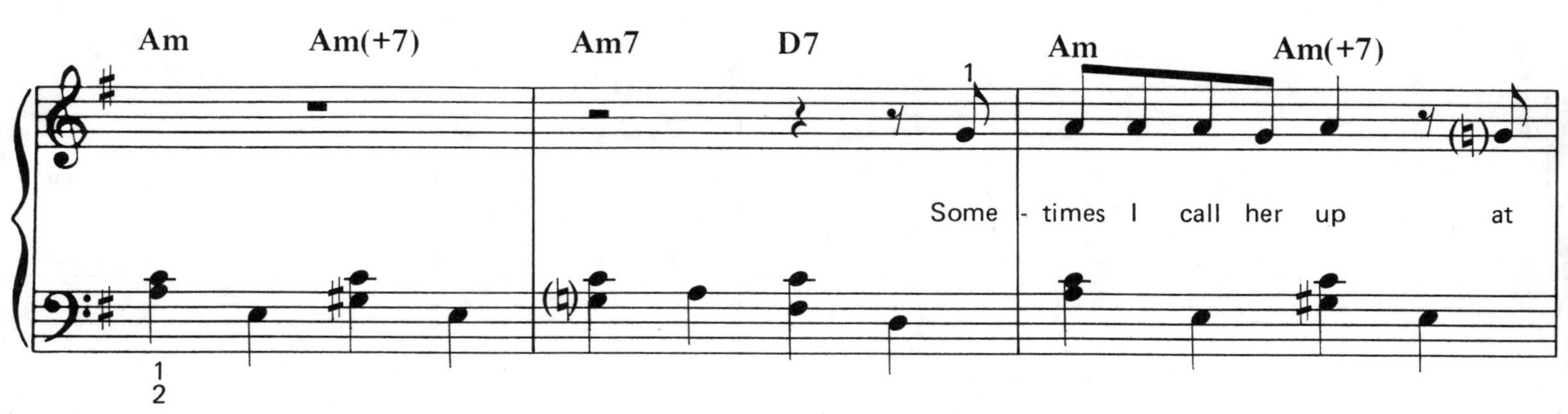
Am
Am(+7)
Am7
D7
Am
Am(+7)
Some - times I call her up at

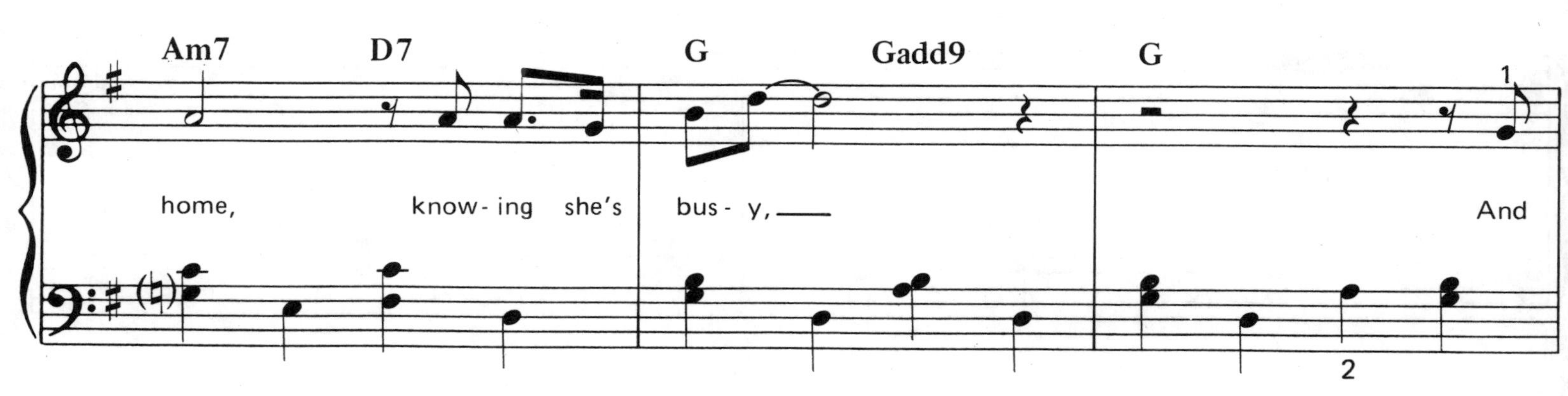
Am7
D7
G
Gadd9
G
home, know - ing she's bus - y, And

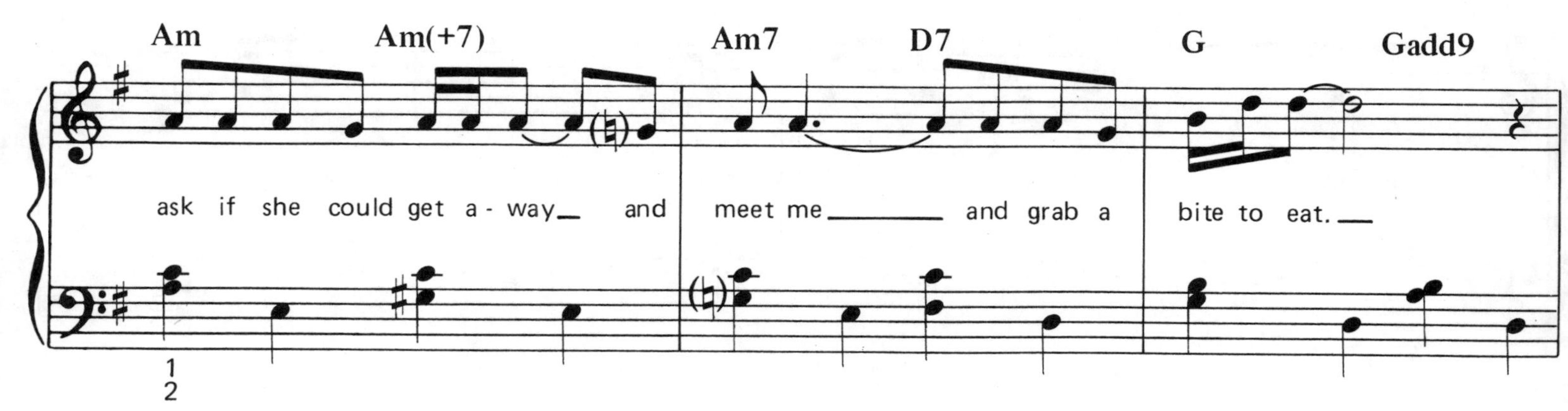
Am
Am(+7)
Am7
D7
G
Gadd9
ask if she could get a - way and meet me and grab a bite to eat.

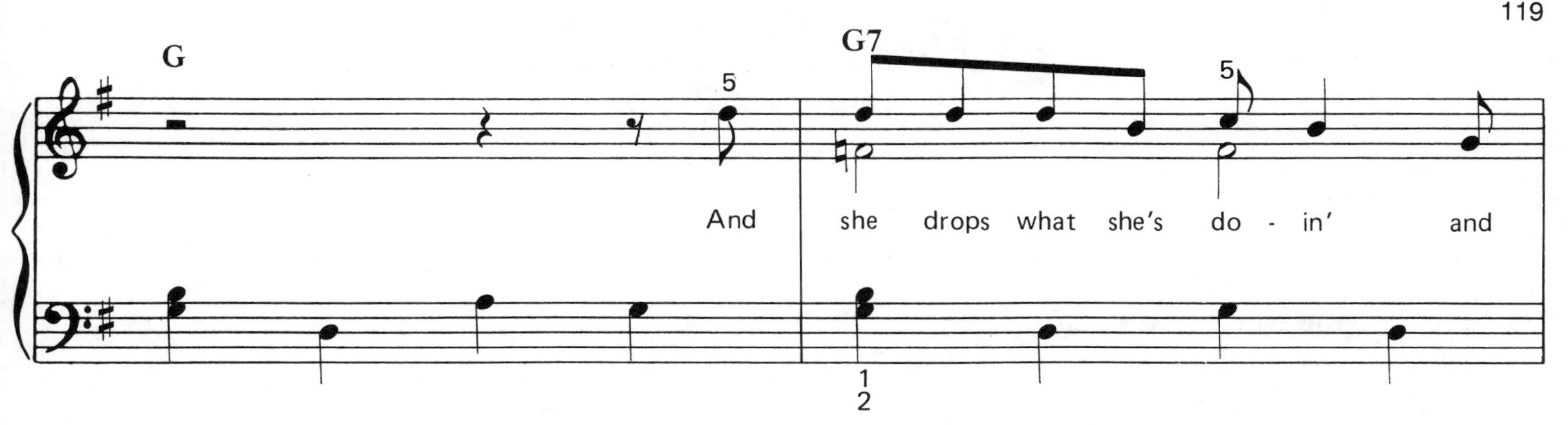
G
G7
5
5
And
she drops what she's do - in' and
1
2

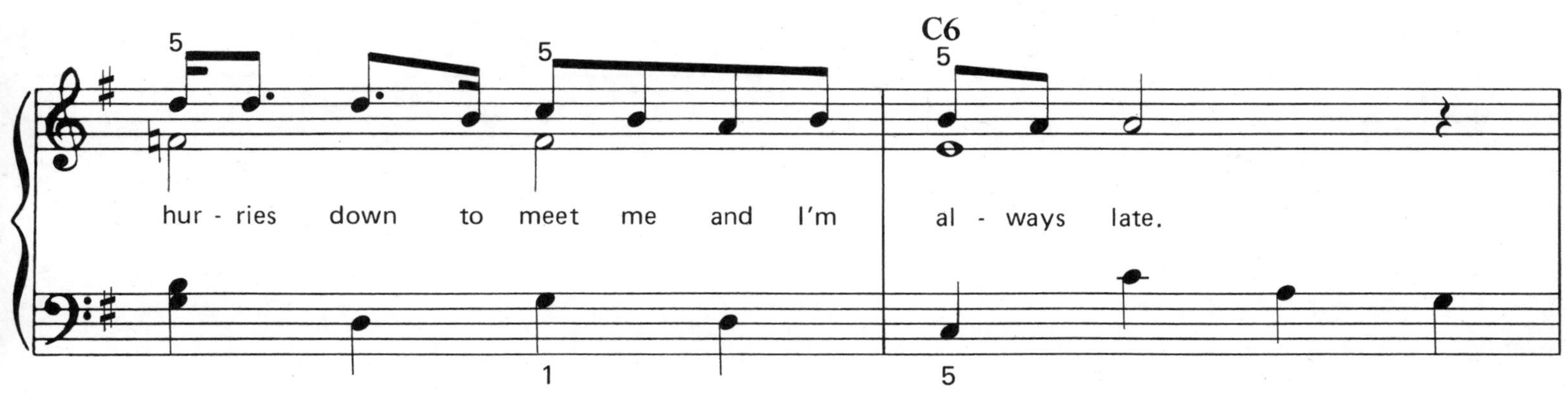
C6
5
5
5
hur - ries down to meet me and I'm
al - ways late.
1
5

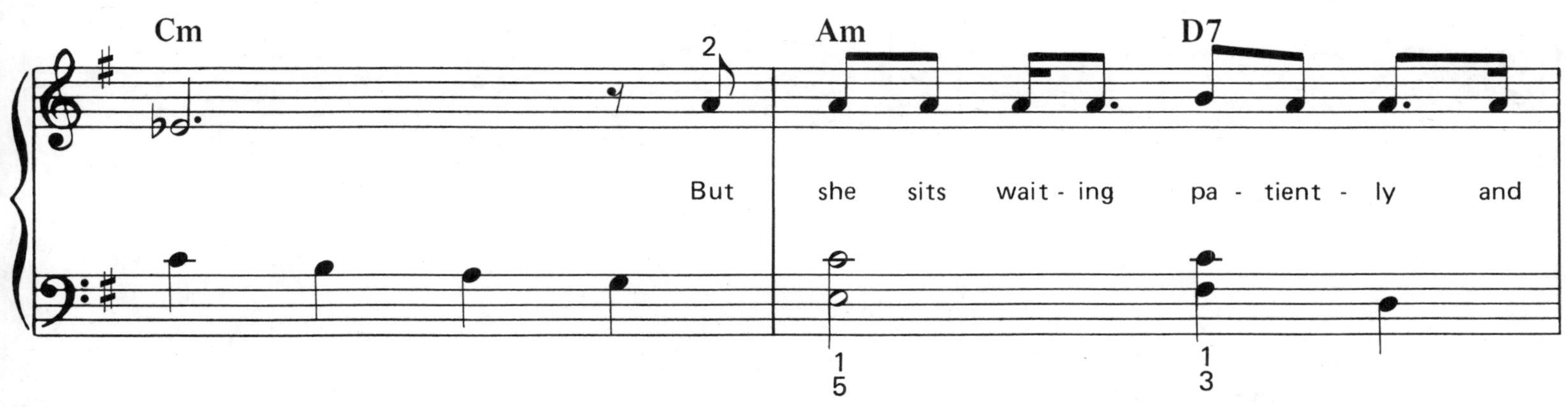
Cm
Am
D7
2
But
she sits wait - ing pa - tient - ly and
1
5
1
3

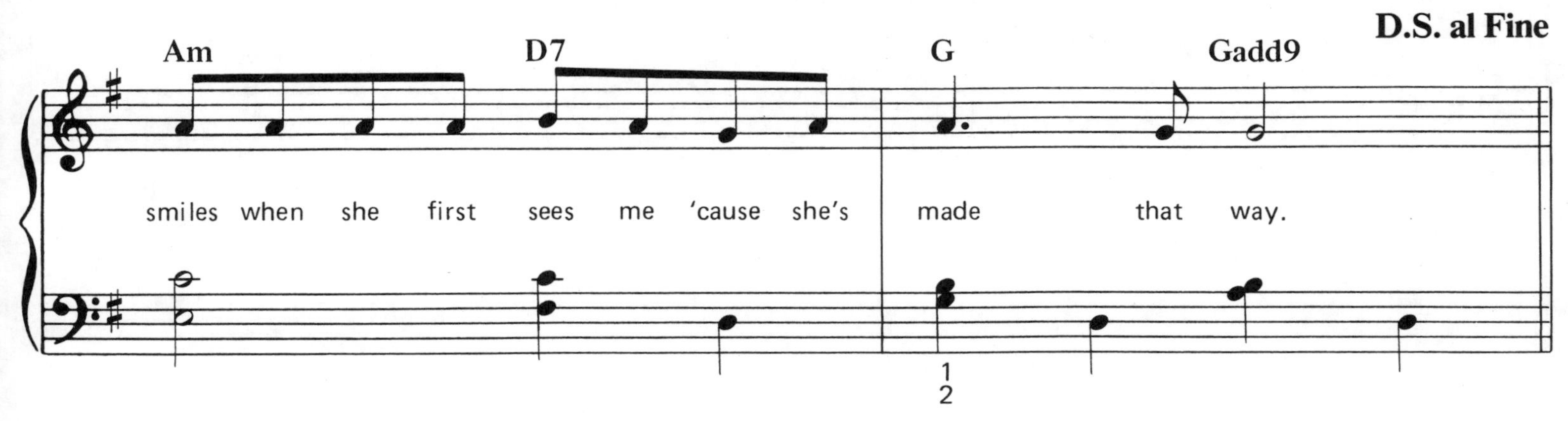
D.S. al Fine
Am
D7
G
Gadd9
smiles when she first sees me 'cause she's
made that way.
1
2

LOVE IS BLUE
(L'amour Est Bleu)

English Lyric by BRIAN BLACKBURN
Original French Lyric by PIERRE COUR
Music by ANDRE POPP

Moderately slow, easy feel

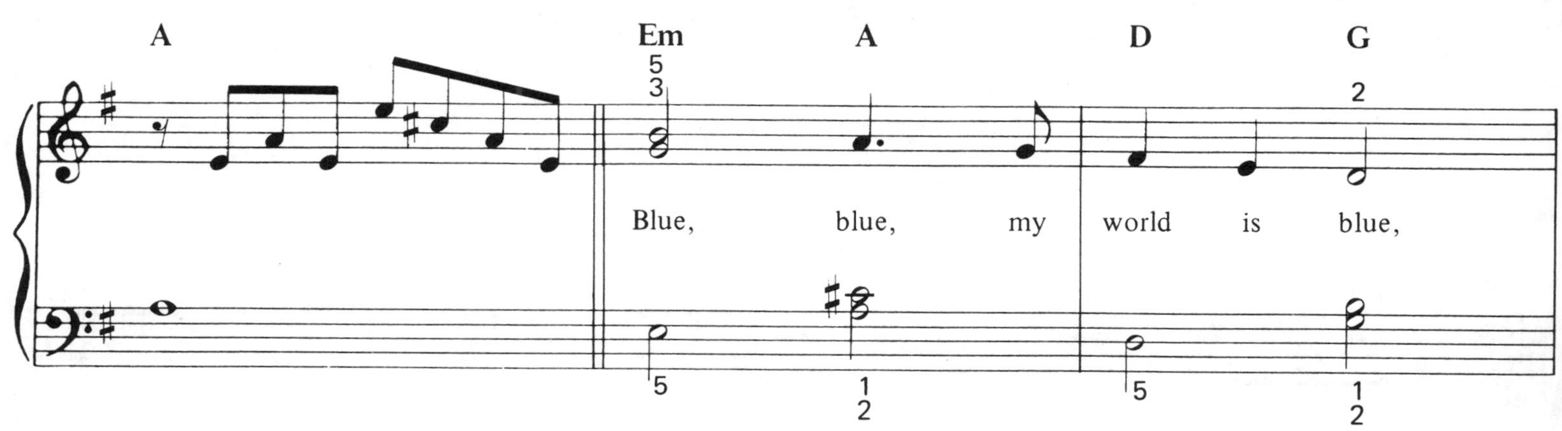

D G Em C B7 Em
life is grey, Cold is my heart since you went a - way.

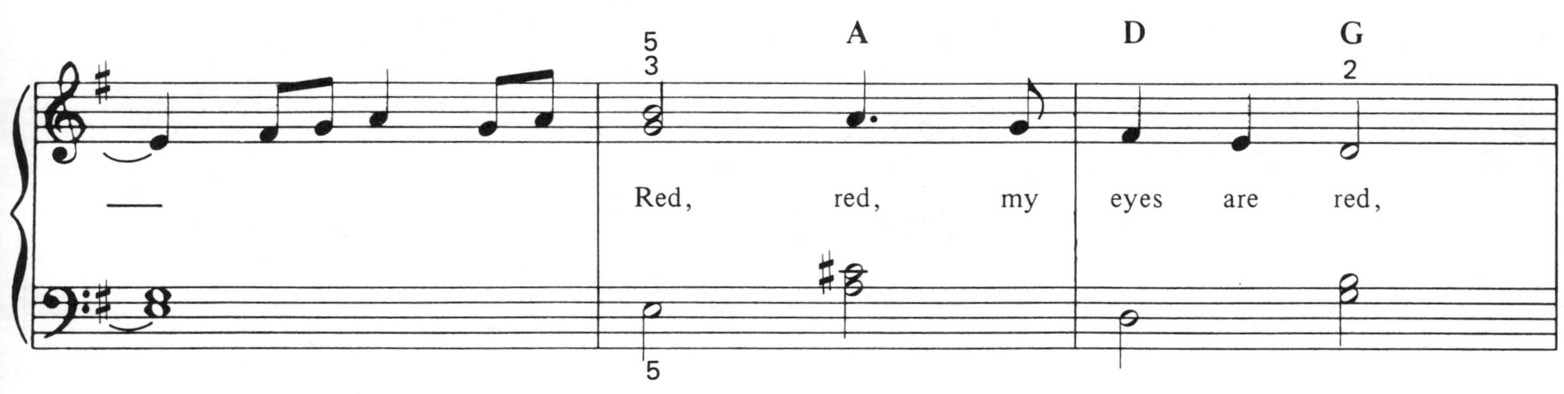
A D G
Red, red, my eyes are red,

Em C D G Em A
Cry - ing for you a - lone in my bed. Green, green, my

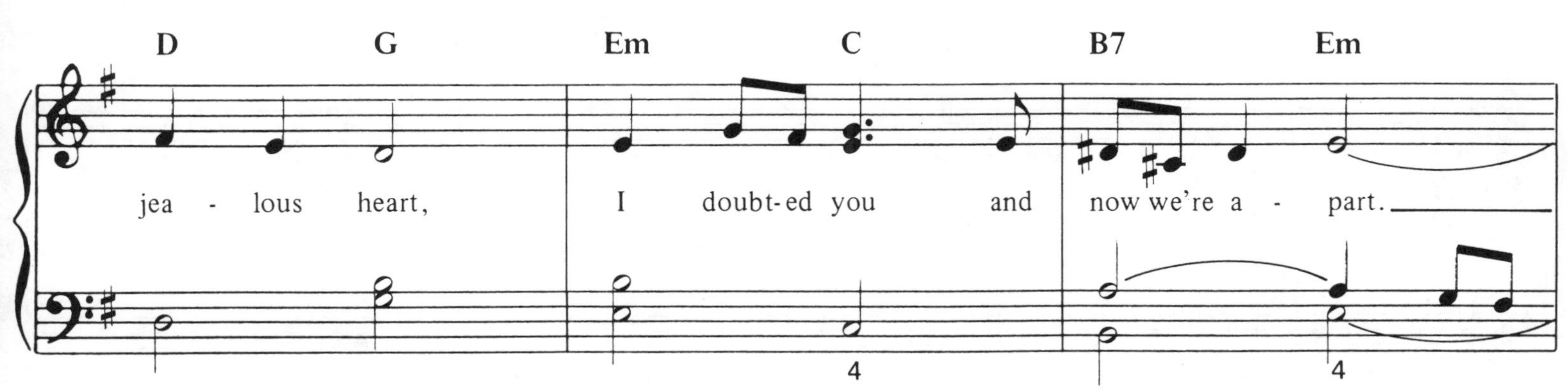
D G Em C B7 Em
jea - lous heart, I doubt-ed you and now we're a - part.

More broadly
E
B7
E
L.H.
When we met, how the

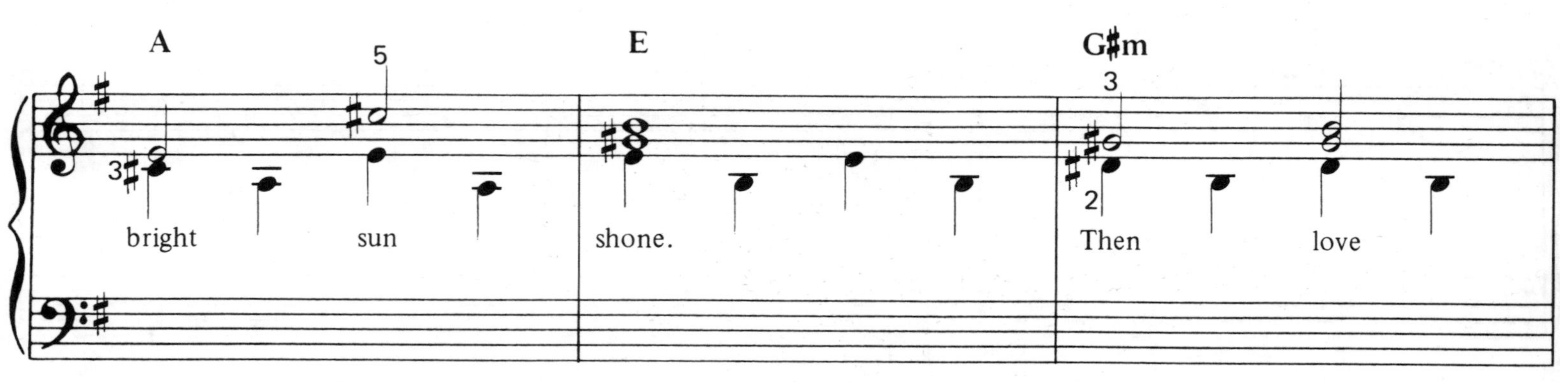
A
E
G♯m
bright sun shone. Then love

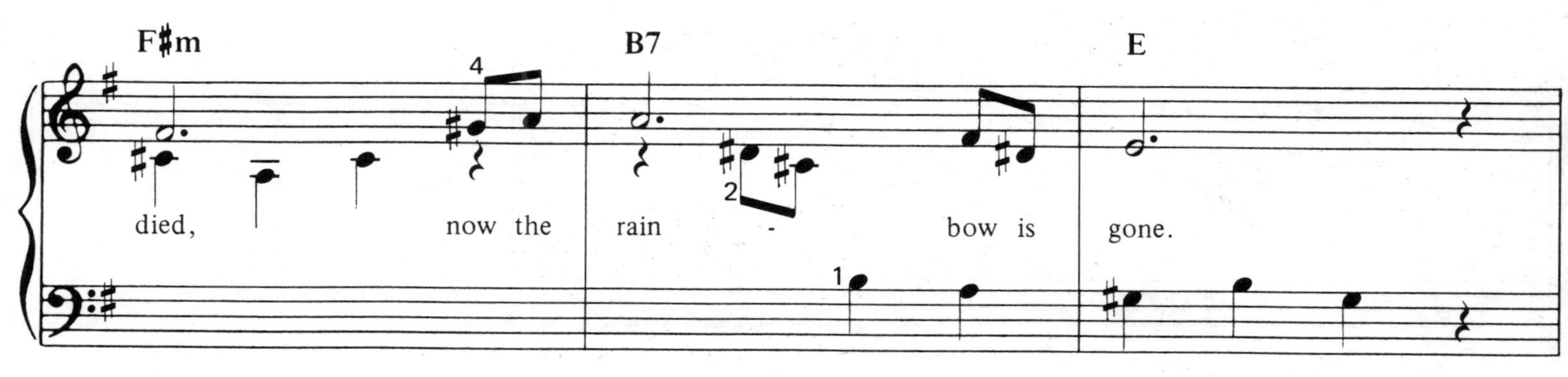
F♯m
B7
E
died, now the rain - bow is gone.

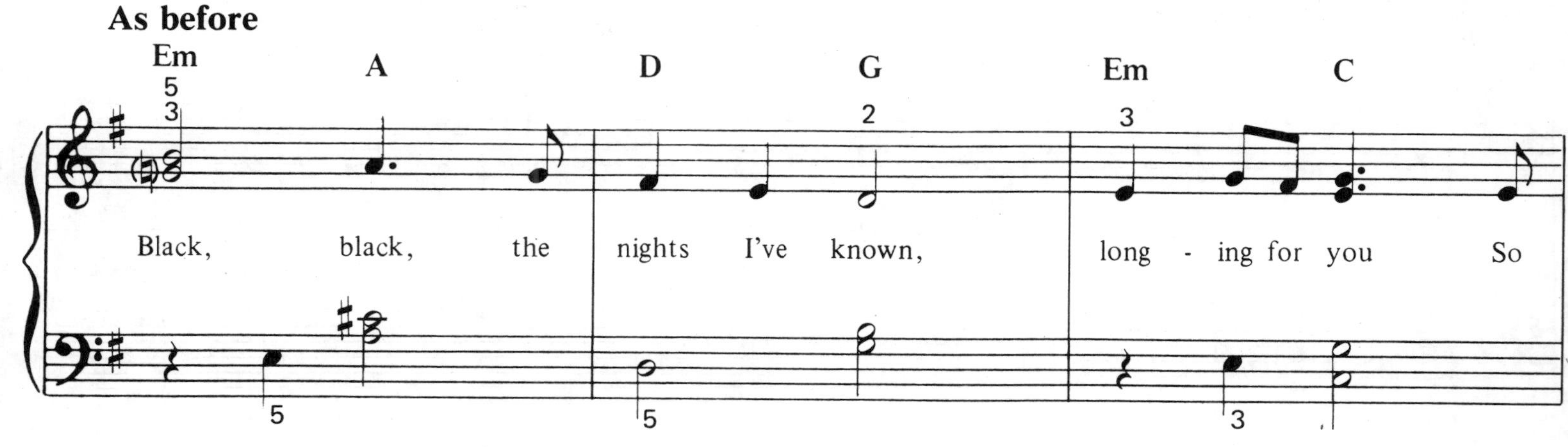
As before
Em
A
D
G
Em
C
Black, black, the nights I've known, long - ing for you So

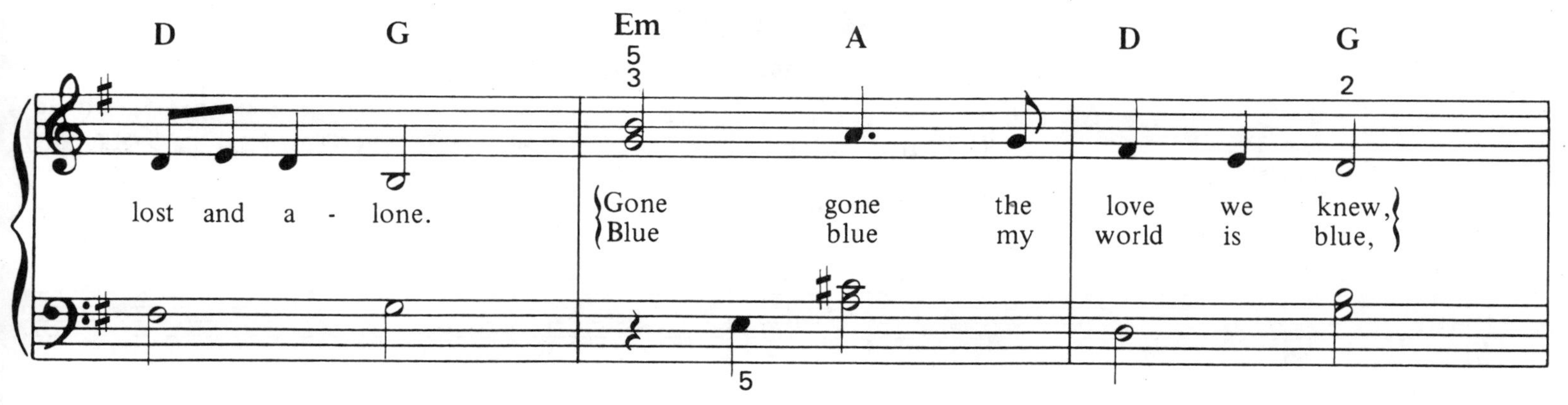
D
G
Em
A
D
G
lost and a - lone.
Gone gone the love we knew,
Blue blue my world is blue,

Em
C
1 B7
E
Blue is my world now I'm with - out you.

2 B7
E
I'm with-out you.
rall.

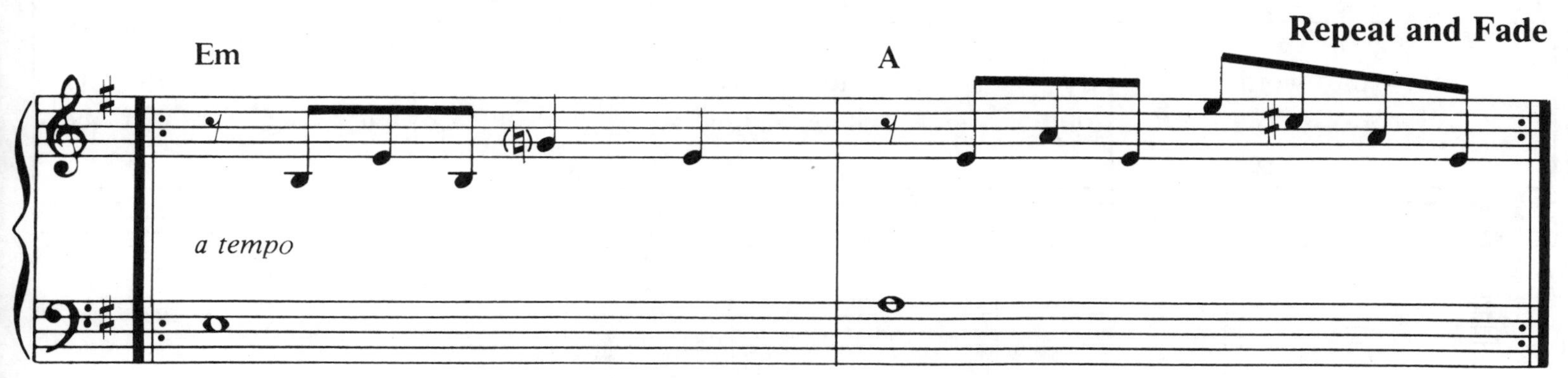
Repeat and Fade
Em
A
a tempo

MORE
(Theme From "MONDO CANE")

English Words by NORMAN NEWELL
Music by RIZ ORTOLANI and NINO OLIVIERO

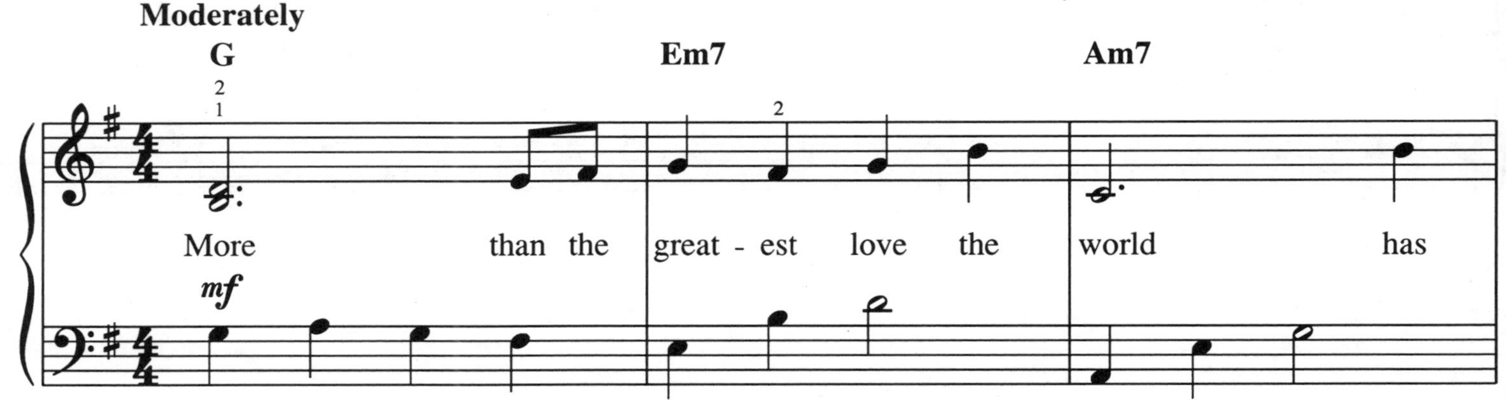

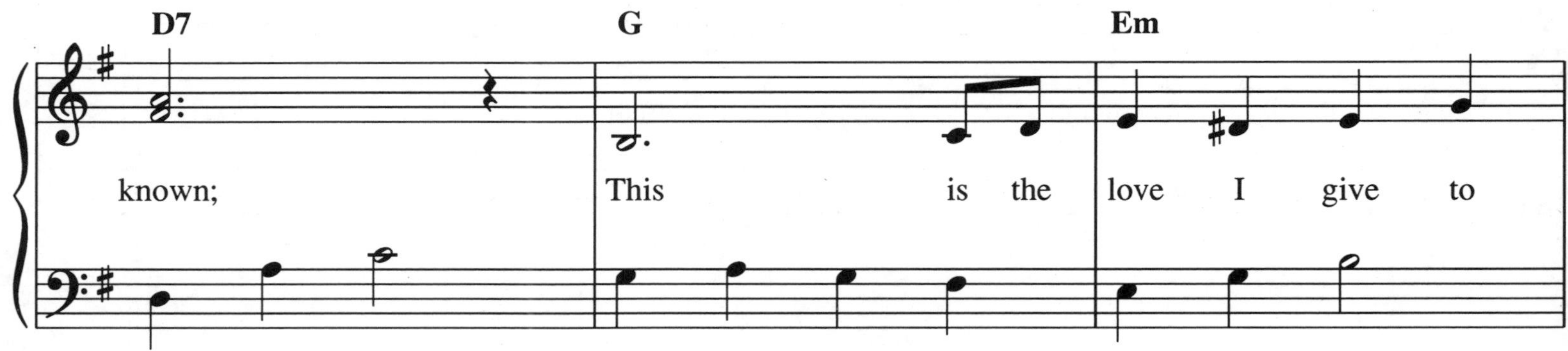

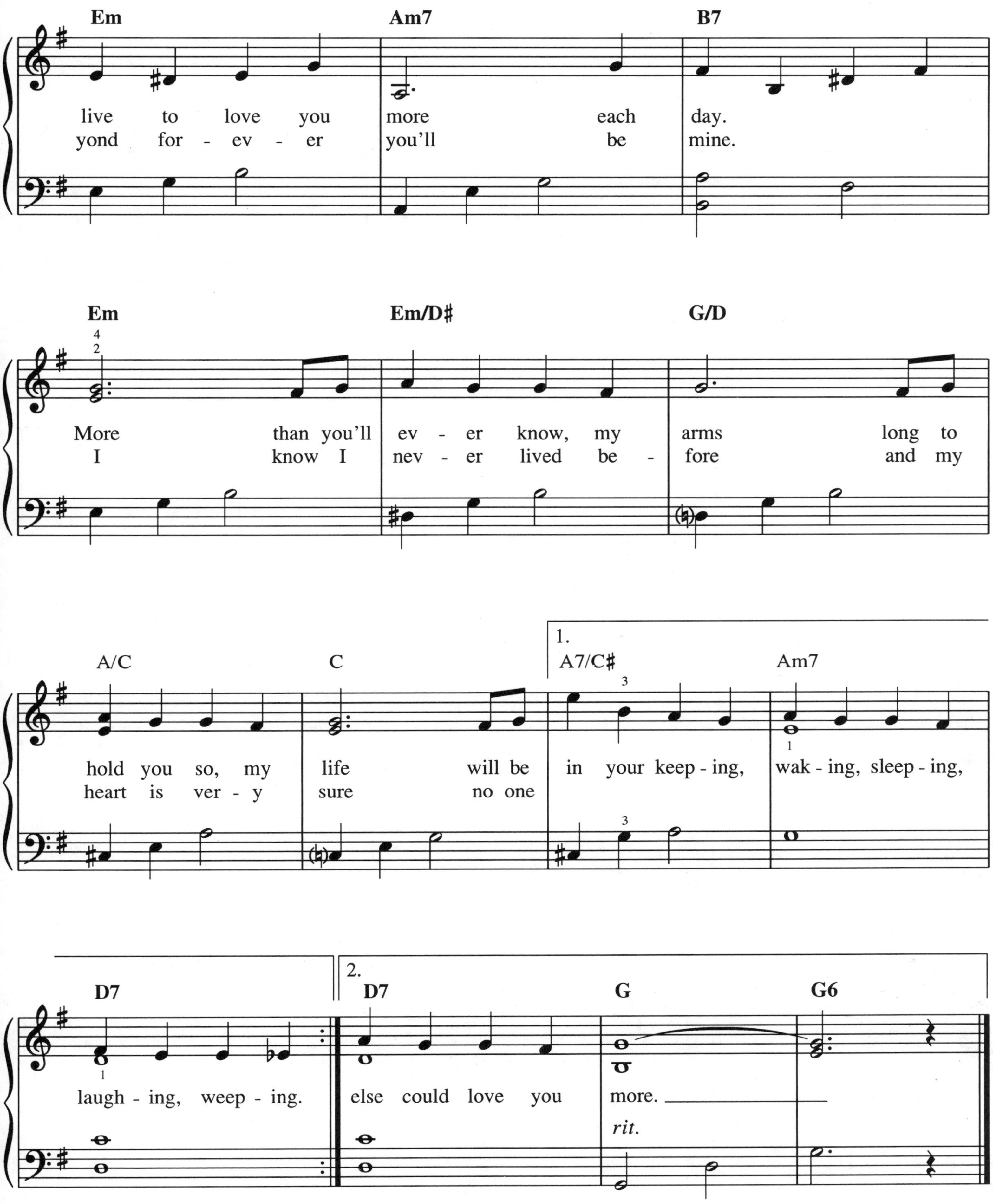

Em Am7 B7

live to love you more each day.

yond for - ev - er you'll be mine.

Em Em/D♯ G/D

More than you'll ev - er know, my arms long to

I know I nev - er lived be - fore and my

A/C C 1. A7/C♯ Am7

hold you so, my life will be in your keep - ing, wak - ing, sleep - ing,

heart is ver - y sure no one

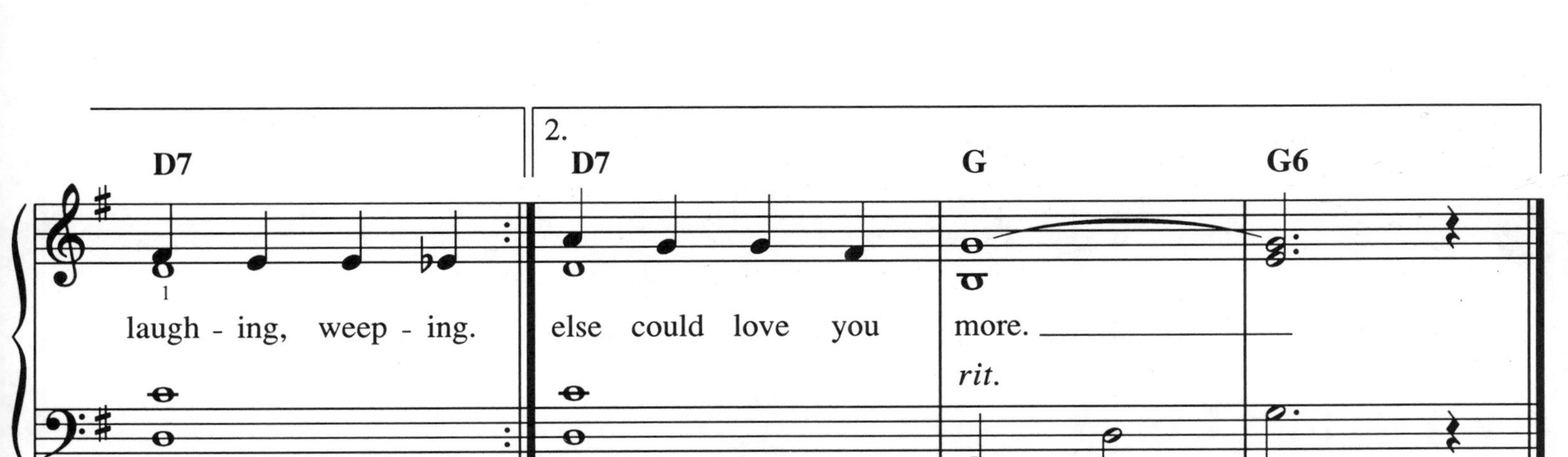

MY COLORING BOOK

Words and Music by FRED EBB
and JOHN KANDER

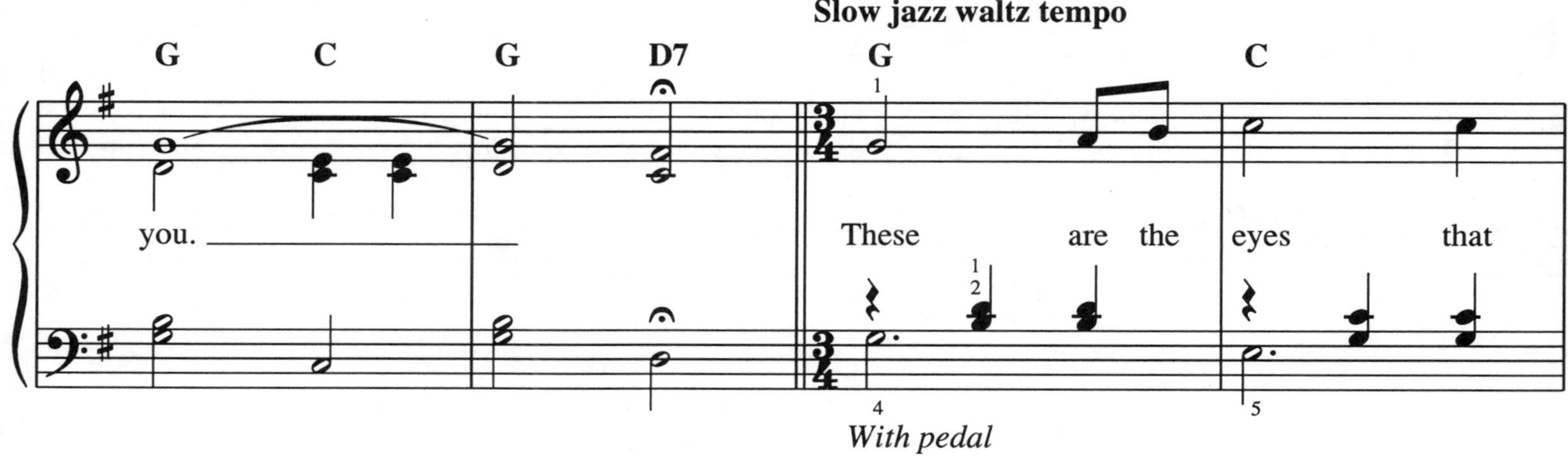

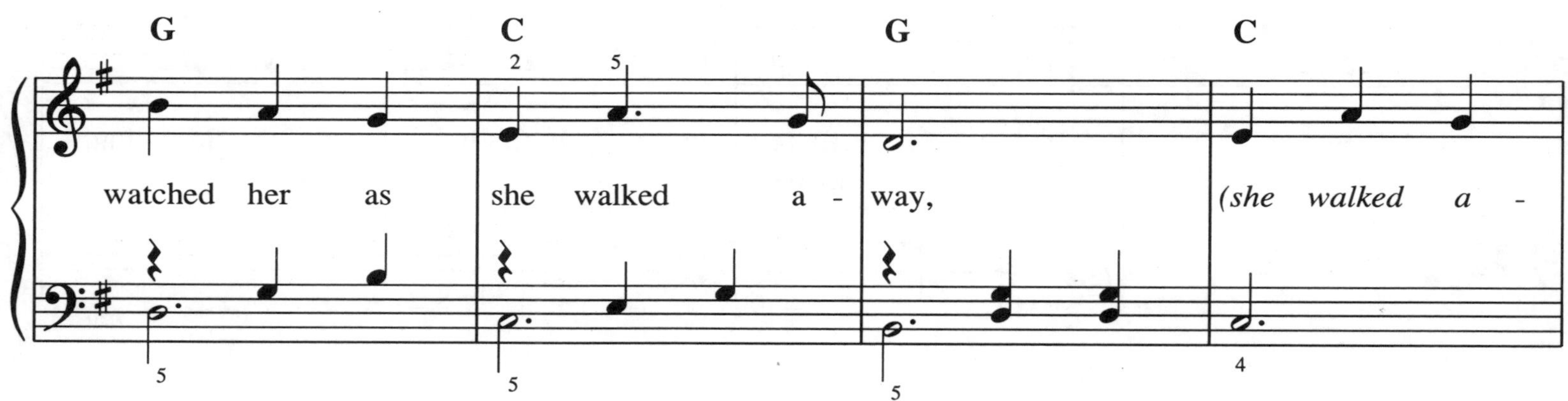

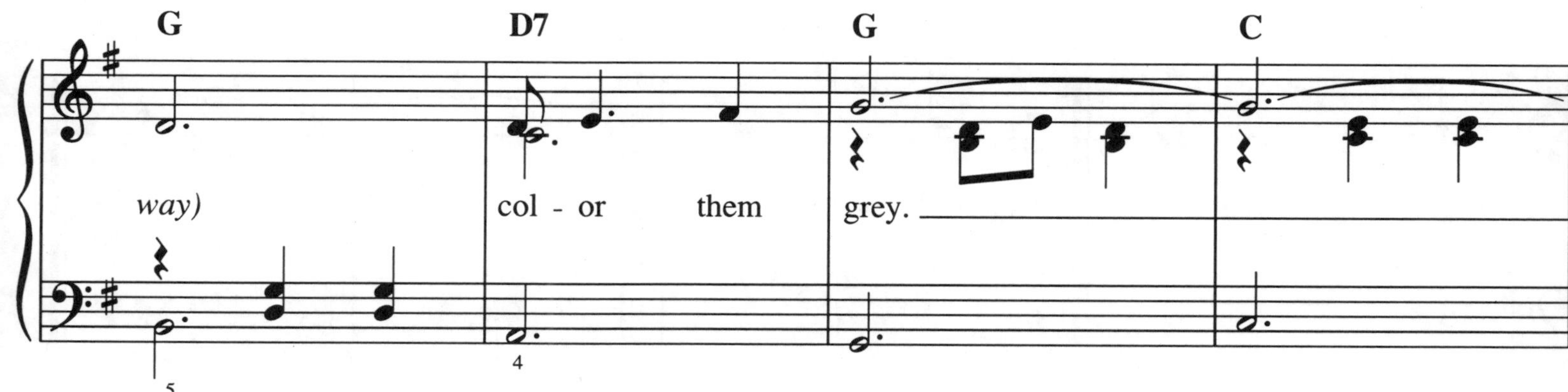

G D7 G C
This is the heart that
These are the beads she
G C G
thought she would al - ways be true,
more un - til he came be - tween,
C G D7
(al - ways be true) col - or it
(he came be - tween) col - or them
G C G G7
blue.
green.
These are the
This is the

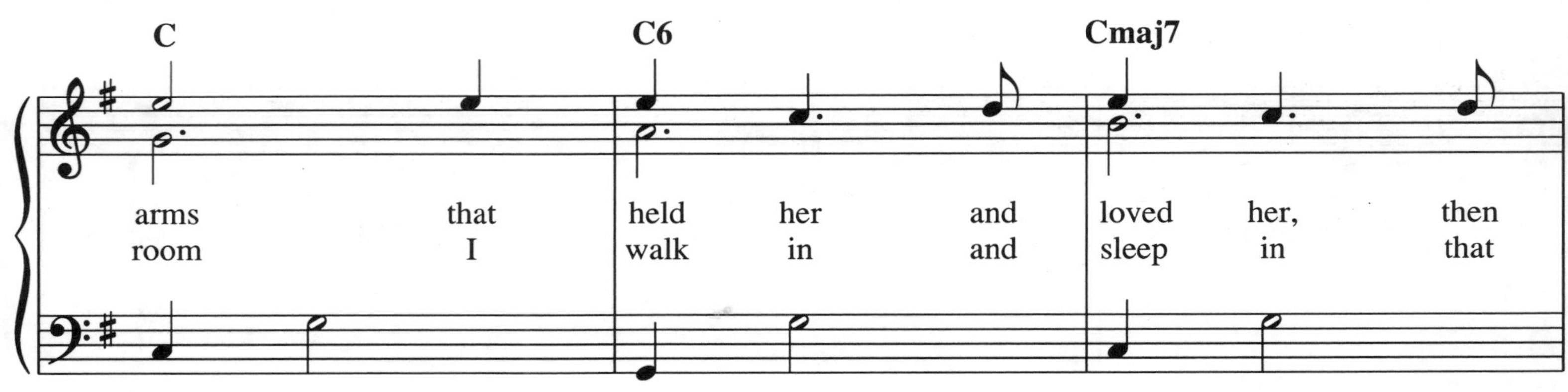
C
C6
Cmaj7
arms that held her and loved her, then
room I walk in and sleep in that

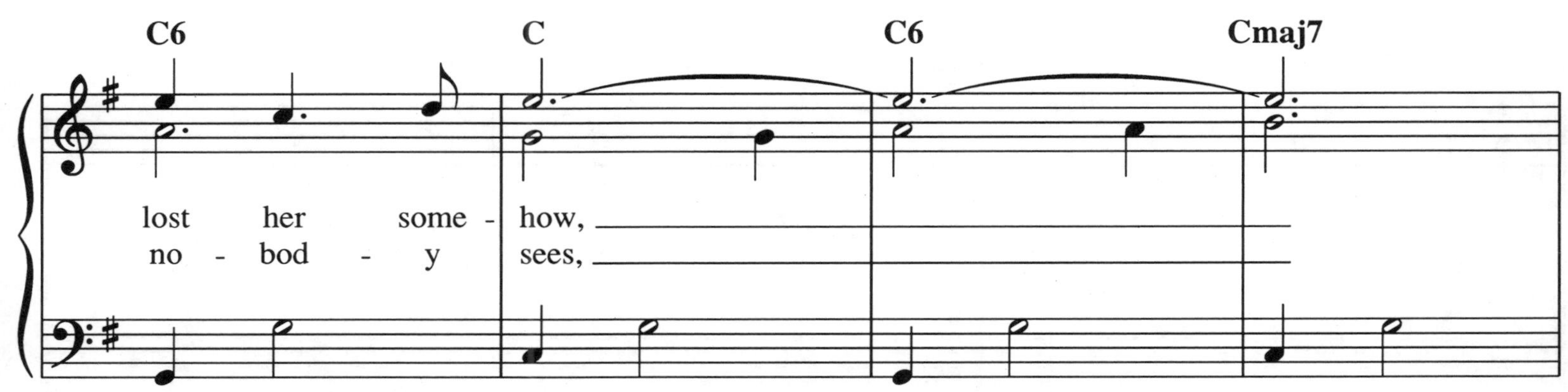
C6
C
C6
Cmaj7
lost her some - how,
no - bod - y sees,

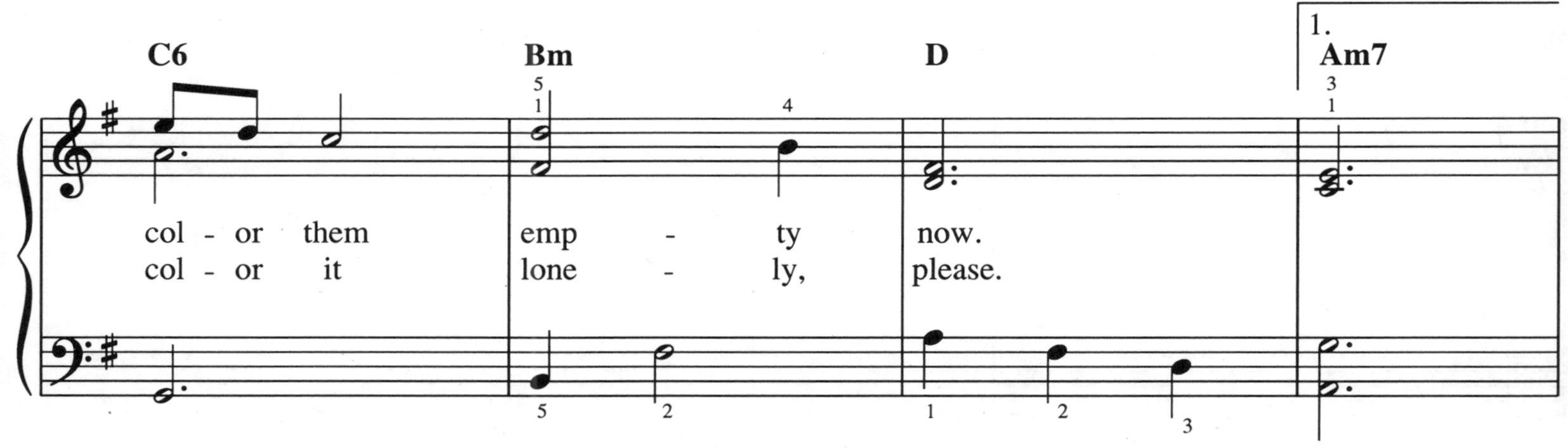
C6
Bm
D
1.
Am7
col - or them emp - ty now.
col - or it lone - ly, please.

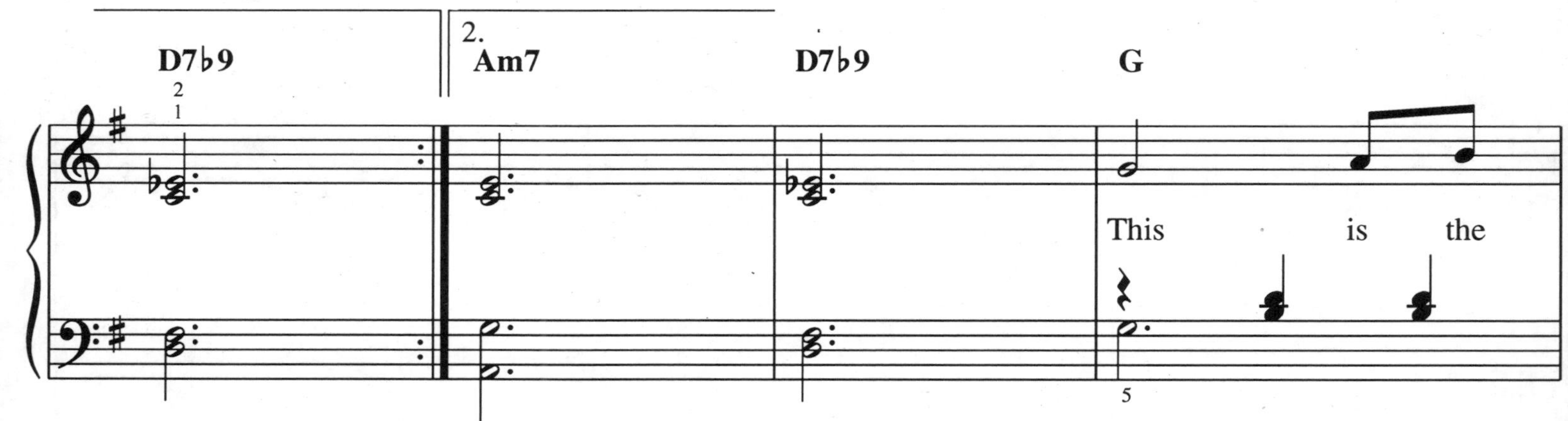
D7♭9
2.
Am7
D7♭9
G
This is the

C
G
C
girl whose love I de - pend - ed up -
G
C
G
D7
on, col - or her
G
C
G
D7
gone.
G

MY CUP RUNNETH OVER

(From "I DO! I DO!")

Words by TOM JONES
Music by HARVEY SCHMIDT

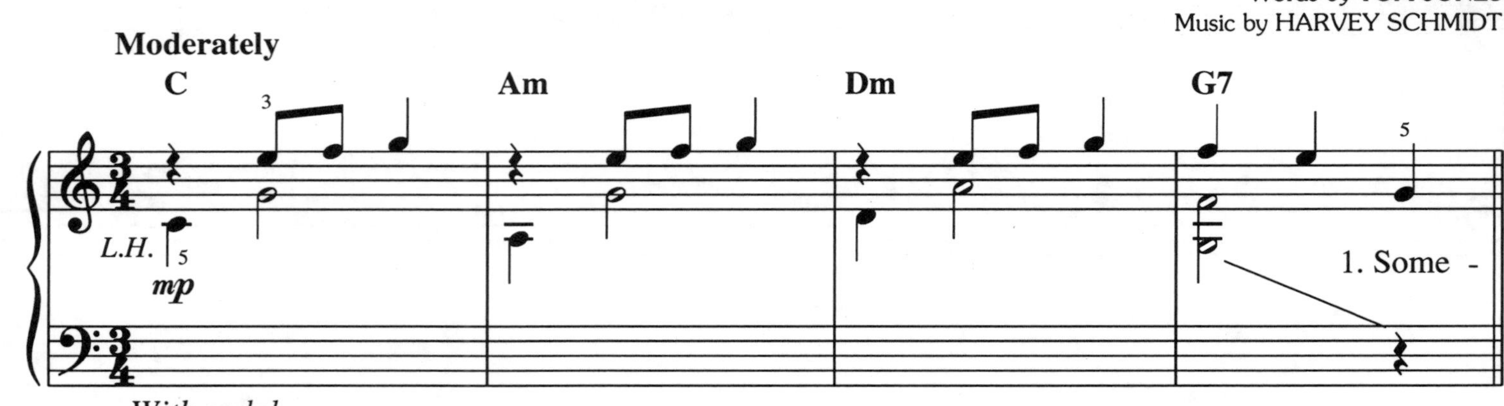

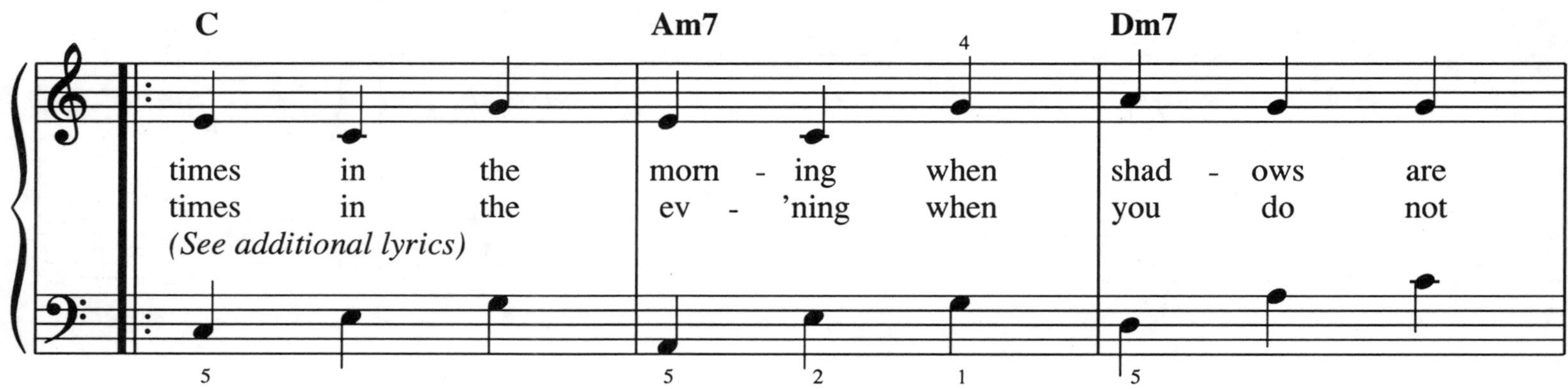

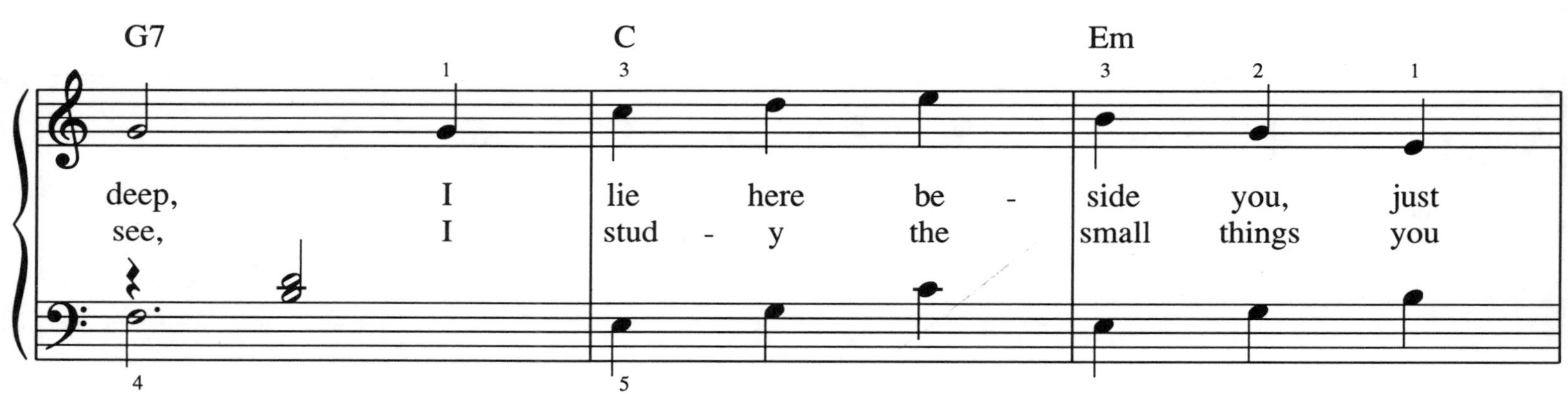

Em
Dm7
Em7
whis - per what I'm think - ing of; my
mo - ments that I'm fond - est of; my
Dm7
G7
C
cup run - neth o - ver with love.
cup run - neth o - ver with love.
Am7
Dm7
1., 2.
G7
C
Am7
Dm
G7
2. Some -
3. In

Additional Lyrics

In only a moment we both will be old;
We won't even notice the world turning cold.
And so in this moment with sunlight above.
My cup runneth over with love, with love.

NA NA HEY HEY KISS HIM GOODBYE

Words and Music by GARY DeCARLO,
PAUL LEKA and DALE FRASHUER

Gm7 C F Gm7 C
love you the way that I love you,
near you to com - fort and cheer you.
F Dm Gm
'cause if he did no, no, he would - n't make you
When all those sad tears are falling baby
C B♭ A
cry. He might be thrill - ing bab - by, but
from your eyes.
Dm Gm F
my love's so dog - gone will - ing. So kiss him,

B♭
B♭m
C
F
go on and kiss him, good - bye. Na na
A♭
1.
E♭
F
na na, Hey Hey Hey, good - bye. Na na
2.
E♭
F
hey, hey, Good - bye. Na na na na, na na
A♭
E♭
F
Repeat and Fade
na na, Hey Hey Hey, Good - bye. Na na

ONE TIN SOLDIER

Words and Music by DENNIS LAMBERT
and BRIAN POTTER

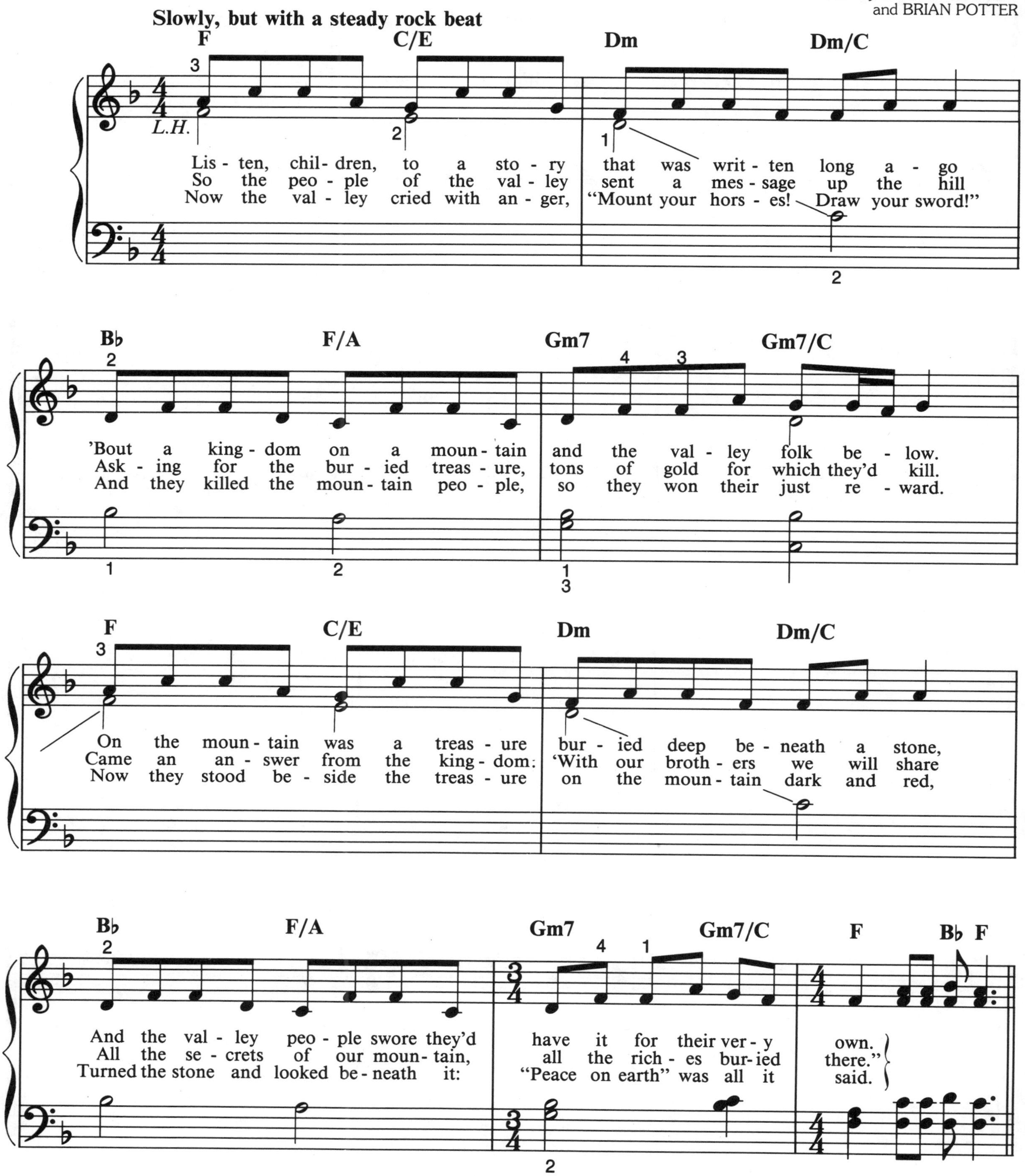

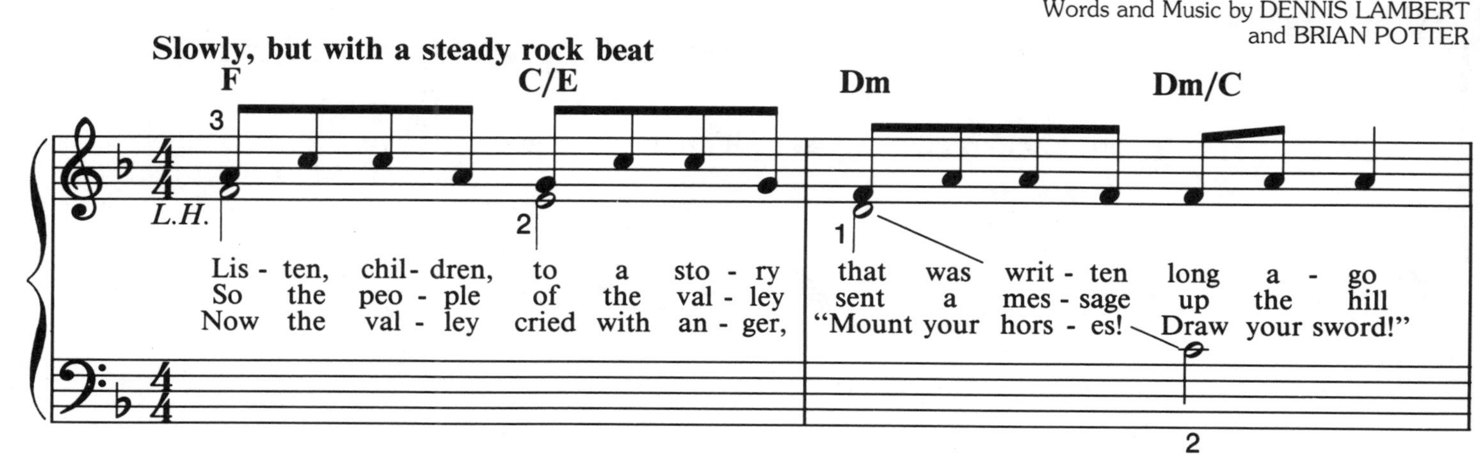

Slowly, but with a steady rock beat
F
C/E
Dm
Dm/C
L.H.
Lis - ten, chil - dren, to a sto - ry that was writ - ten long a - go
So the peo - ple of the val - ley sent a mes - sage up the hill
Now the val - ley cried with an - ger, "Mount your hors - es! Draw your sword!"
B♭
F/A
Gm7
Gm7/C
'Bout a king - dom on a moun - tain and the val - ley folk be - low.
Ask - ing for the bur - ied treas - ure, tons of gold for which they'd kill.
And they killed the moun - tain peo - ple, so they won their just re - ward.
F
C/E
Dm
Dm/C
On the moun - tain was a treas - ure bur - ied deep be - neath a stone,
Came an an - swer from the king - dom: 'With our broth - ers we will share
Now they stood be - side the treas - ure on the moun - tain dark and red,
B♭
F/A
Gm7
Gm7/C
F
B♭ F
And the val - ley peo - ple swore they'd have it for their ver - y own.
All the se - crets of our moun - tain, all the rich - es bur - ied there."
Turned the stone and looked be - neath it: "Peace on earth" was all it said.

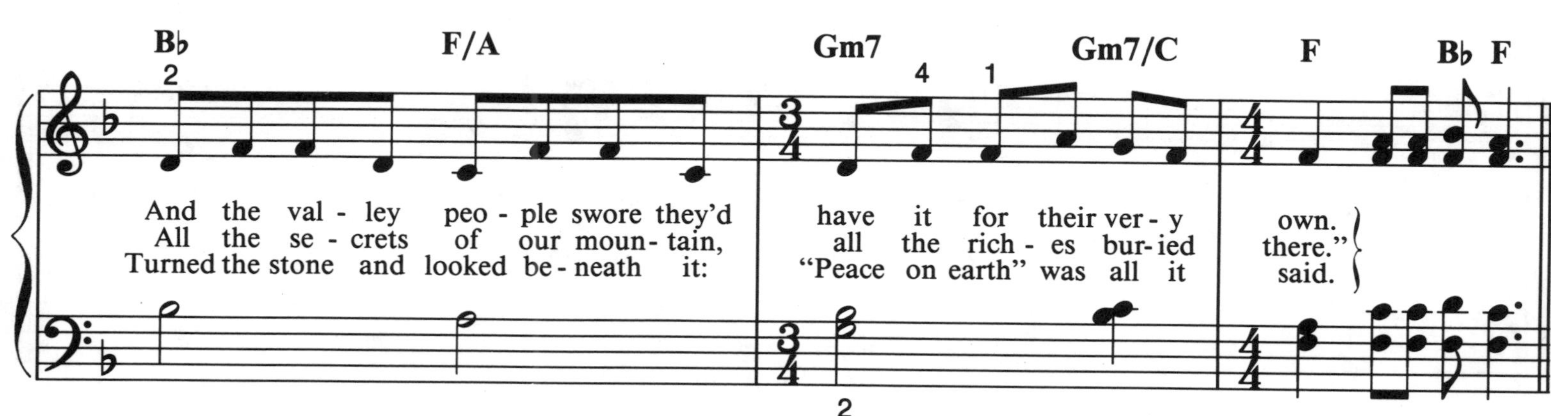

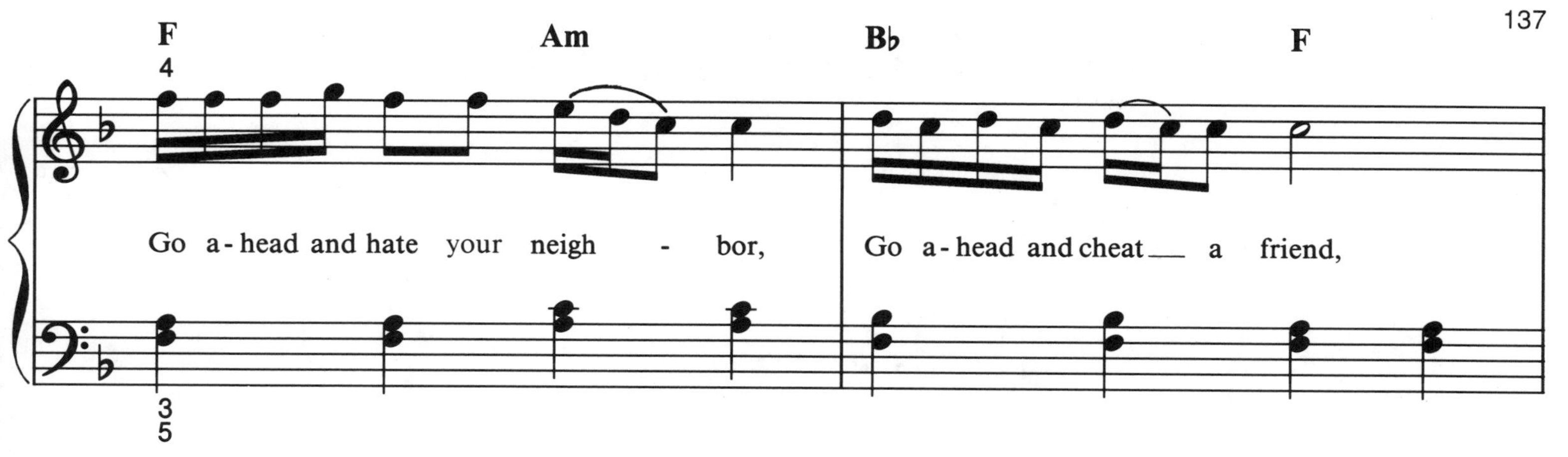
F
Am
B♭
F
4
Go a-head and hate your neigh - bor,
Go a-head and cheat a friend,
3
5

F
Am
B♭
F
Do it in the name of heav - en,
Jus-ti-fy it in the end. There

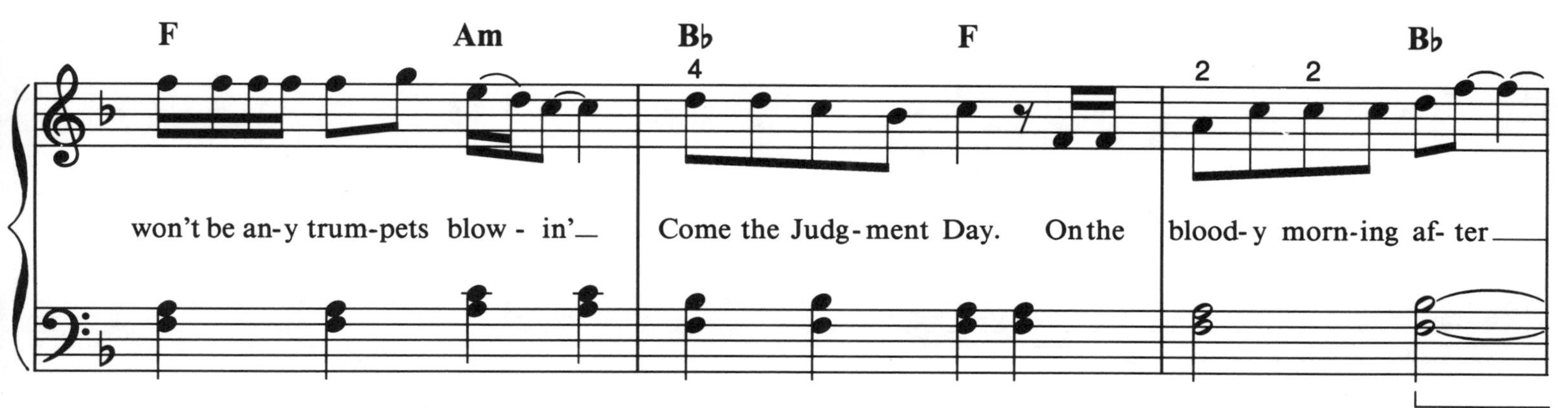
F
Am
B♭
F
B♭
4
2 2
won't be an-y trum-pets blow - in'
Come the Judg-ment Day. On the
blood-y morn-ing af- ter

Gm7/C
F
B♭
F
B♭
F
One tin sold - dier rides a - way.

OUR DAY WILL COME

Words by BOB HILLIARD
Music by MORT GARSON

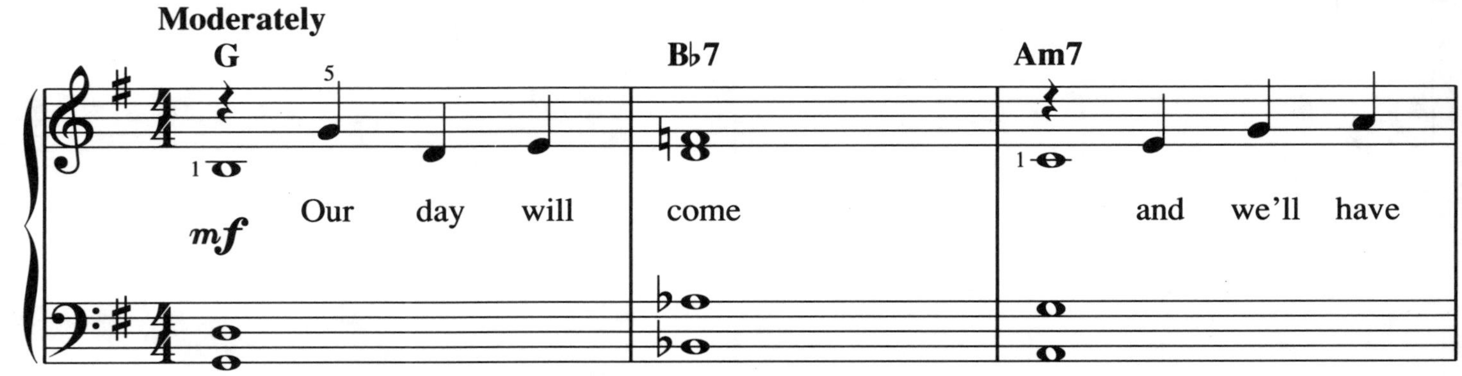

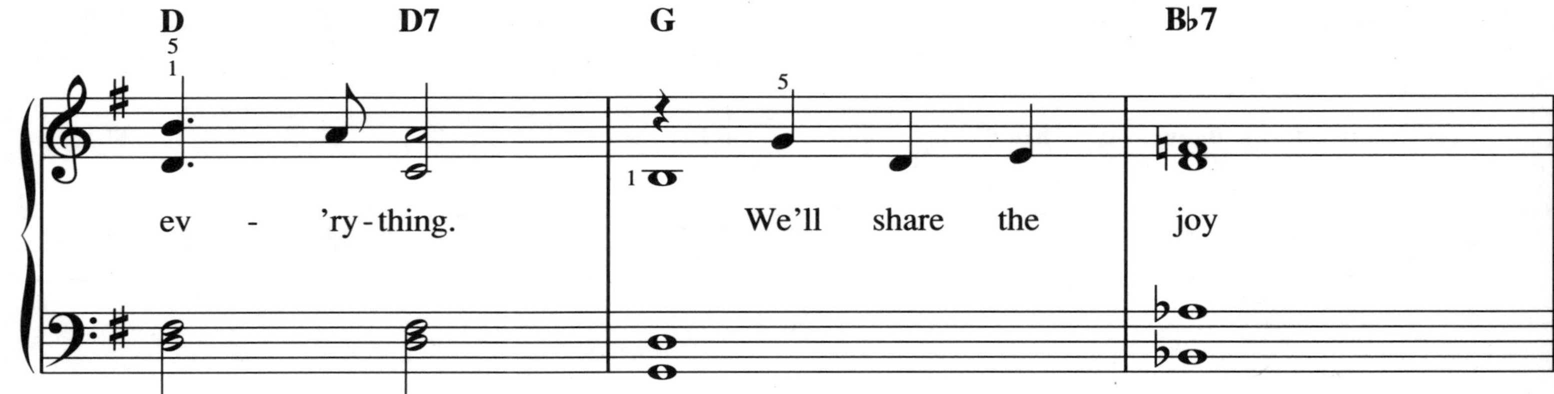

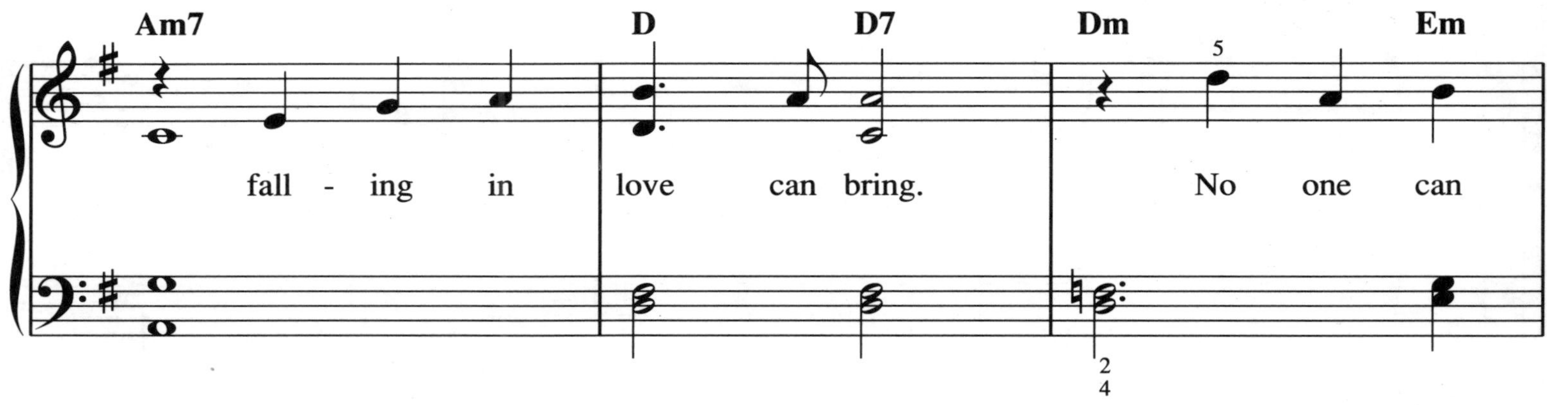

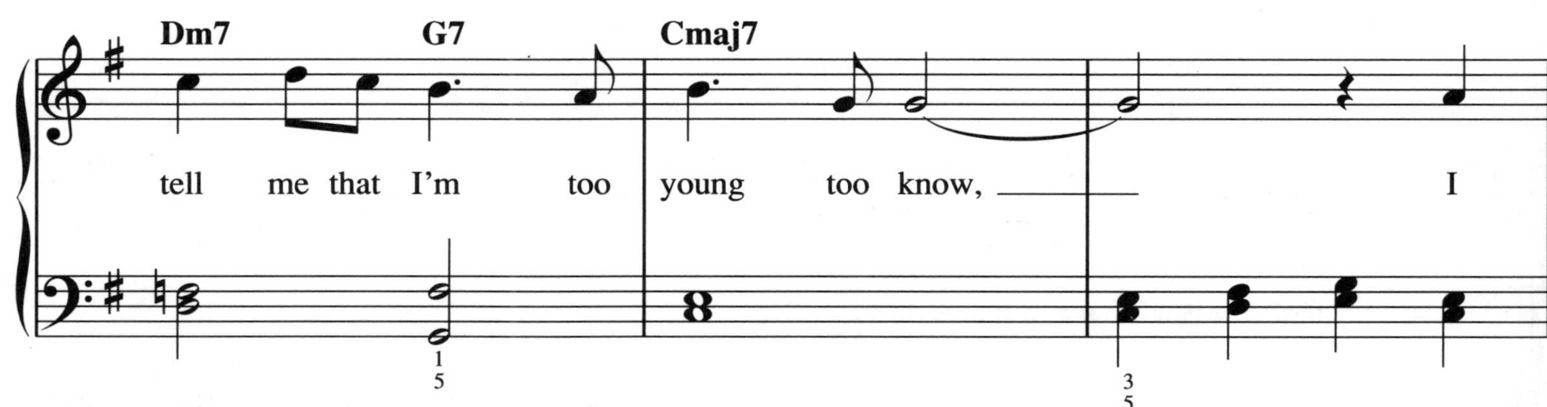

Cm7
love you so ___ and you love
Bm7
B♭7
me.
Am7
D7
G
B♭7
Our day will
come
Am7
if we just
D
D7
wait a - while.
G
No tears for
B♭7
us,
Am7
think love and
D
D7
wear a smile.

Dm
Em
Our dreams have
Dm7
G7
mag - ic be - cause we'll
Cmaj7
al - ways stay in
Cm7
love this way,
Bm7
E7
our day
Am7
A♭7
will
1.
G
E7(♭9)
come.
Am7
D7
2. G
B♭7
A♭7
Gmaj7
come.
molto rit.

PEOPLE
(From "FUNNY GIRL")

Words by BOB MERRILL
Music by JULE STYNE

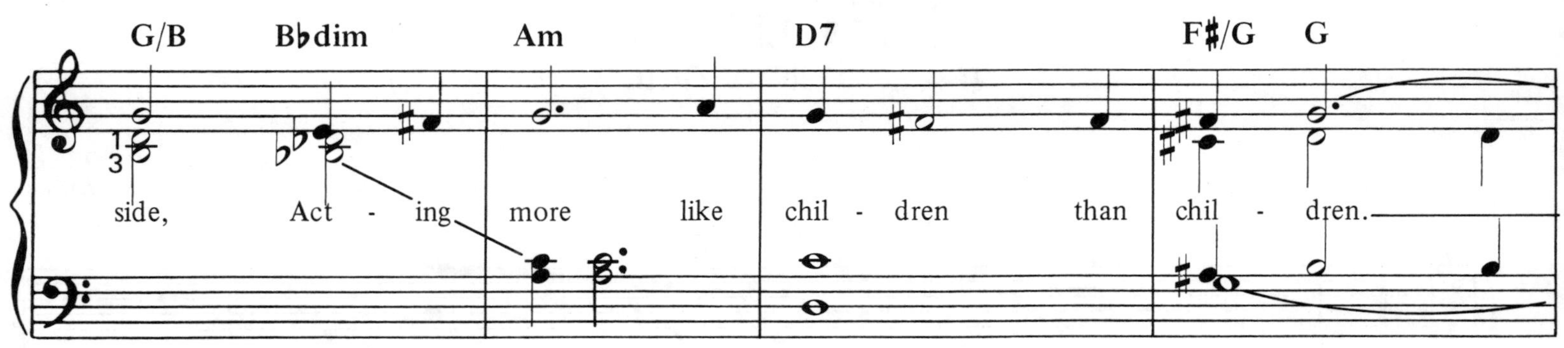
G/B
B♭dim
Am
D7
F♯/G
G
side, Act - ing more like chil - dren than chil - dren.

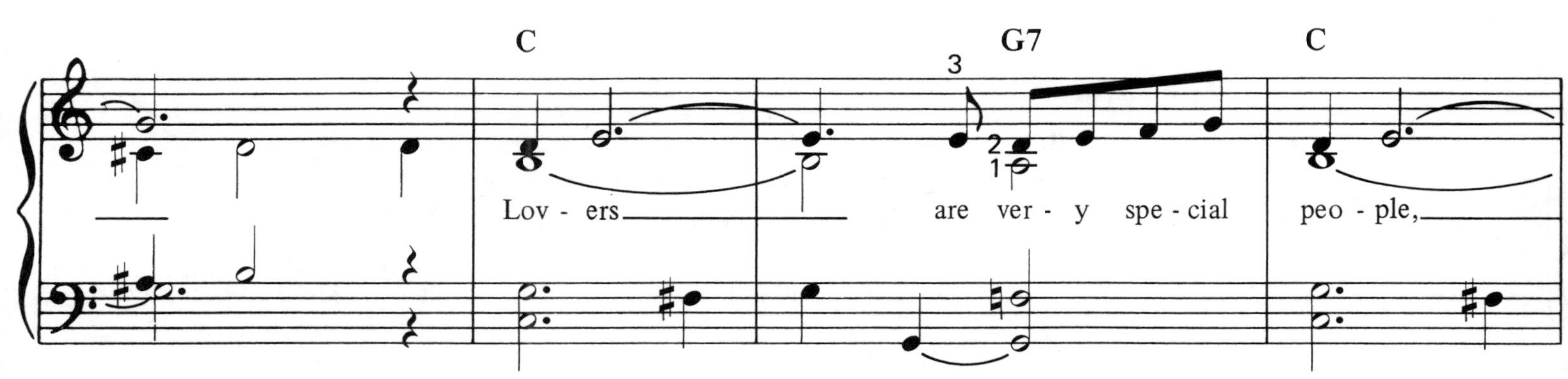
C
G7
C
Lov - ers are ver - y spe - cial peo - ple,

F
G
F
C
Gm7
They're the luck - i - est peo - ple in the world.

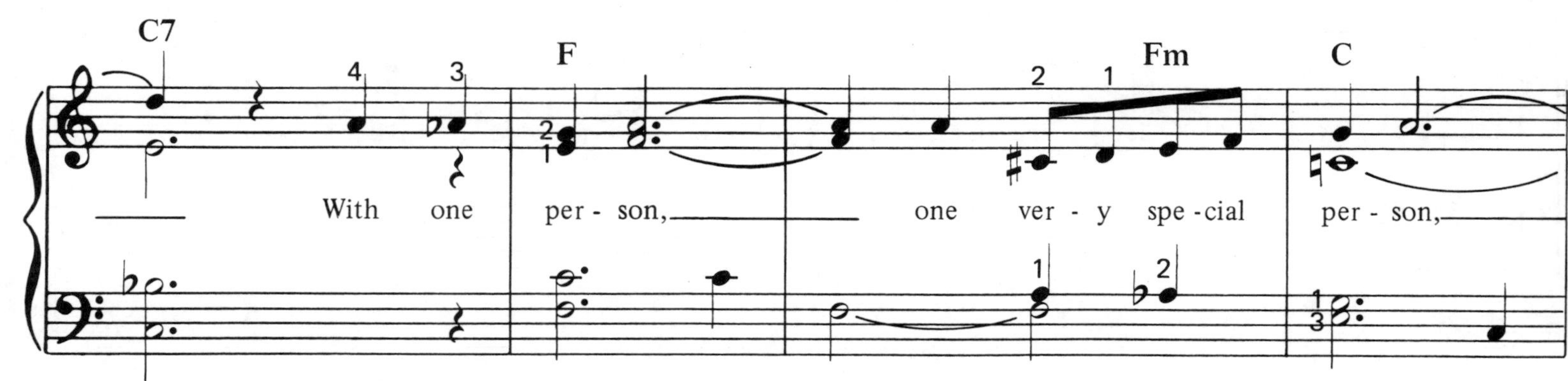
C7
F
Fm
C
With one per - son, one ver - y spe - cial per - son,

Gm7
F
G/F
C/E
A feel - ing deep in your soul says, "You were half, now you're whole."

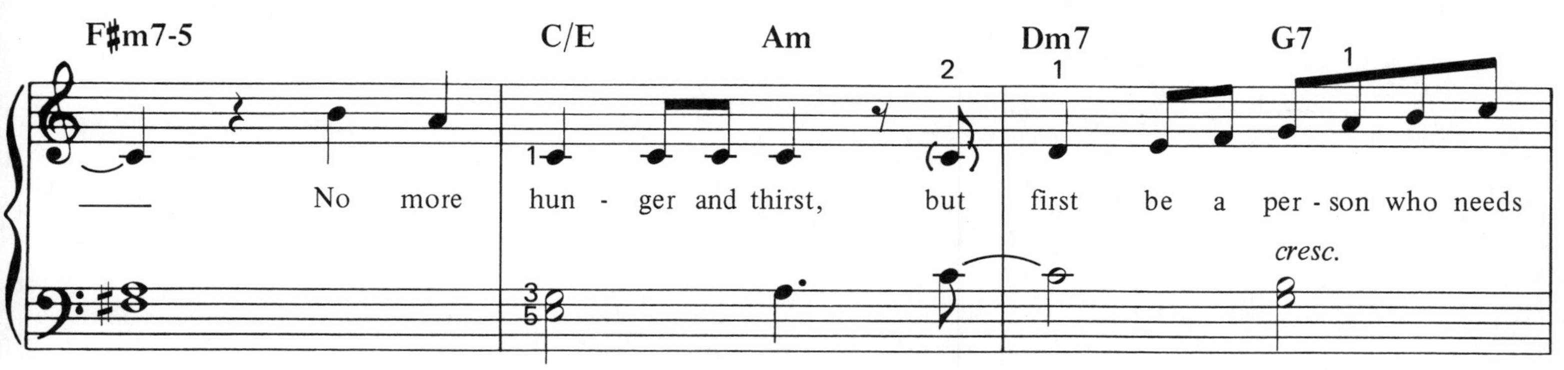
F♯m7-5
C/E
Am
Dm7
G7
No more hun - ger and thirst, but first be a per - son who needs
cresc.

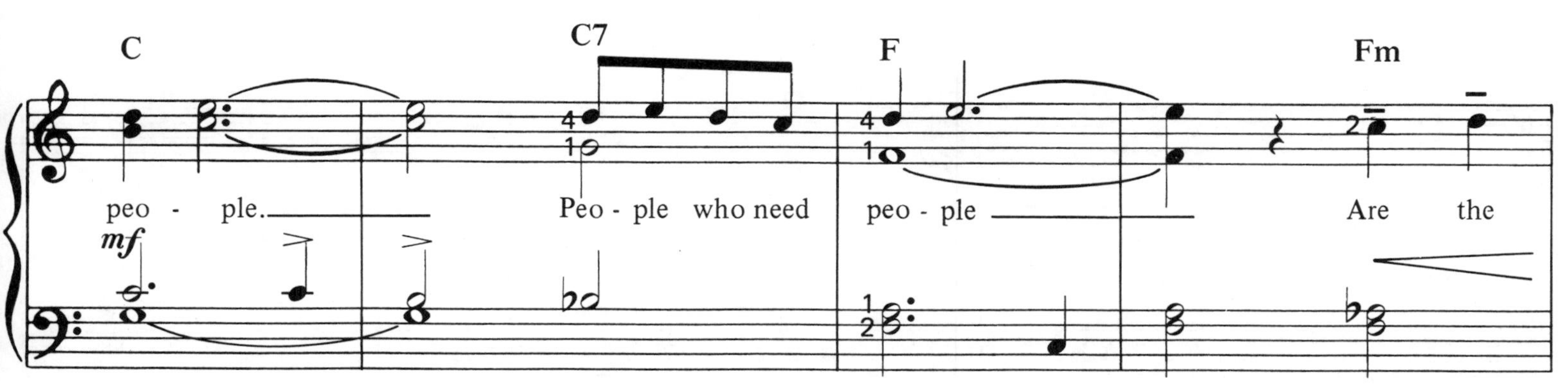
C
C7
F
Fm
peo - ple. Peo - ple who need peo - ple Are the
mf

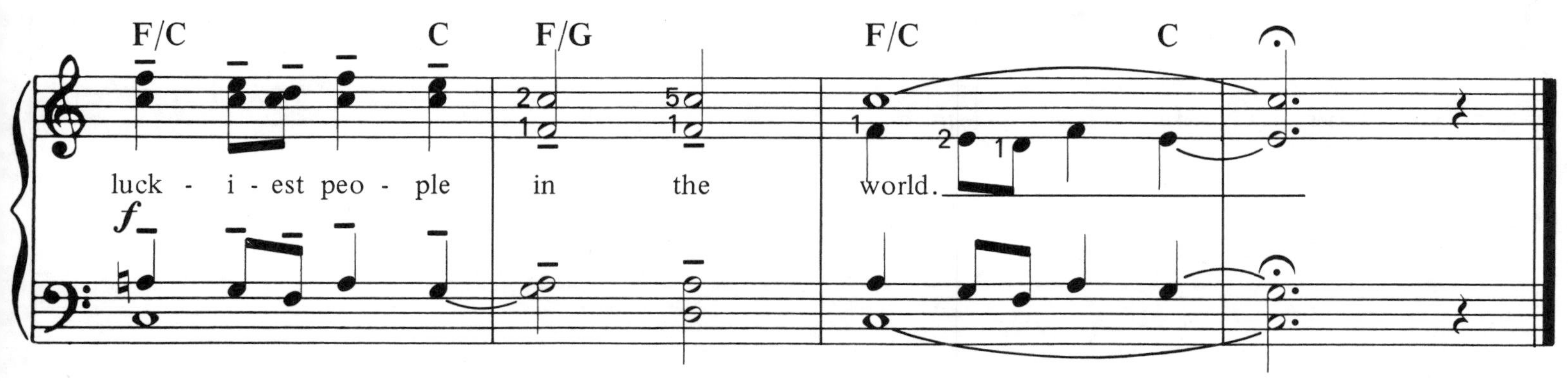
F/C
C
F/G
F/C
C
luck - i - est peo - ple in the world.
f

PAPER ROSES

Words by JANICE TORRE
Music by FRED SPIELMAN

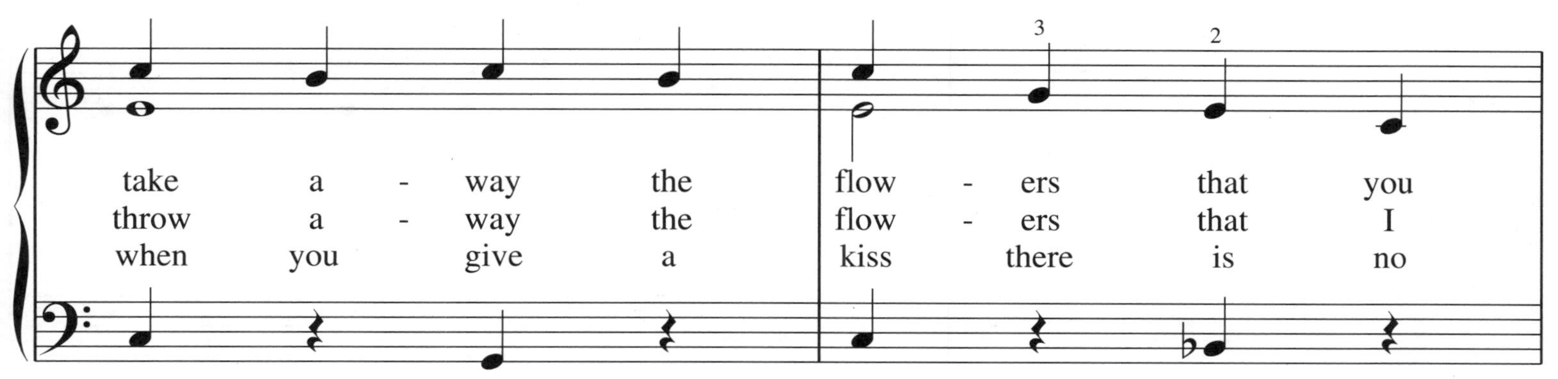
3
2
take a - way the flow - ers that you
throw a - way the flow - ers that I
when you give a kiss there is no

F
5
G7
gave me and
gave you. I'll
feel - ing, it's
send the kind that
just a stiff and
2
1
2

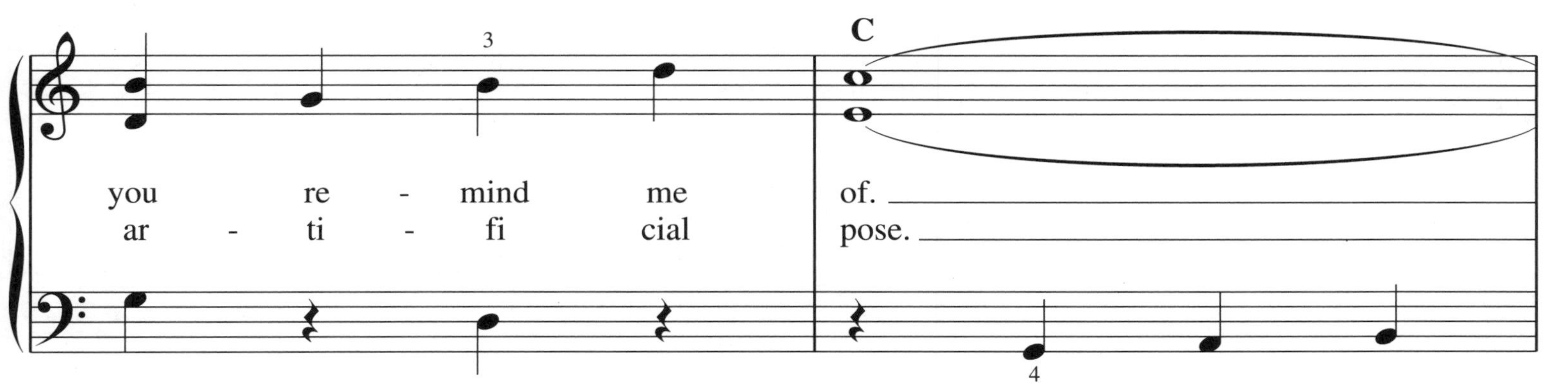
3
C
you re - mind me of.
ar - ti - fi cial pose.
4

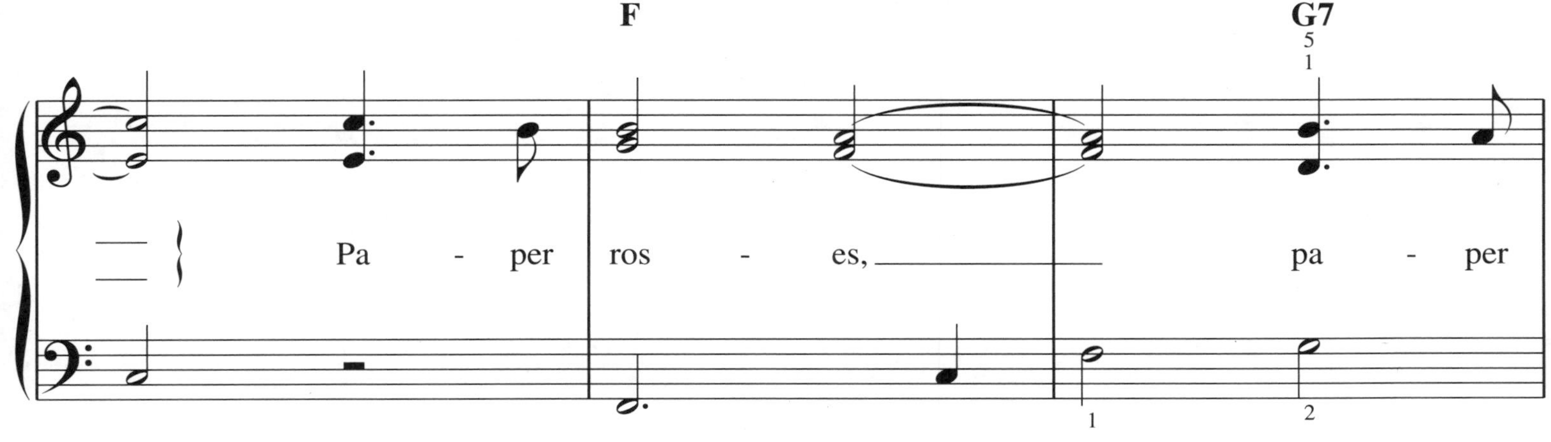
F
G7
5
1
Pa - per ros - es, pa - per
1
2

C
A7
Dm
ros - es, oh, how real those ros - es
1
3

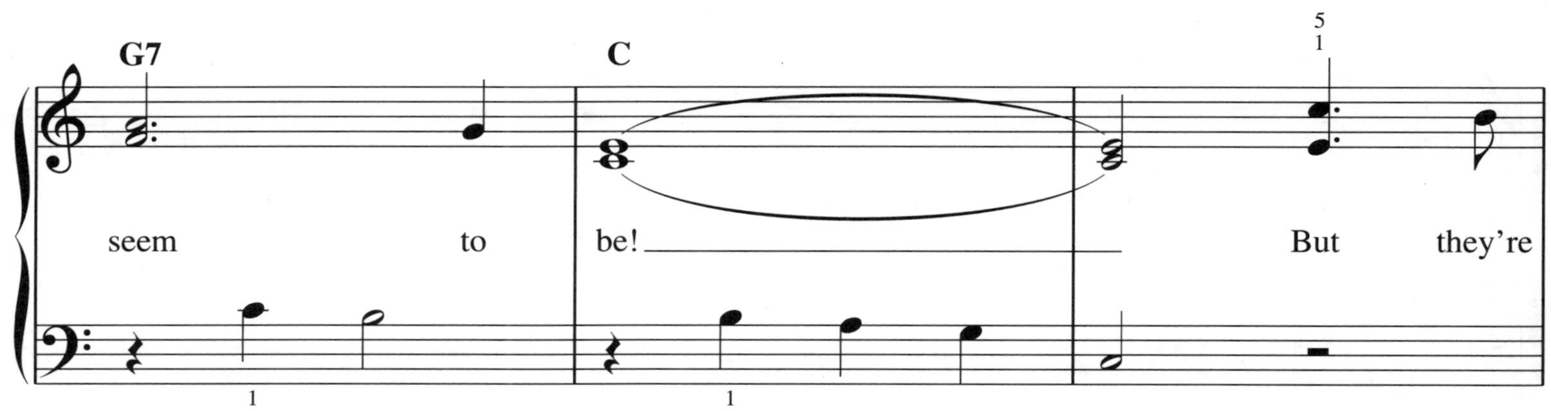
G7
C
5
1
seem to be! But they're
1
1

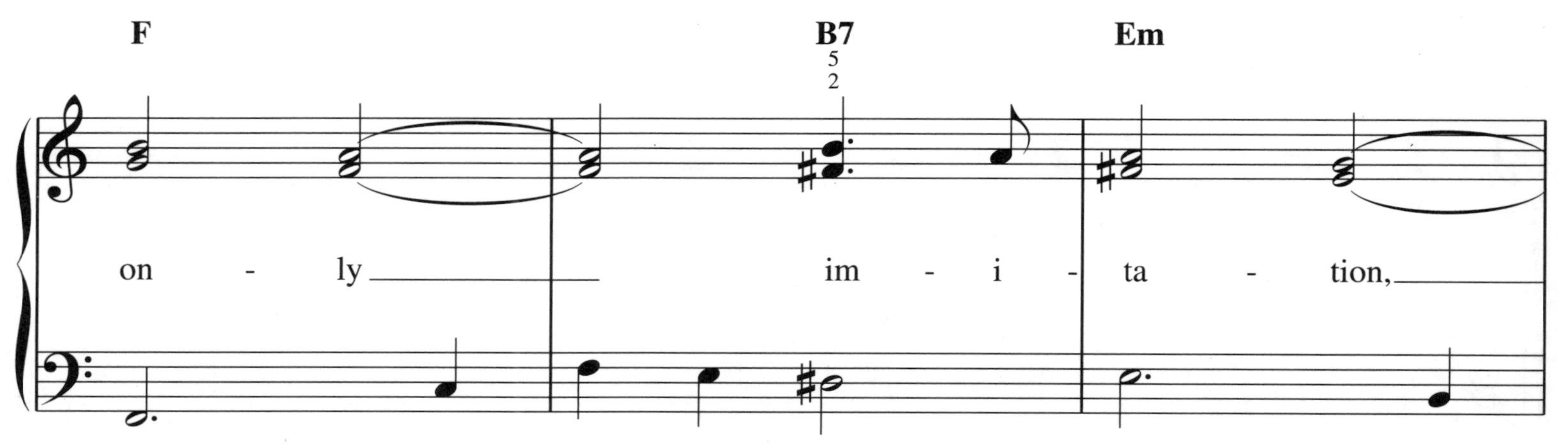
F
B7
5
2
Em
on - ly im - i - ta - tion,

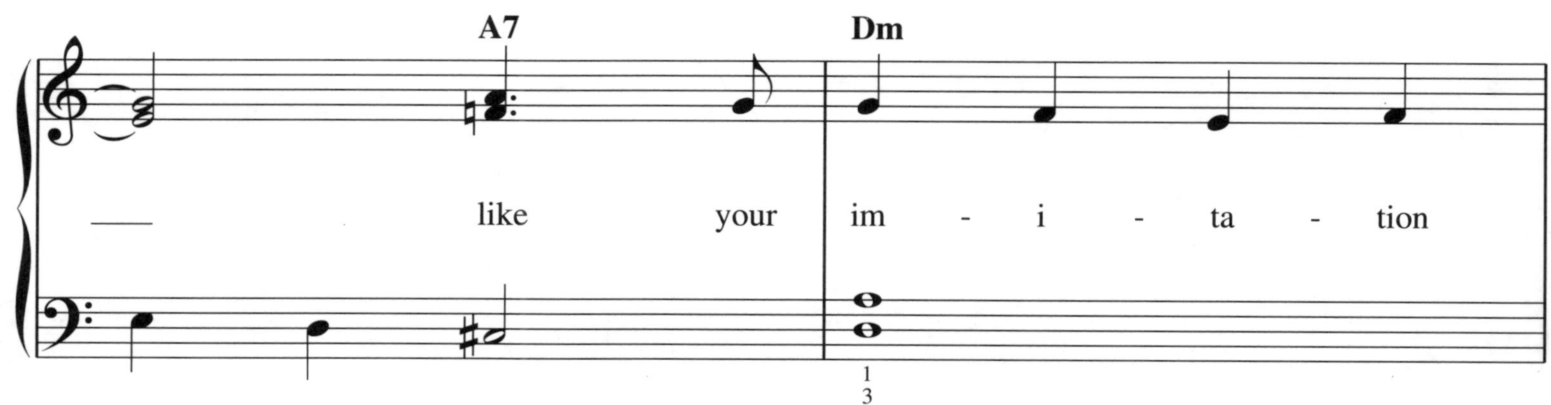
A7
Dm
like your im - i - ta - tion
1
3

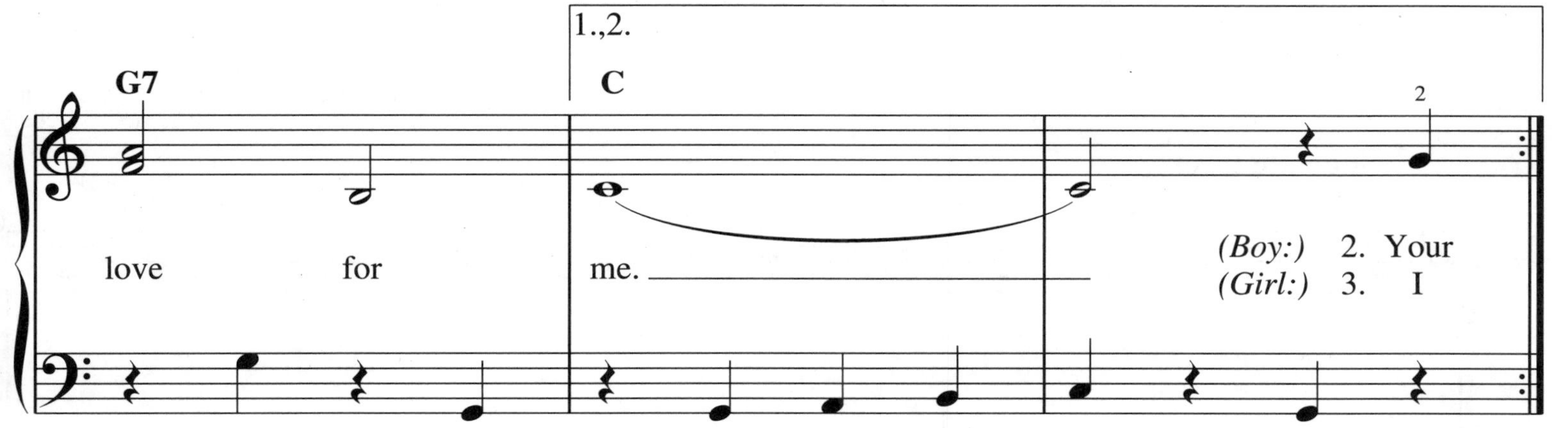

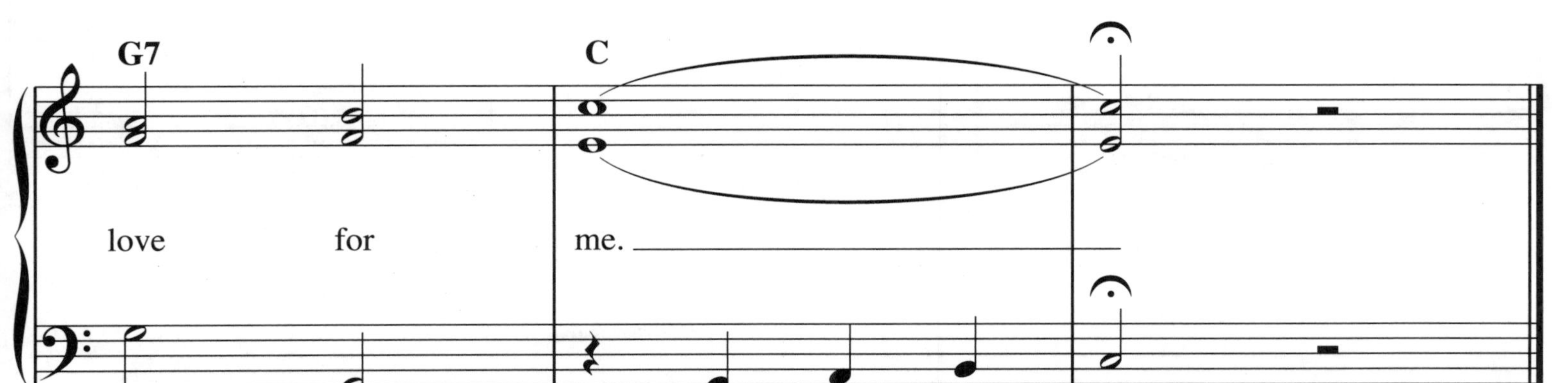

Additional Lyrics

3. I thought that you would be a perfect lover,
you seemed so full of sweetness as the start.
But like a big red rose that's made of paper,
there isn't any sweetness in your heart.

PLEASE PLEASE ME

Words and Music by JOHN LENNON
and PAUL McCARTNEY

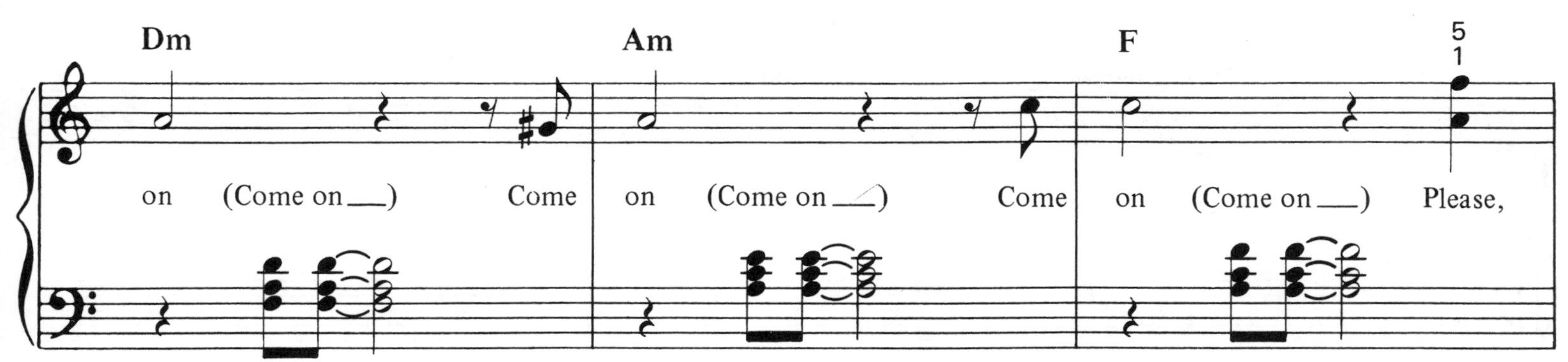
Dm
Am
F
5
1
on (Come on __) Come on (Come on __) Come on (Come on __) Please,

C
5
1
Last time
To Coda
F
3
1
G
C
5
please me, wo yeah, like I please you.

1.
2.
F
3
I don't want to sound com-plain-ing

G7
C
but you know there's al - ways rain in my ___ heart.

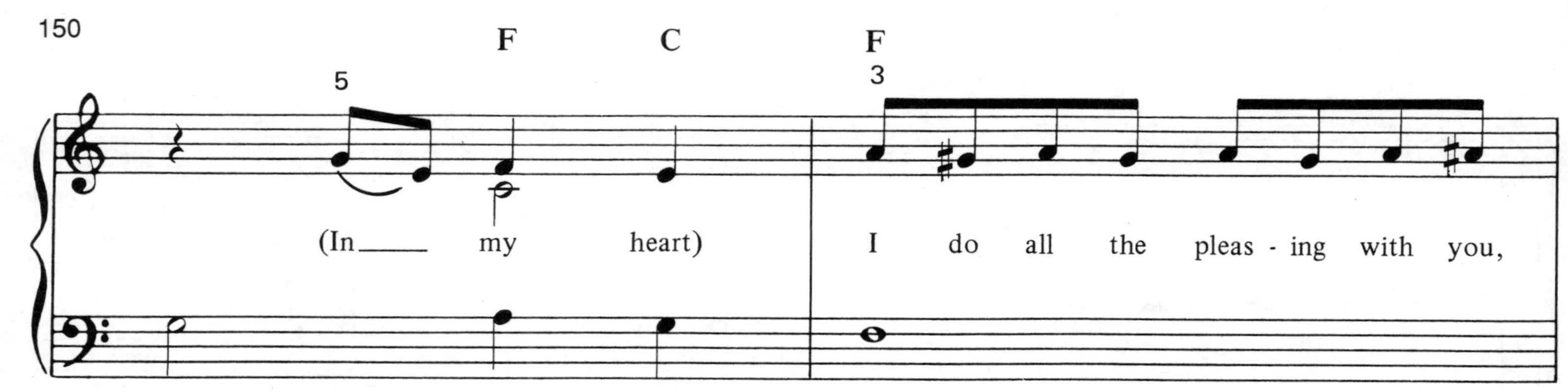
F
C
F
5
3
(In__ my heart)
I do all the pleas - ing with you,

G7
C
F
G
4
it's so hard to rea - son with
you, wo
yeah, why do you make me

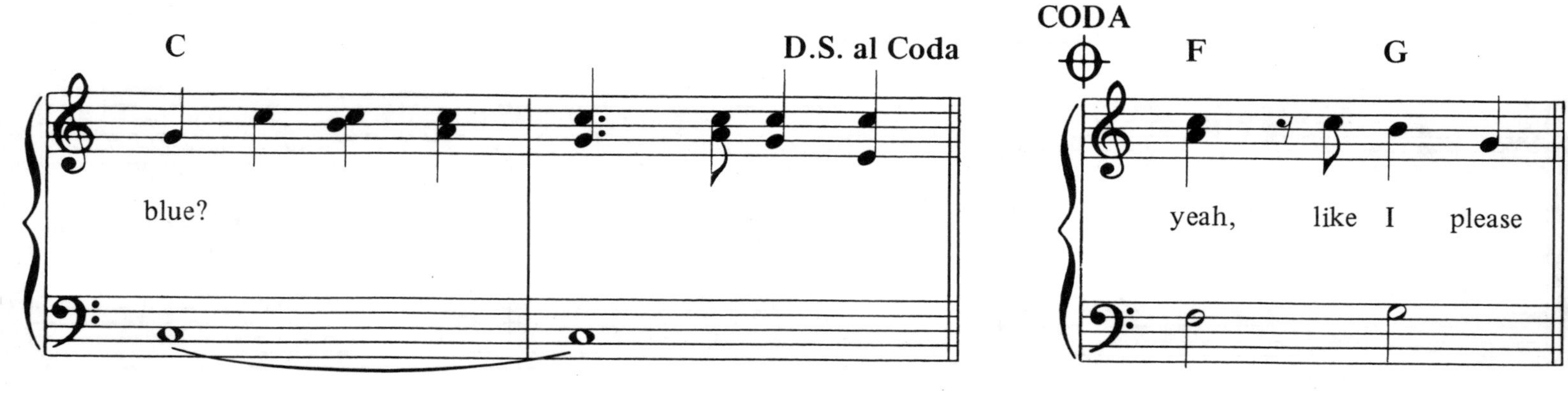
C
D.S. al Coda
CODA
F
G
blue?
yeah, like I please

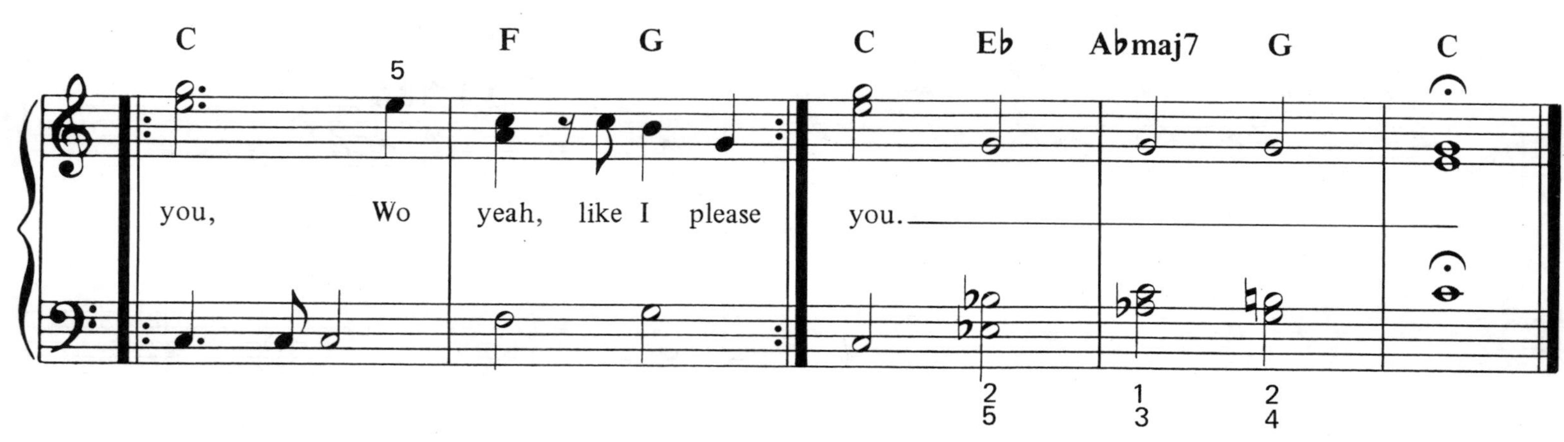
C
F
G
C
E♭
A♭maj7
G
C
5
you, Wo
yeah, like I please
you.

STRANGERS IN THE NIGHT

Moderately slow

Words by CHARLES SINGLETON and EDDIE SNYDER
Music by BERT KAEMPFERT

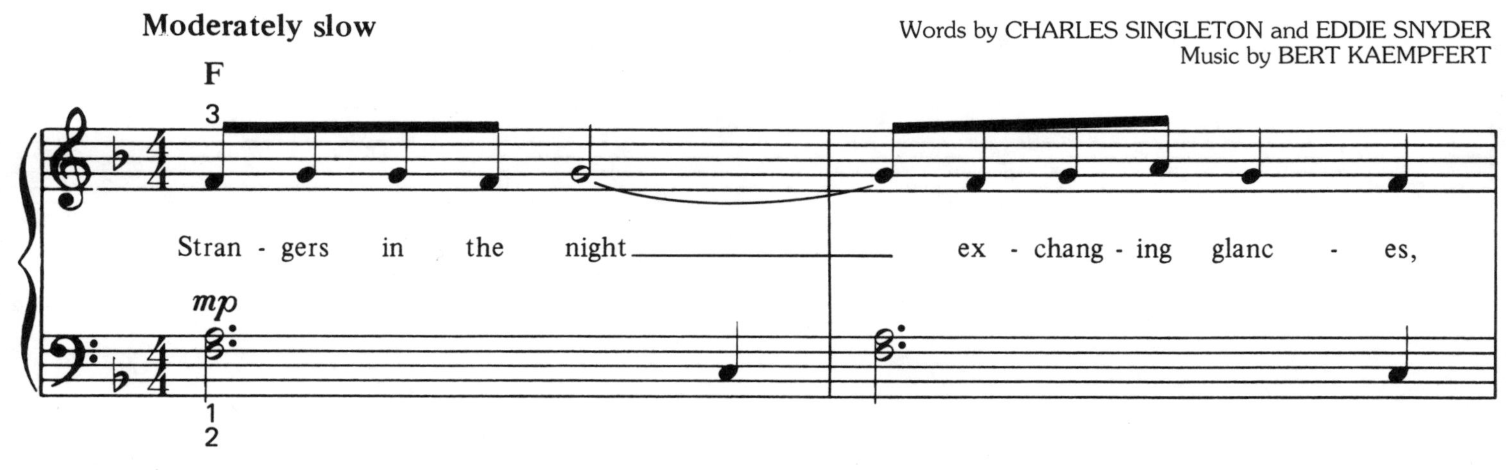

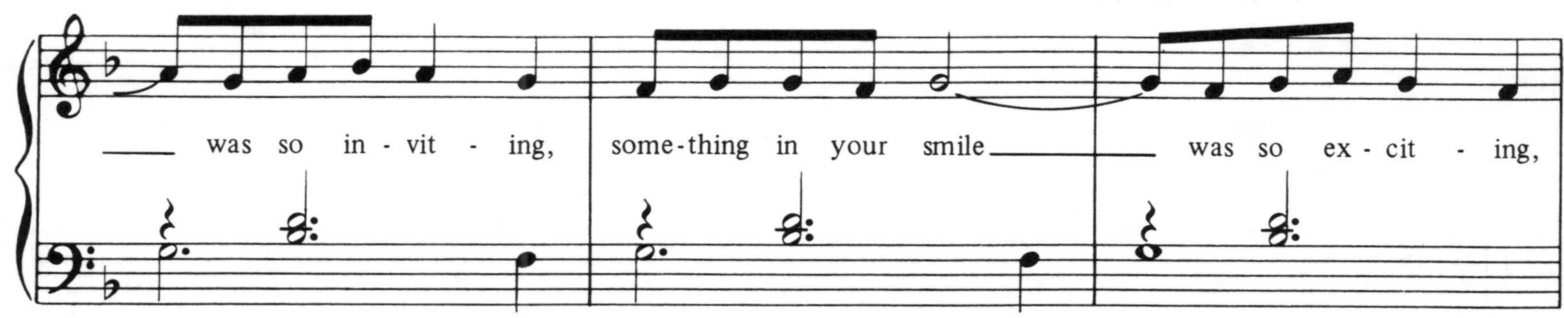
was so in - vit - ing,
some-thing in your smile
was so ex - cit - ing,

C9
3
1
F
some-thing in my heart
told me I must have
you.

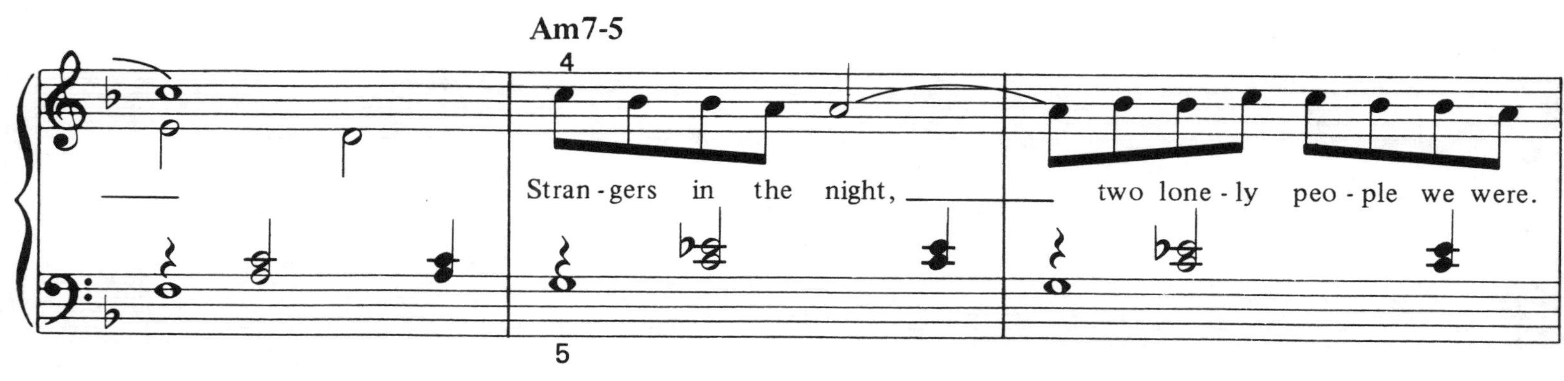
Am7-5
4
Stran - gers in the night,
two lone - ly peo - ple we were.
5

D7
Stran - gers in the night
up to the mo - ment when we

Gm
Bbm
F/C
Dm7
said our first hel - lo.
Lit - tle did we know
love was just a glance a - way, a

Gm
C7
F
warm em - brac - ing dance a - way, And
ev - er since that night
we've been to - geth - er,

C7
lov - ers at first sight
in love for - ev - er.
It turned out so right

F
for stran - gers in the
night.

SAN FRANCISCO

(Be Sure To Wear Some Flowers In Your Hair)

Words and Music by
JOHN PHILLIPS

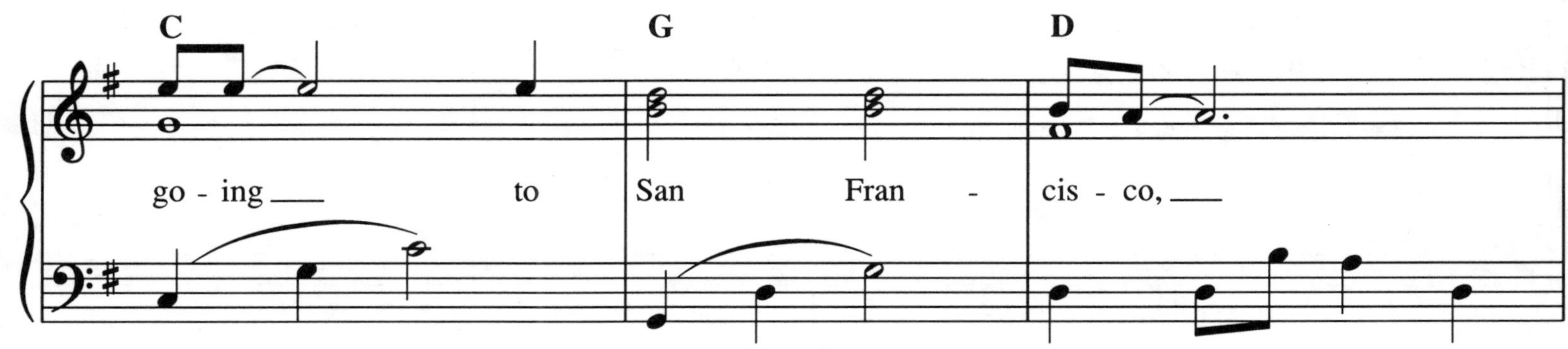

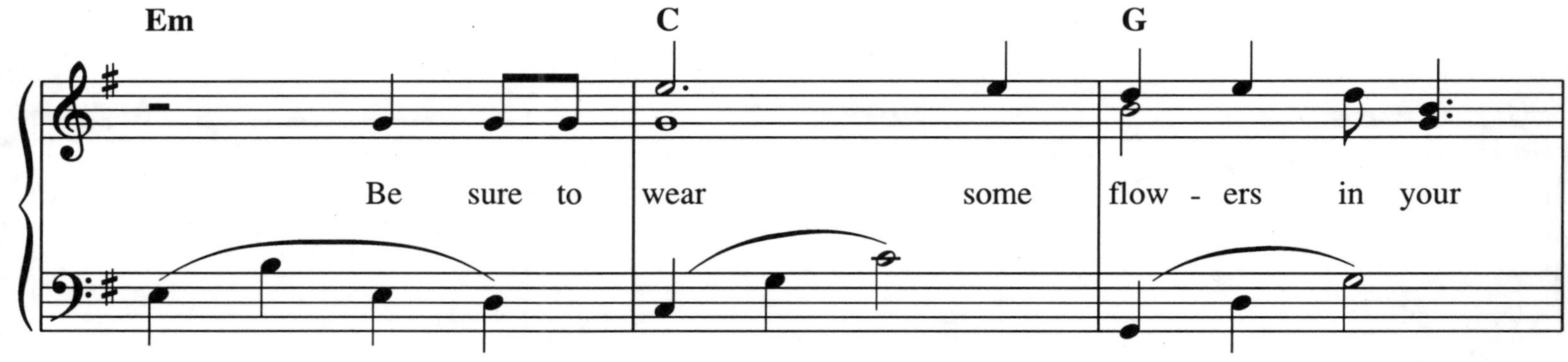

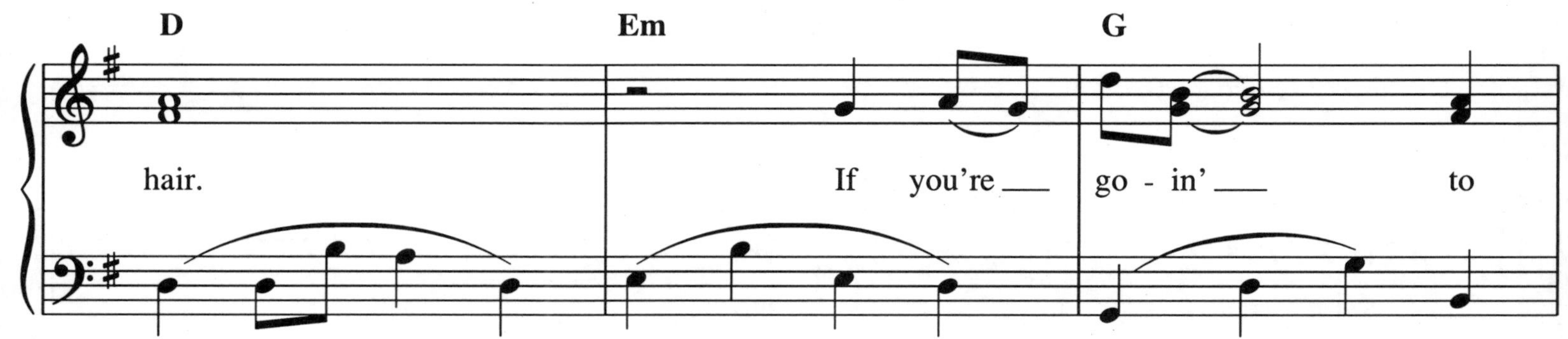

C
G
G6/D
3
San Fran - cis - co,
You're gon - na
Bm
Em7
D
meet some gen - tle peo - ple there.
Em
C
For those who come to
For those who come to
G
D
San Fran - cis - co,
San Fran - cis - co,

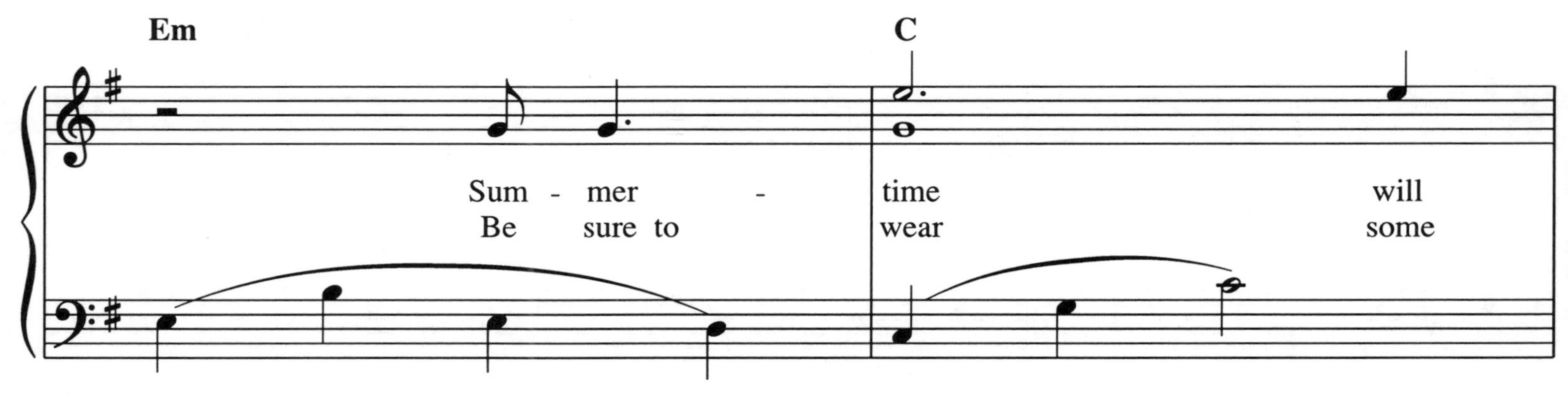
Em
C
Sum - mer - time will
Be sure to wear some

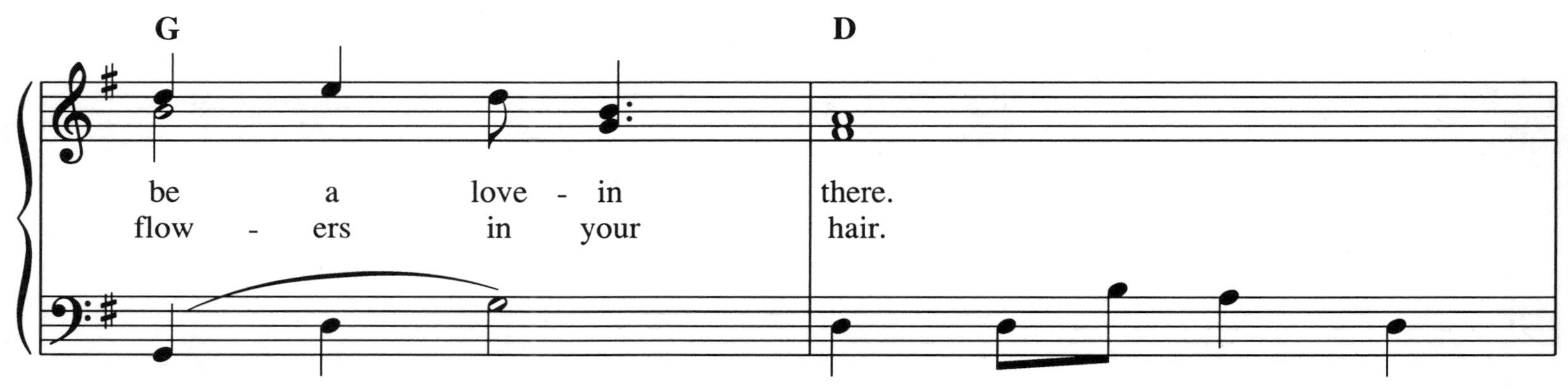
G
D
be a love - in there.
flow - ers in your hair.

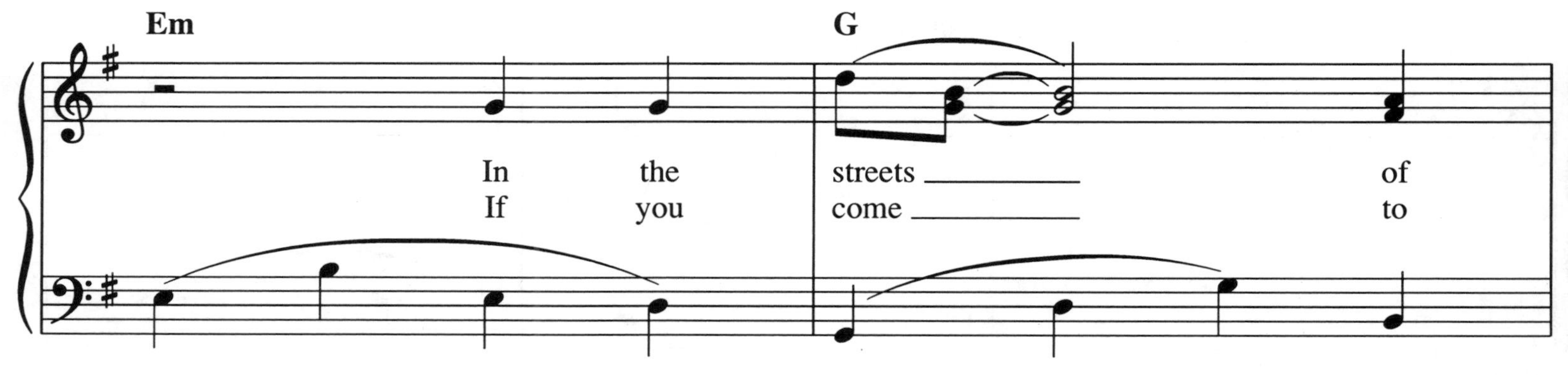
Em
G
In the streets of
If you come to

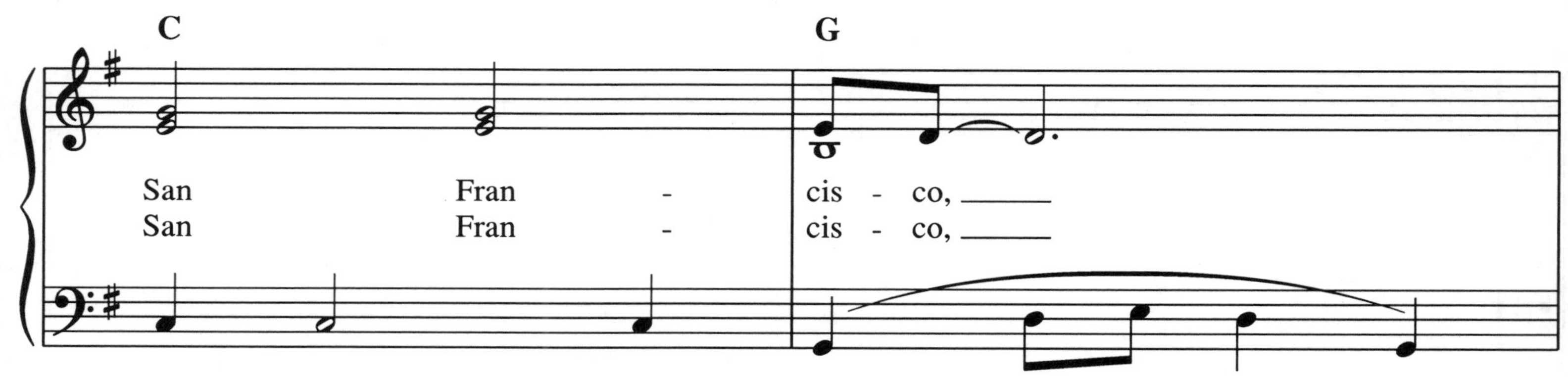
C
G
San Fran - cis - co,
San Fran - cis - co,

G6/D
Bm
Gen - tle
peo - ple
with
Sum - mer -
time
will
To Coda
Em7
D
flow - ers
in their
hair.
be a
love - in
F
Dm
F
All a - cross the
na - tion,
Such a strong vi -
Dm
G
bra - tion:
Peo - ple in
mo - tion.

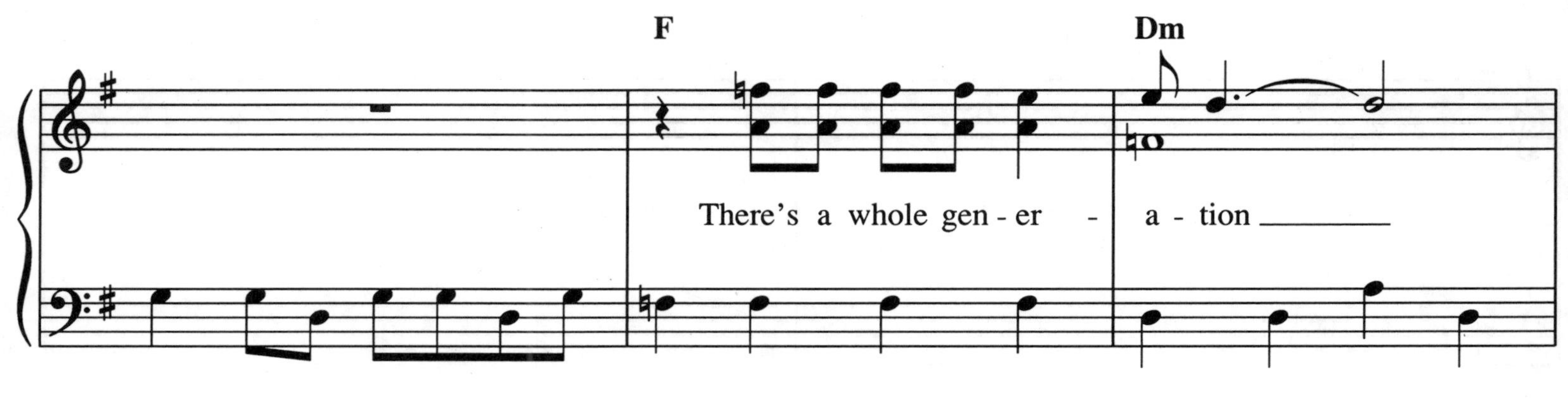
F
Dm
There's a whole gen - er - a - tion

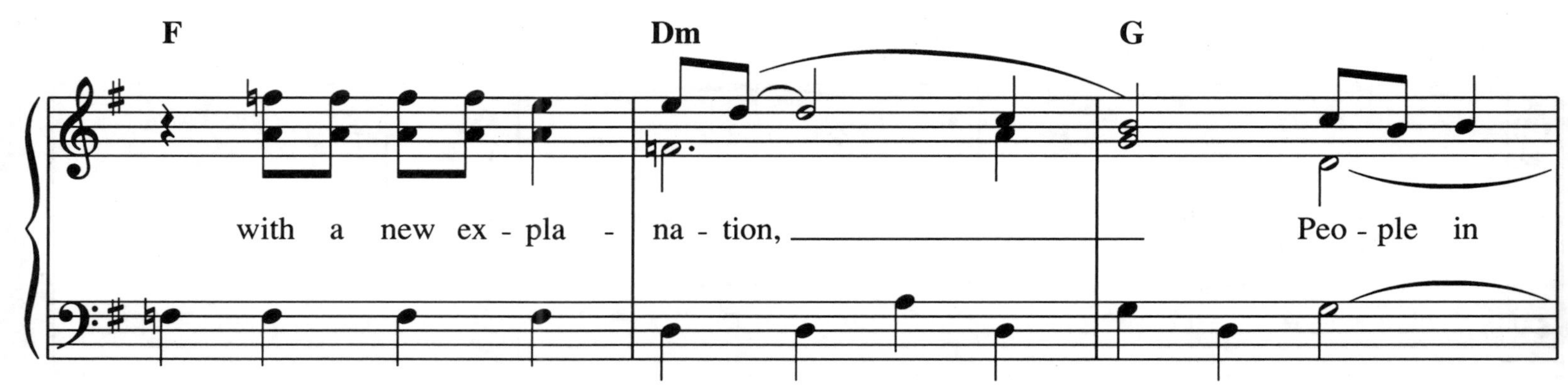
F
Dm
G
with a new ex - pla - na - tion,
Peo - ple in

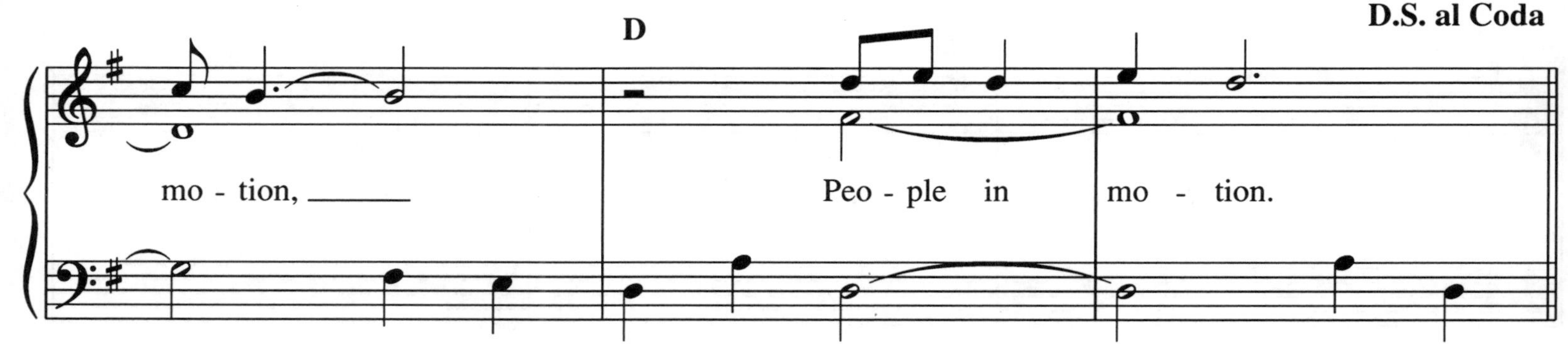
D
D.S. al Coda
mo - tion,
Peo - ple in mo - tion.

CODA
G
Em
there.

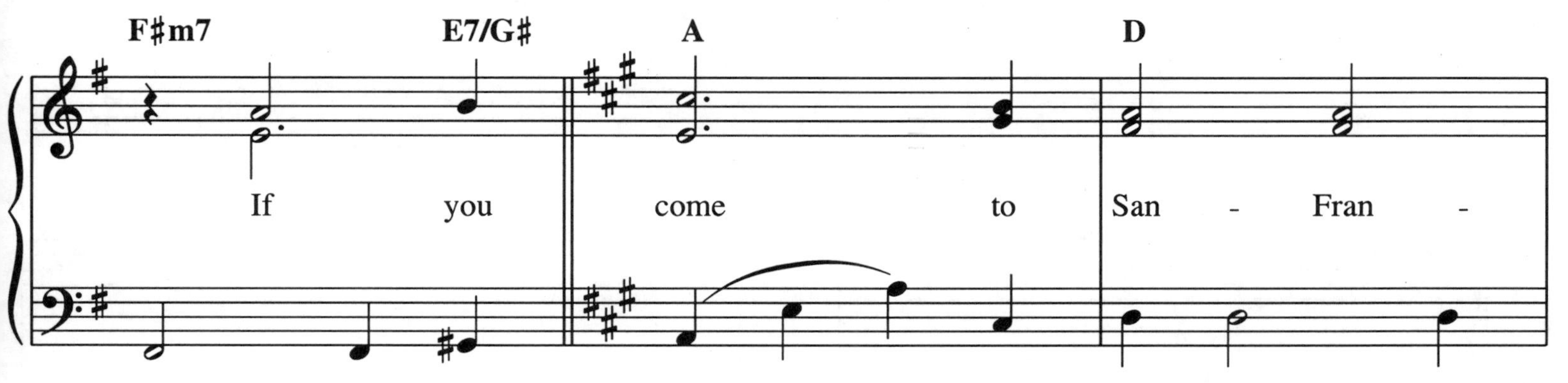
F♯m7
E7/G♯
A
D
If you come to San - Fran -

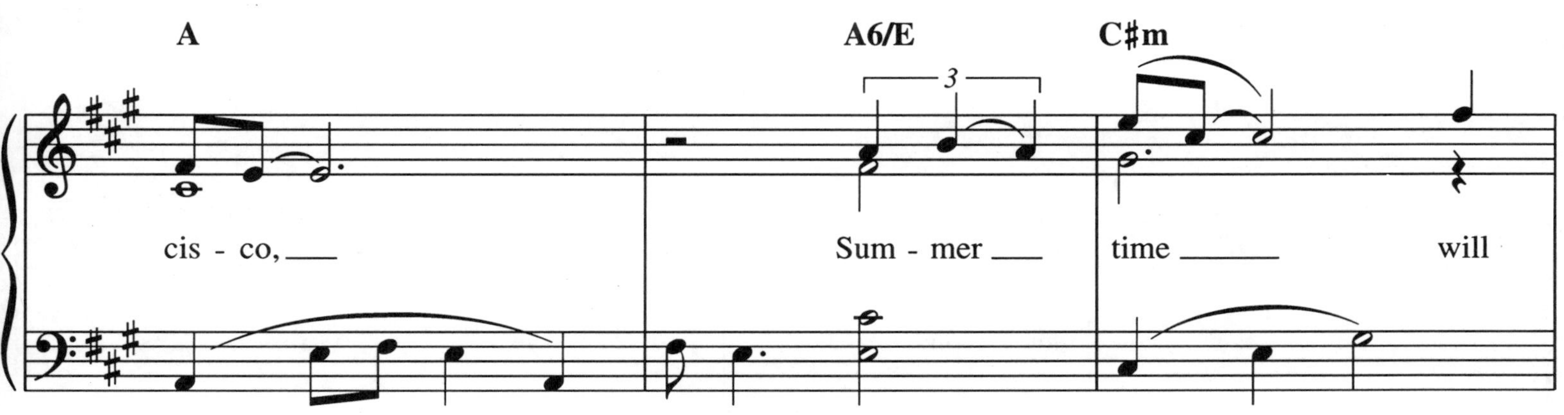
A
A6/E
C♯m
3
cis - co,
Sum - mer
time
will

F♯m7
E7
A
E
be a love - in
there.

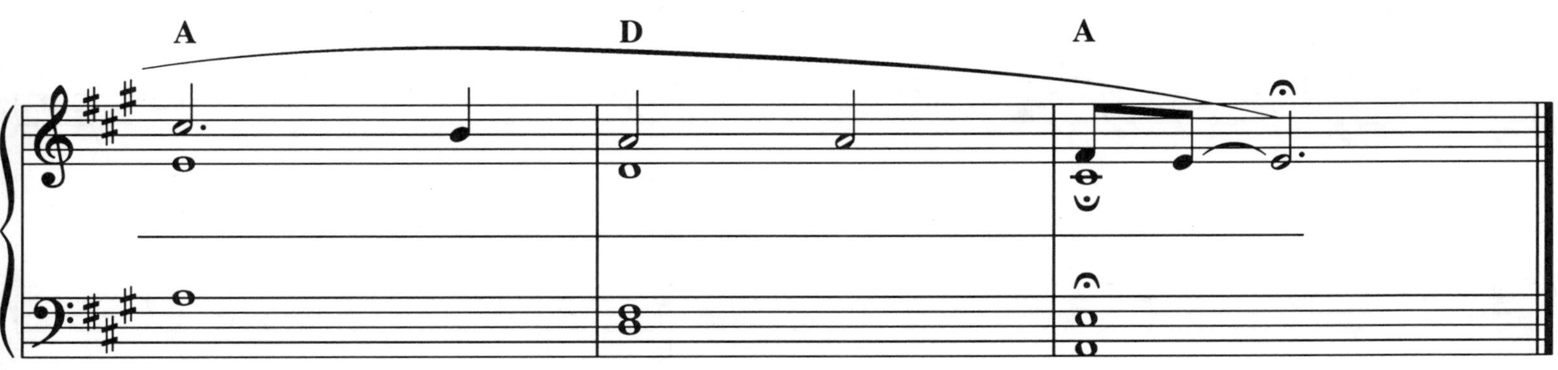
A
D
A

SHE LOVES YOU

Words and Music by JOHN LENNON
and PAUL McCARTNEY

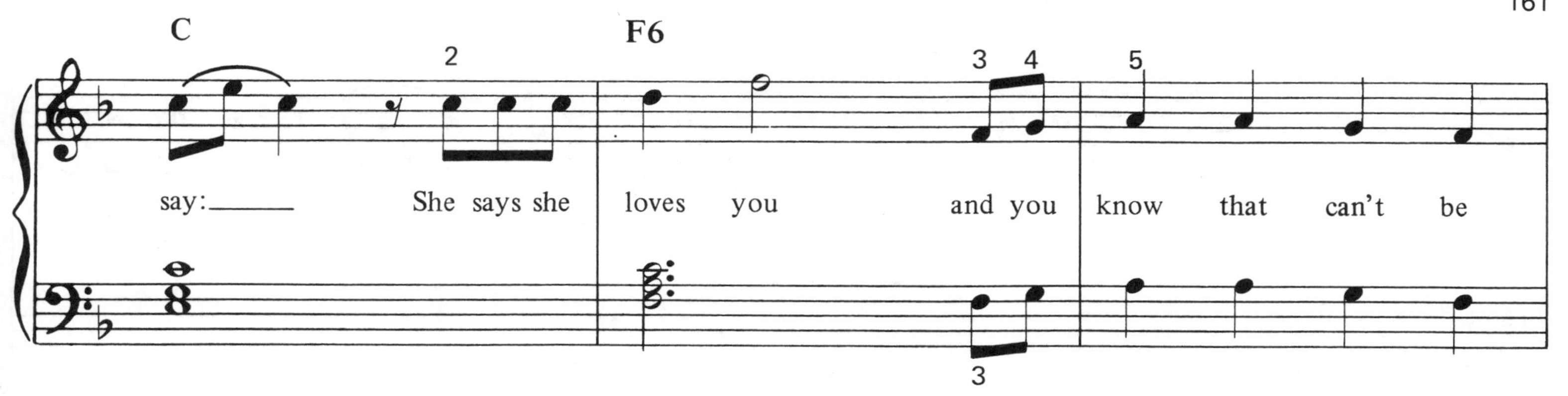
C
F6
say:
She says she
loves you
and you
know that can't be

Dm
B♭m
bad.
Yes, she
loves you
and you
know you should be

C
F
Dm7
glad.
She
said you hurt her
know it's up to
so,
you,
She
I

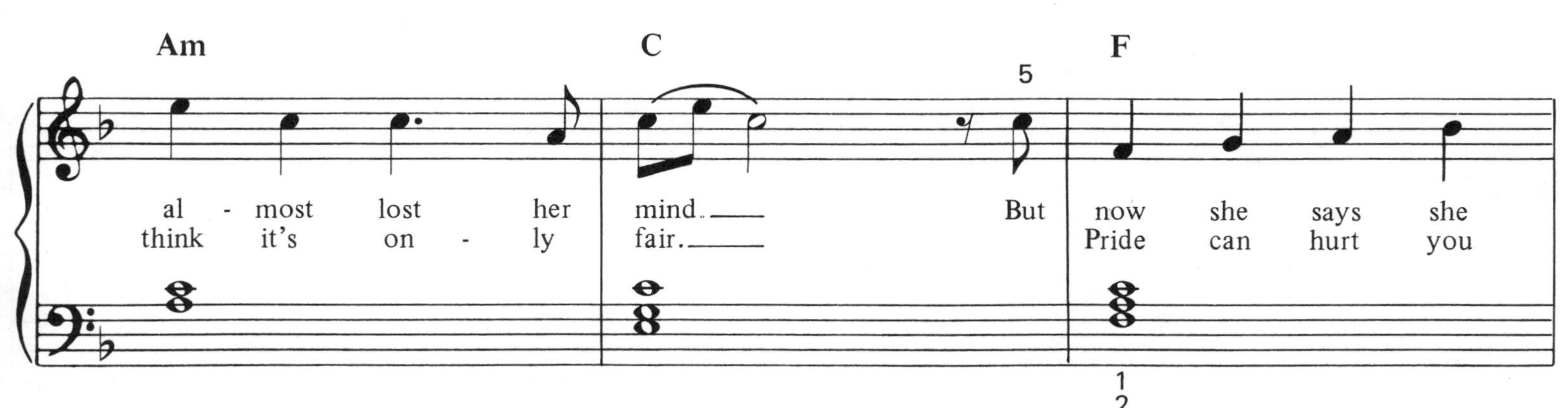
Am
C
F
al - most lost her
think it's on - ly
mind.
fair.
But
now she says she
Pride can hurt you

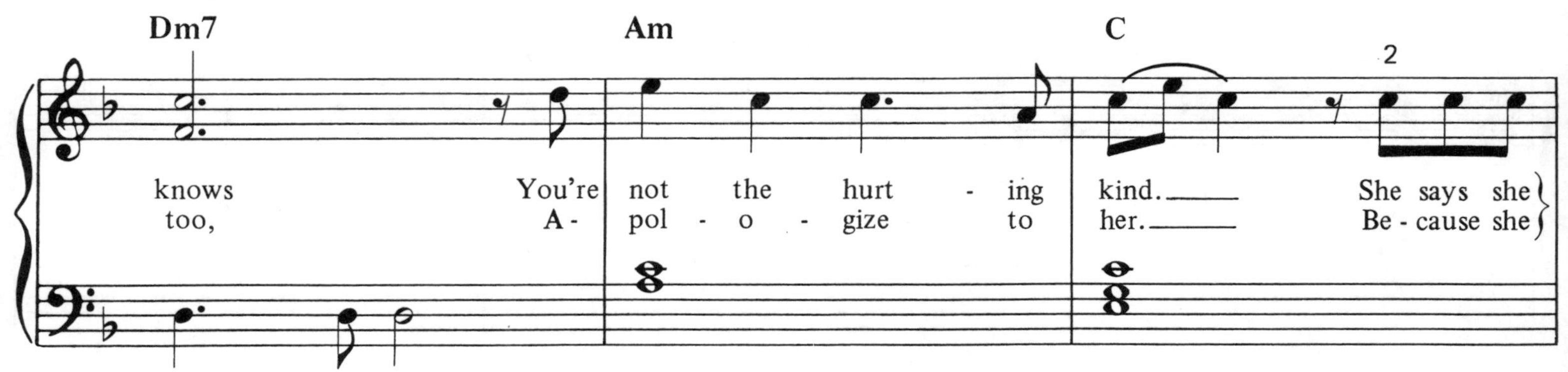
Dm7
Am
C
2
knows You're not the hurt - ing kind.___ She says she
too, A - pol - o - gize to her.___ Be - cause she

F6
Dm
3
loves you and you know that can't be bad. Yes, she
3

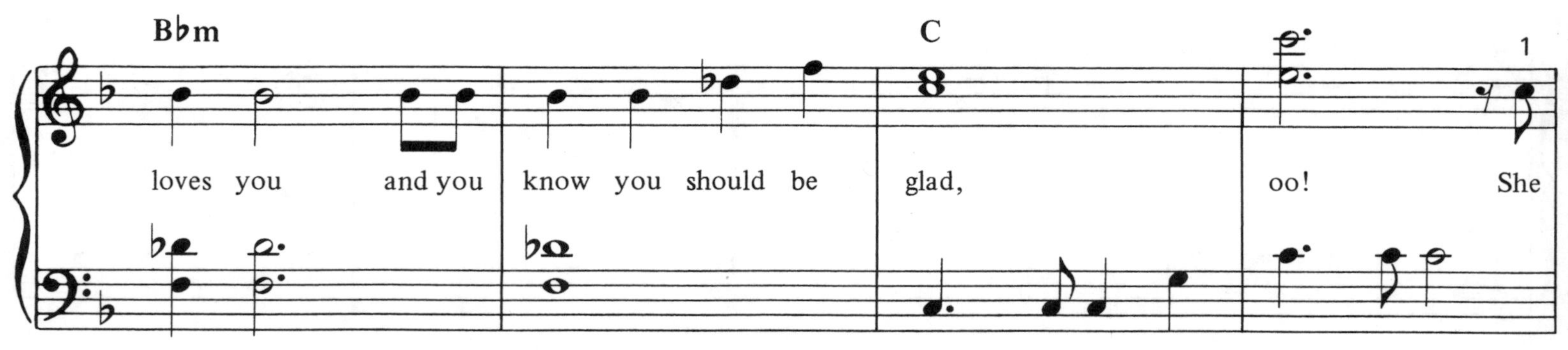
B♭m
C
1
loves you and you know you should be glad, oo! She

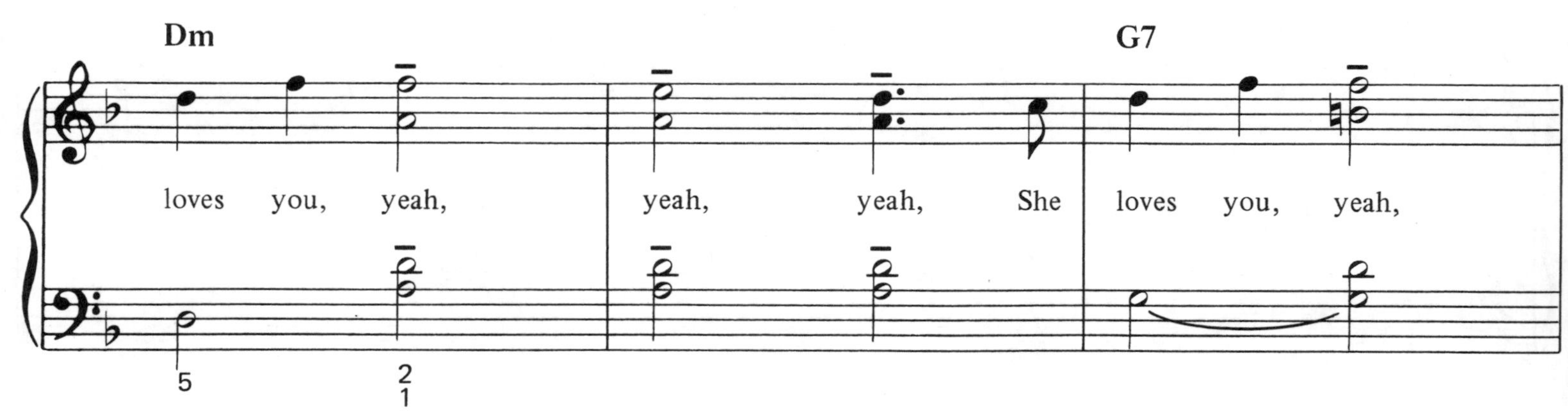
Dm
G7
loves you, yeah, yeah, yeah, She loves you, yeah,
5
2
1

Bbm
C+
yeah, yeah. And with a love like that you know you should be

1. F
2. F
glad. You glad, With a

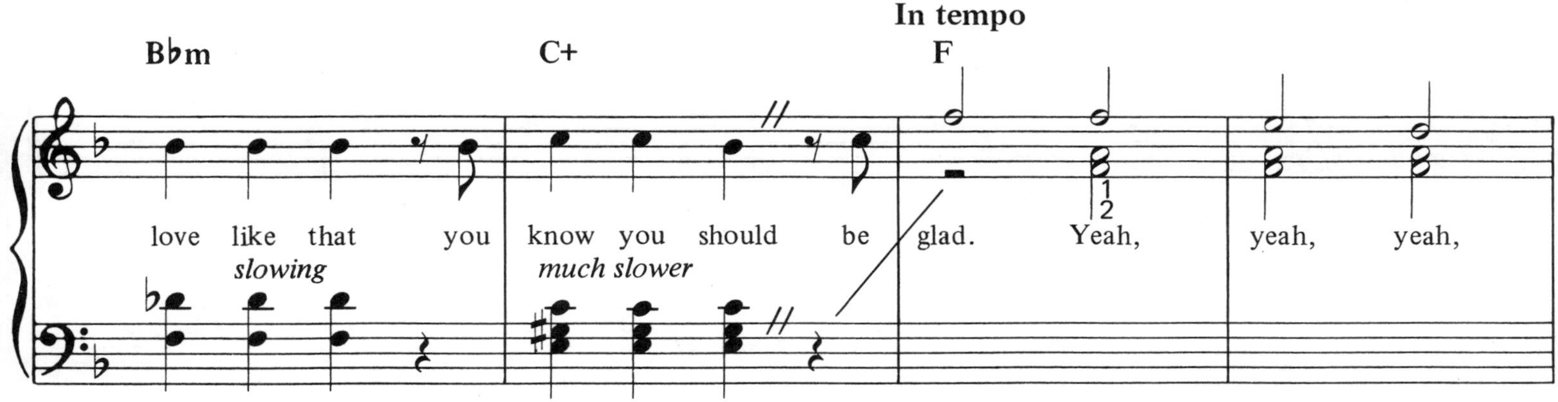
In tempo
Bbm
C+
F
love like that you know you should be glad. Yeah, yeah, yeah,
slowing
much slower

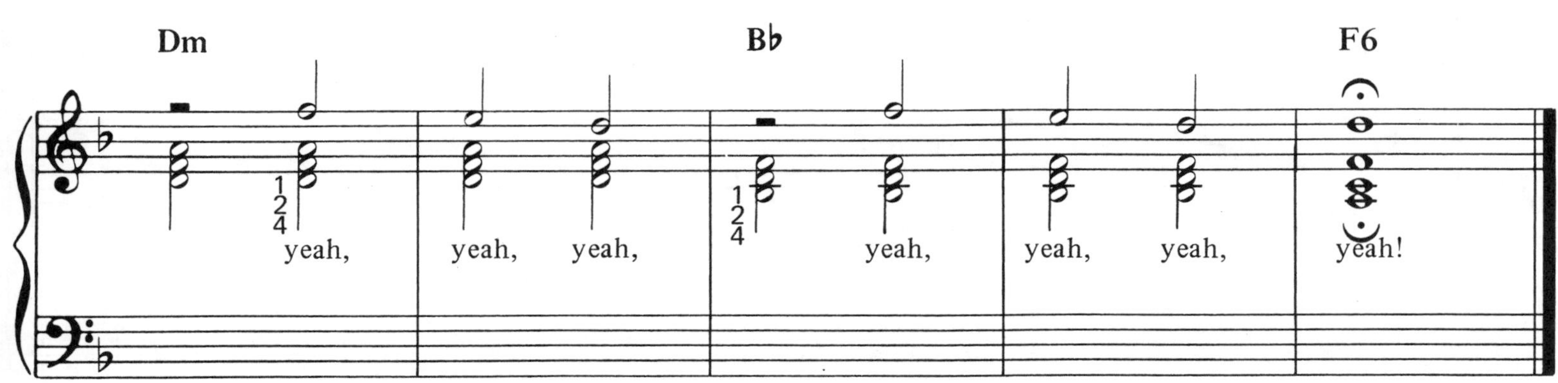
Dm
Bb
F6
yeah, yeah, yeah, yeah, yeah, yeah, yeah!

THAT'S LIFE

Words and Music by DEAN KAY
and KELLY GORDON

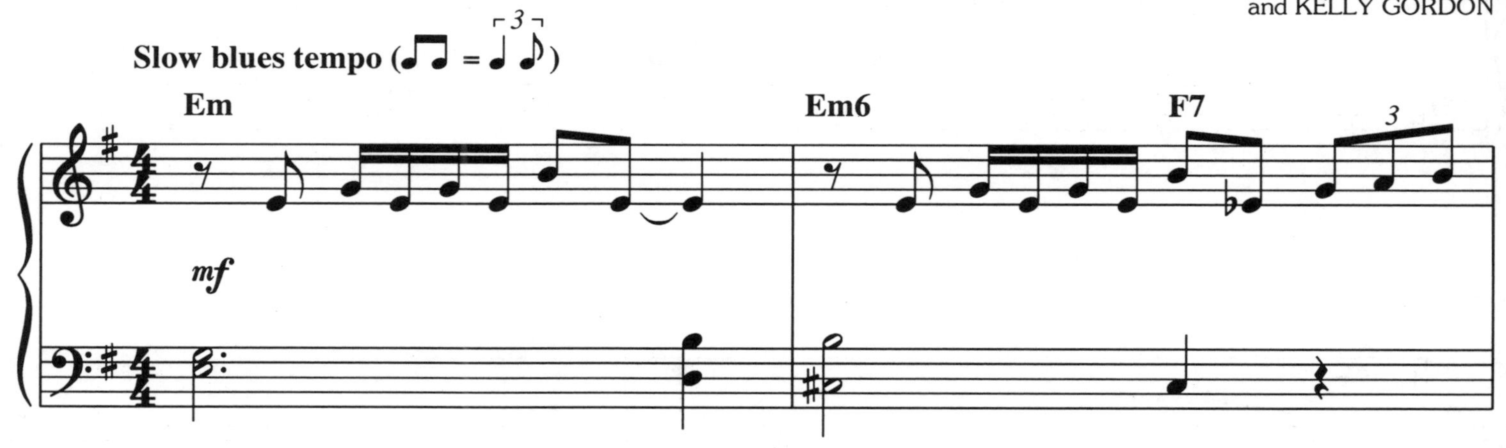

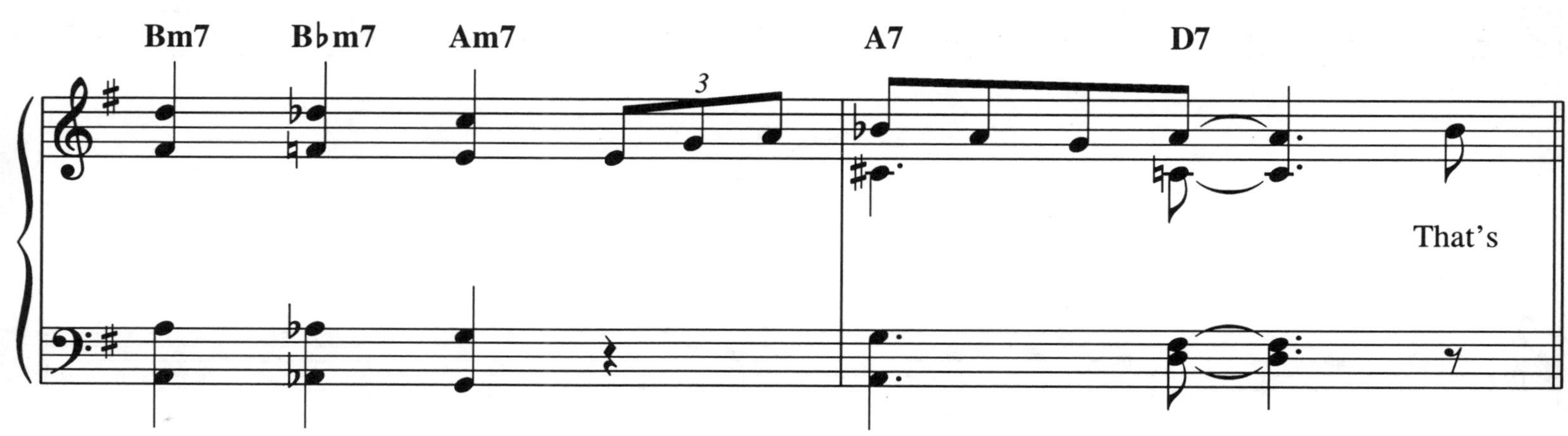

Em
B♭7
A7
Cm6
You're rid - in' high in A - pril,
Shot down in May; But I
G/D
Cmaj7
B7(♯5)
Em
Em6
know I'm gon - na change that tune, When I'm
A9
Am7
D7
G
back on top in June. That's life,
B7
Em
B♭7
Fun - ny as it seems,
Some peo - ple get their kicks

A7
Gmaj7
F#m7
F7
step - pin' on dreams; But I don't let it get me
Em
Em6
Am7
A7
D7
down, 'Cause this ol' world keeps go - ing a -
G
G7
round. I've been a pup-pet, a pau-per, a pi - rate, a po - et, a
C6
pawn and a king. I've been up and down and o - ver and out And

Bb7
A13
I know one thing;
Each time I find my - self
flat on my face,
I
D7
pick my - self up and get
D7(#5)
G
back in the race.
That's
life
B7
I can't de - ny it,
Em
I thought of quit - ting, but my

A7
Gmaj7
F♯m7
F7
heart just won't buy it. If I
did - n't think it was worth a
Em
Em6
A7
D7
try,
I'd
roll my - self up in a big ball and
1.
G
F9
A7
D7
die.
That's
2.
G
C7
D7(♯9)
G13(♯11)
die.
rit.

THINGS

Words and Music by
BOBBY DARIN

Moderately

F

p

F

Ev - 'ry night I sit here by the win - dow (win - dow.)
Mem - o - ries are all I have to cling to (cling to) And

mf

Star - ing at the lone - ly av - e -
heart - aches are the friends I'm talk - ing

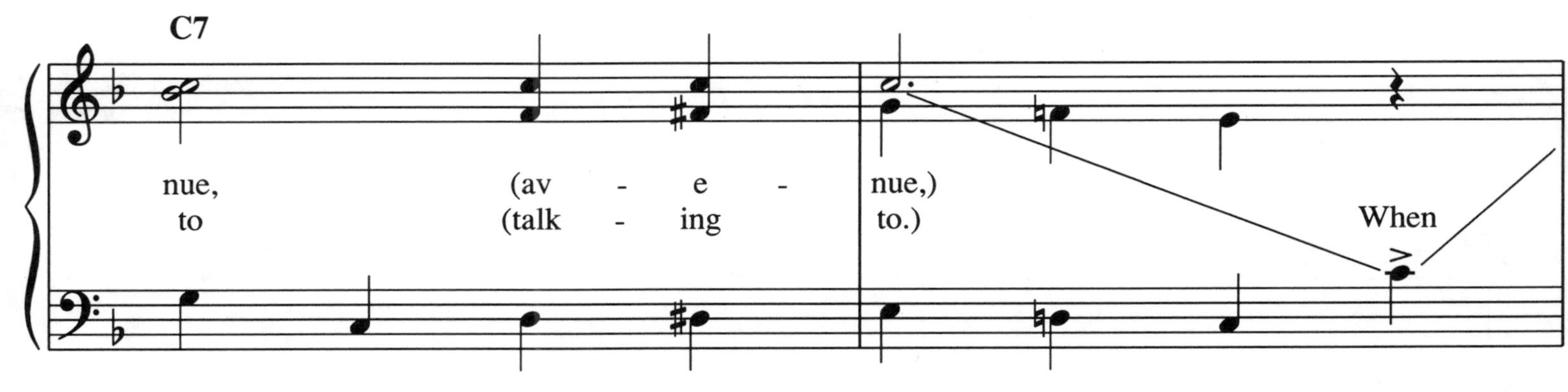
C7
nue, (av - e - nue,)
to (talk - ing to.) When

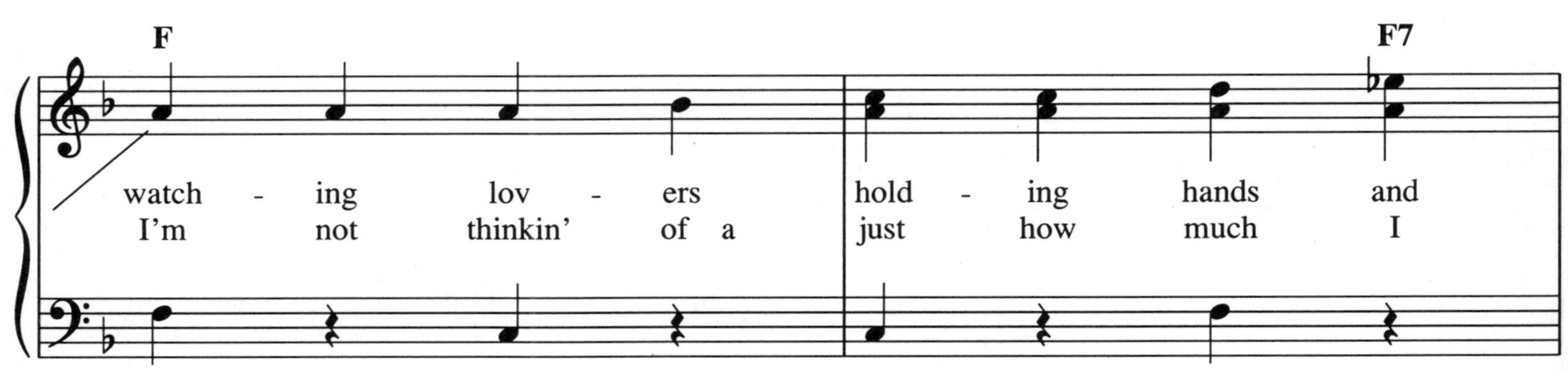
F
F7
watch - ing lov - ers hold - ing hands and
I'm not thinkin' of a just how much I

B♭
laugh - ing (laugh - ing) And
love you, (love you,) Well, I'm

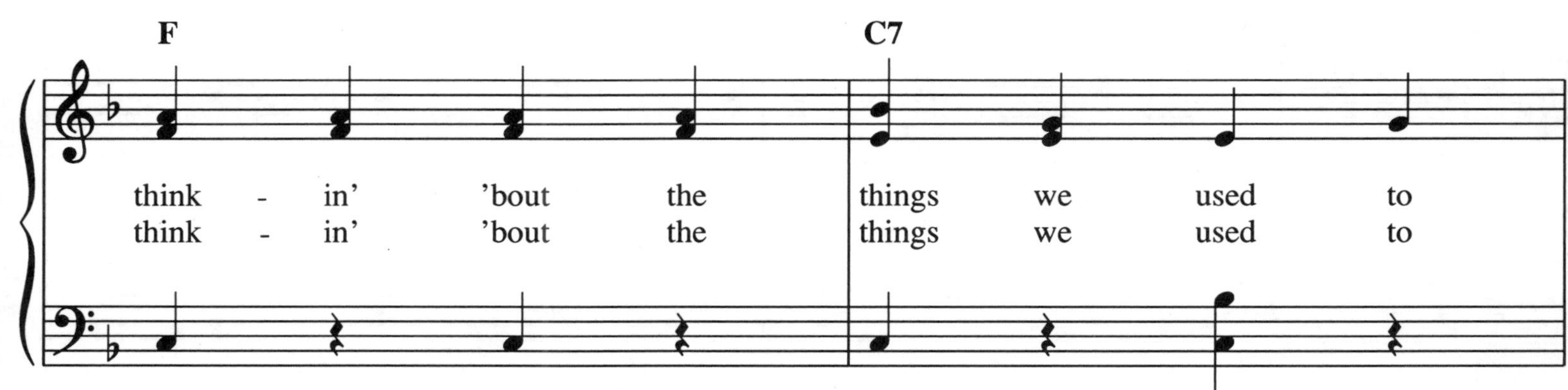
F
C7
think - in' 'bout the things we used to
think - in' 'bout the things we used to

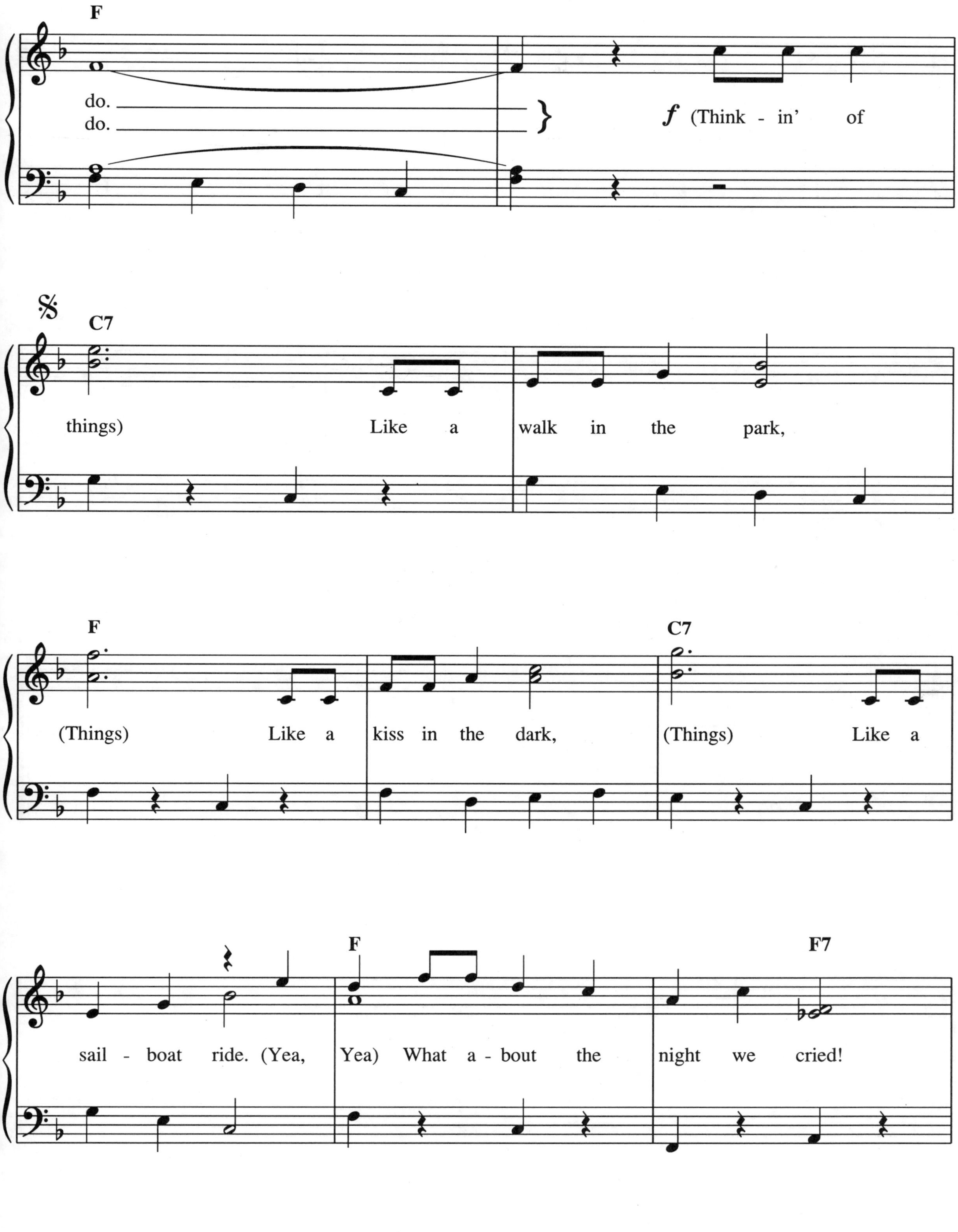

F

do. ______________________
do. ______________________ }

f (Think - in' of

C7

things) Like a walk in the park,

F

(Things) Like a kiss in the dark,

C7

(Things) Like a

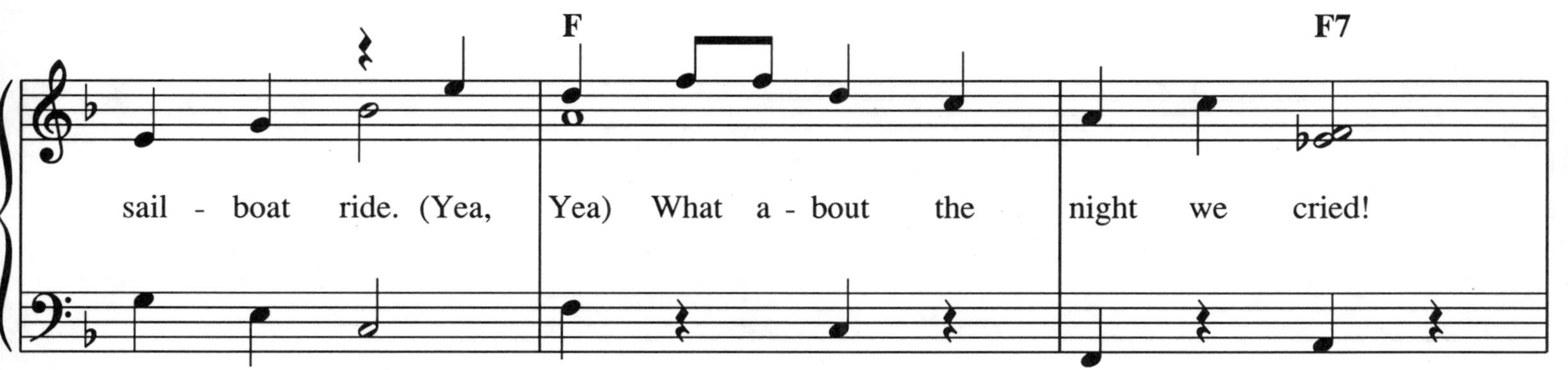

B♭
F
Things like a lov - er's vow, Things that we

Gm7
C7
To Coda
don't do now, Think - in' 'bout the things we used to

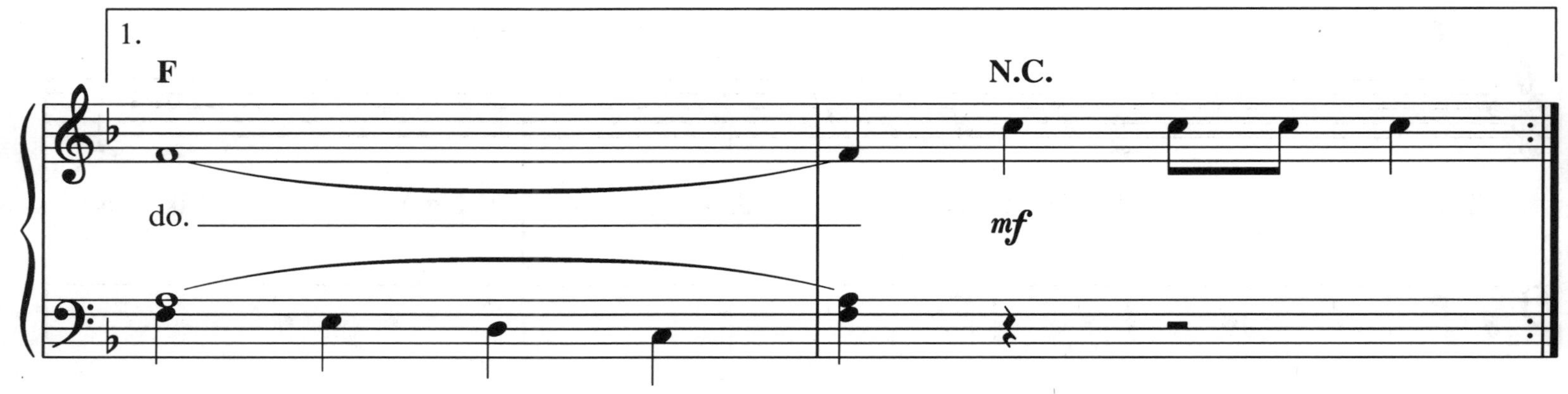
1.
F
N.C.
do.
mf

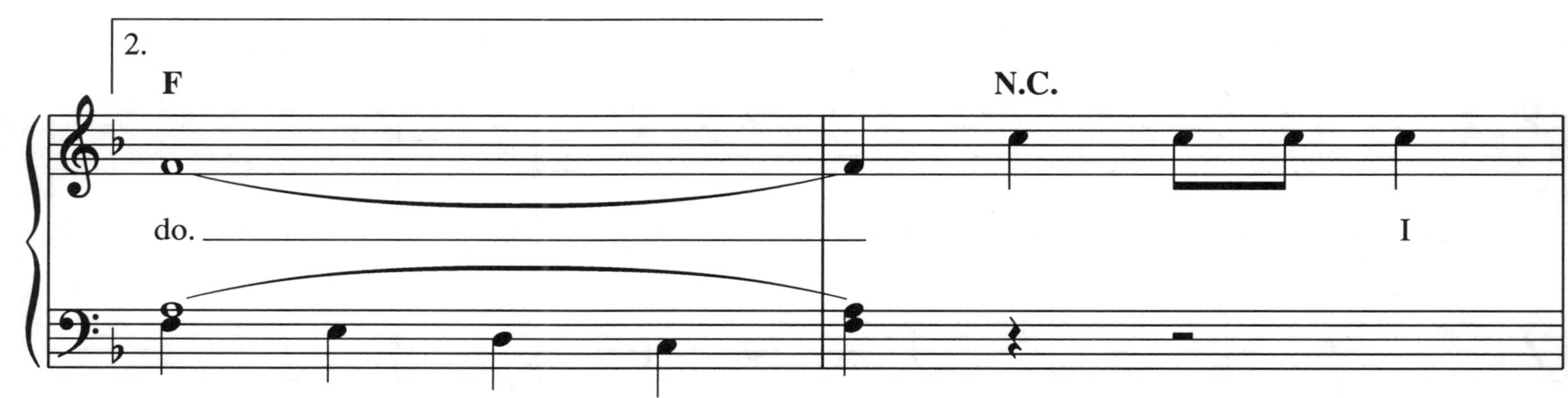
2.
F
N.C.
do.
I

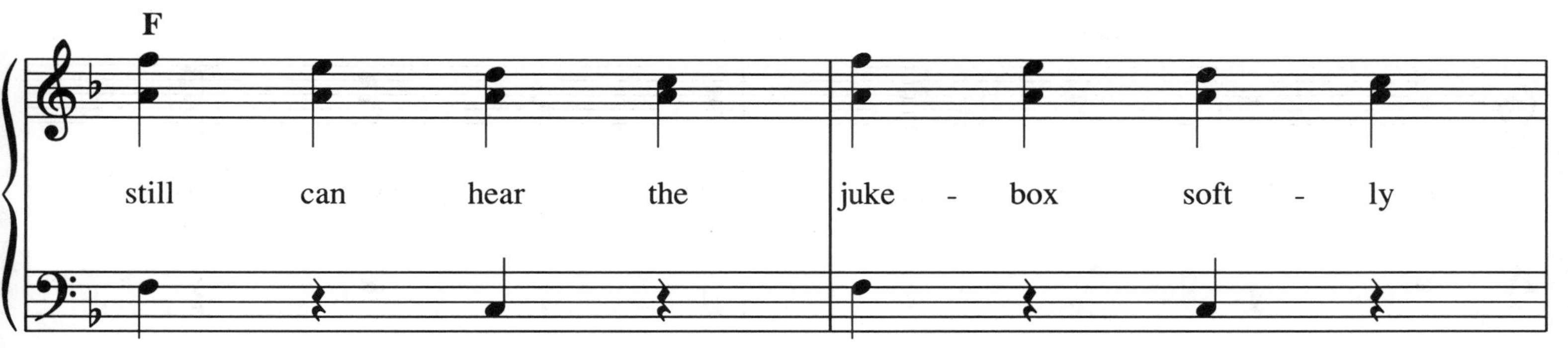
F
still can hear the juke - box soft - ly

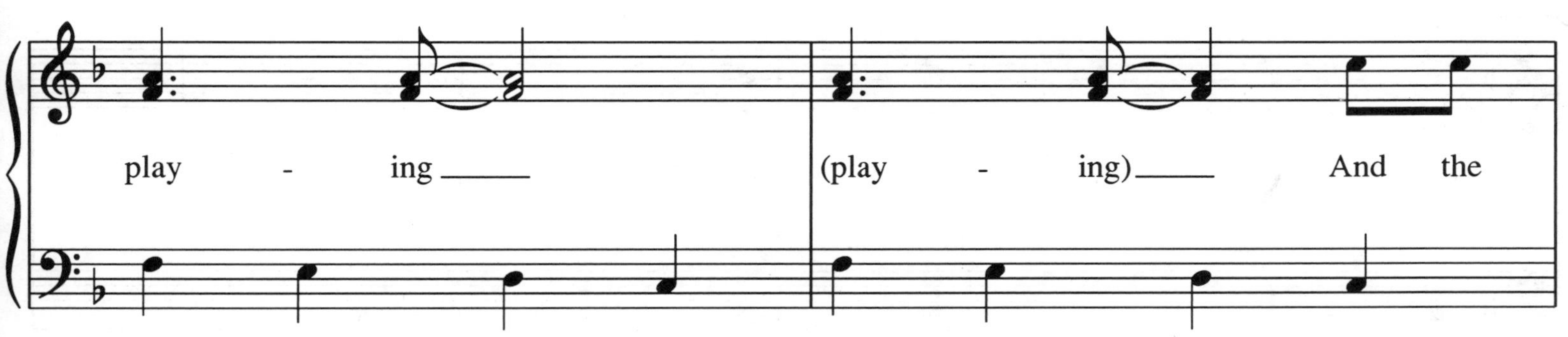
play - ing
(play - ing) And the

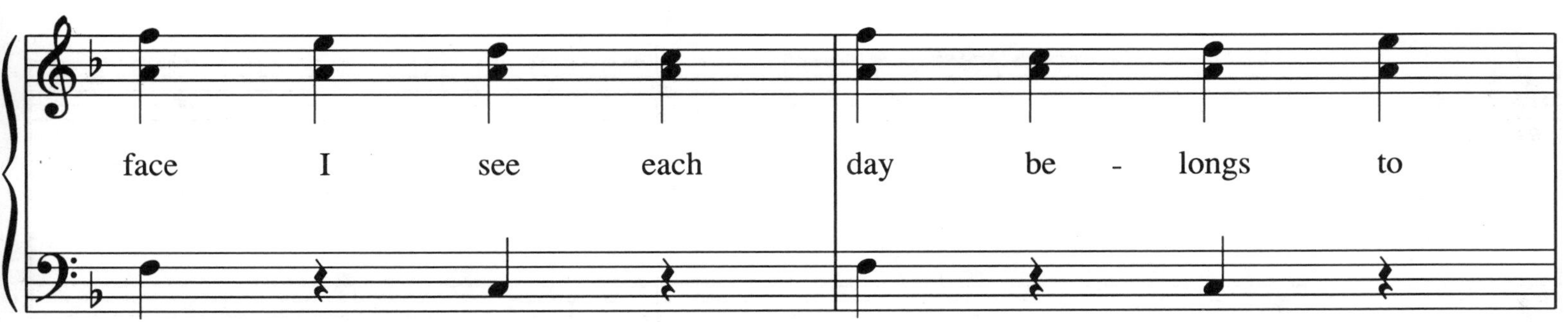
face I see each day be - longs to

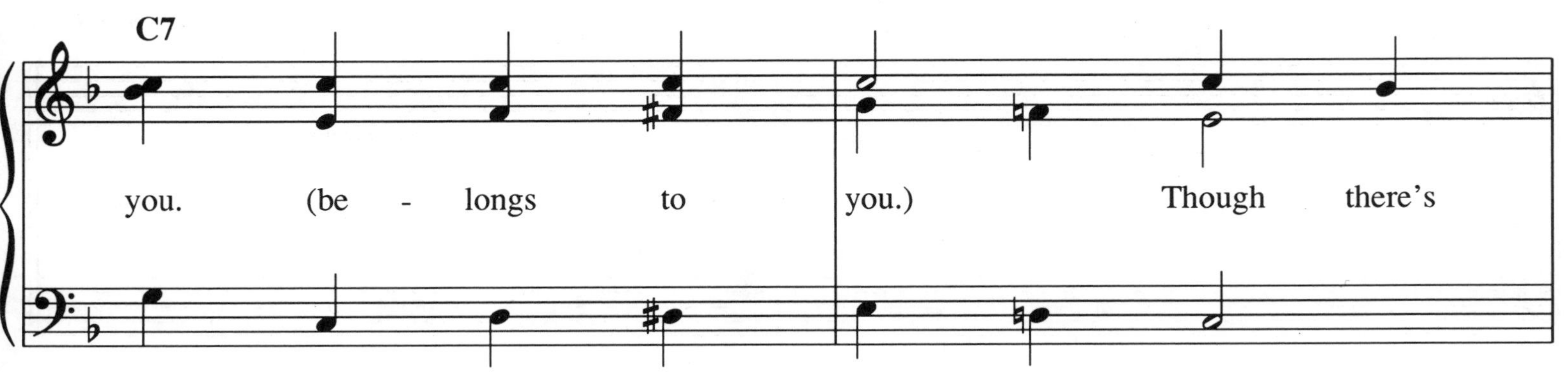
C7
you. (be - longs to you.) Though there's

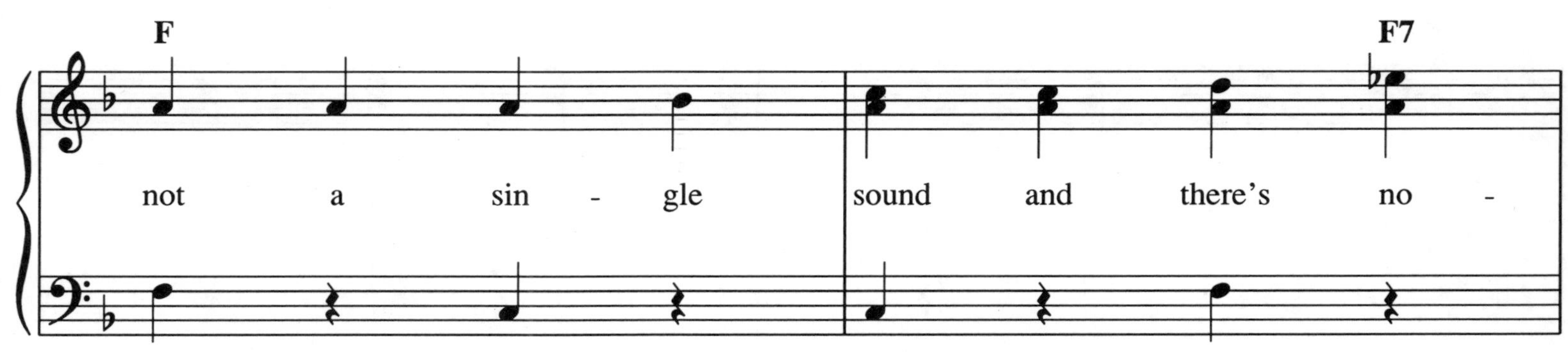
F
F7
not a sin - gle
sound and there's no -

B♭
bod - y else a -
round, well, there's a -

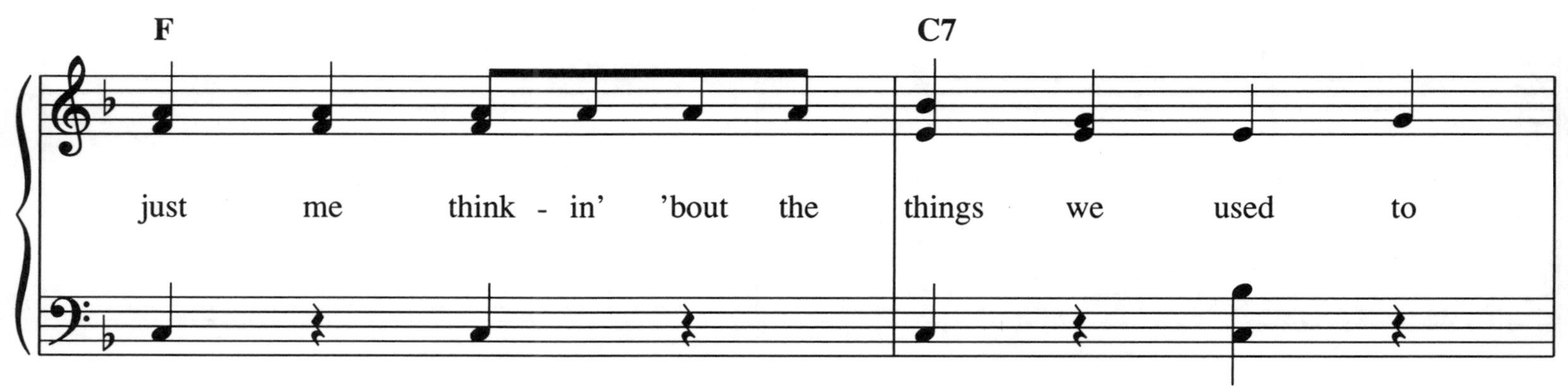
F
C7
just me think - in' 'bout the
things we used to

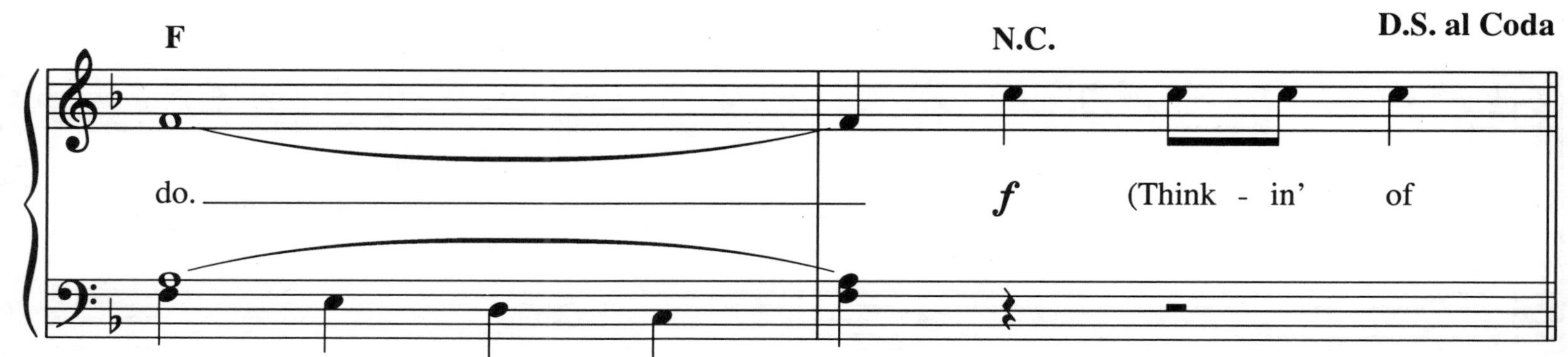
F
N.C.
D.S. al Coda
do.
f
(Think - in' of

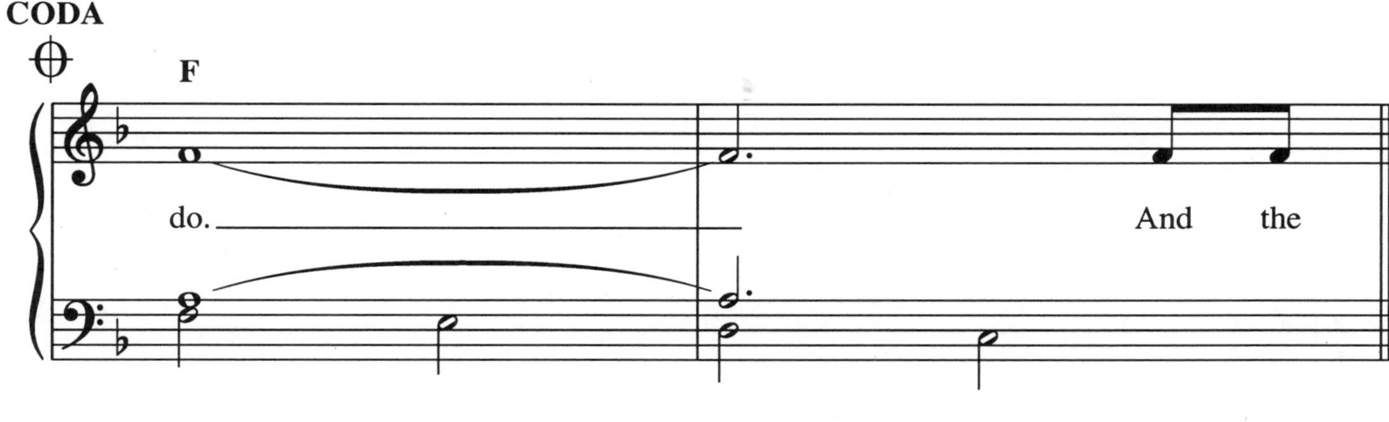
CODA
F
do.
And the

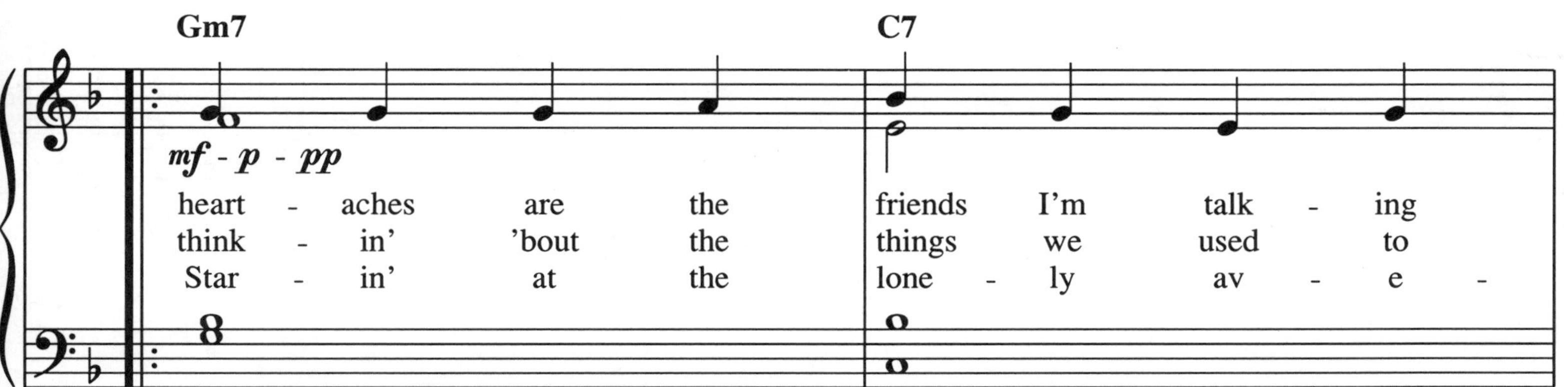
Gm7
C7
mf - p - pp
heart - aches are the friends I'm talk - ing
think - in' 'bout the things we used to
Star - in' at the lone - ly av - e -

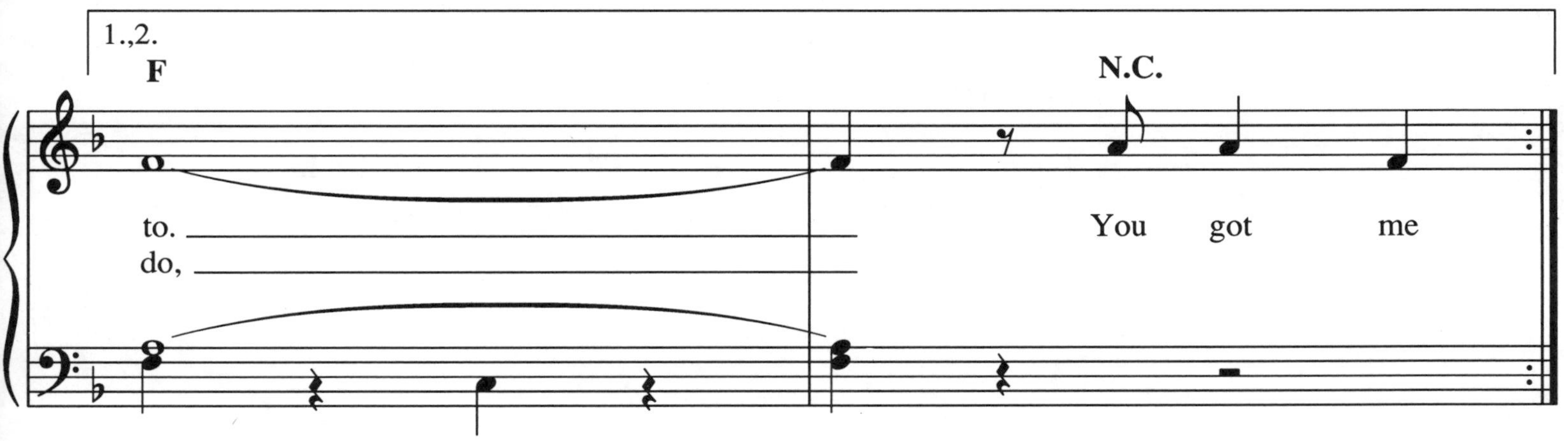
1.,2.
F
N.C.
to.
do,
You got me

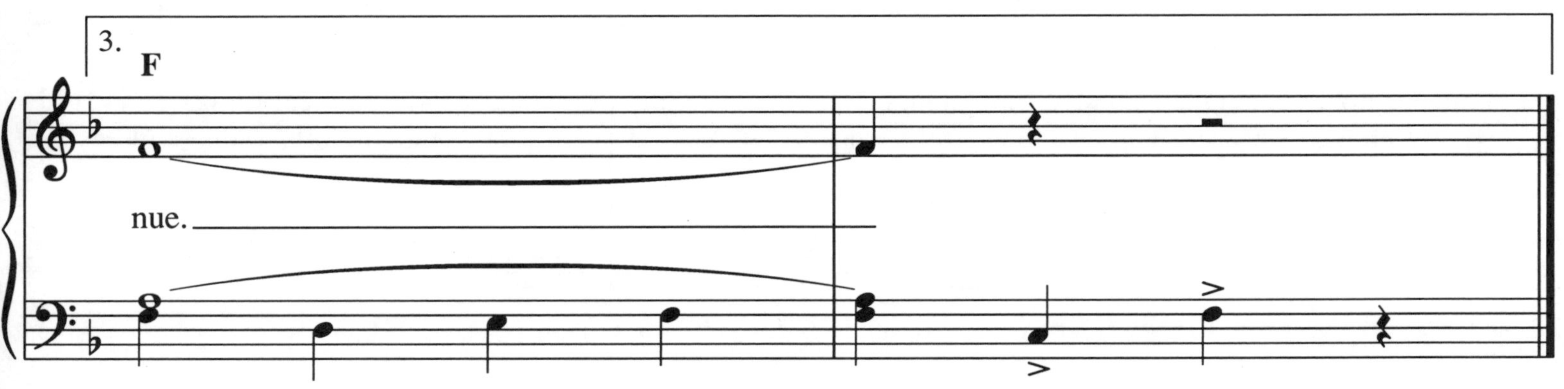
3.
F
nue.

THOSE WERE THE DAYS

Words and Music by
GENE RASKIN

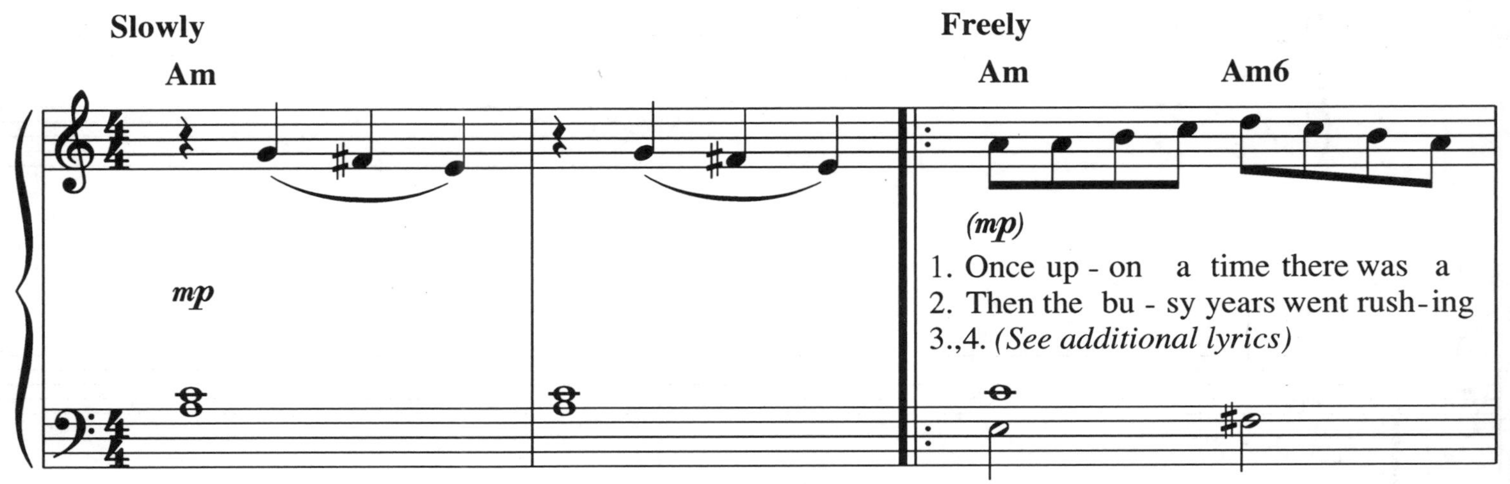

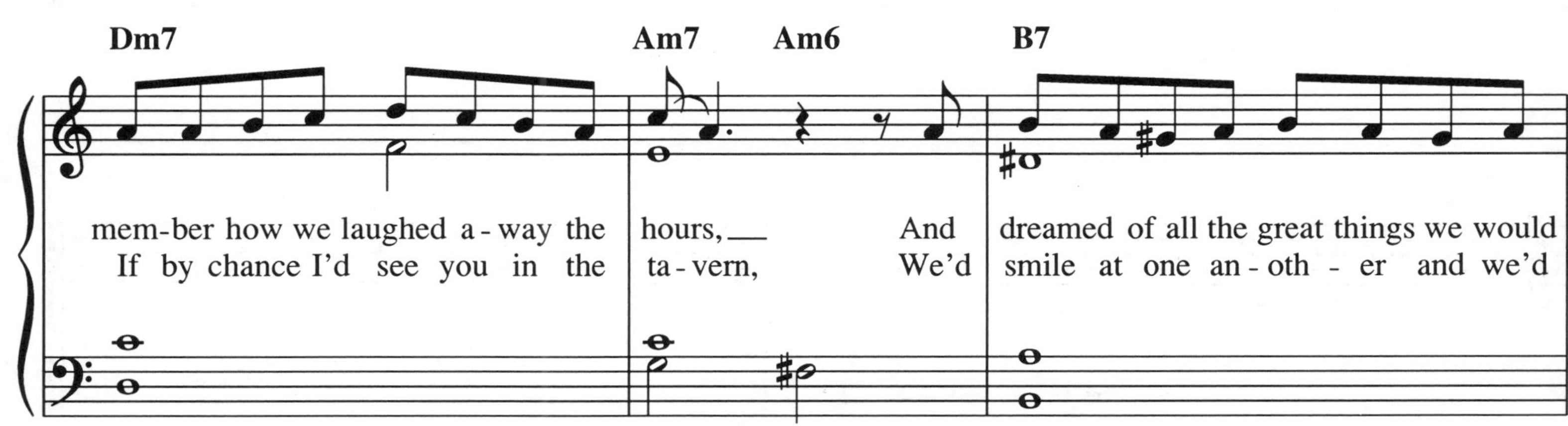

E7
Am
do.
say:
Those were the days, my friend,
mf
a tempo

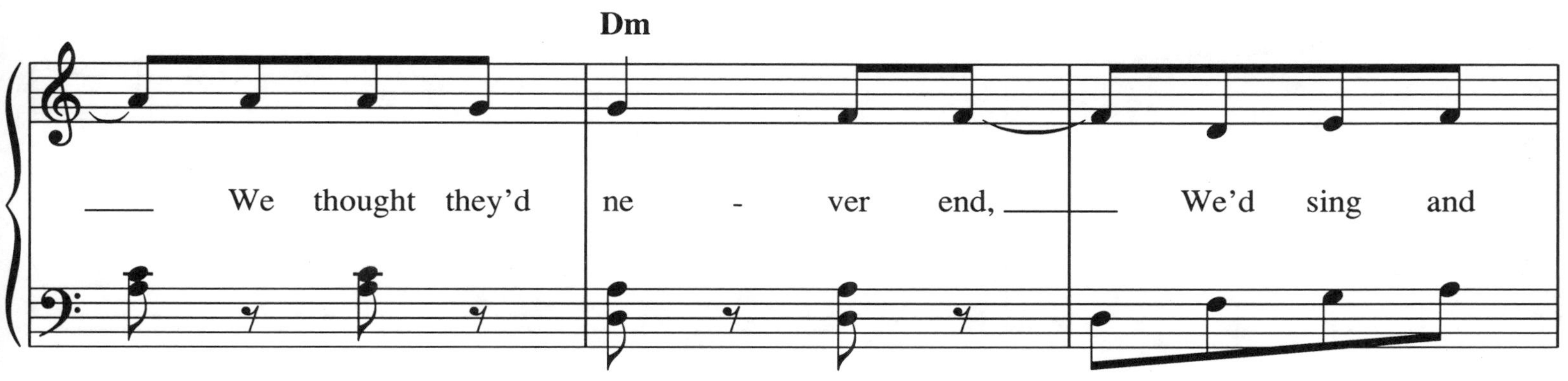
Dm
We thought they'd ne - ver end,
We'd sing and

G
C
dance for - e - ver and a day;

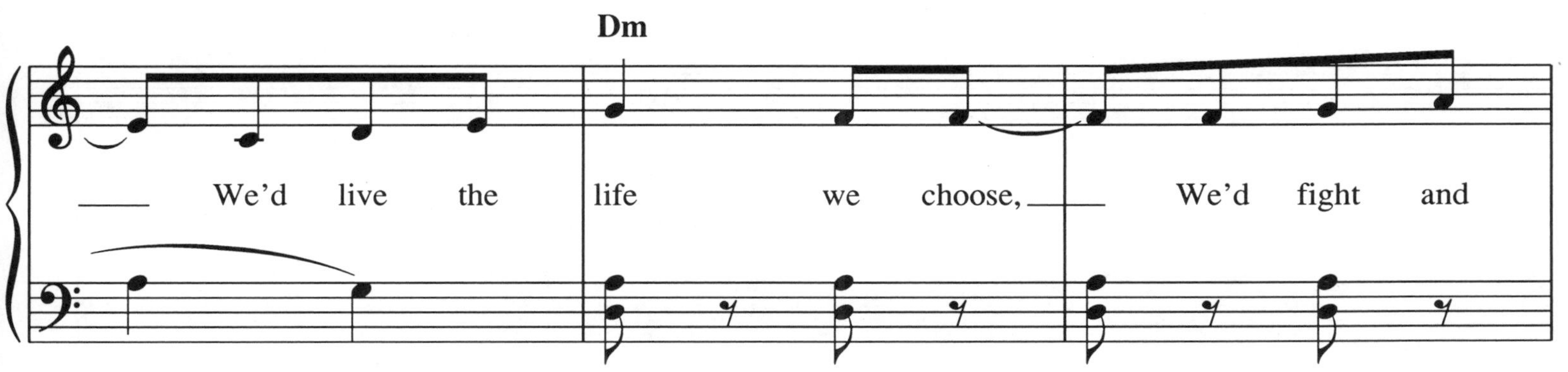
Dm
We'd live the life we choose,
We'd fight and

Am
E7
ne - ver lose,
For we were
young and sure

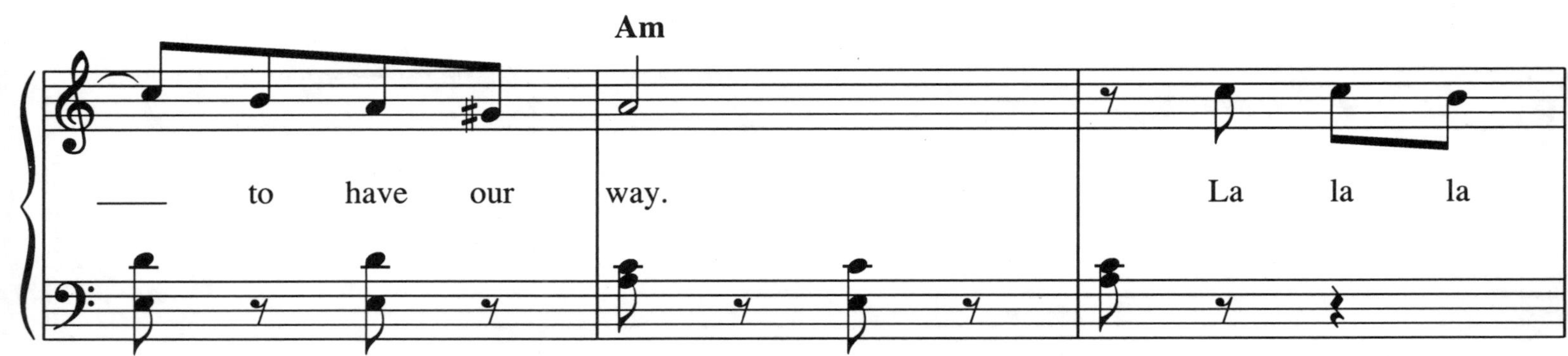
Am
to have our
way.
La la la

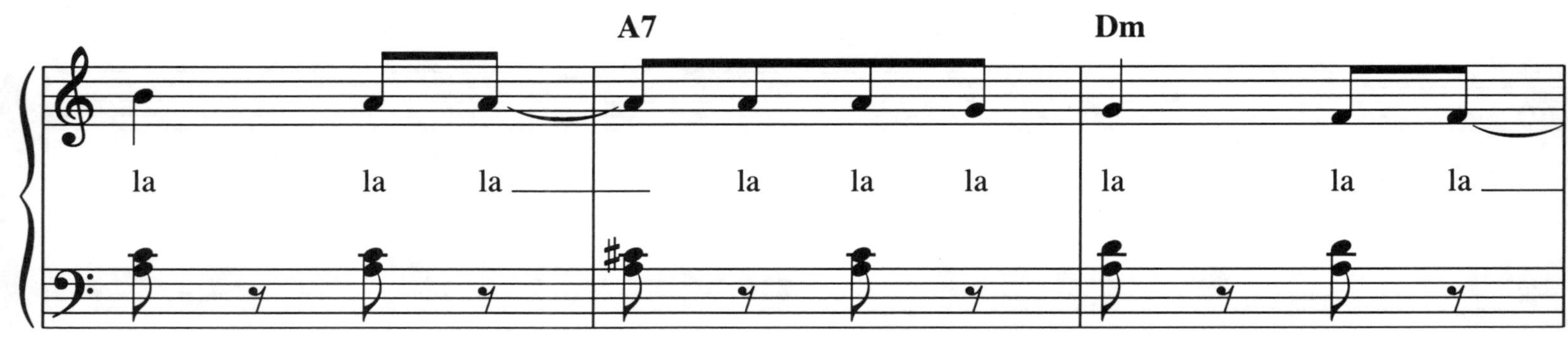
A7
Dm
la la la
la la la
la la la

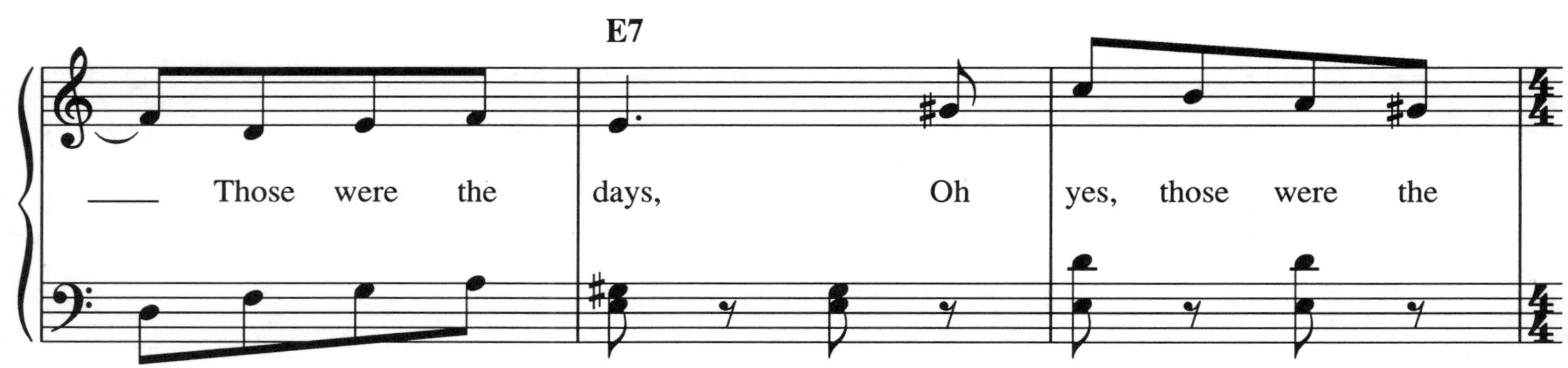
E7
Those were the
days, Oh
yes, those were the

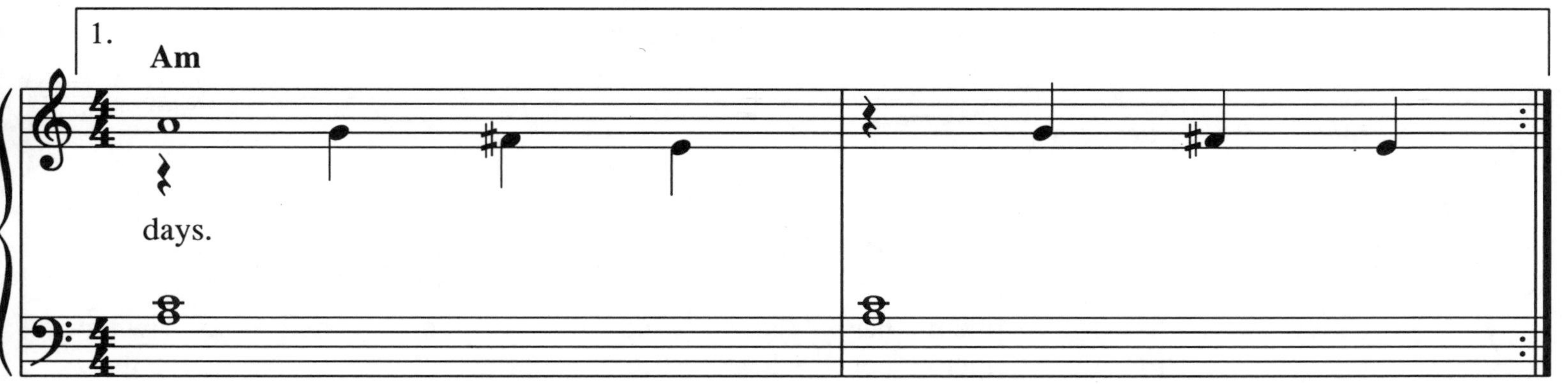

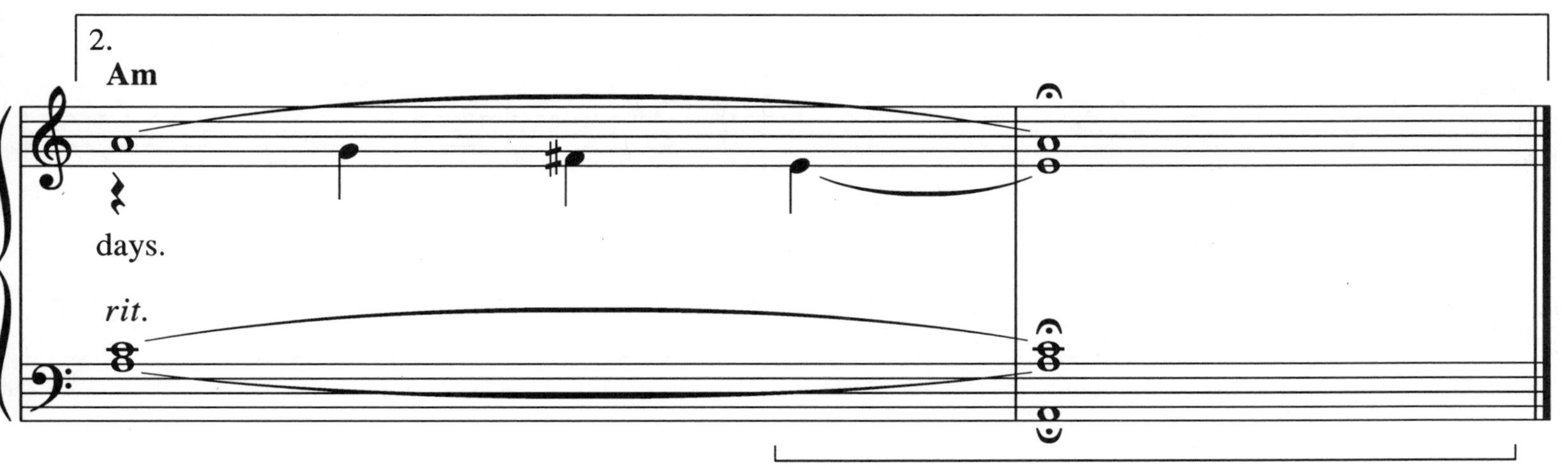

Additional Lyrics

3. Just tonight I stood before the tavern,
Nothing seemed the way it used to be.
In the glass I saw a strange reflection,
Was that lonely fellow really me?

4. Through the door there came familiar laughter,
I saw your face and heard you call my name.
Oh my friends we're older but no wiser,
For in our hearts the dreams are still the same.

TRY TO REMEMBER
(From "THE FANTASTICKS")

Slowly, with tenderness

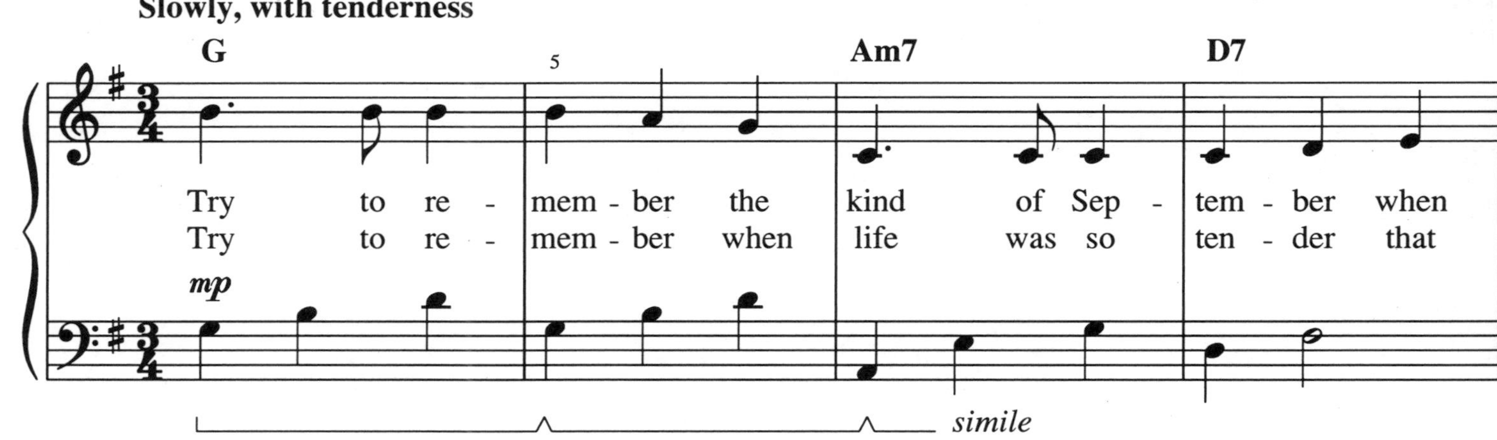

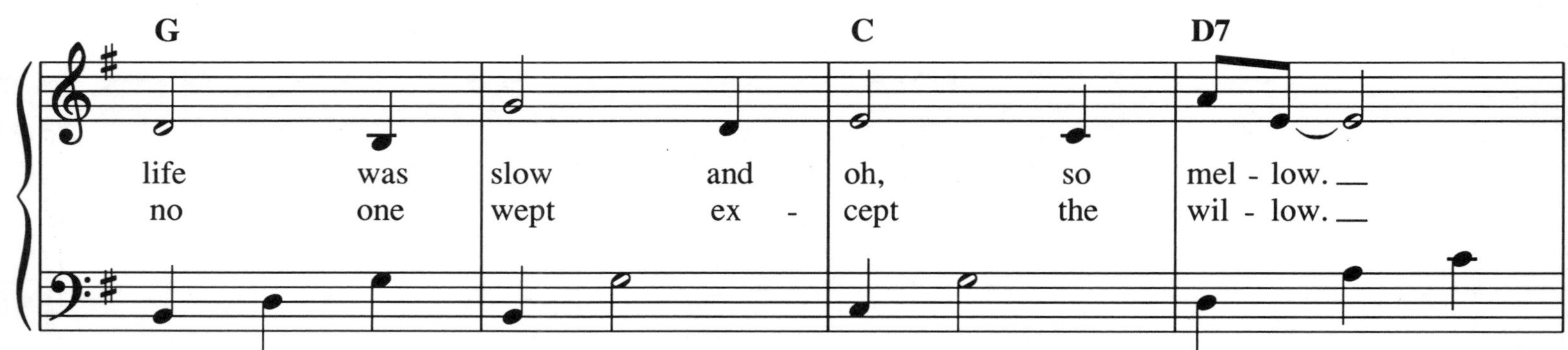

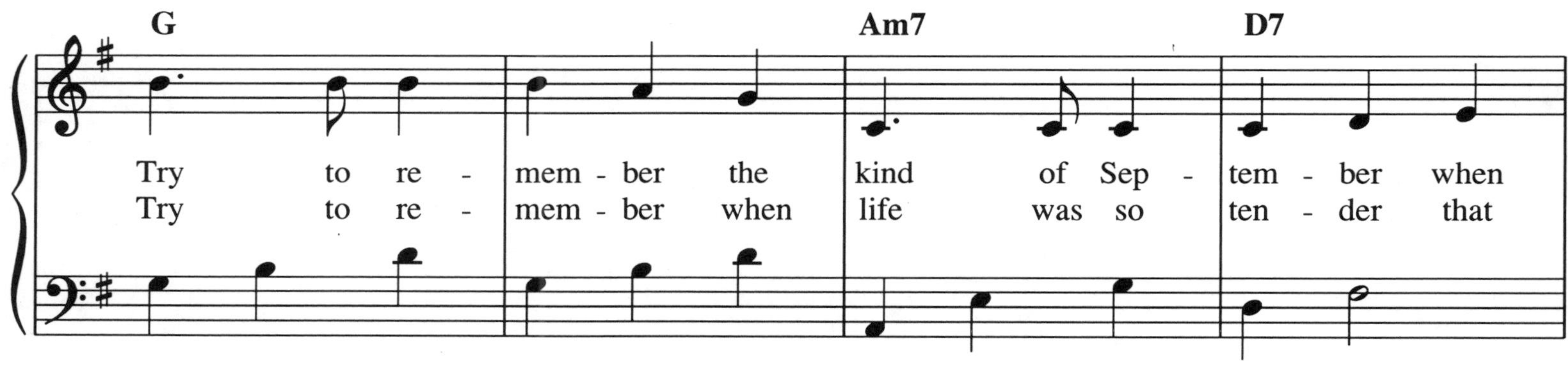

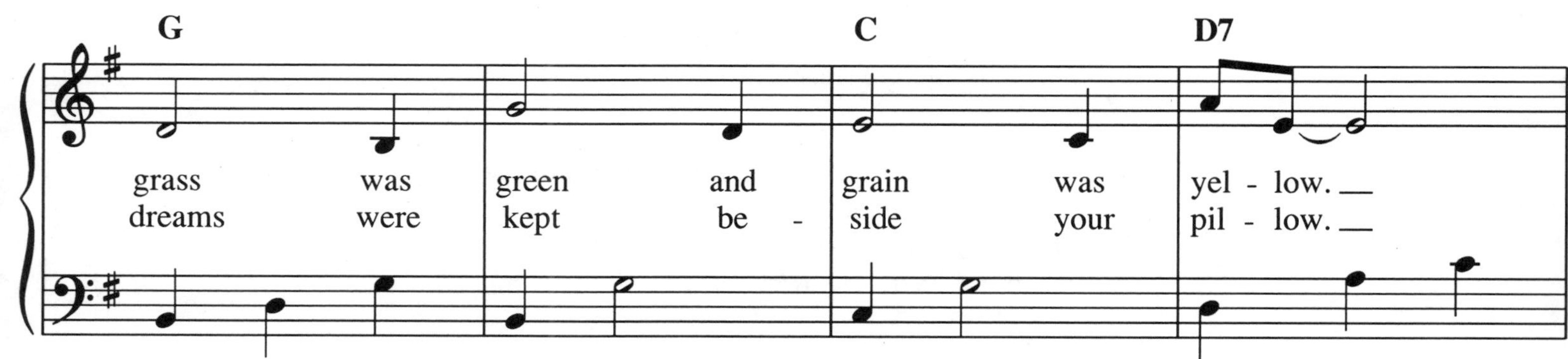

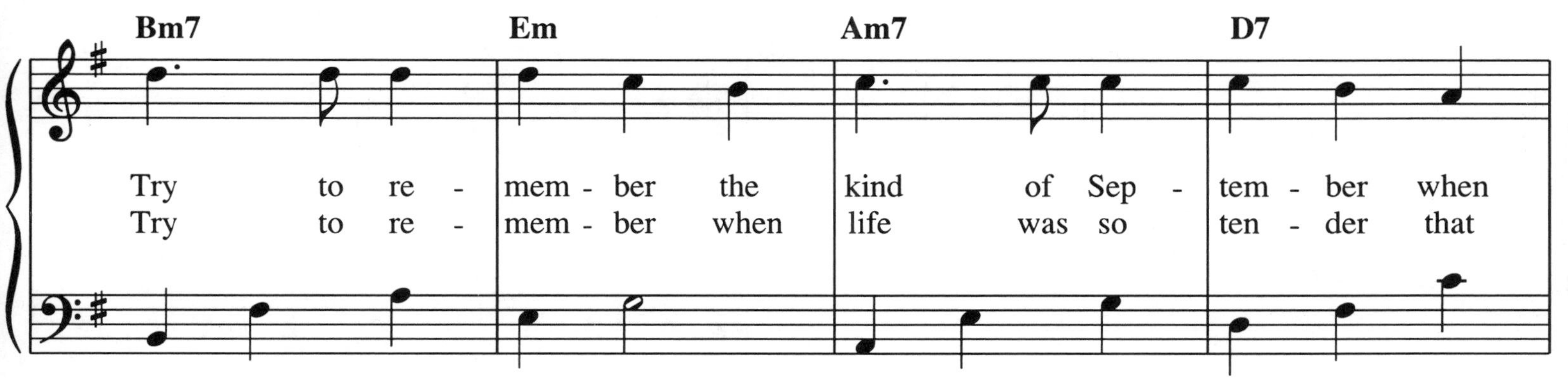
Bm7
Em
Am7
D7
Try to re - mem - ber the kind of Sep - tem - ber when
Try to re - mem - ber when life was so ten - der that

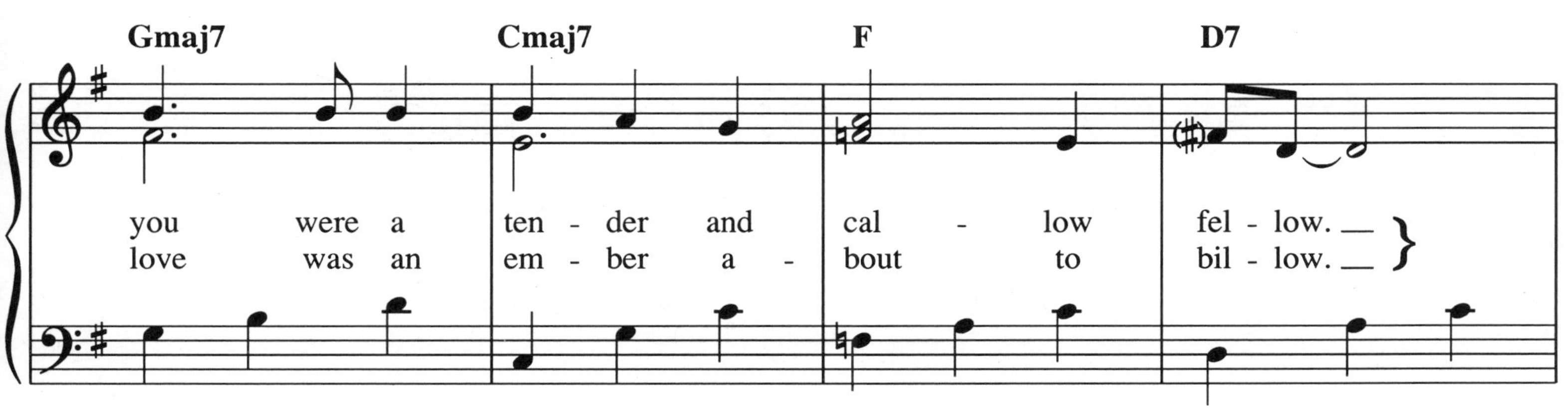
Gmaj7
Cmaj7
F
D7
you were a ten - der and cal - low fel - low.
love was an em - ber a - bout to bil - low.

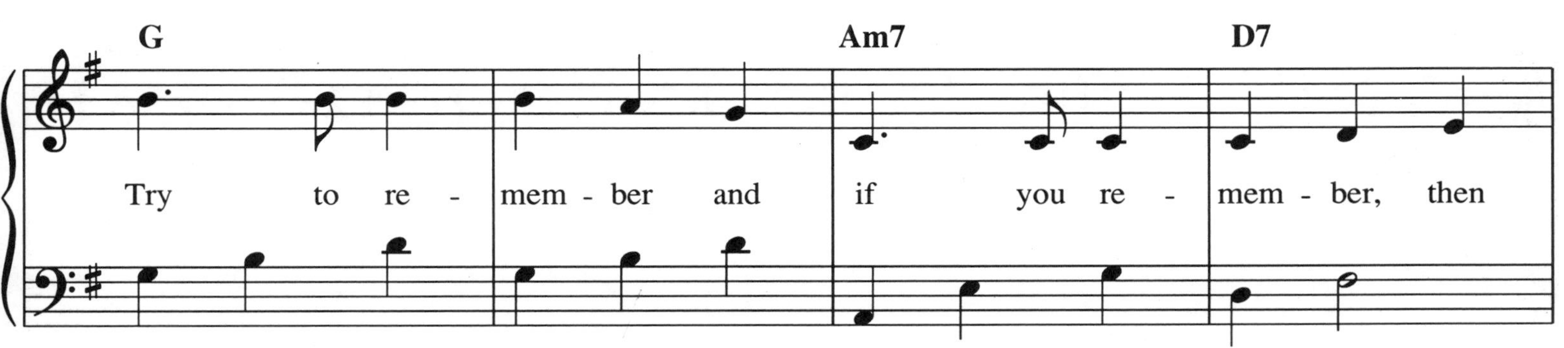
G
Am7
D7
Try to re - mem - ber and if you re - mem - ber, then

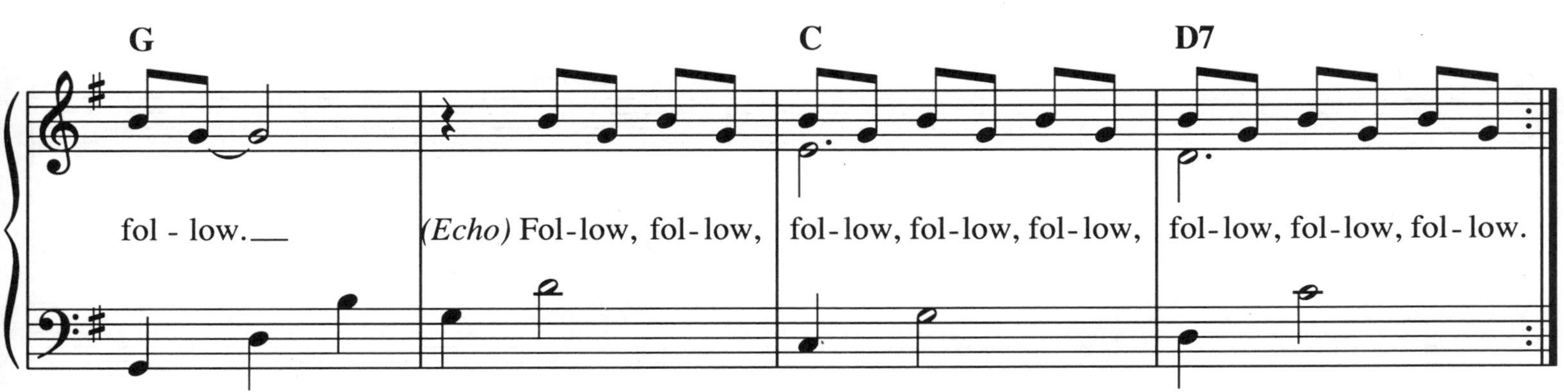
G
C
D7
fol - low.
(Echo) Fol-low, fol-low, fol-low, fol-low, fol-low, fol-low, fol-low, fol-low.

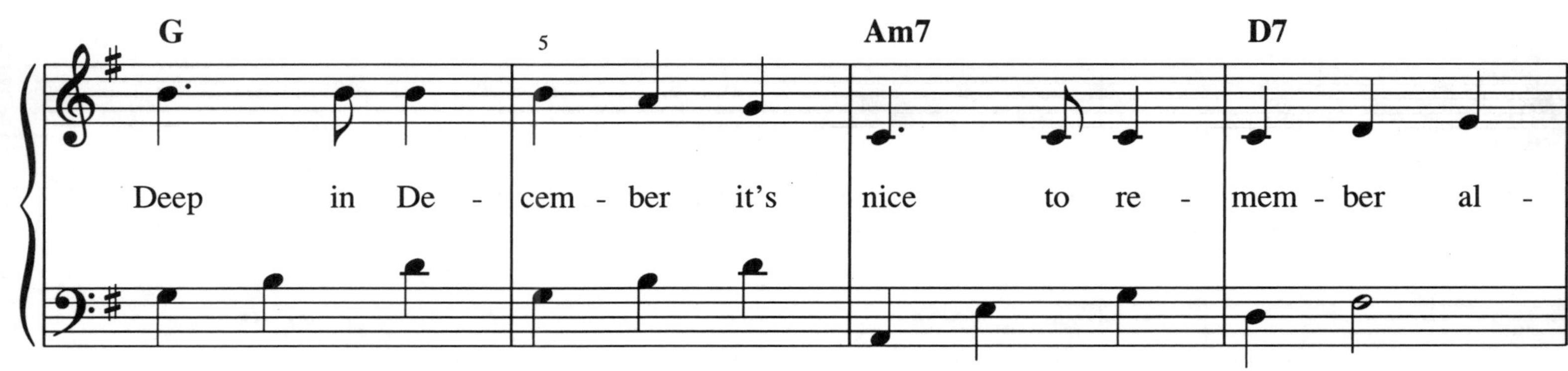
G
5
Am7
D7
Deep in De - cem - ber it's nice to re - mem - ber al -

G
C
D7
tho' you know the snow will fol - low. __

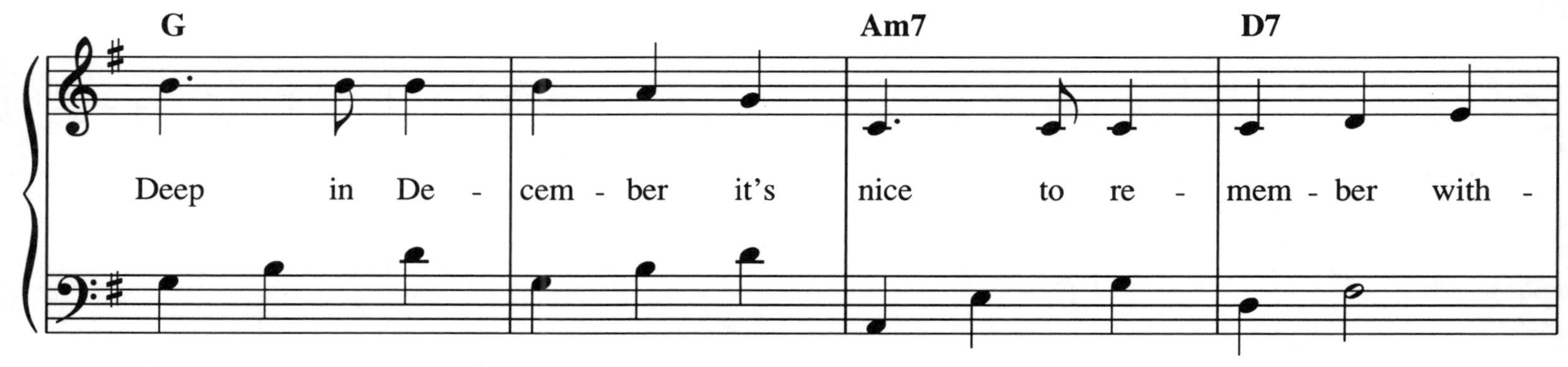
G
Am7
D7
Deep in De - cem - ber it's nice to re - mem - ber with -

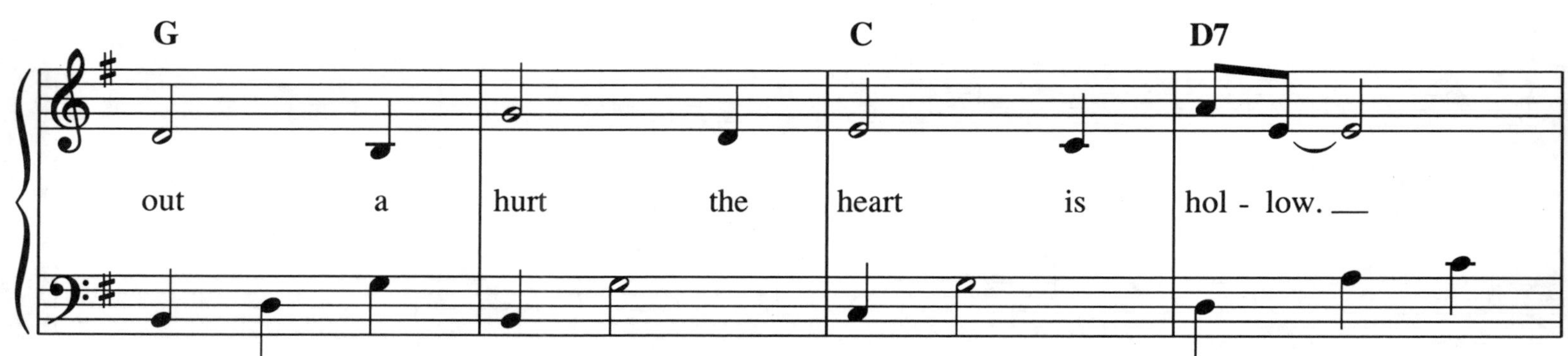
G
C
D7
out a hurt the heart is hol - low. __

Bm7
Em
Am7
D7
Gmaj7
Deep in De - cem - ber, it's nice to re - mem - ber the fire of Sep -

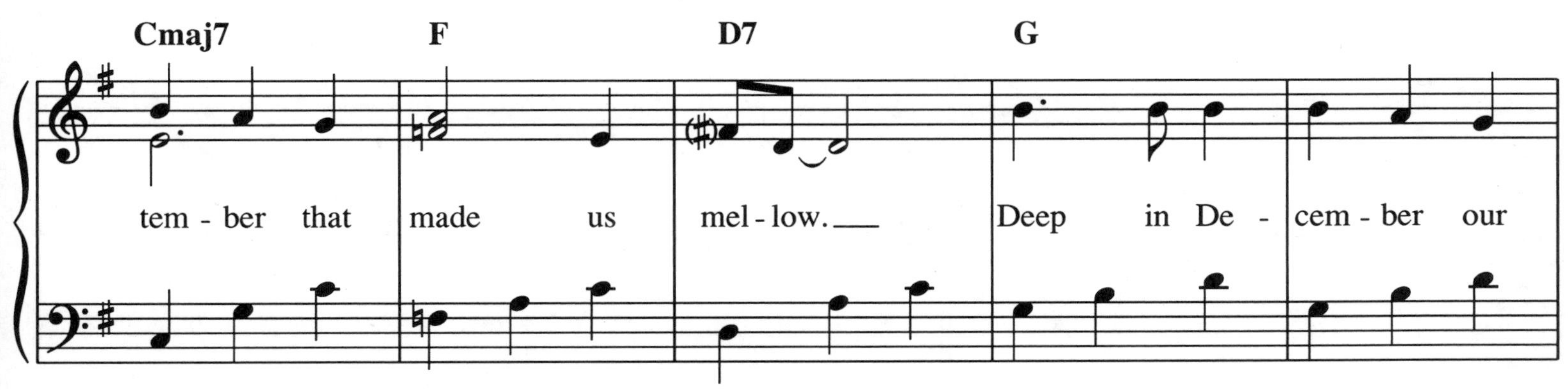
Cmaj7
F
D7
G
tem - ber that made us mel - low.
Deep in De - cem - ber our

Am7
D7
G
hearts should re - mem - ber and fol - low.
(Echo) Fol - low, fol - low,

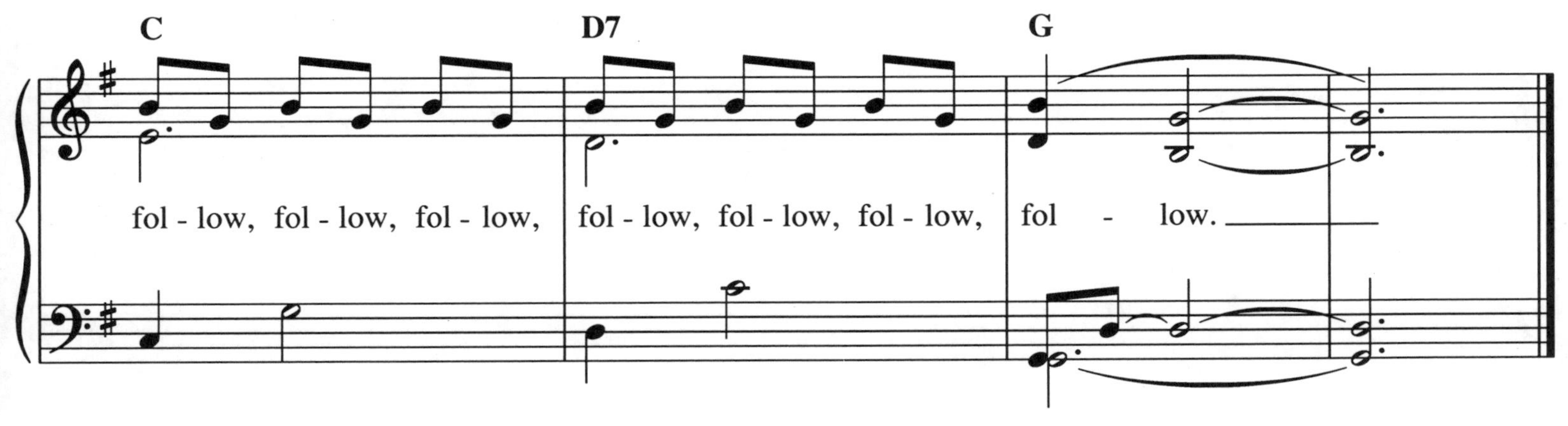
C
D7
G
fol - low, fol - low, fol - low, fol - low, fol - low, fol - low, fol - low.

TURN! TURN! TURN!
(To Everything There Is A Season)

Words from the Book of Ecclesiastes
Adaptation and Music by PETE SEEGER

Moderately slow, in 2

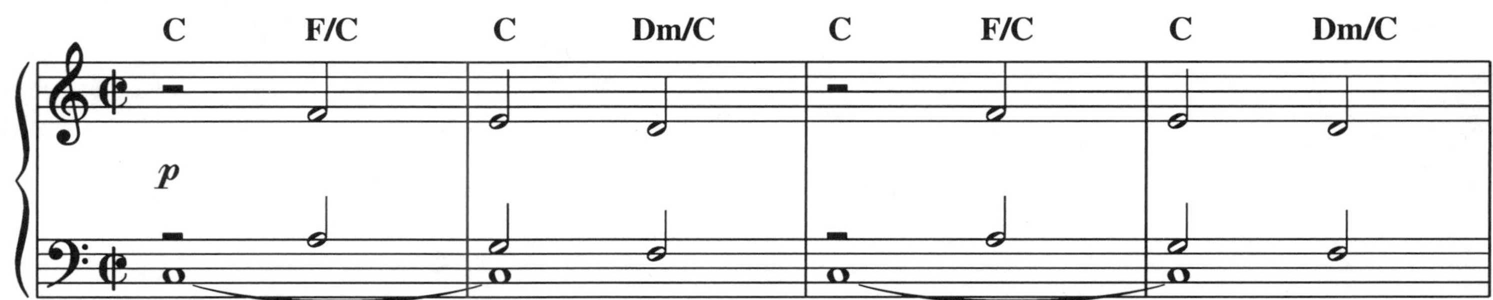

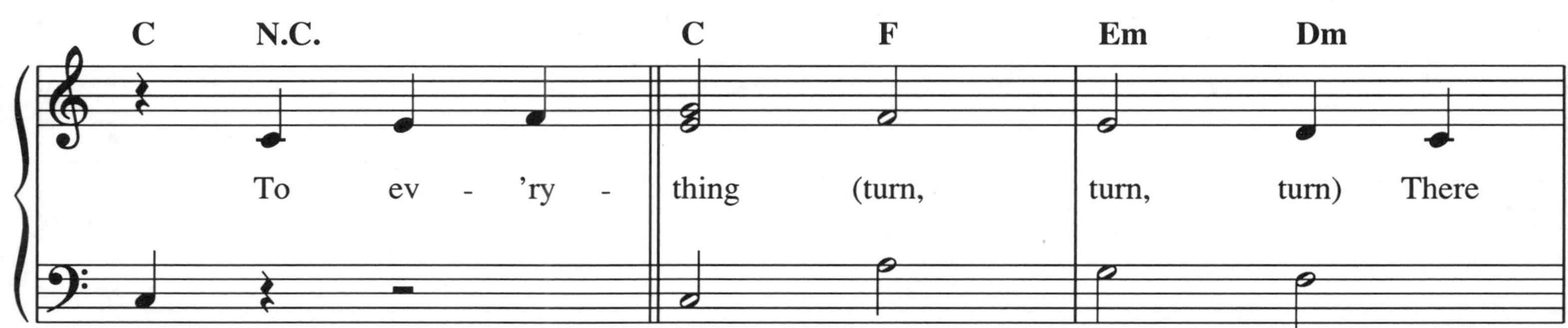

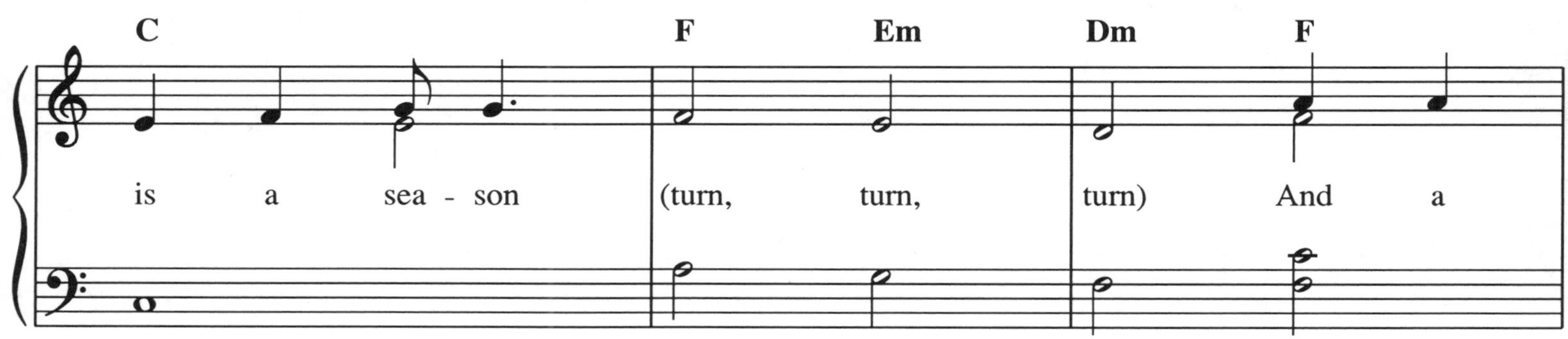

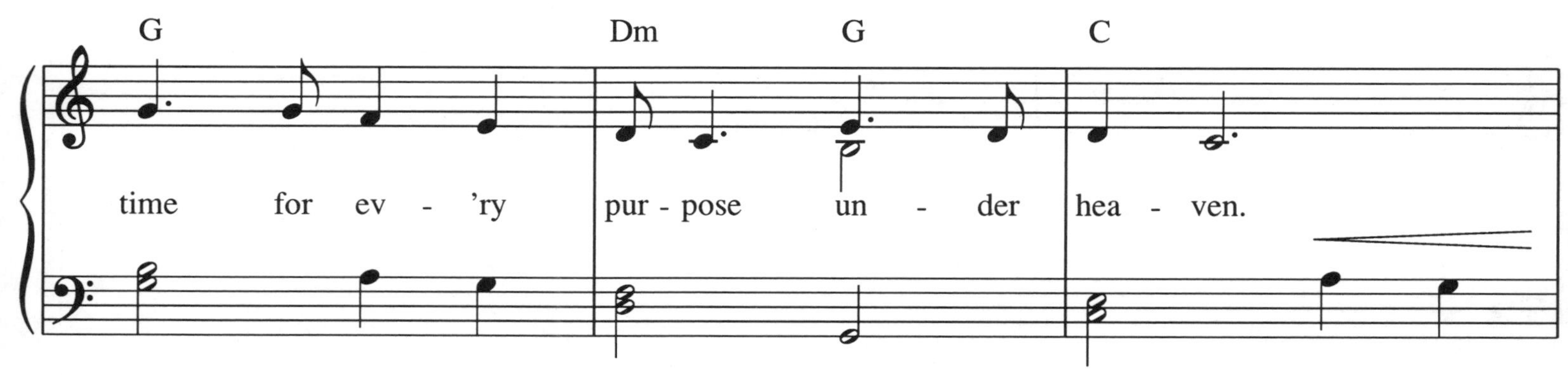

G7
C
mf
A time to be born, a time to die; a time to

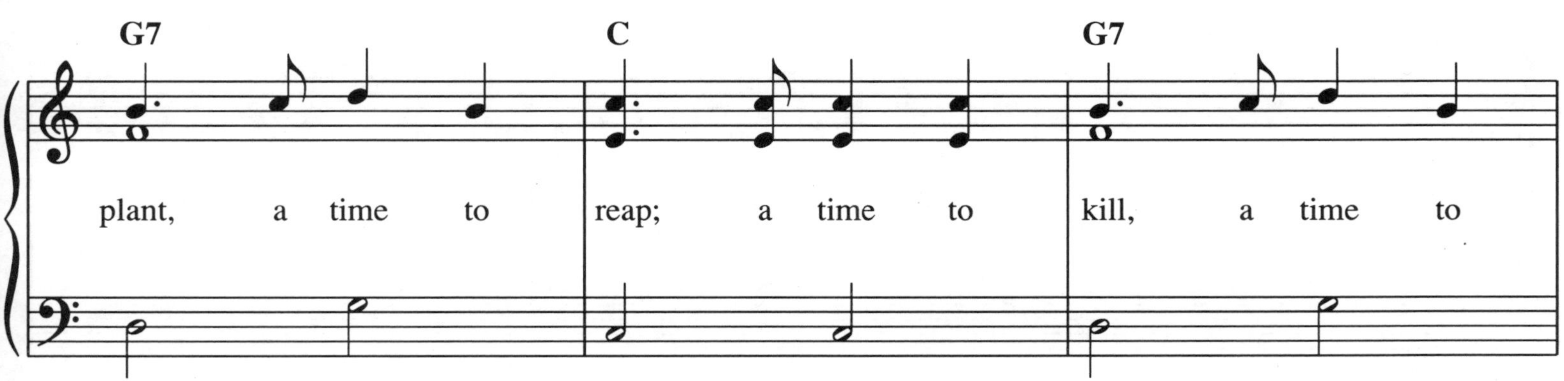
G7
C
G7
plant, a time to reap; a time to kill, a time to

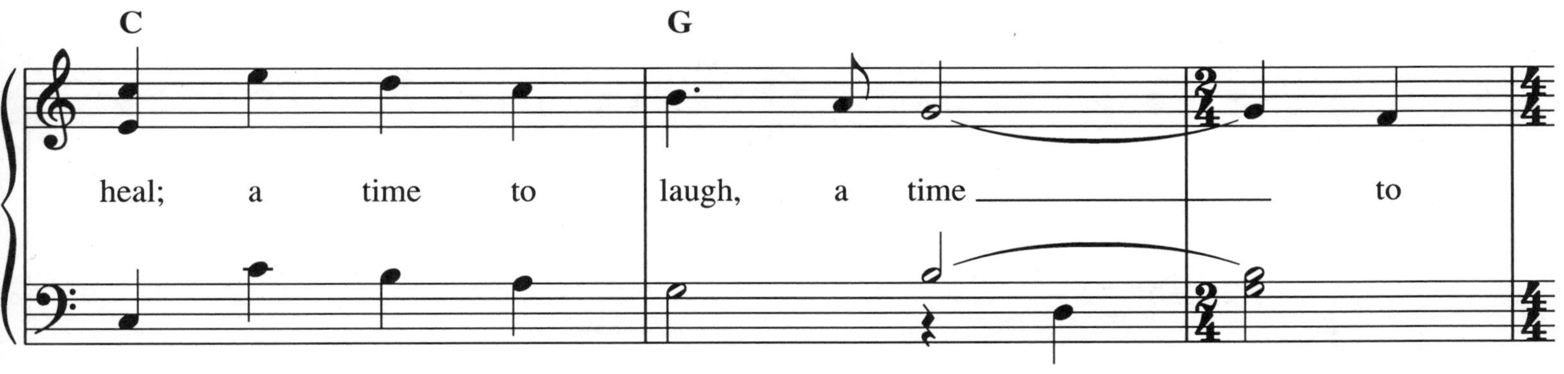
C
G
heal; a time to laugh, a time to

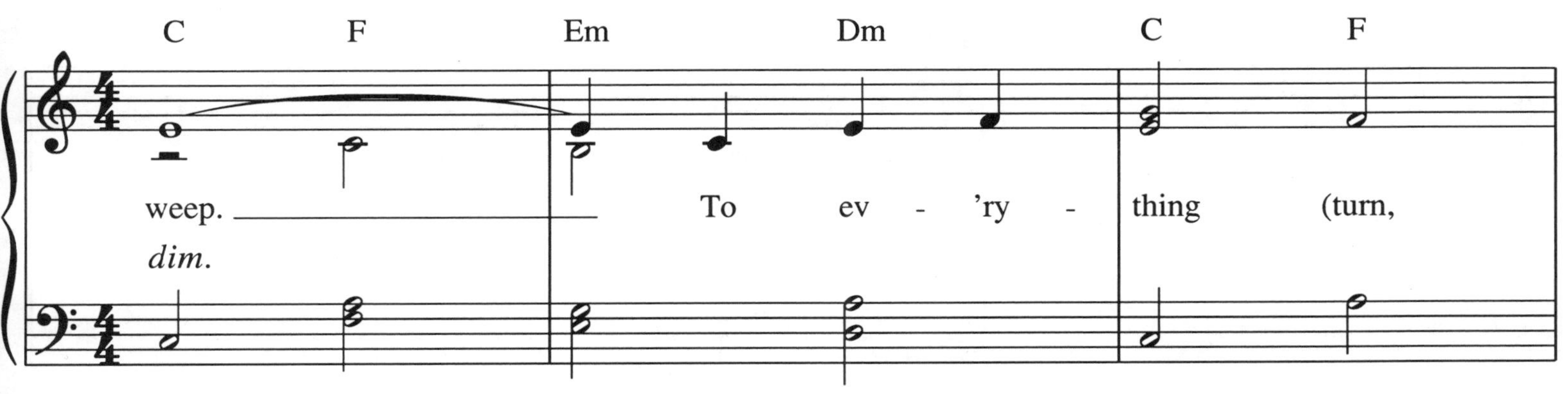
C
F
Em
Dm
C
F
weep. To ev - 'ry - thing (turn,
dim.

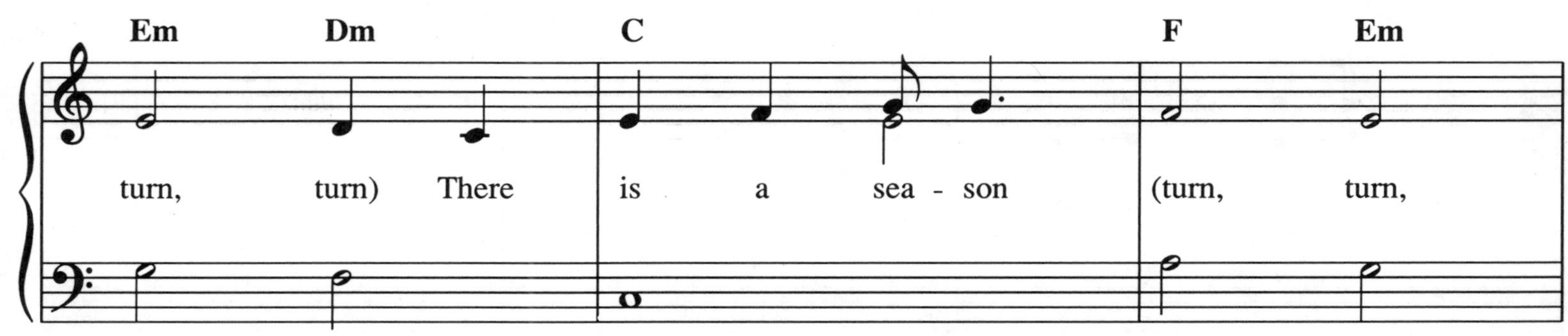
Em Dm C F Em
turn, turn) There is a sea - son (turn, turn,

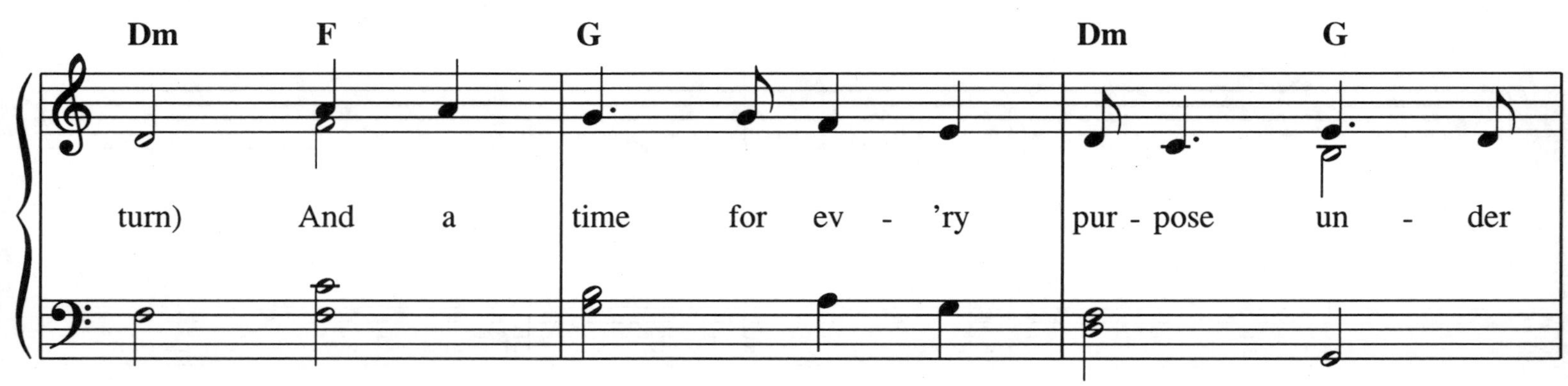
Dm F G Dm G
turn) And a time for ev - 'ry pur - pose un - der

C G7
heav - en. A time to build up, a time to break
mf

C G7 C
down; a time to dance, a time to mourn; a

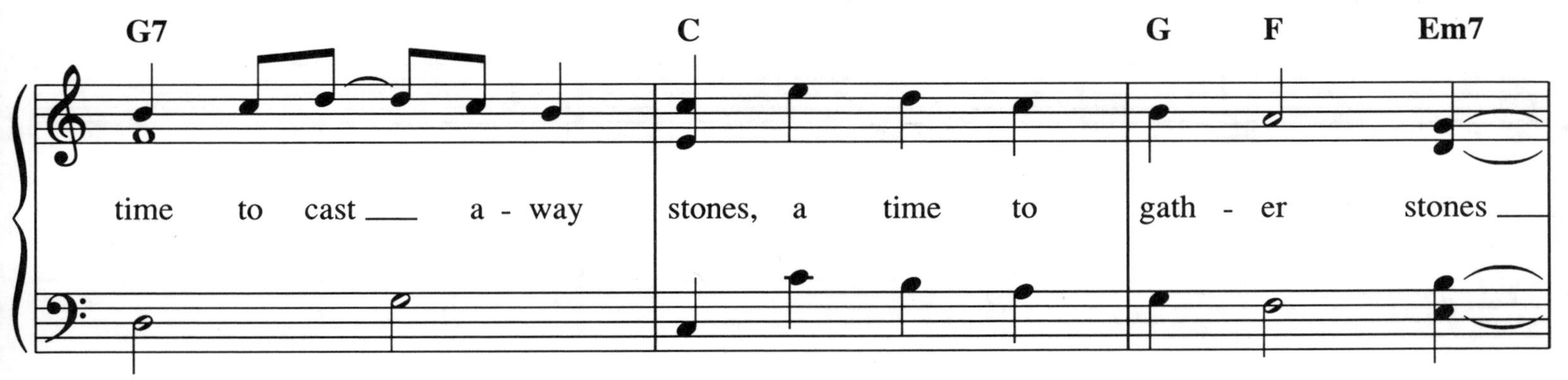
G7
C
G
F
Em7
time to cast ___ a - way
stones, a time to
gath - er stones ___

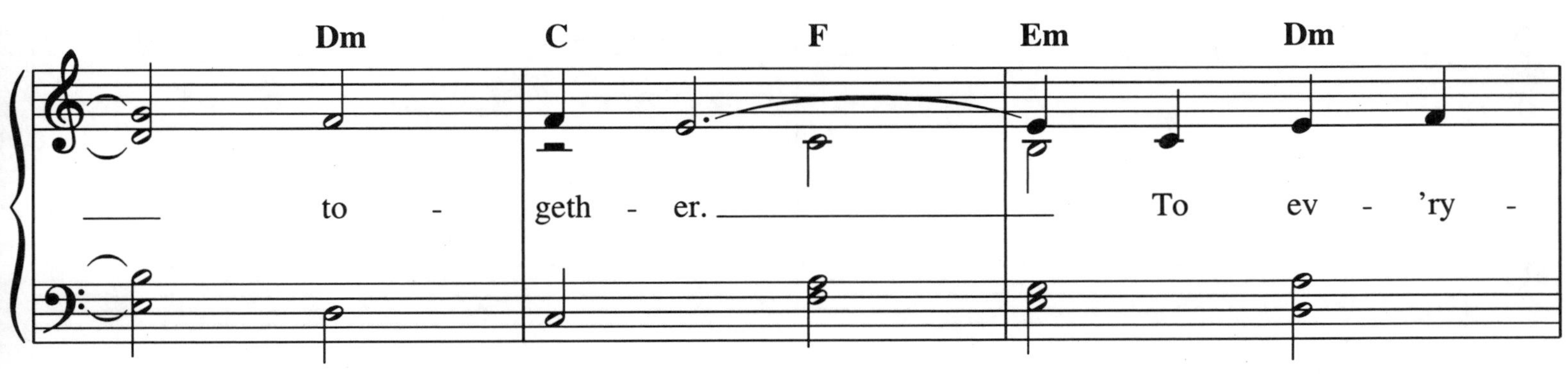
Dm
C
F
Em
Dm
___ to -
geth - er. ___
To ev - 'ry -

C
F
Em
Dm
C
thing (turn,
turn, turn) There
is a sea - son

F
Em
Dm
F
G
(turn, turn,
turn) And a
time for ev - 'ry

Dm
G
pur - pose
un - der
heav - en.
A time of
A time to

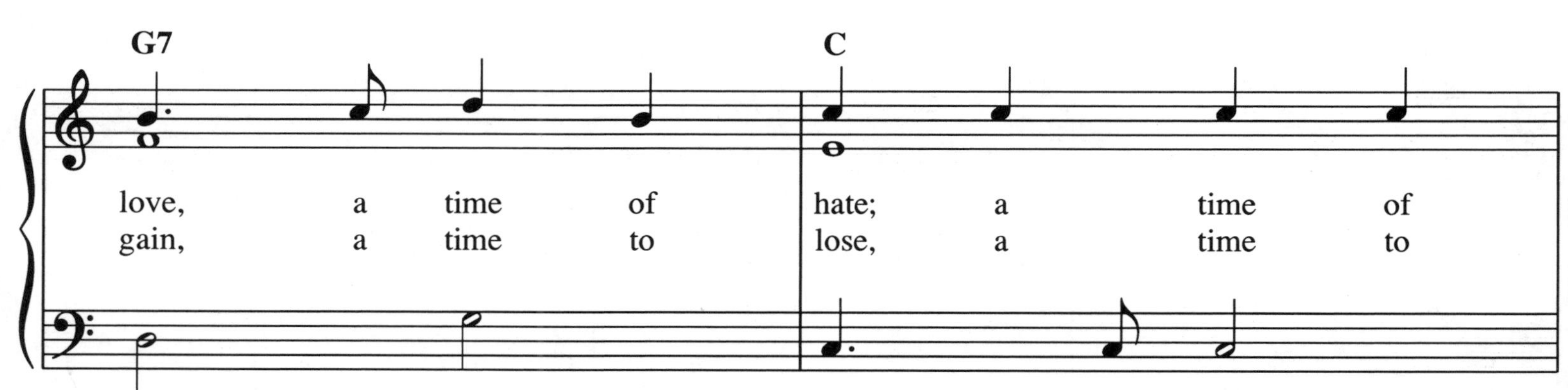
G7
C
love, a time of
gain, a time to
hate; a time of
lose, a time to

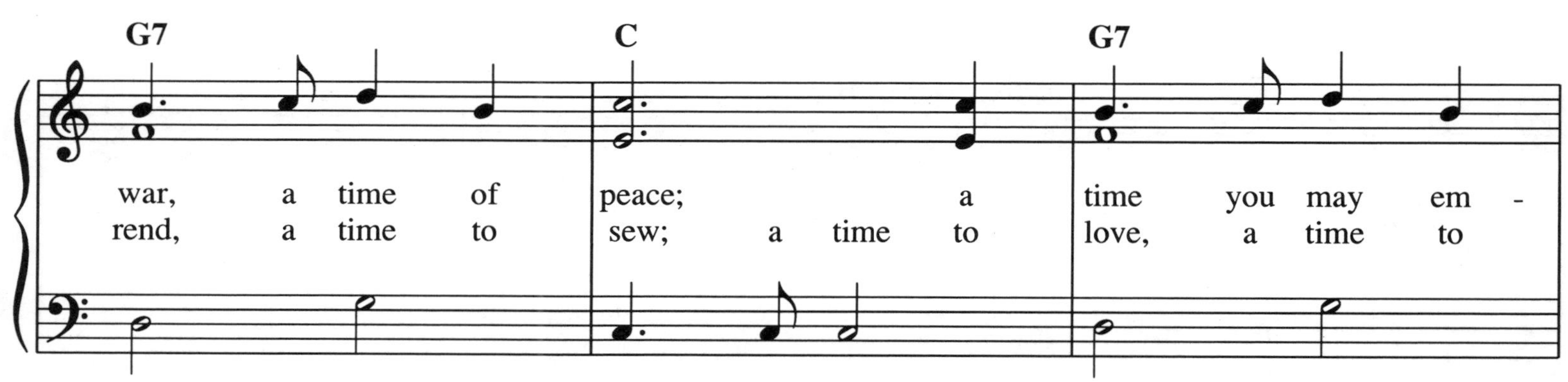
G7
C
G7
war, a time of
rend, a time to
peace; a
sew; a time to
time you may em -
love, a time to

C
G
F
G
brace, a time to
hate, a time for
re - frain
peace I
from em -
swear it's not too

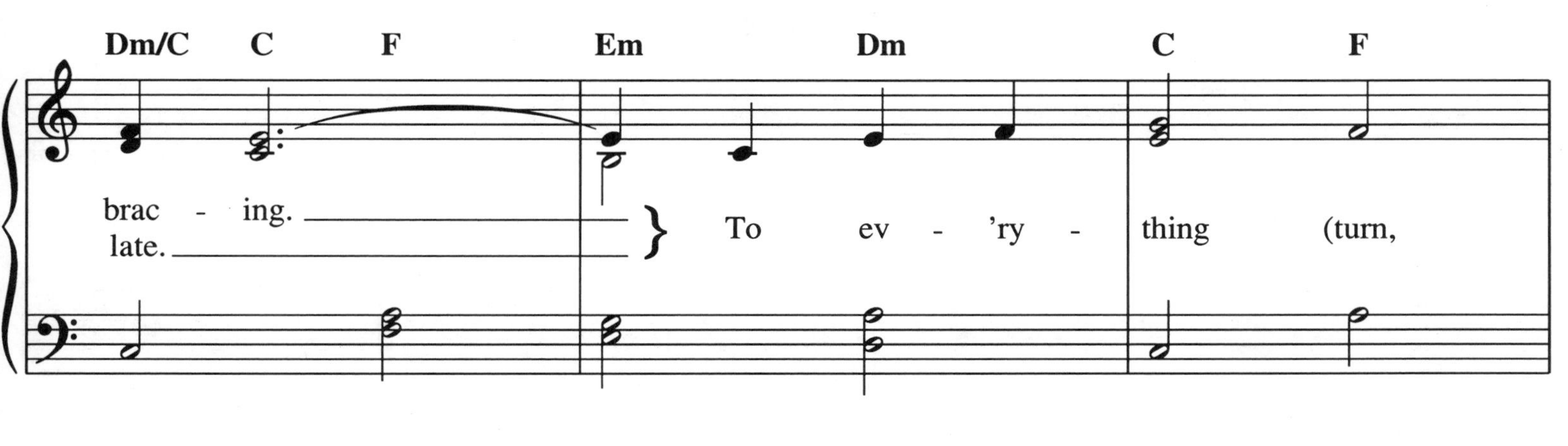
Dm/C
C
F
Em
Dm
C
F
brac - ing.
late.
To ev - 'ry - thing (turn,

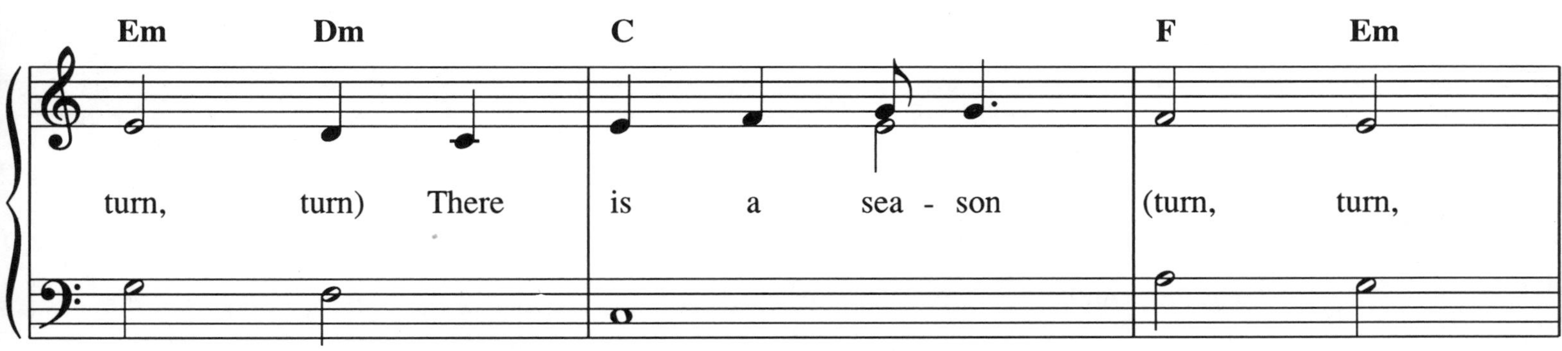
Em
Dm
C
F
Em
turn, turn) There is a sea - son (turn, turn,

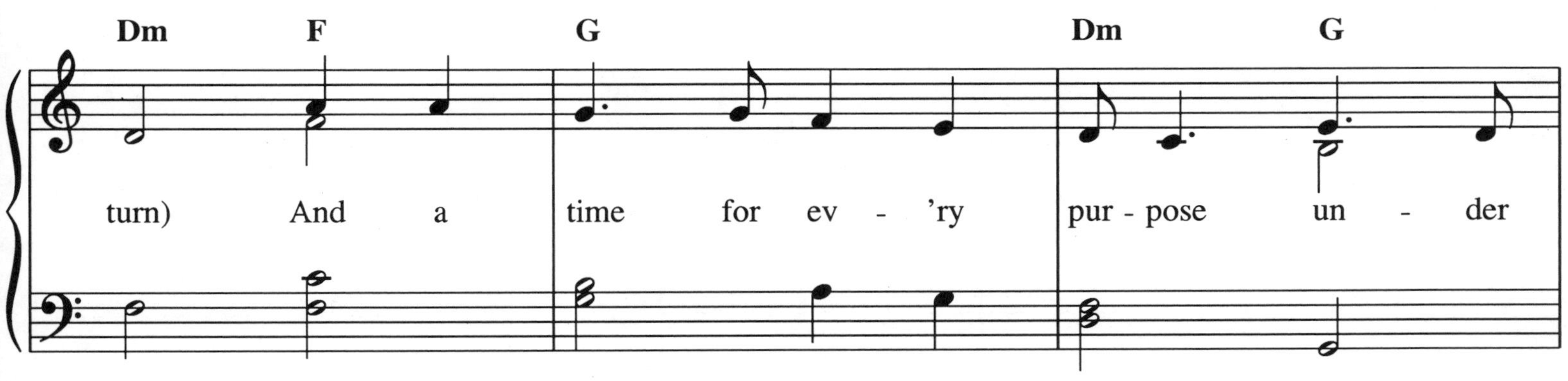
Dm
F
G
Dm
G
turn) And a time for ev - 'ry pur - pose un - der

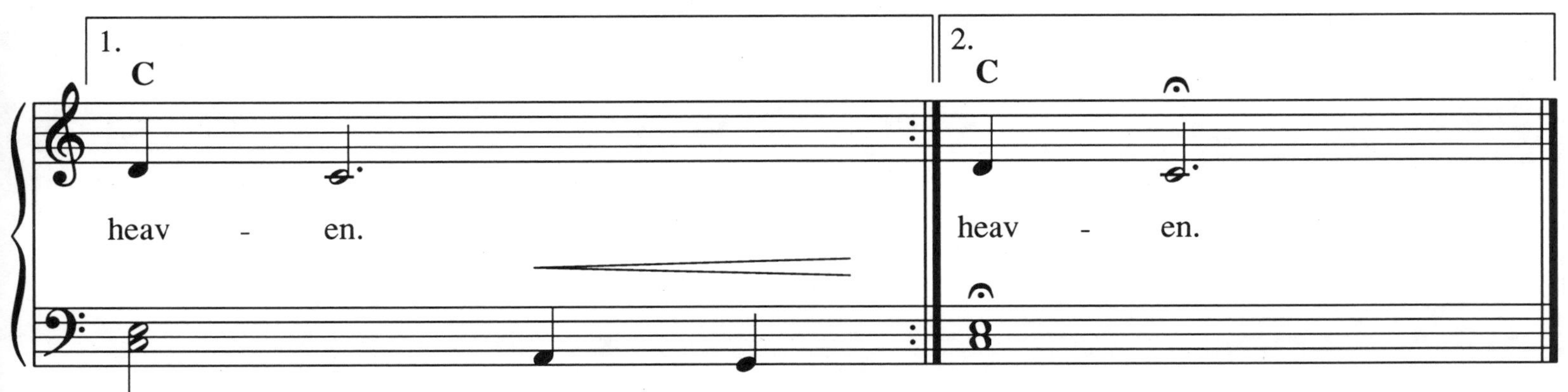
1.
C
heav - en.
2.
C
heav - en.

THE TWIST

Words and Music by
HANK BALLARD

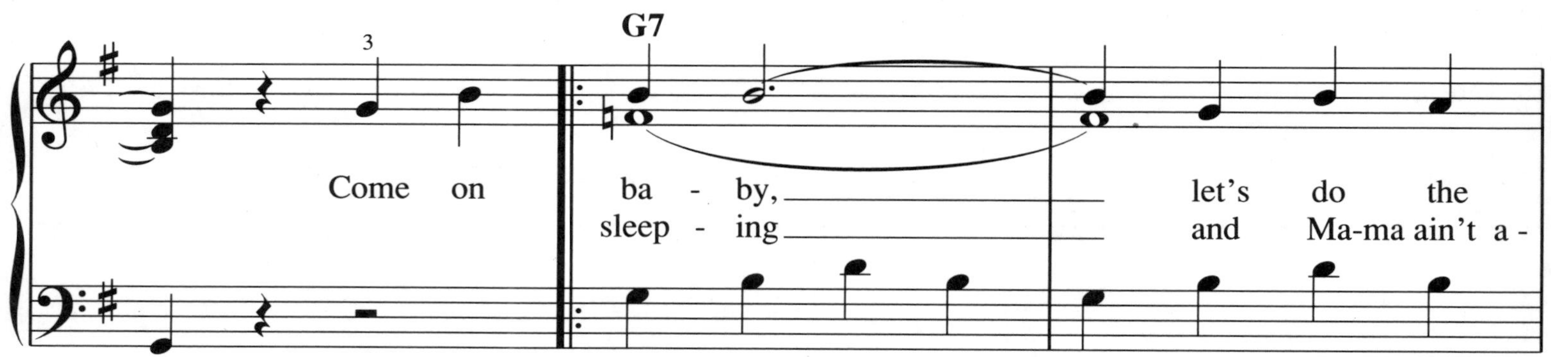

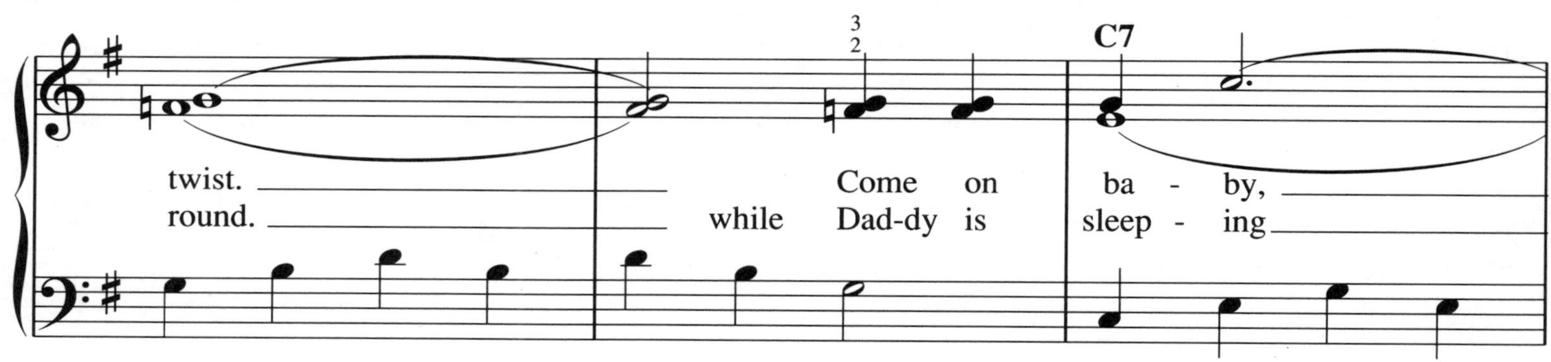

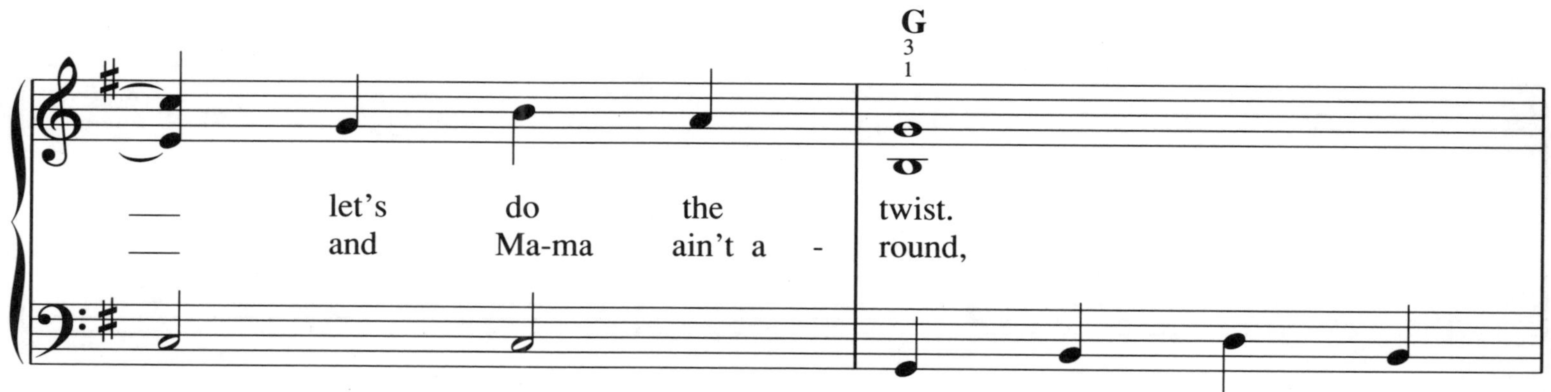

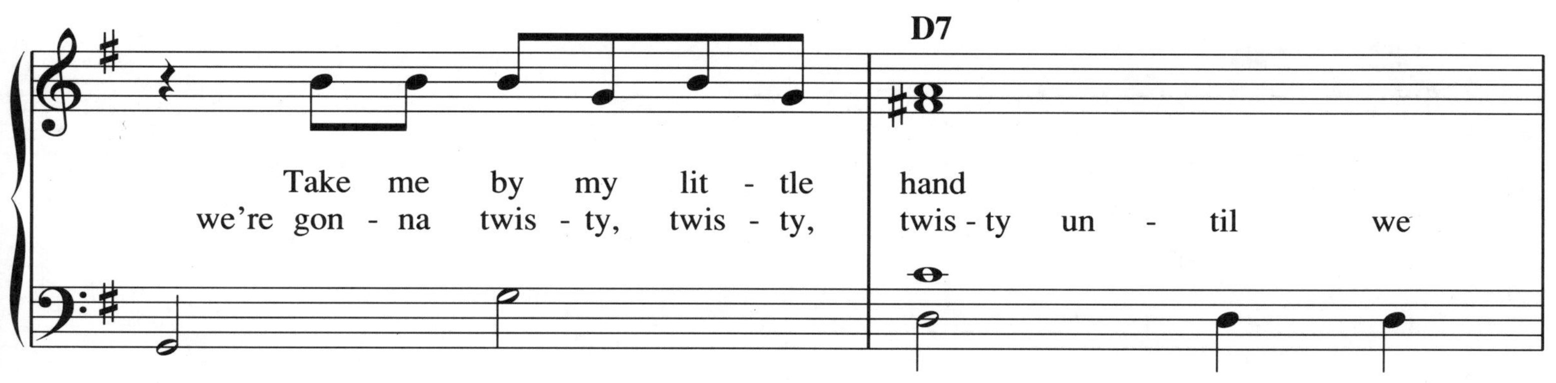
D7
Take me by my lit - tle
hand
we're gon - na twis - ty, twis - ty,
twis - ty un - til we

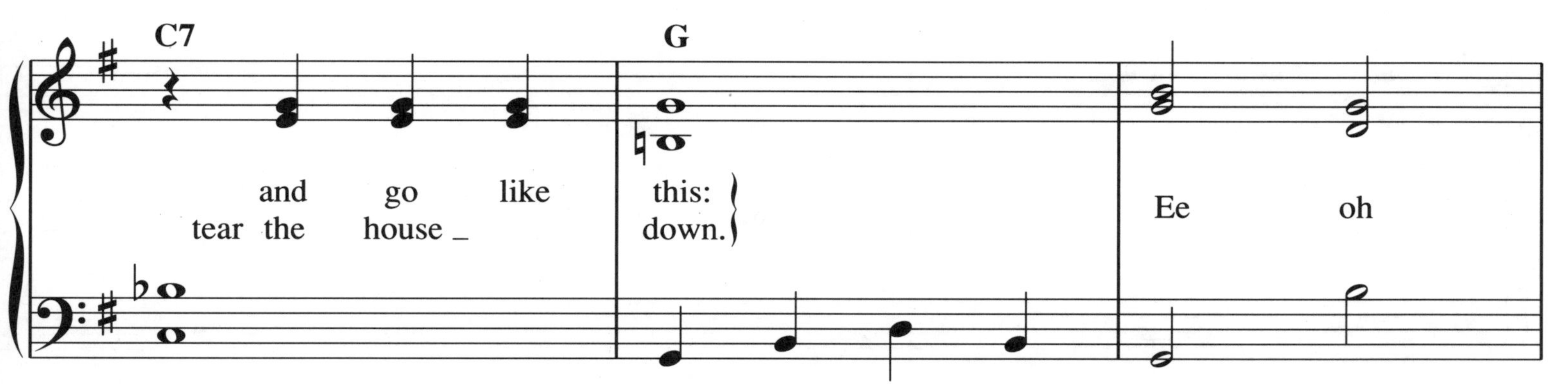
C7
G
and go like
this:
tear the house
down.
Ee oh

G7
Twist,
ba - by, ba - by,
Twist, ('round and a -
1 2 3 5 3

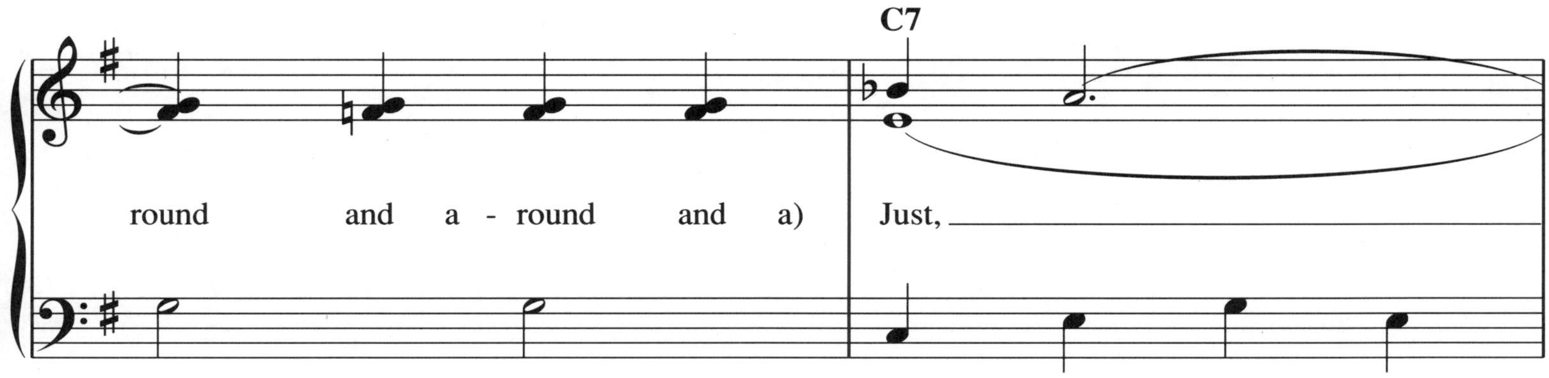
C7
round and a - round and a)
Just,

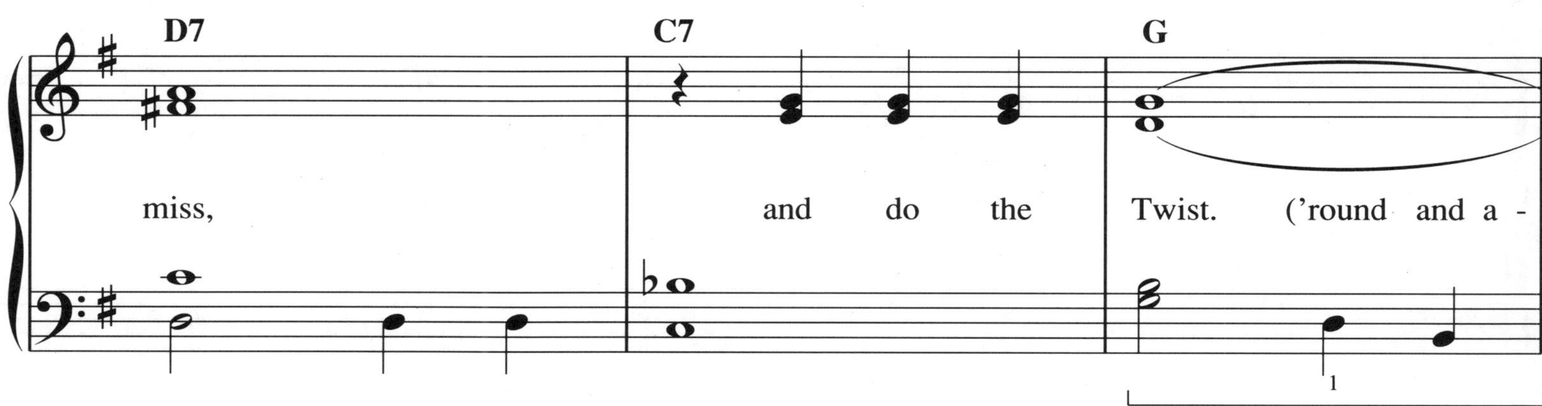

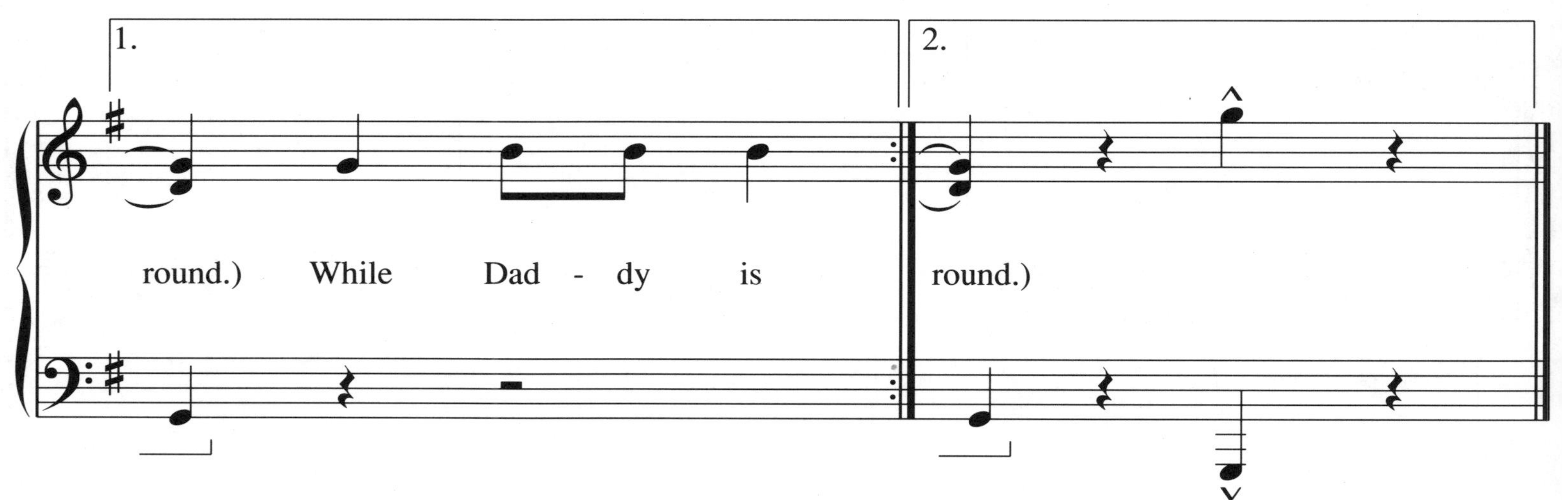

Additional Lyrics

3. You should see my little sis.
You should see my little sis.
She knows how to rock and she knows how to Twist.

WATCH WHAT HAPPENS

English Words by NORMAN GIMBEL
French Text by JACQUES DEMY
Music by MICHEL LEGRAND

Gm9
C11
1.
Fmaj7
G♭maj7
Gmaj7
G♭maj7
hand,
heart,
let him touch you and
let him find you and
watch what hap - pens.

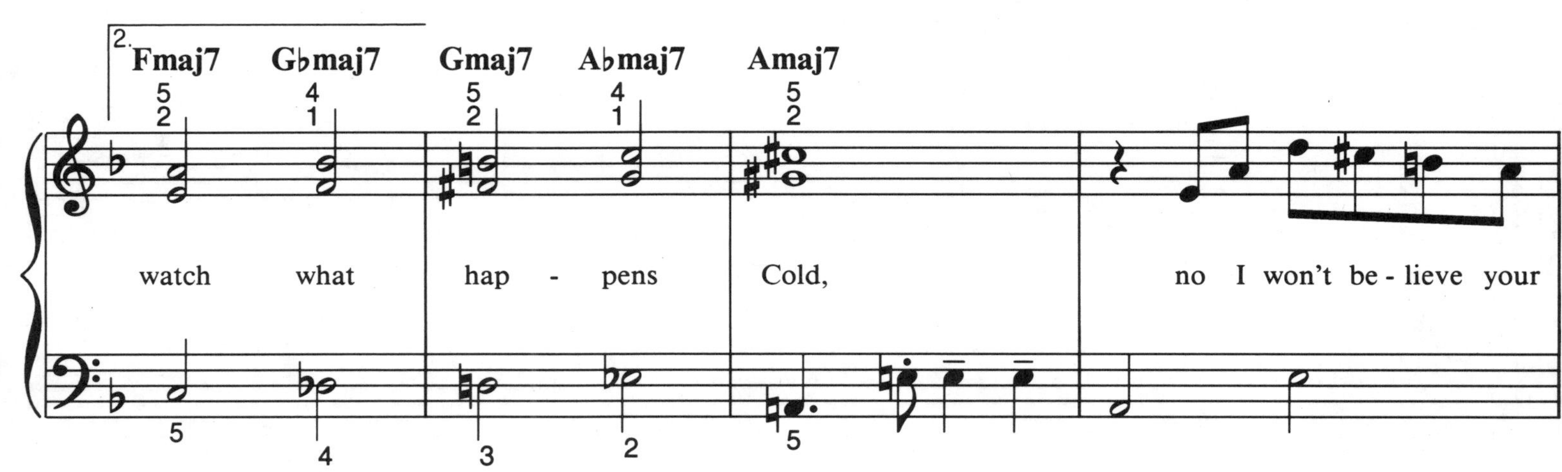
2.
Fmaj7
G♭maj7
Gmaj7
A♭maj7
Amaj7
watch what hap - pens Cold,
no I won't be - lieve your

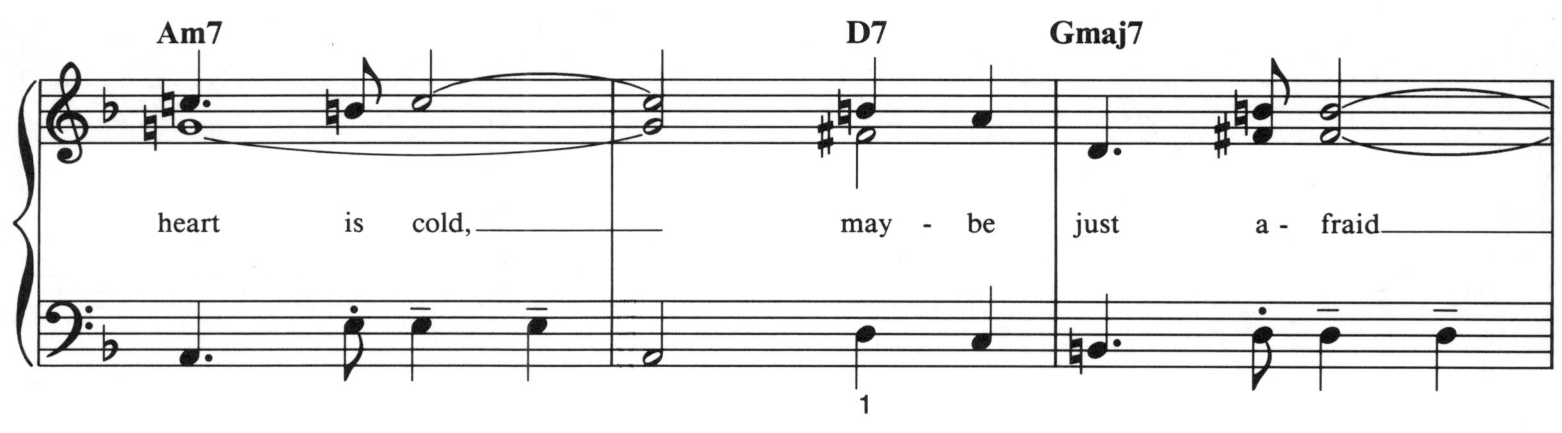
Am7
D7
Gmaj7
heart is cold,
may - be just a - fraid

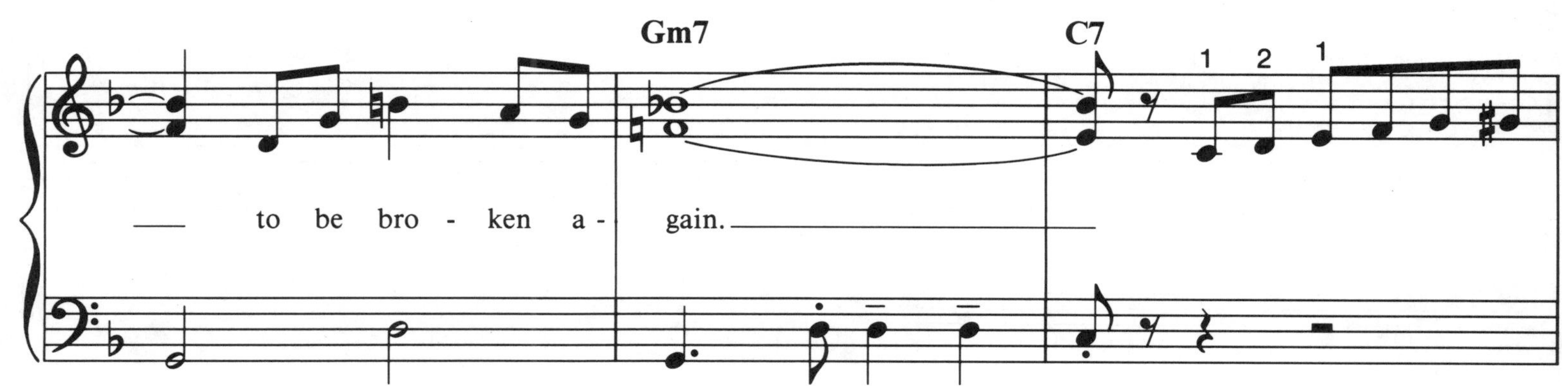
Gm7
C7
to be bro - ken a - gain.

F
G9
Let some- one with a deep love to give

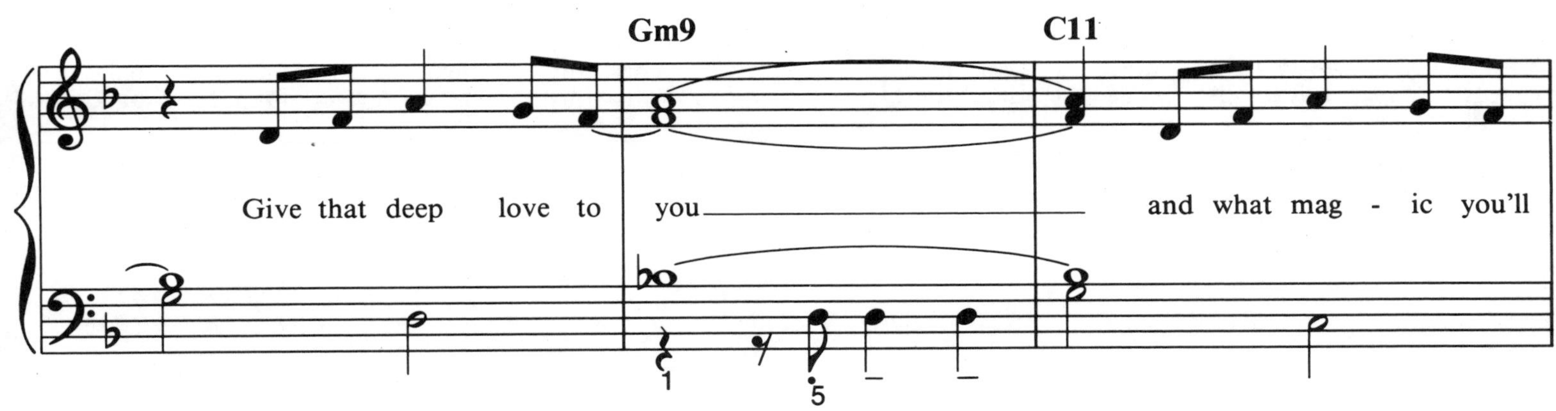
Gm9
C11
Give that deep love to you and what mag - ic you'll

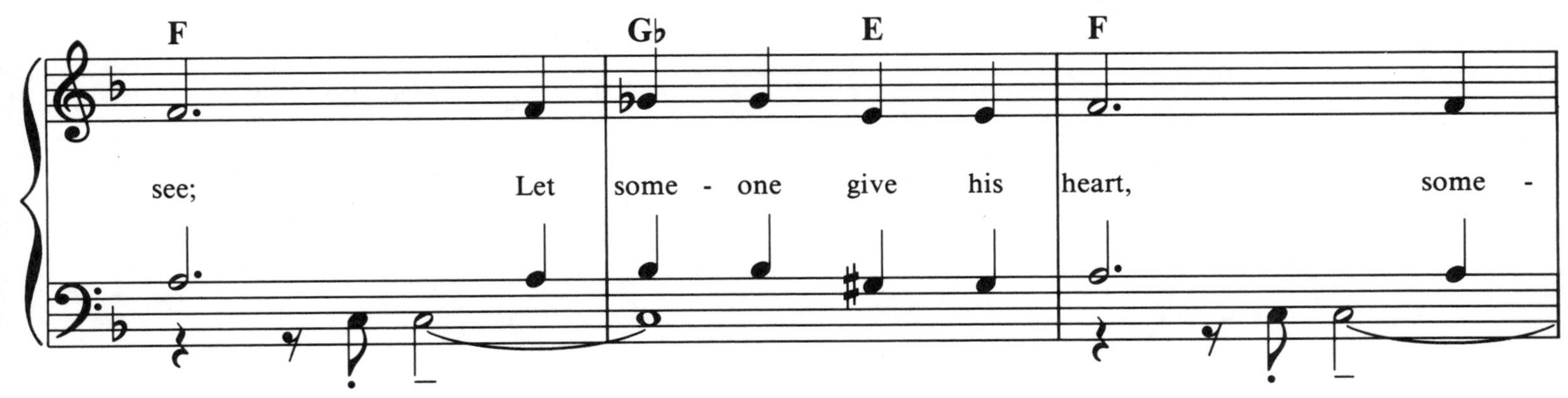
F
G♭
E
F
see; Let some - one give his heart, some -

G♭
E
F
one who cares like me.

UP, UP AND AWAY

Words and Music by JIM WEBB

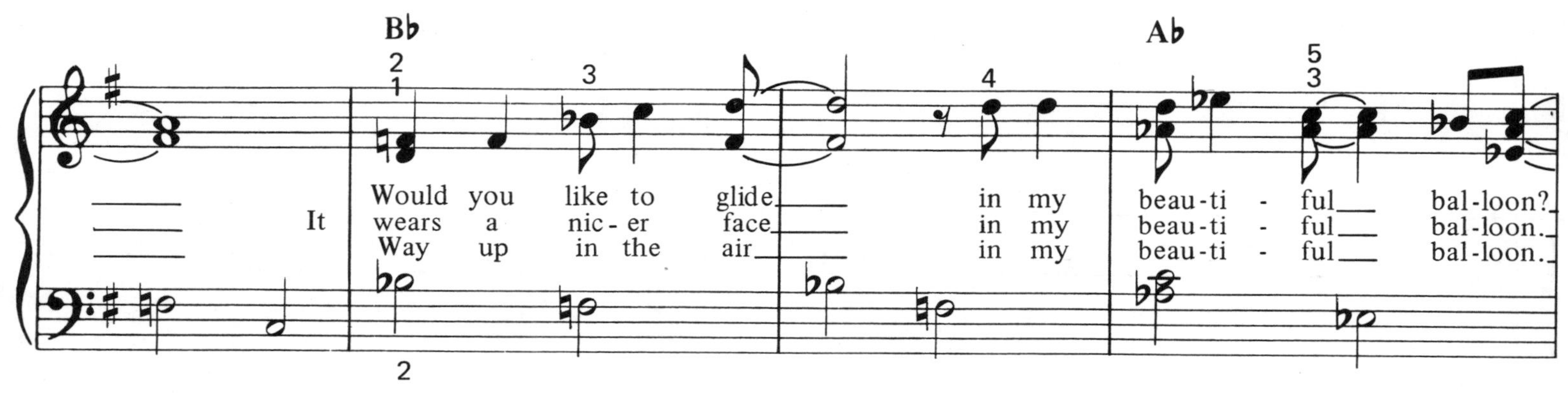

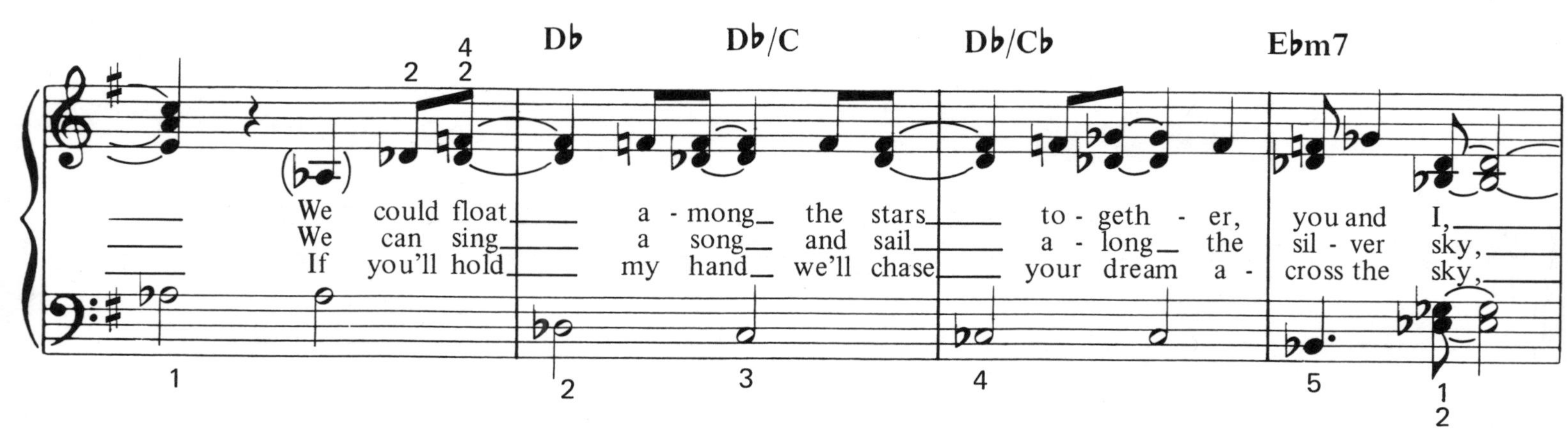

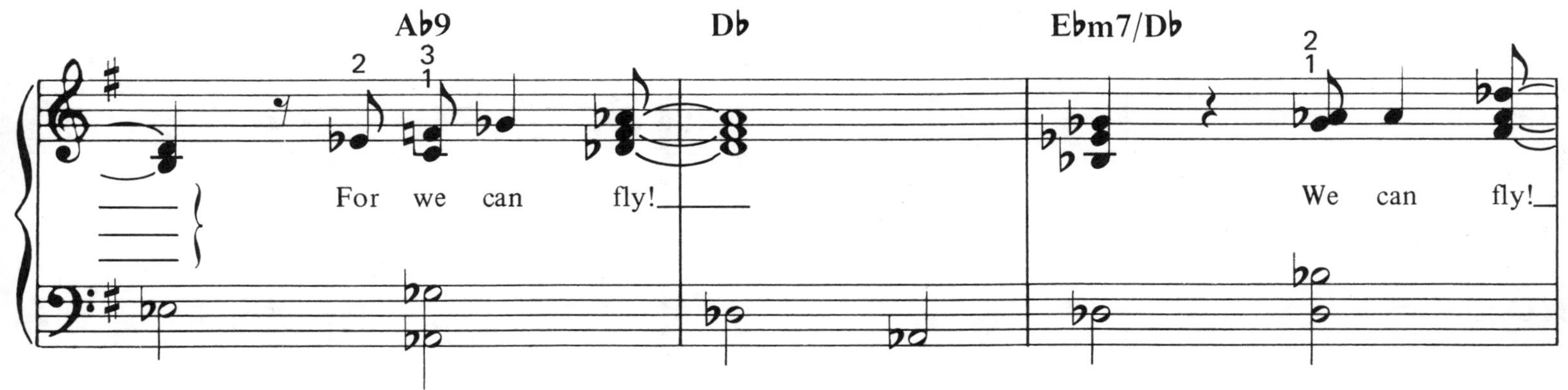
Ab9
Db
Ebm7/Db
For we can fly!
We can fly!

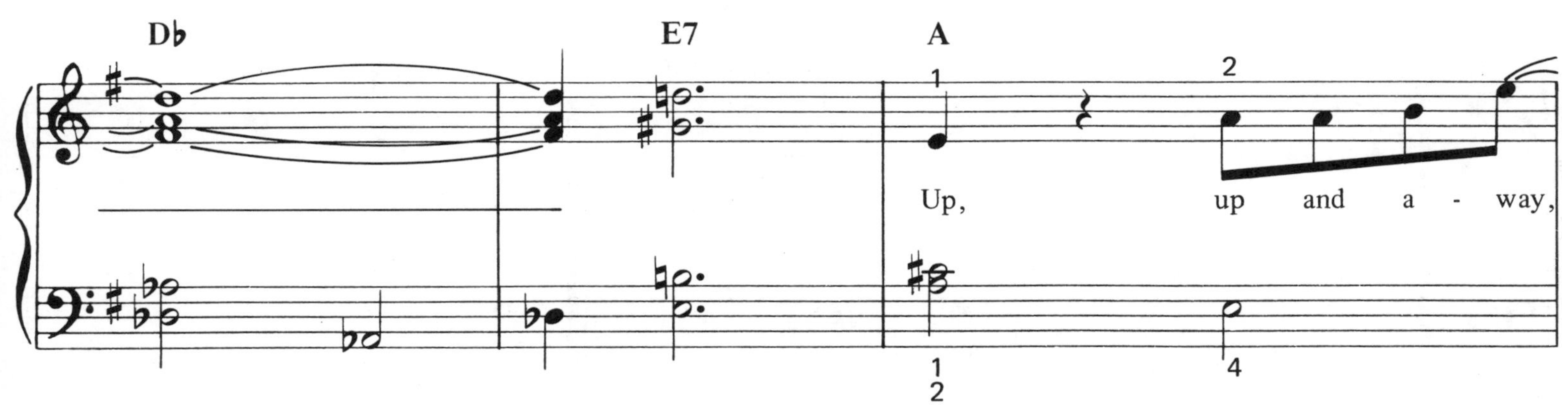
Db
E7
A
Up, up and a - way,

D
my beau - ti - ful, my

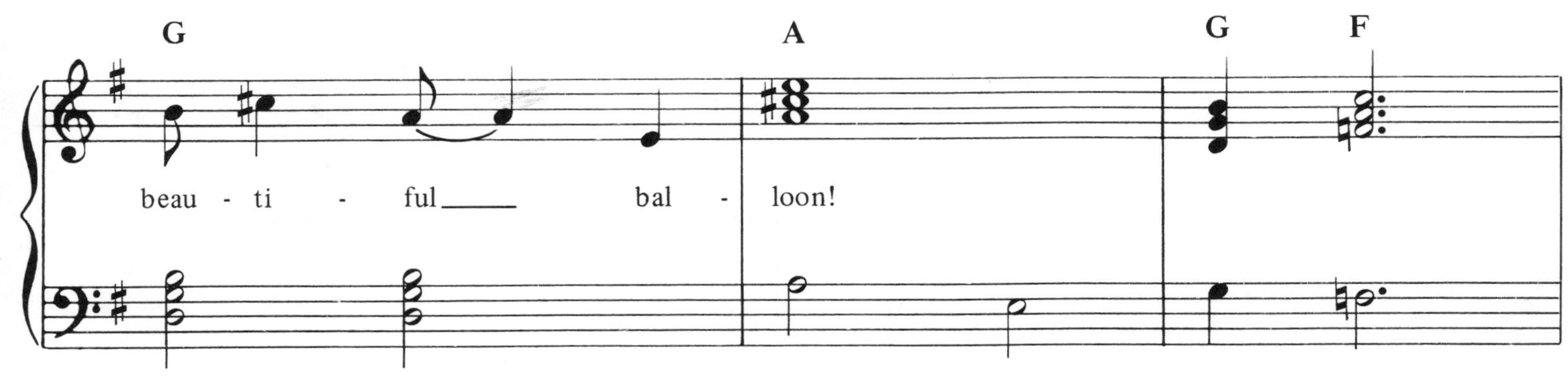
G
A
G
F
beau - ti - ful bal - loon!

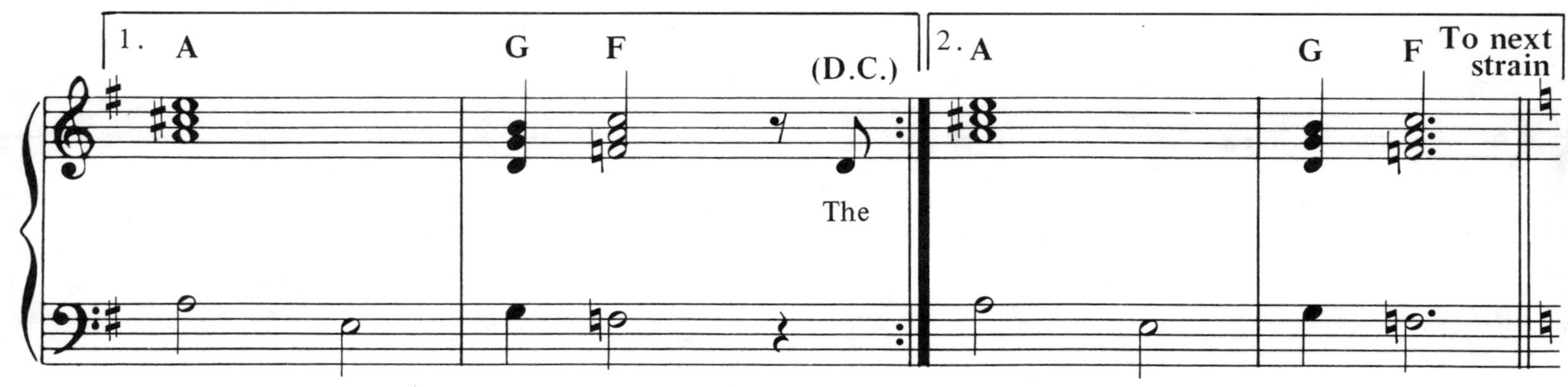
1.
A
G
F
(D.C.)
The
2.
A
G
F
To next strain

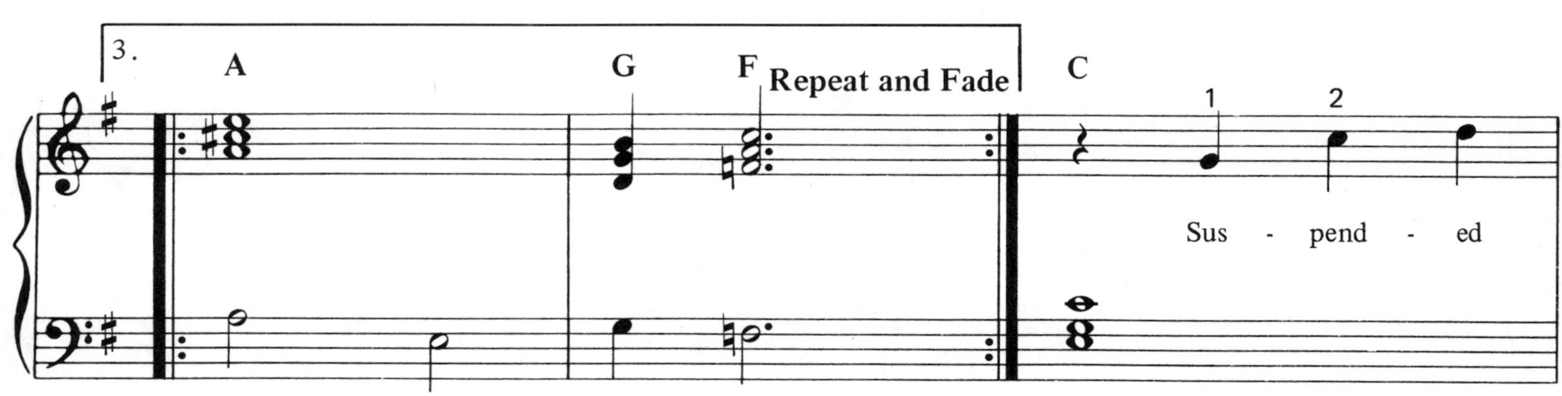
3.
A
G
F
Repeat and Fade
C
1
2
Sus - pend - ed

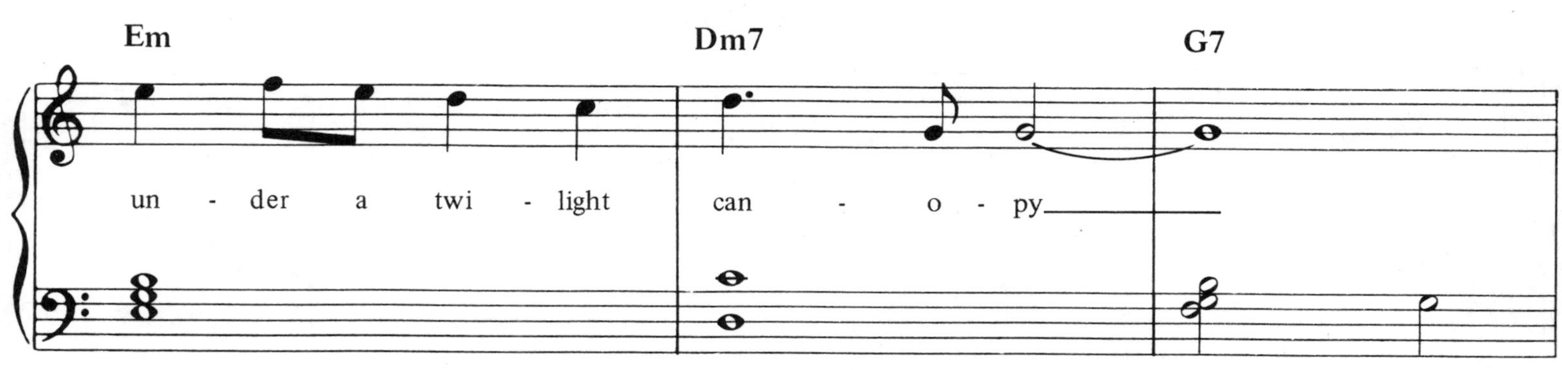
Em
Dm7
G7
un - der a twi - light can - o - py

C
We'll search the clouds for a star to

Dm7
G7
Eb
guide us.
If by some

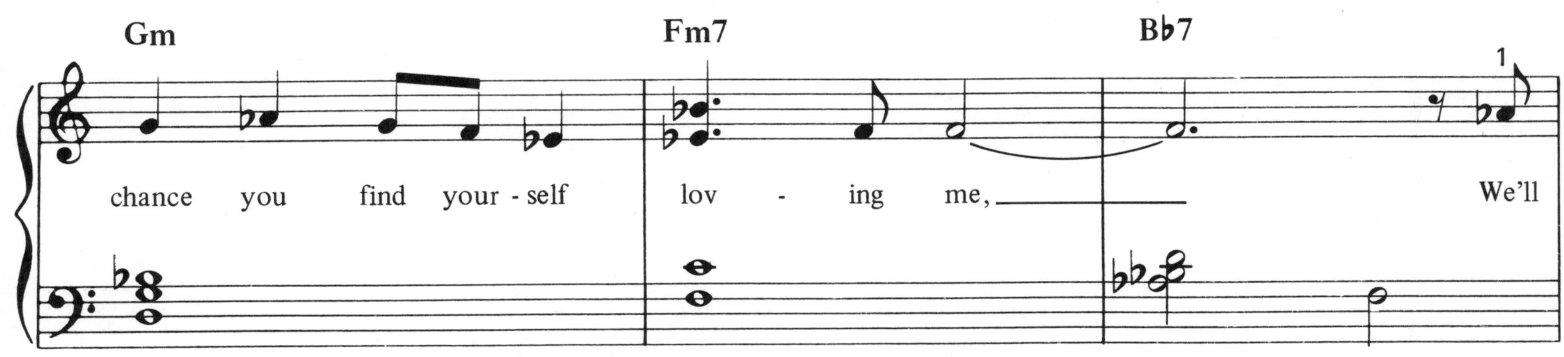
Gm
Fm7
Bb7
chance you find your - self
lov - ing me,
We'll

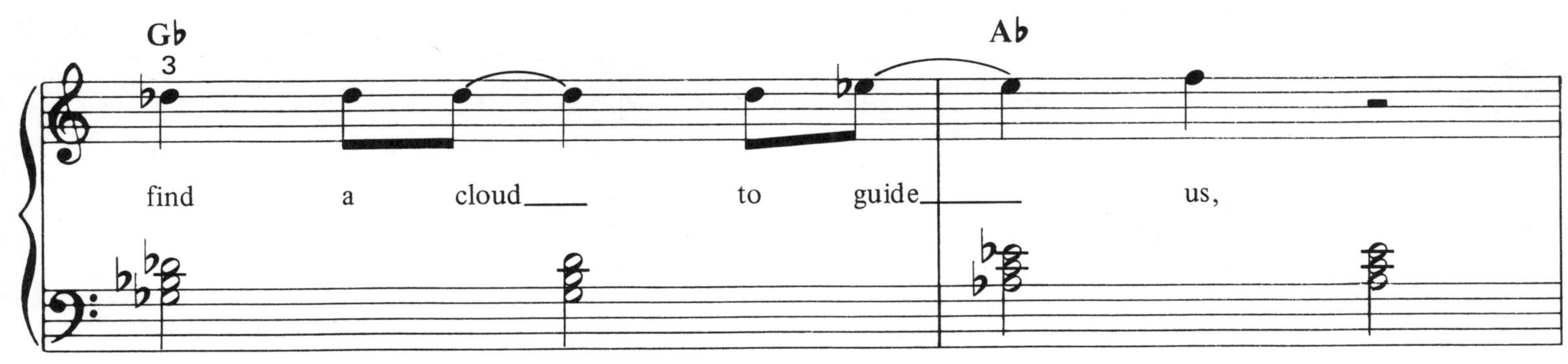
Gb
Ab
find a cloud to guide us,

G
F
Eb
D.C. al
3rd Ending
Keep the moon be - side us.

WHAT KIND OF FOOL AM I?

(From the Musical Production "STOP THE WORLD - I WANT TO GET OFF")

Words and Music by LESLIE BRICUSSE
and ANTHONY NEWLEY

Moderately slow

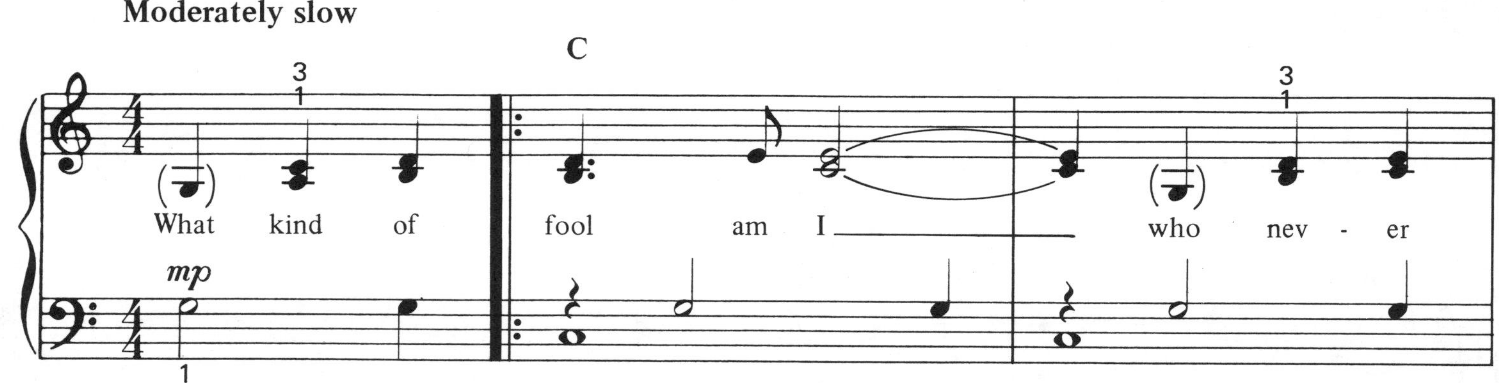

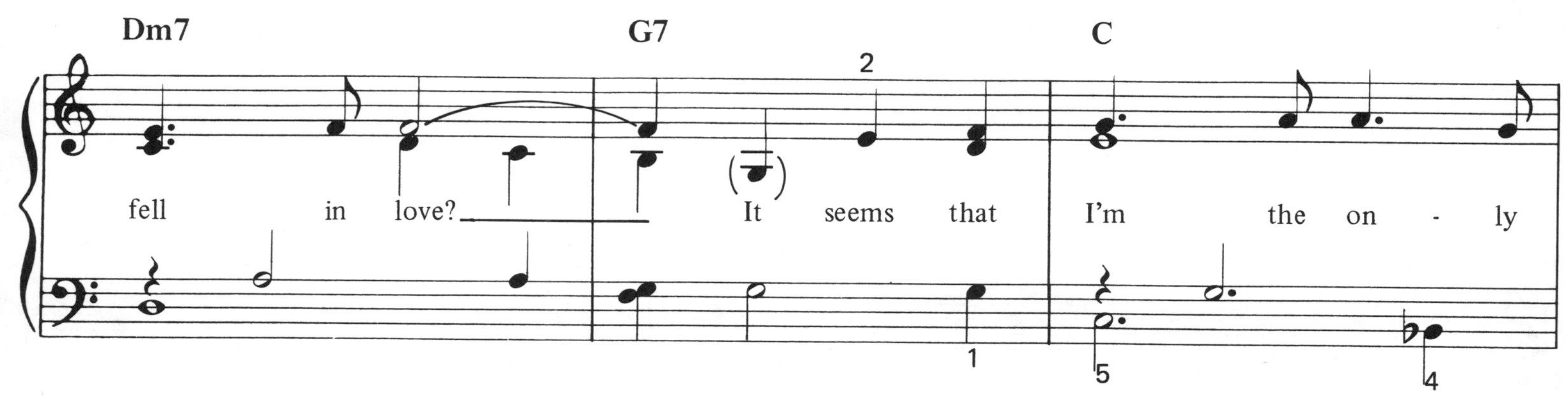

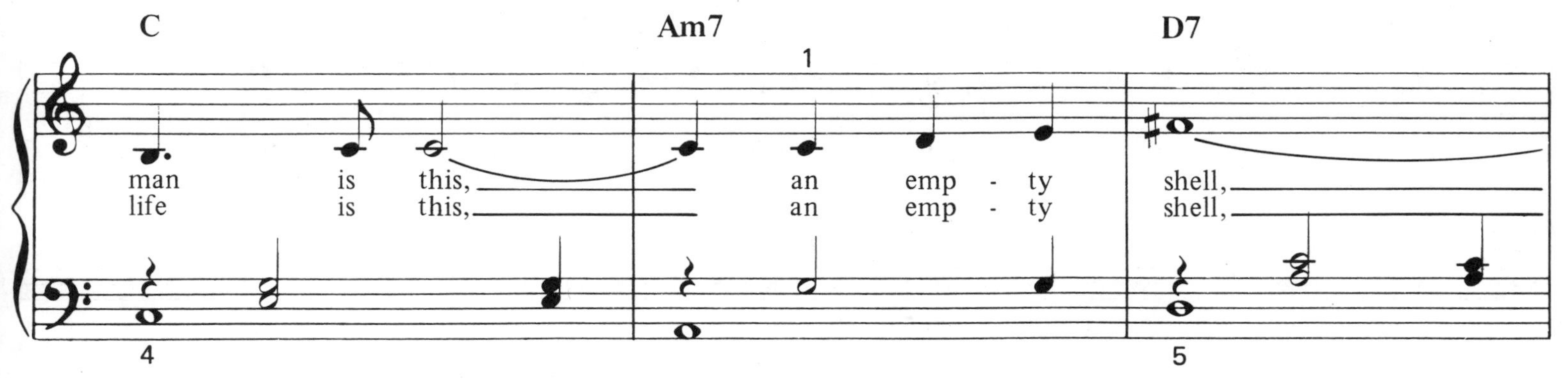
C
Am7
D7
1
man is this, an emp - ty shell,
life is this, an emp - ty shell,
4
5

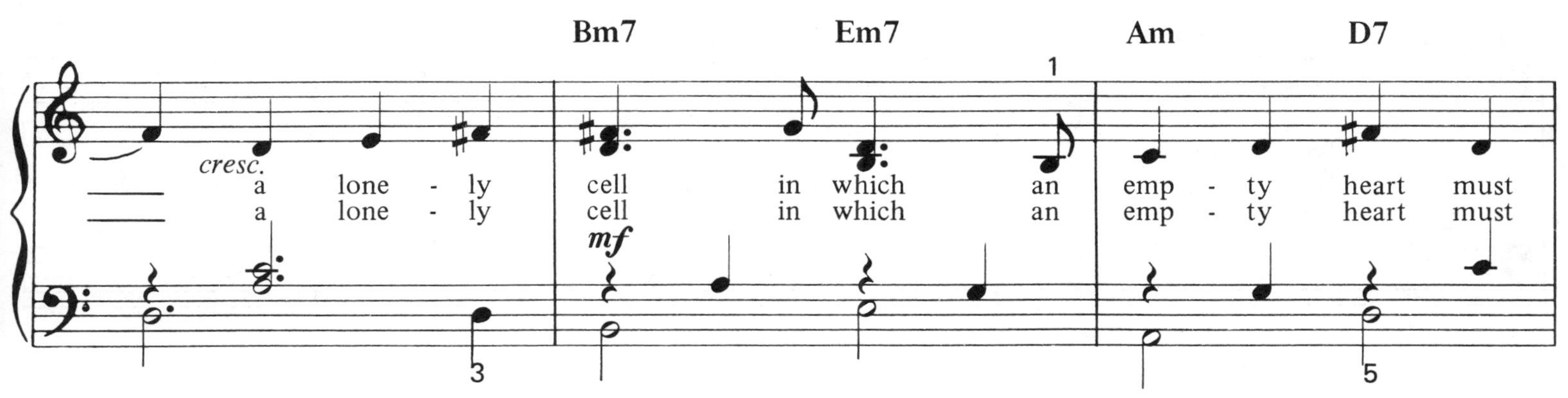
Bm7
Em7
Am
D7
1
cresc.
a lone - ly cell in which an emp - ty heart must
a lone - ly cell in which an emp - ty heart must
mf
3
5

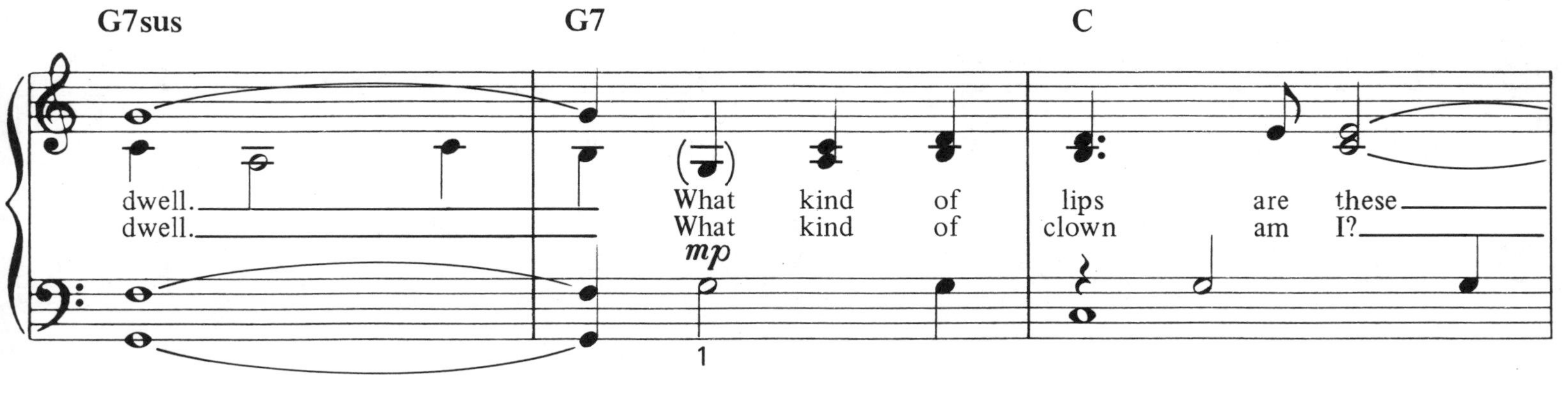
G7sus
G7
C
dwell. What kind of lips are these
dwell. What kind of clown am I?
mp
1

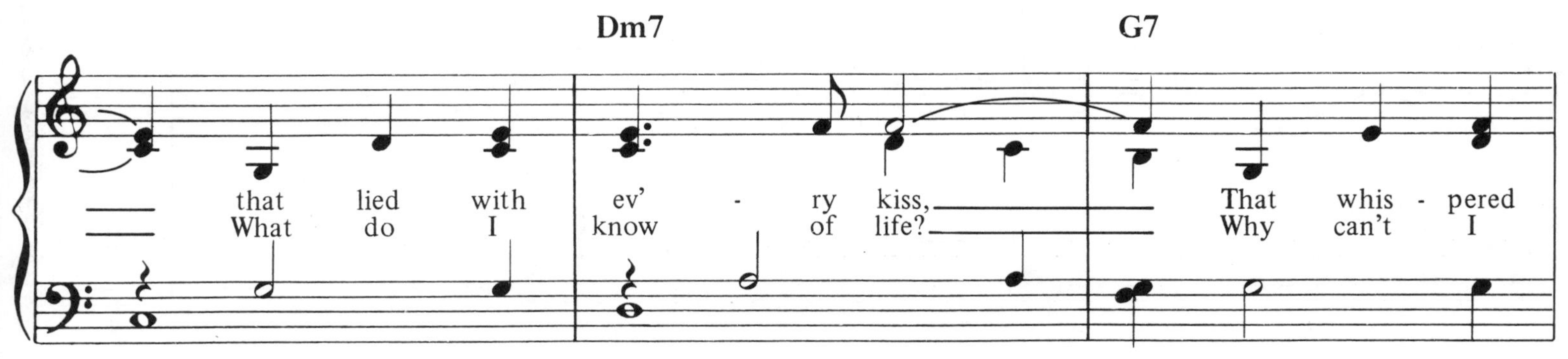
Dm7
G7
that lied with ev' - ry kiss, That whis - pered
What do I know of life? Why can't I

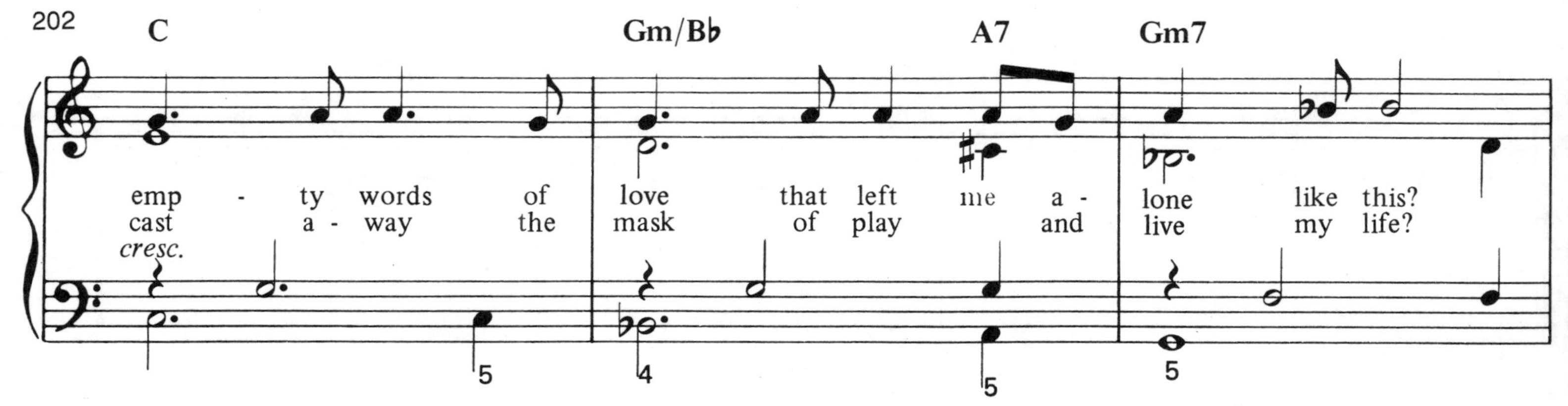
C
Gm/B♭
A7
Gm7
emp - ty words of love that left me a - lone like this?
cast a - way the mask of play and live my life?
cresc.

C7
F
Fm
Why can't I fall in love like an - y
Why can't I fall in love 'til I don't
ff

C/E
D7
Dm7
F/G
G7
oth - er man, And may - be then I'll know what kind of fool I
give a damn, And may - be then I'll know what kind of fool I

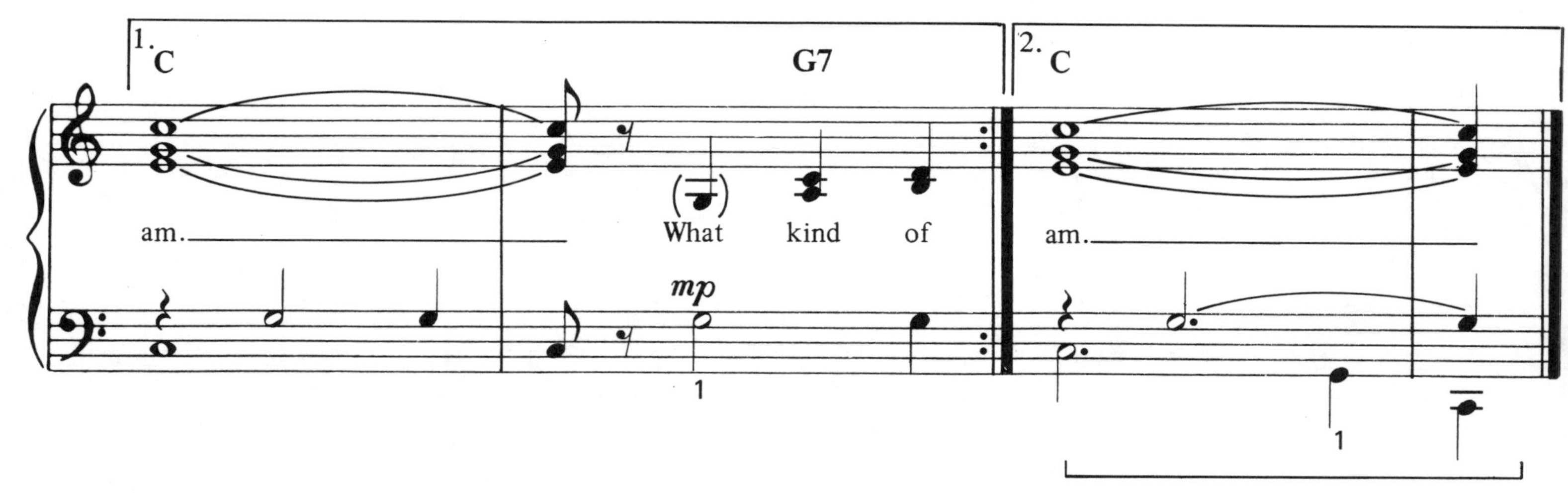
1.
C
G7
2.
C
am. (What) kind of
am.
mp

WHO CAN I TURN TO (WHEN NOBODY NEEDS ME)

(From "THE ROAR OF THE GREASEPAINT - THE SMELL OF THE CROWD")

Words and Music by LESLIE BRICUSSE
and ANTHONY NEWLEY

Em7
Cmaj7
Am
Fmaj7
Dm6
no one be - side me,
I'll
go on my way and

Em7
A7
Dm
G7
af - ter the day the
dark - ness will hide me.
And

C
Dm7
G7
may - be to-mor - row
I'll
find what I'm af - ter,

Dm7
G7
C
I'll
throw off my sor - row,
beg steal or bor - row

Gm
C7
F
F+
my share of laugh - ter.
With
you I could learn to,

Dm6
E7
Am
Am+7
Am7
with
you on a new day,
But

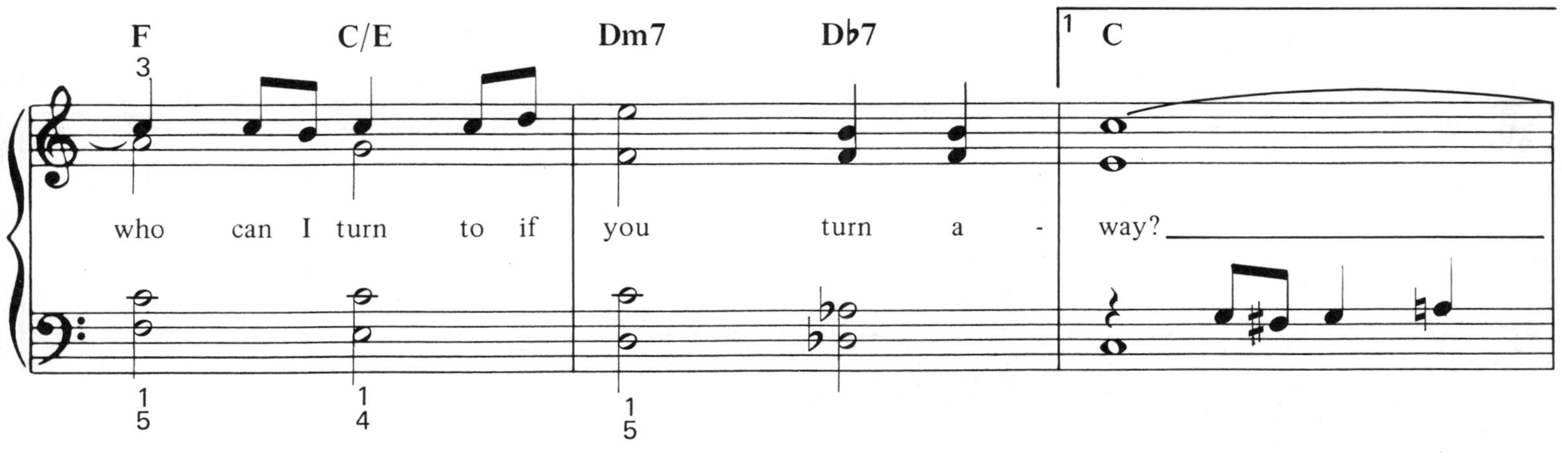
F
C/E
Dm7
D♭7
C
who can I turn to if
you turn a - way?

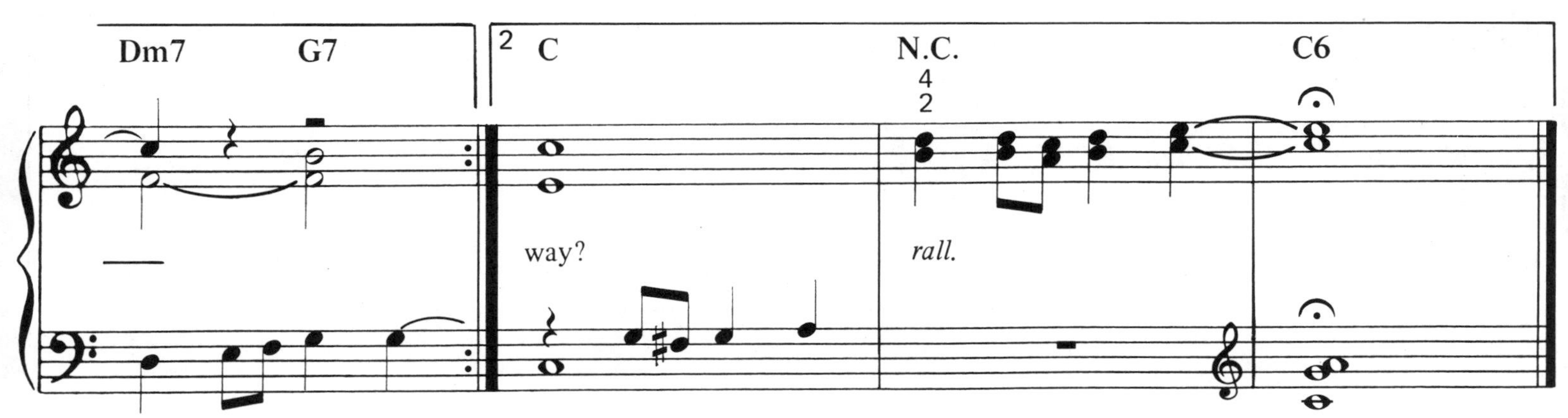
Dm7
G7
C
N.C.
C6
way?
rall.

WHERE HAVE ALL THE FLOWERS GONE?

Words and Music by
PETE SEEGER

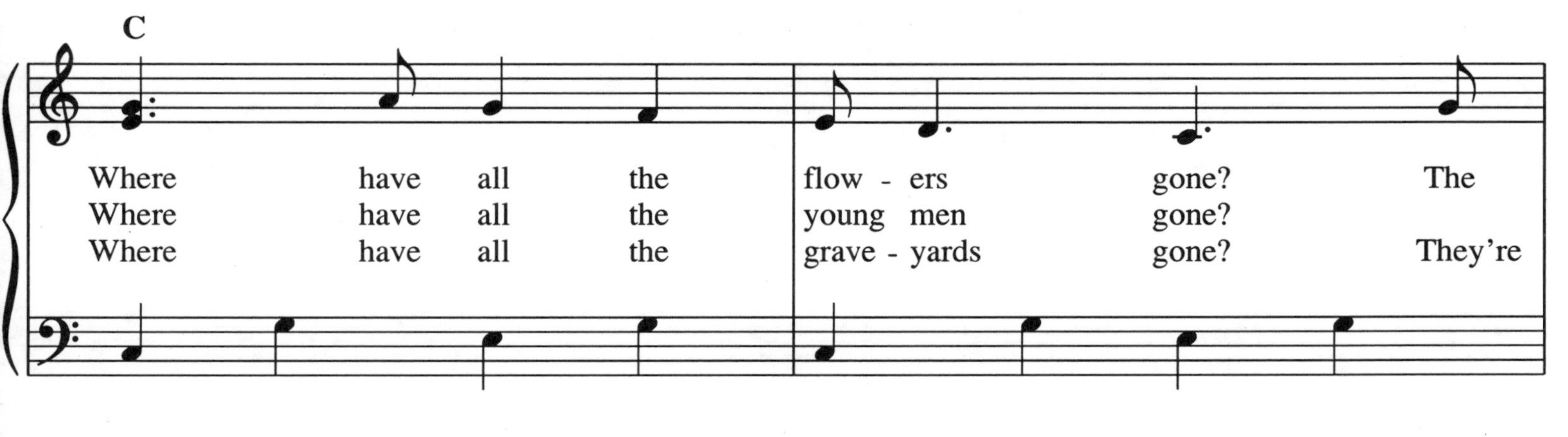
C
Where have all the flow - ers gone? The
Where have all the young men gone?
Where have all the grave - yards gone? They're

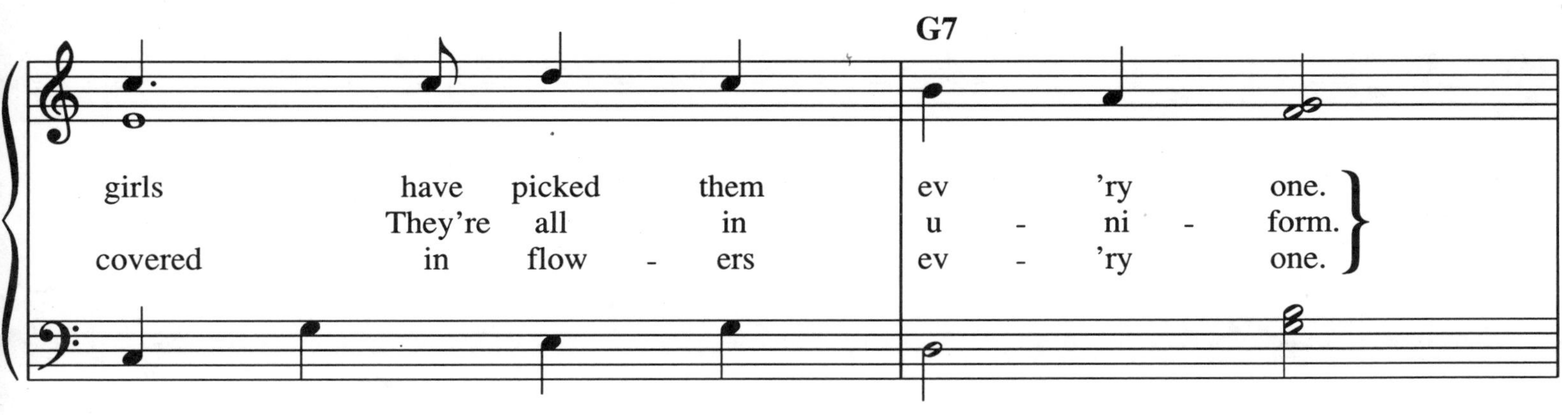
G7
girls have picked them ev 'ry one.
They're all in u - ni - form.
covered in flow - ers ev - 'ry one.

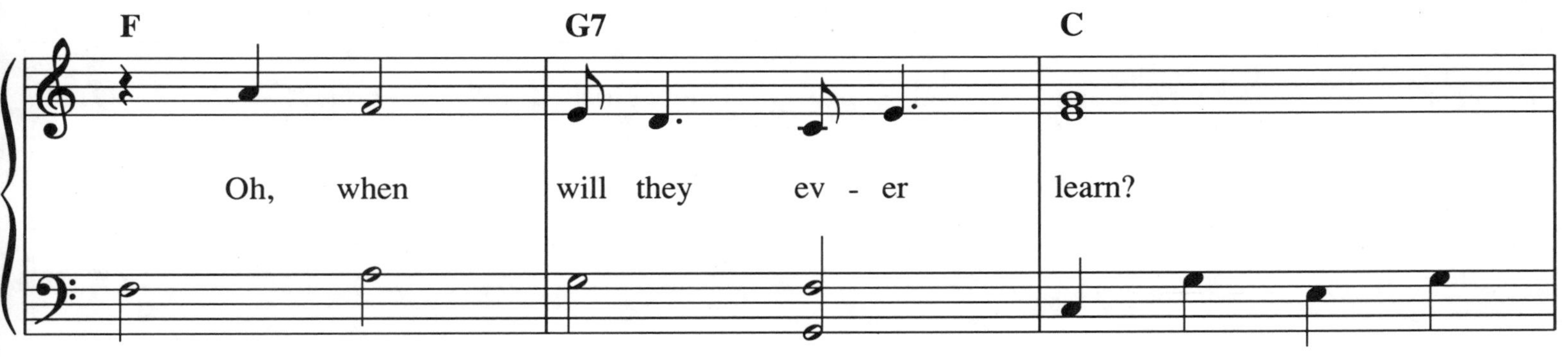
F
G7
C
Oh, when will they ev - er learn?

F
G7
Oh, when - will they ev - er

C
learn?
2. Where have all the
4. Where have all the
6. Where have all the
D7
G
G7
young girls gone? Long time pas - sing.
sol - diers gone? Long time pas - sing.
flow - ers gone? Long time pas - sing.
C
Where have all the young girls gone?
Where have all the sol - diers gone?
Where have all the flow - ers gone?
F
G
G7
C
Long time a - go. Where have all the
Long time a - go. Where have all the
Long time a - go. Where have all the

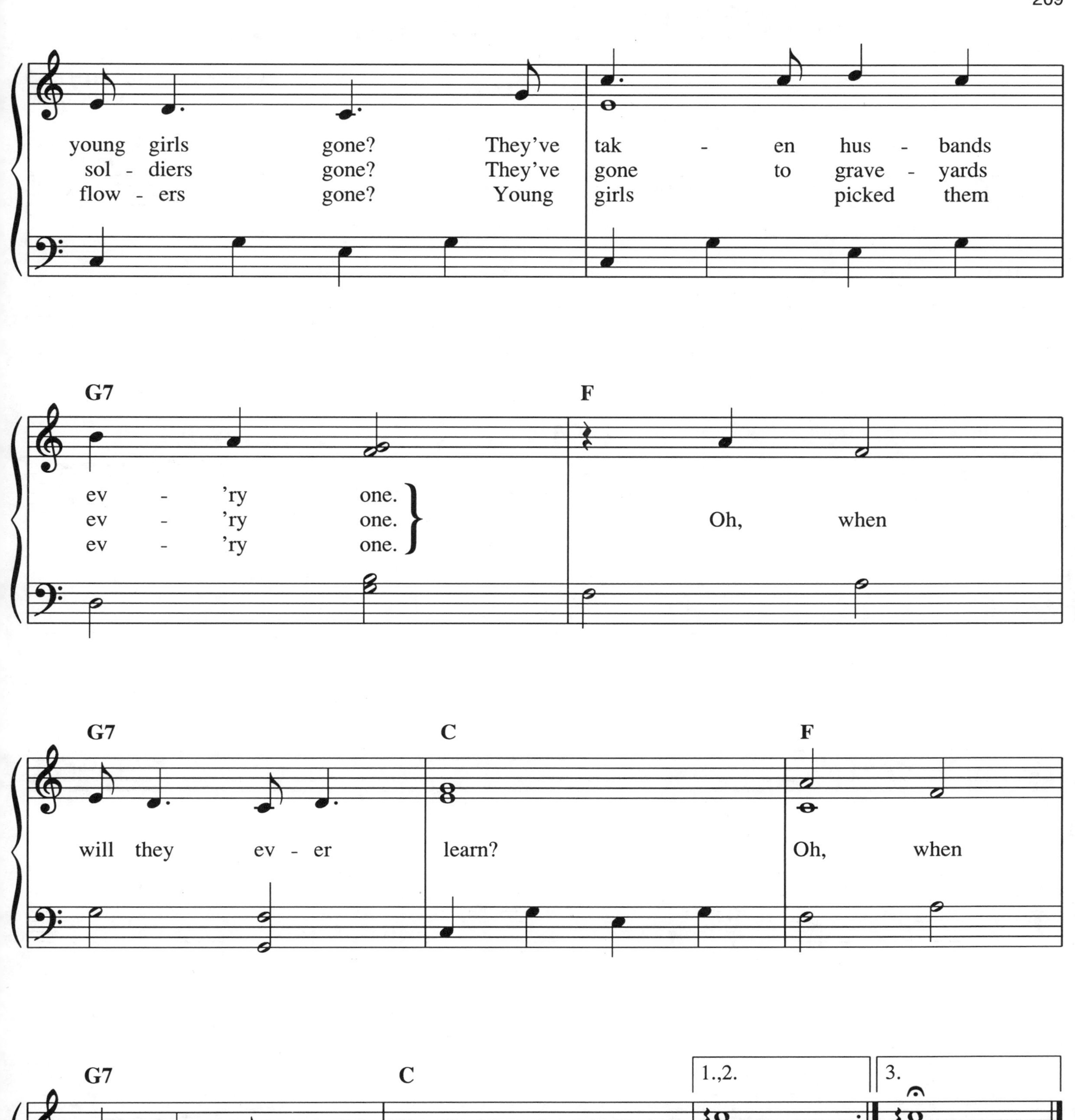
young girls gone? They've tak - en hus - bands
sol - diers gone? They've gone to grave - yards
flow - ers gone? Young girls picked them
G7
ev - 'ry one.
ev - 'ry one.
ev - 'ry one.
F
Oh, when
G7
will they ev - er
C
learn?
F
Oh, when
G7
will they ev - er
C
rit.
learn?
1.,2.
3.

A WHITER SHADE OF PALE

Words and Music by KEITH REID
and GARY BROOKER

Dm7
G
G/F
floor;
I was feel - ing kind of
sea;
So I took her by the
Em
G7/D
C
C/B
sea - sick,
the crowd called out for
look - ing glass
and forced her to a -
Am
Em/G
F
F/E
more.
The room was hum - ming
gree.
Say-ing "You must be the
Dm7
G
G/F
hard - er
as the ceil - ing flew a -
mer - maid
who took Nep - tune for a

Em G7/D C C/B
way. ride,"
When we called out for an - but she smiled at me so
Am Em/B F F/E
oth - er drink sad - ly
the wait - er brought a that my an - ger straight - way
Dm7 Em/G C6 C/B
tray. died.
And so it
was that
3
3
Am C/G F F/E Dm7
la - ter as the mil - ler told his tale,

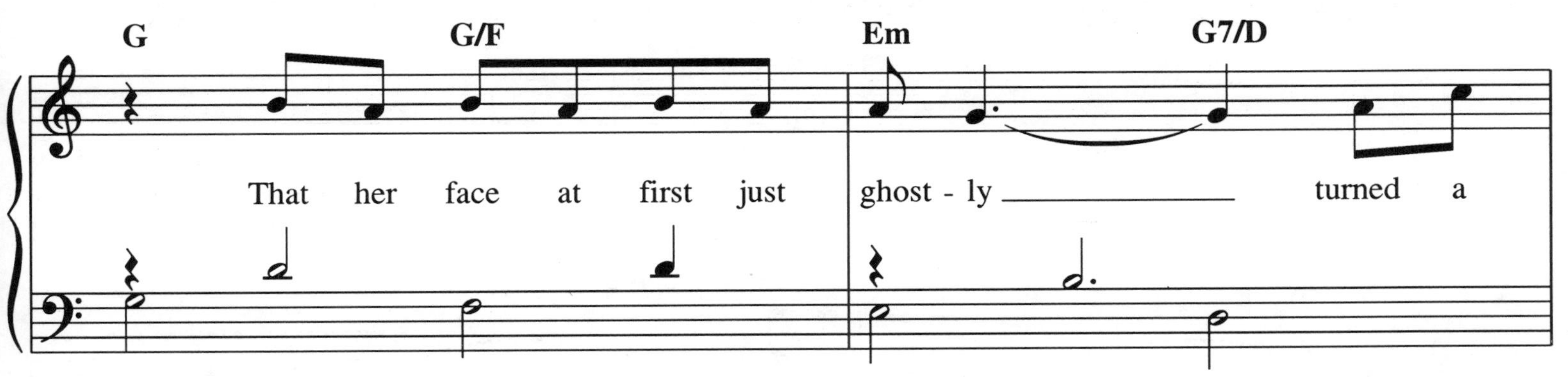

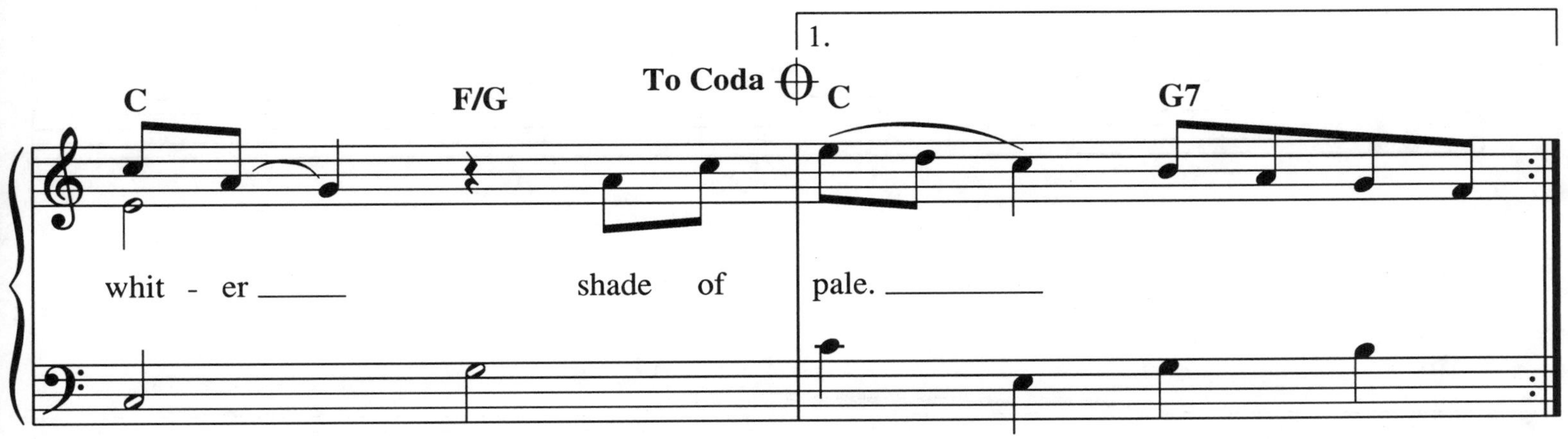

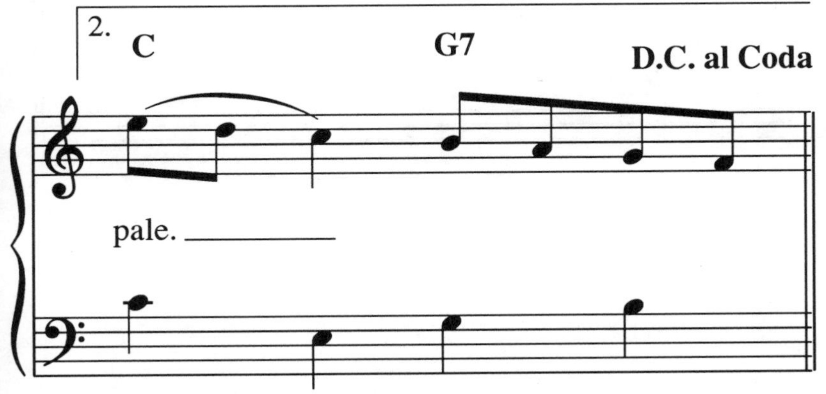

Additional Lyrics

She said, "There is no reason,
and the truth is plain to see,"
But I wandered through my playing cards
and would not let her be
one of the sixteen vestal virgins
who were leaving for the coast.
And although my eyes were open
they might just as well been closed.

YESTERDAY, WHEN I WAS YOUNG

(Hier Encore)

English lyrics by HERBERT KRETZMER
Original French Text and Music by
CHARLES AZNAVOUR

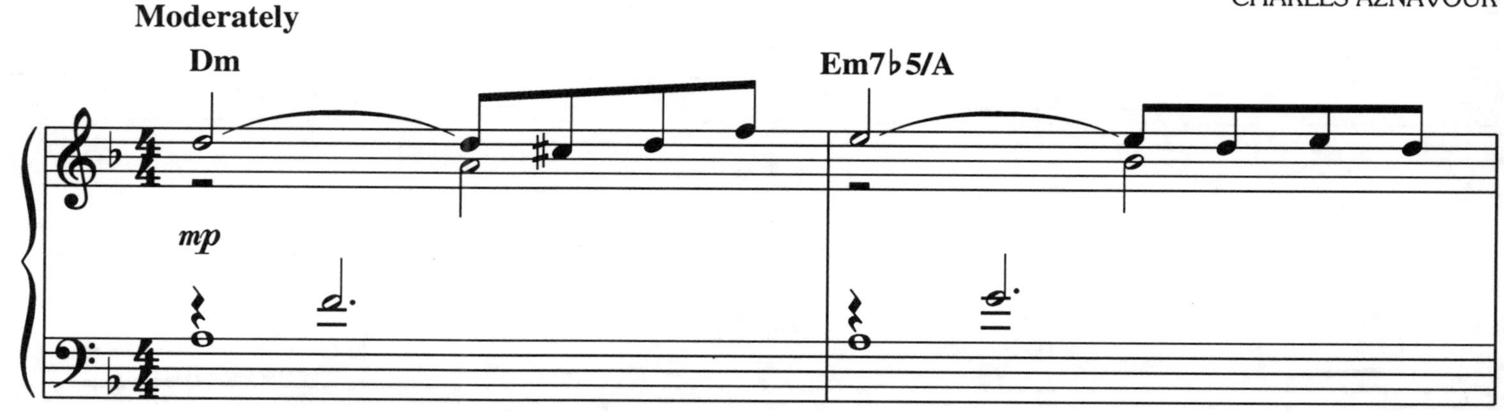

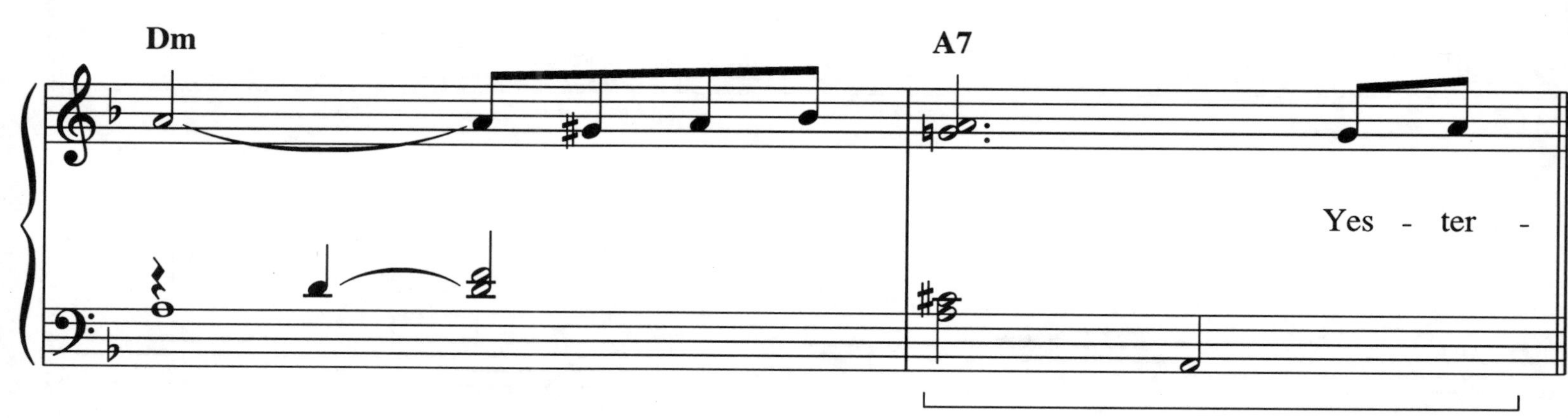

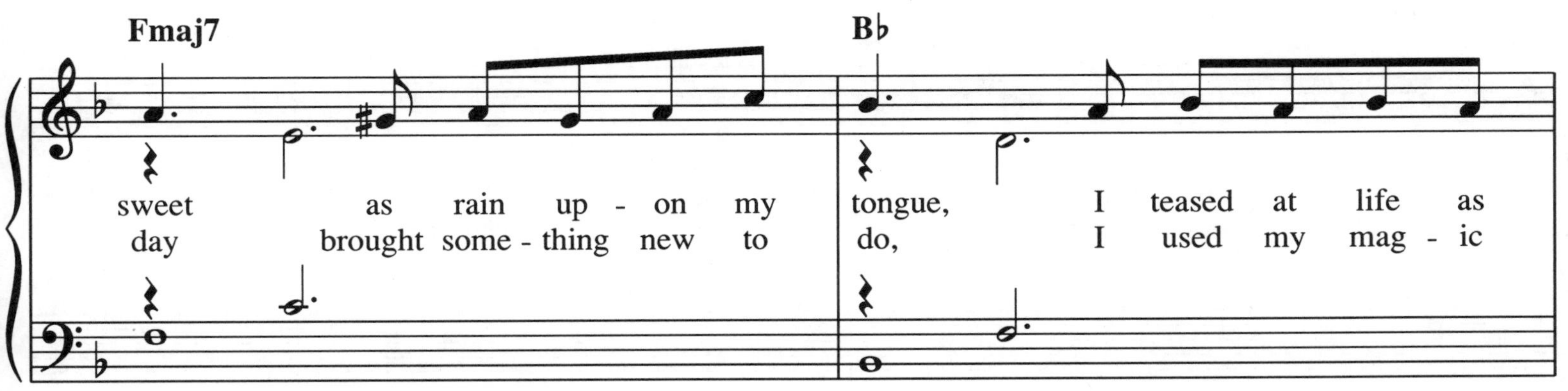
Fmaj7
Bb
sweet as rain up - on my tongue, I teased at life as
day brought some - thing new to do, I used my mag - ic

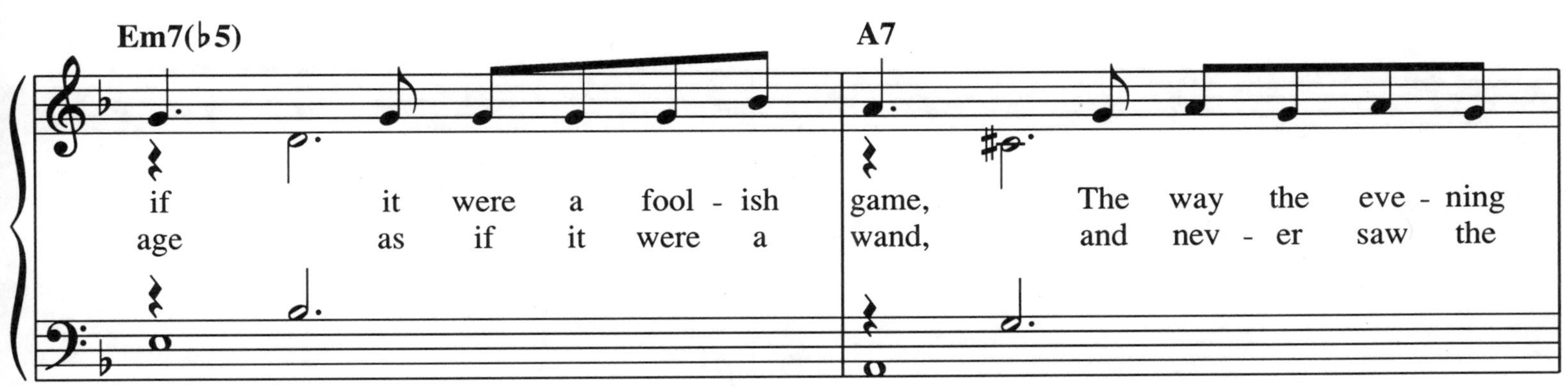
Em7(b5)
A7
if it were a fool - ish game, The way the eve - ning
age as if it were a wand, and nev - er saw the

Dm
breeze may tease a can - dle flame; The thou - sand dreams I
waste and emp - ti - ness be - yond; The game of love I

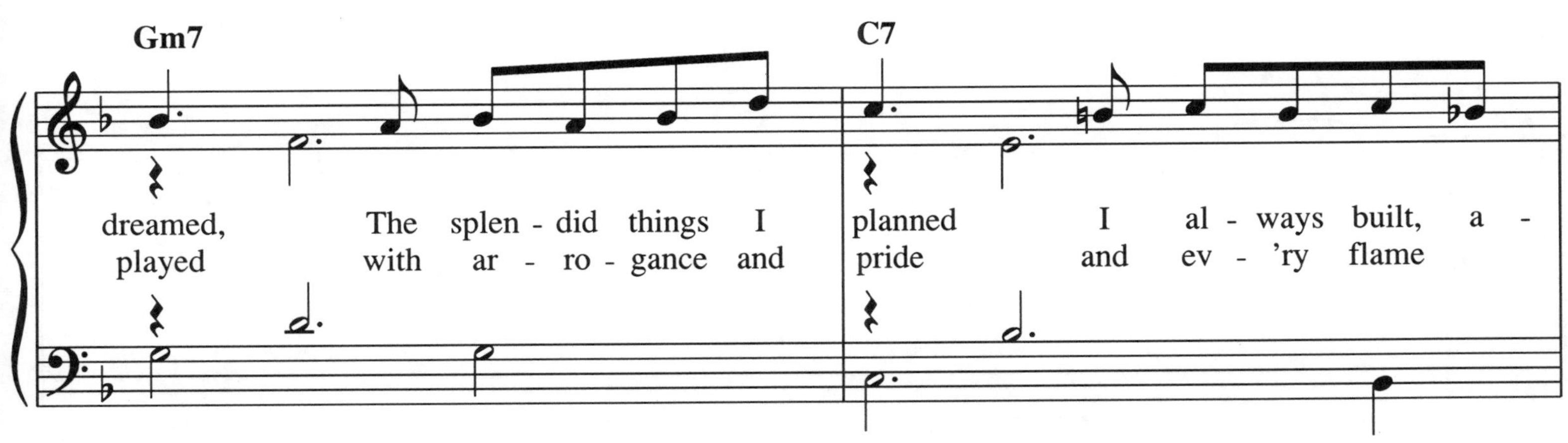
Gm7
C7
dreamed, The splen - did things I planned I al - ways built, a -
played with ar - ro - gance and pride and ev - 'ry flame

Fmaj7
Bb
las, on weak and shift - ing sand; I lived by night and
lit too quick - ly quick - ly died; The friends I made all
Em7(b5)
A7
shunned the na - ked light of day And on - ly now I
seemed some - how to drift a - way And on - ly I am
Dm
To Coda
see how the years ran a - way. Yes - ter -
left on stage to end the
Gm7
C7
day when I was young, So man - y drink - ing

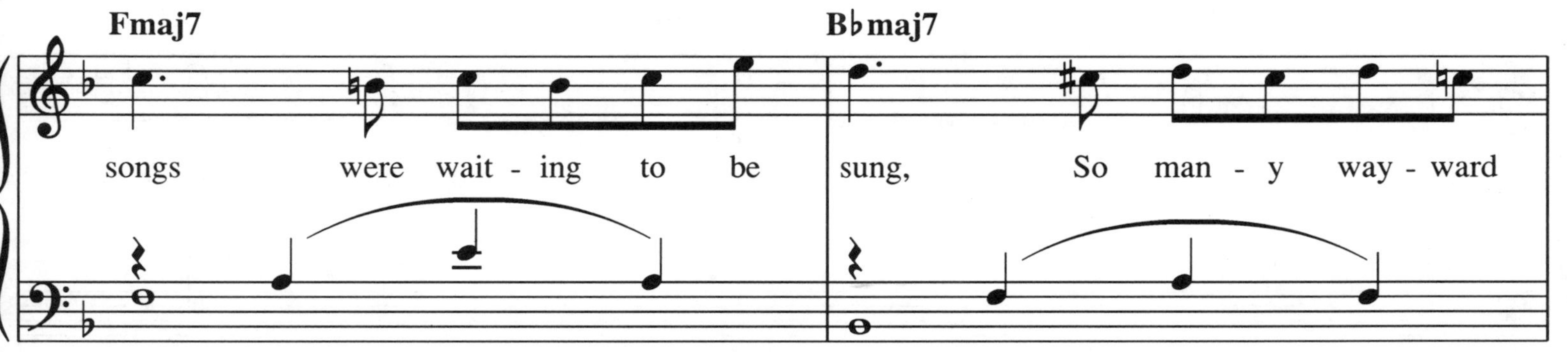
Fmaj7
Bbmaj7
songs were wait - ing to be sung, So man - y way - ward

Gm
A7(b9)
plea - sures lay in store for me And so much pain my

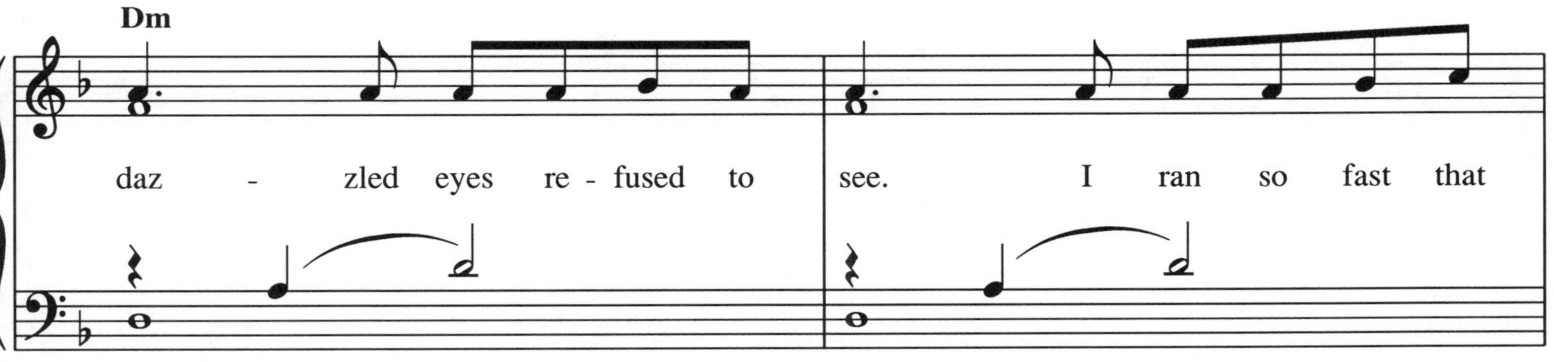
Dm
daz - zled eyes re - fused to see. I ran so fast that

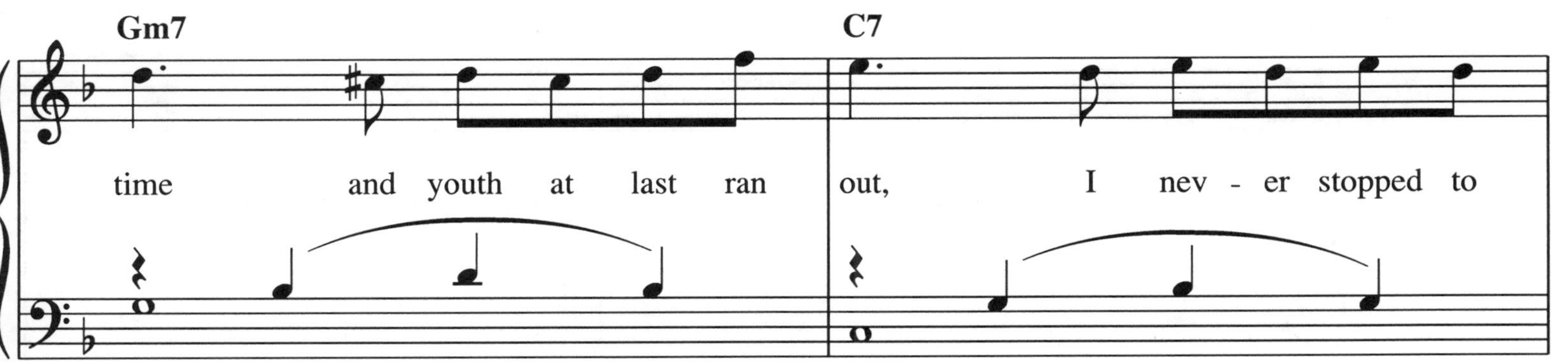
Gm7
C7
time and youth at last ran out, I nev - er stopped to

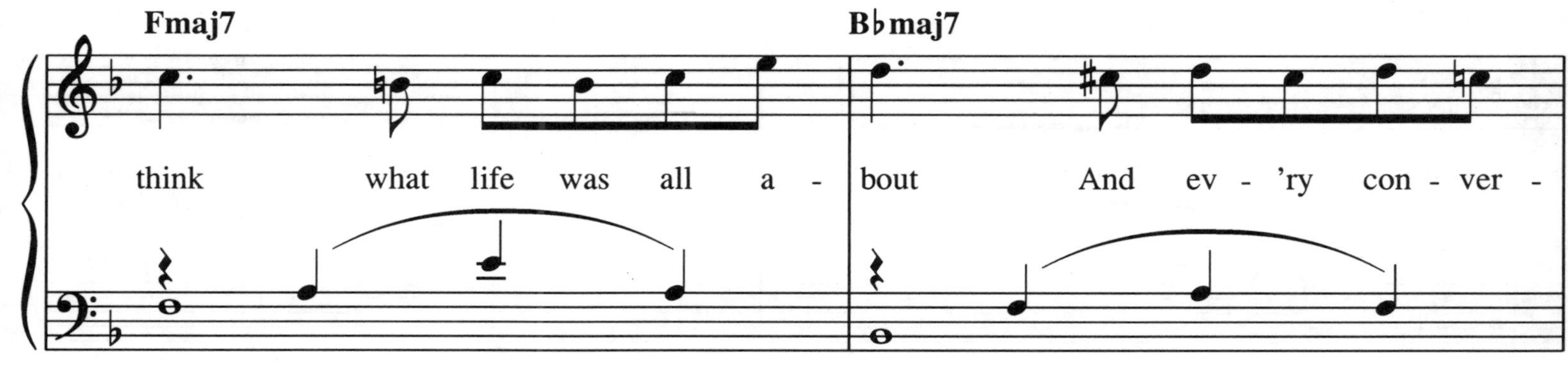
Fmaj7
B♭maj7
think what life was all a - bout And ev - 'ry con - ver -

Gm
A7(♭9)
sa - tion I can now re - call con - cerned it - self with

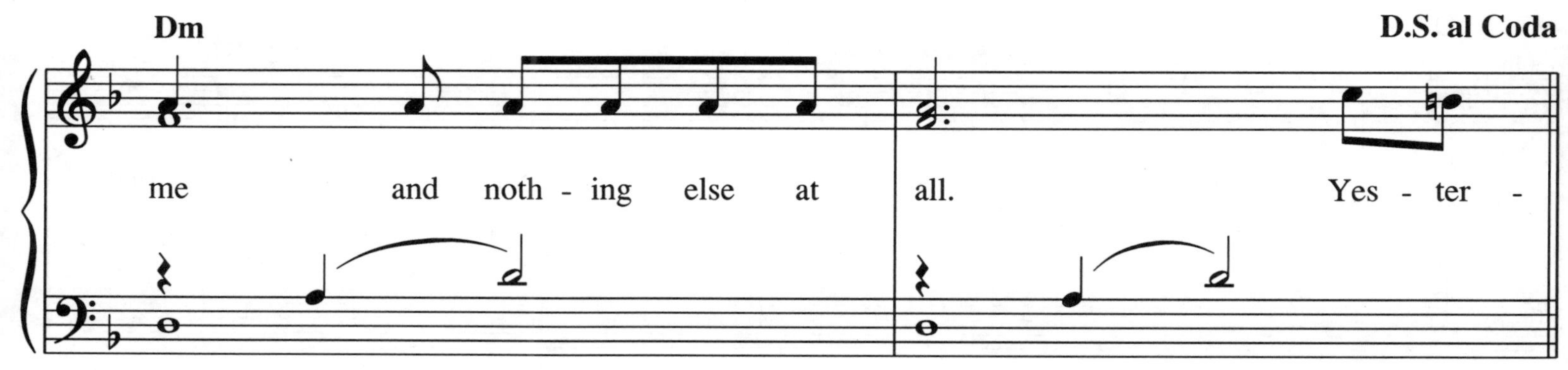
Dm
D.S. al Coda
me and noth - ing else at all. Yes - ter -

CODA
Dm
Gm
play. There are so man - y songs in me that won't be

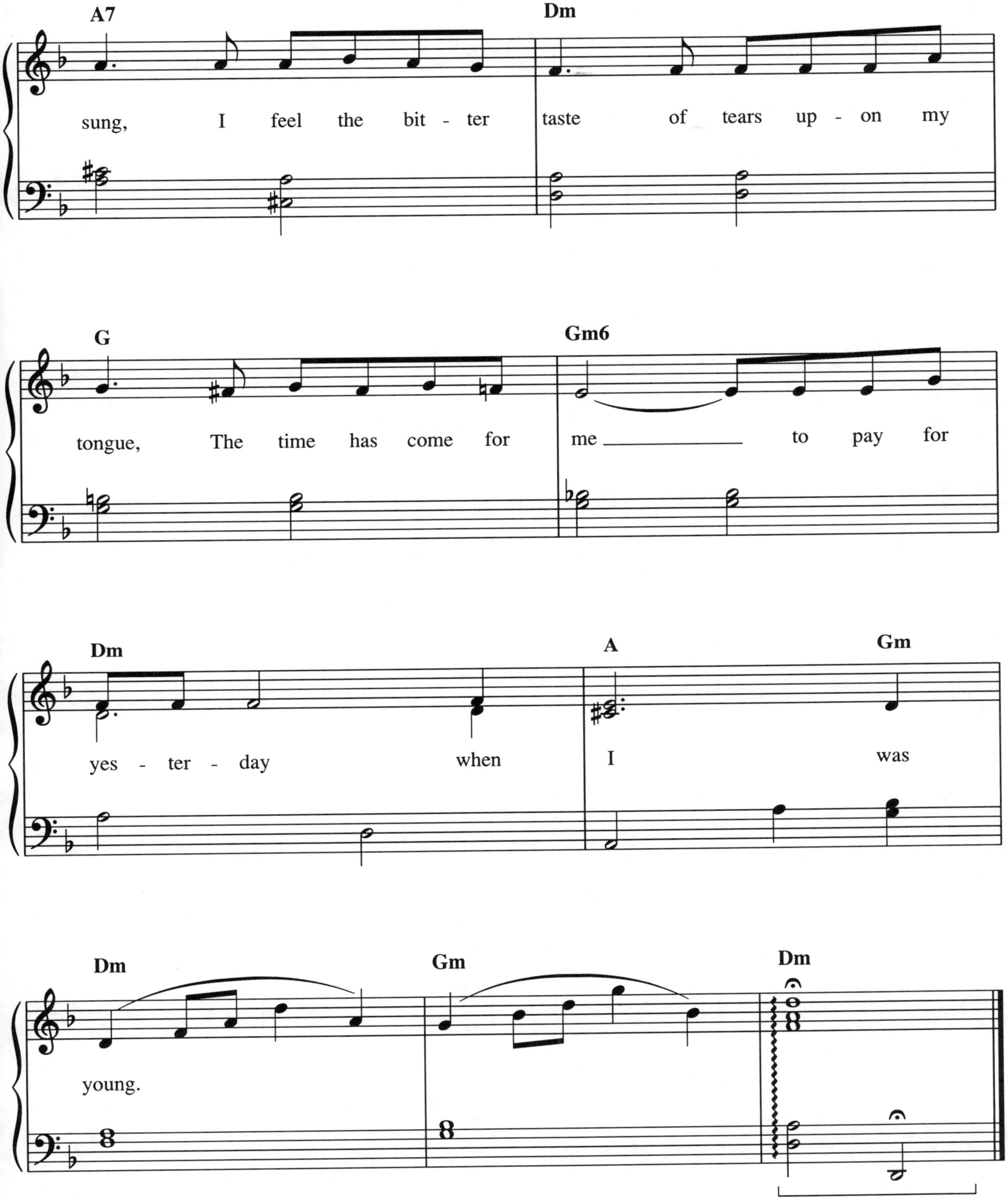

A7 Dm

sung, I feel the bit - ter taste of tears up - on my

G Gm6

tongue, The time has come for me ___ to pay for

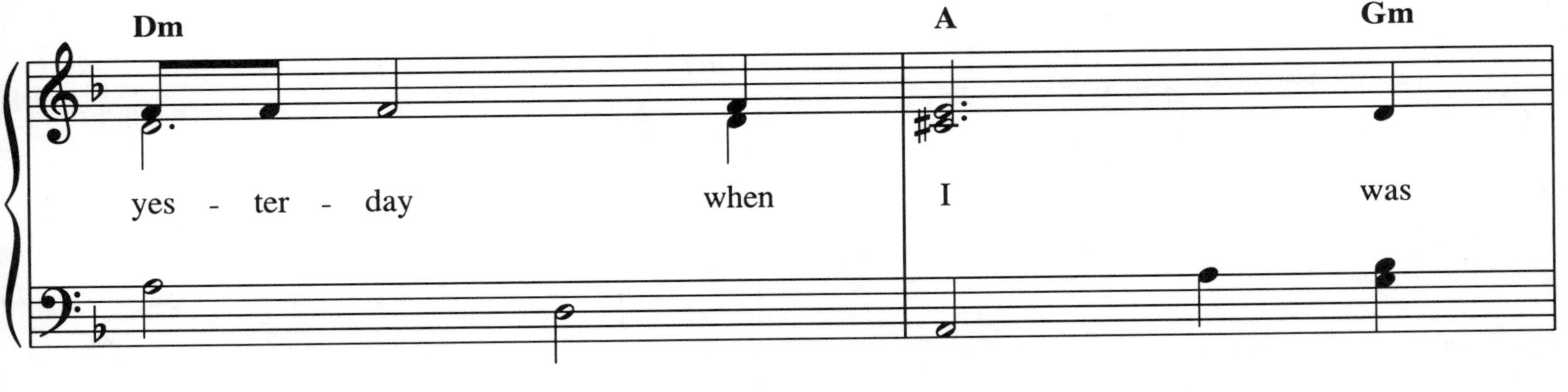

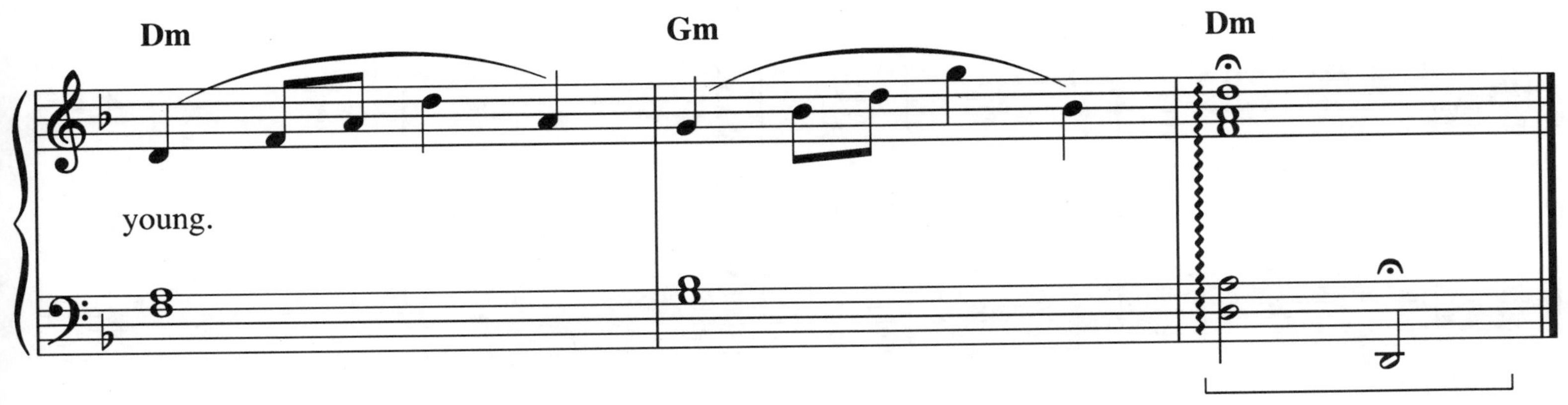

WOODEN HEART

Words and Music by BEN WEISMAN, KAY TWOMEY,
FRED WISE and BERTHOLD KAEMPFERT

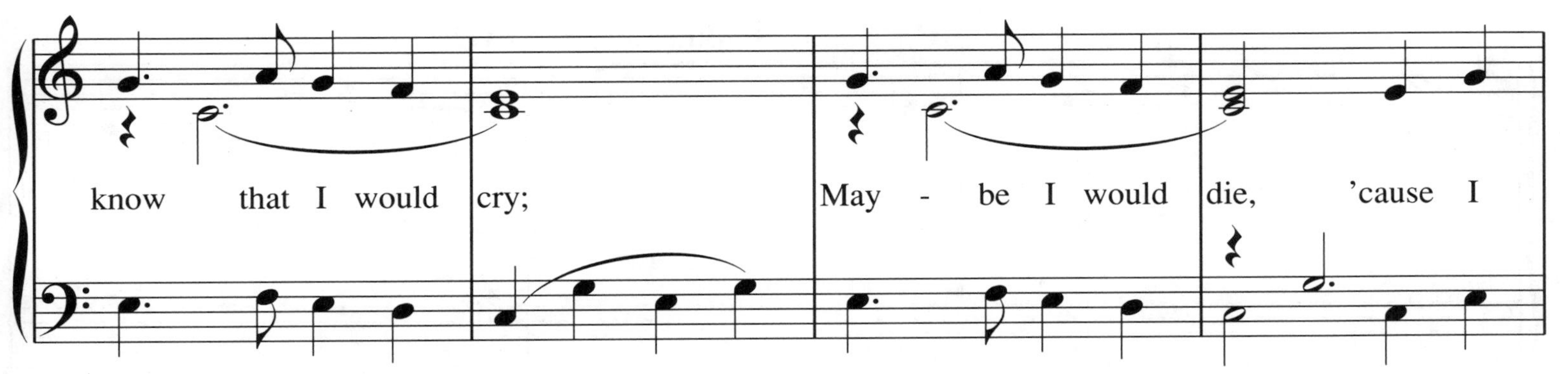
know that I would cry;
May - be I would die, 'cause I

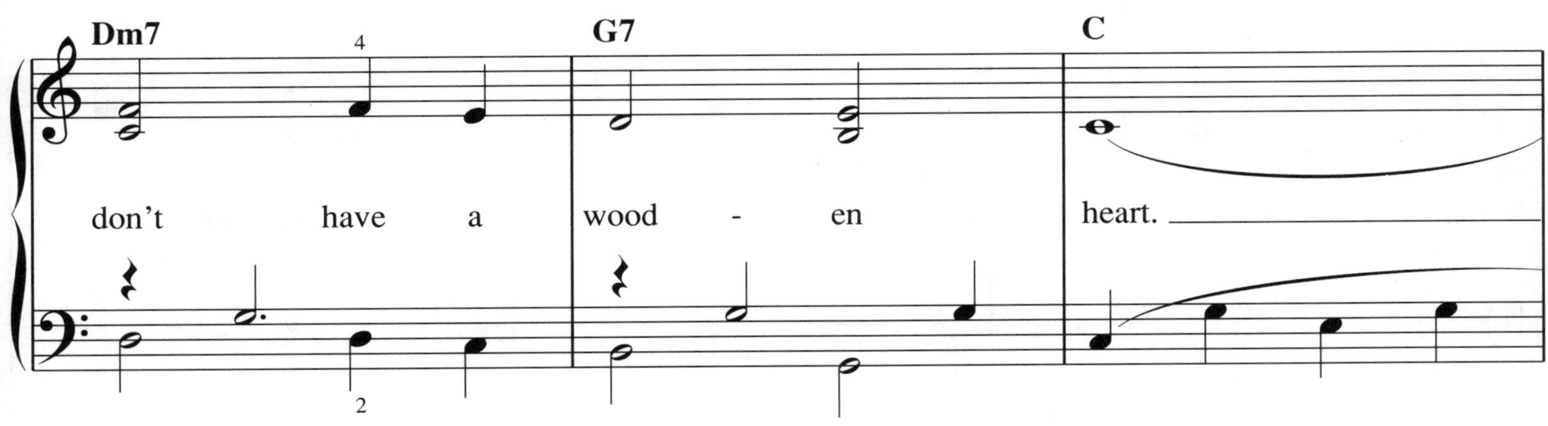
Dm7
G7
C
4
don't have a wood - en heart.
2

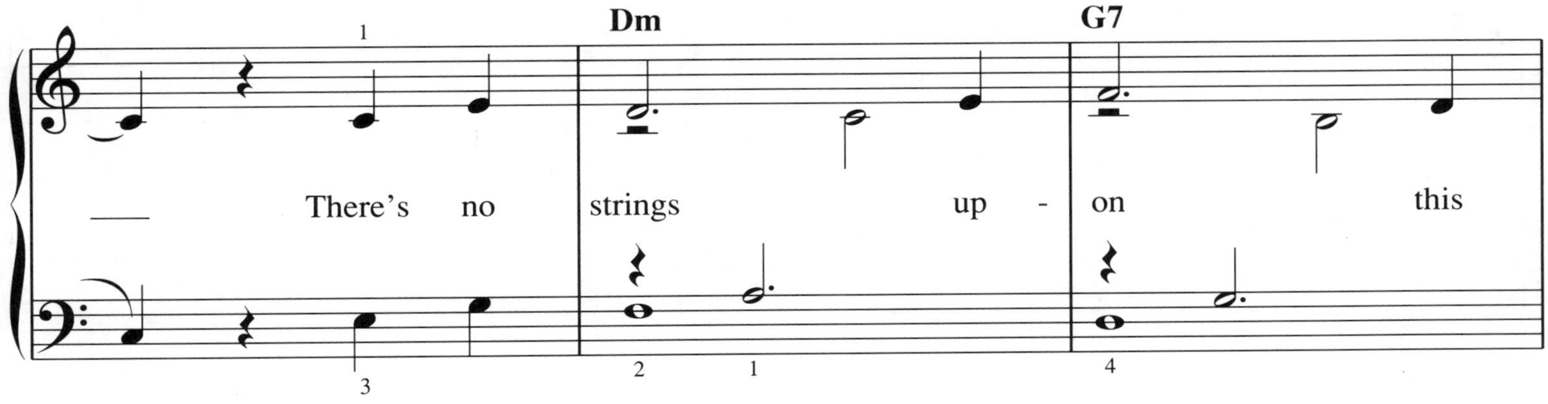
Dm
G7
1
There's no strings up - on this
3
2 1
4

C
F
2
love of mine; It was al - ways
5

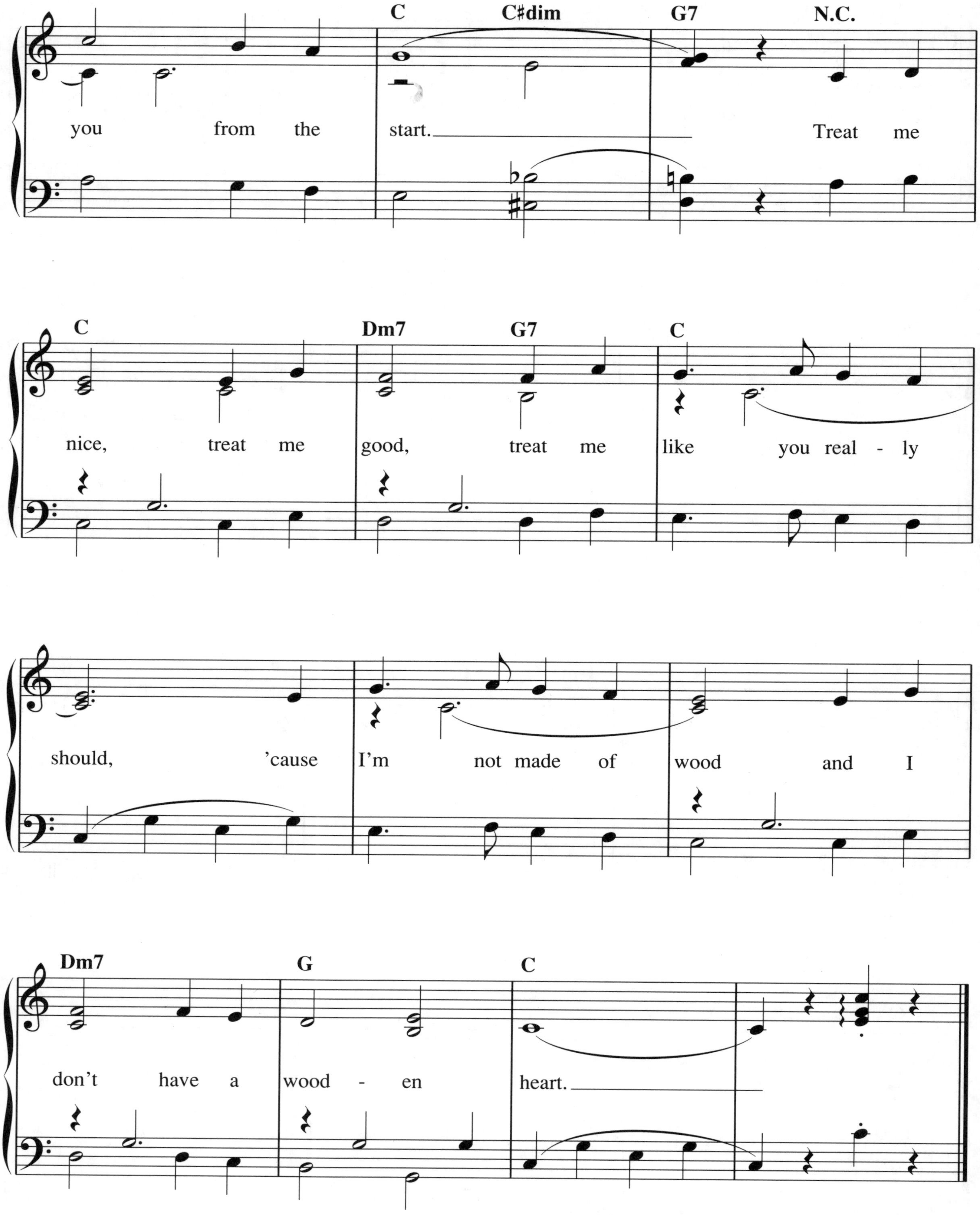

C C#dim G7 N.C.

you from the start. Treat me

C Dm7 G7 C

nice, treat me good, treat me like you real - ly

should, 'cause I'm not made of wood and I

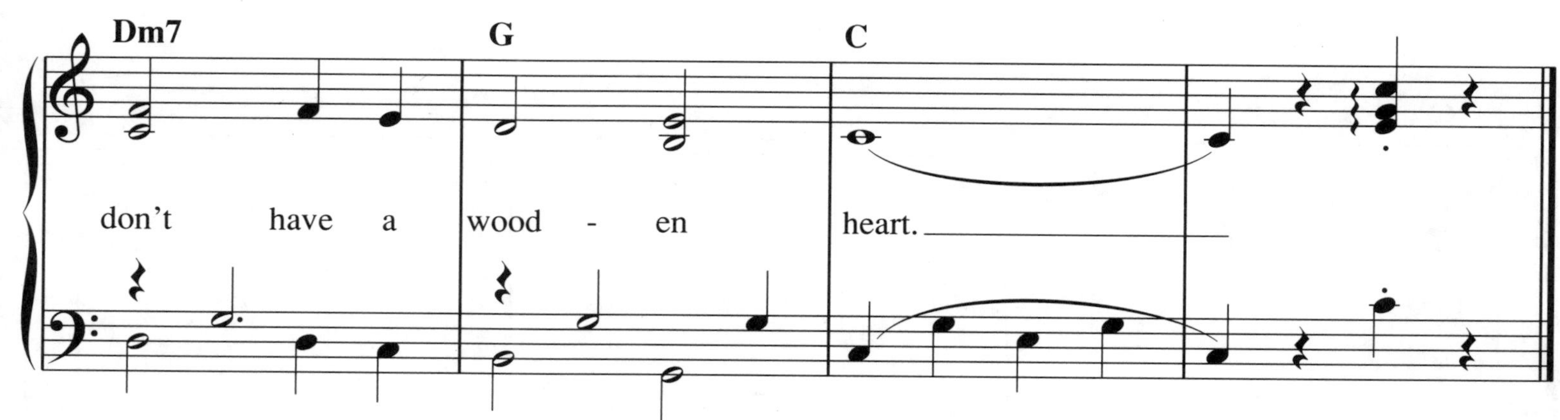